FAIR PLAY
IN THE
MARKETPLACE

The First Battle
for Pure Food and Drugs

Mitchell Okun

1986

NORTHERN ILLINOIS UNIVERSITY PRESS

DEKALB, ILLINOIS

Library of Congress Cataloging-in-Publication Data

Okun, Mitchell.
   Fair play in the marketplace.

   Bibliography: p.
   Includes index.
   1. Food adulteration and inspection—United States—
History—19th century.   2. Food adulteration and
inspection—Law and legislation—United States—History
—19th century.   3. Food adulteration and inspection—
New York (State)—History—19th century.   4. Food
adulteration and inspection—Law and legislation—
New York (State)—History—19th century.   I. Title.
HD9000.9.U5039   1986   363.1'926'0973   85-25921
ISBN 0-87580-115-3

Designed by Jo Aerne

Contents

Illustrations

Preface

There is a gap in the history of American reform that has gone largely unnoticed. Except for a few specialized monographs, studies of the origins of the consumer movement have concentrated on the federal Pure Food and Drug Act of 1906. Yet the conditions that inspired that law had fully developed a generation earlier. The battles over adulteration in the period 1865–1886 were not merely a rehearsal for reform, but anticipated the issues, the arguments, and even the solutions of the Pure Food and Drug Act.

As early as 1820 readers had been warned that the traditional relationship between producer, merchant, and consumer was being threatened by the very "division of labour" that was helping to create a revolution in the trade of industrialized nations. It was feared that the growing complexity of the marketplace, the loss of localism, the dispersion of neighborhood production, and the resulting anonymity of modern business would encourage fraud and immorality. The continuing centralization of the food and drug marketplace after the Civil War revived hoary—and sometimes implausible—anxieties about the quality and reliability of even the most commonplace commodities.

Though the rapid growth of pharmaceutical manufacturing and of food canning, packaging, and wholesale distribution stimulated concern about a broad variety of consumer goods, attention focused first upon milk, the most basic food item. In urban areas the local dairy, whose cattle once fed off the grass of small open fields and supplied the needs of neighboring residents, had vanished. The rapid rise of urban population, exemplified by New

York's incredible growth beginning in the years just before the war, resulted in the concentration of milch cows in crowded, filthy stables, where they were fed with the vegetable waste of local distilleries in a primitive assembly line.

By the 1870s the efforts of sanitarians—and even more, the economic realities of the age—dictated the development of intensive dairying in neighboring counties, with milk transported over the expanding railway net into New York City. Now unsupervised "creameries" mechanically skimmed the milk for butter and cheese production and sent the residue in forty-gallon cans to itinerant milk dealers, who routinely thinned it with water. No longer could New Yorkers rely on the good faith of neighborhood entrepreneurs, and urban concern over the milk supply resulted in the first modern anti-adulteration laws.

Similarly, accusations had long been made about the adulteration of many other staple goods, such as mustard, ground coffee, and spices. In the 1870s these suspicions intensified. Highly competitive advertising and new techniques of merchandising aroused anxiety about traditional products. There was even more intense concern over food products that were entirely new, technological innovations such as glucose and oleomargarine, which could be manufactured profitably only by large-scale production.

These concerns led, in 1881–1882, to the passage of virtually identical anti-adulteration laws in New York and two neighboring states. In addition, controversy over sugar adulterated with glucose led to one of the earliest federal investigations of a domestic food. Excitement over oleomargarine, a product then made from animal fats and the residue of the slaughterhouses, led to antioleo legislation in virtually every state by 1886, and to the first federal regulation of a domestic food product.

These controversies, fomented by technological and entrepreneurial innovations, provided a testing ground for professionalism. The first adulteration laws coincided with the institutionalization of public health and with the establishment of local and state boards of health throughout the nation. Supervision over the food supply thus fell into the hands of the sanitarians, despite their lack of training or qualification.

In this same era medicine, pharmacy, and chemistry became professionalized and institutionalized. The chemists quickly proved themselves indispensable to the amateur reformers and the medical men who had fought for the health boards, but who now discovered that merely "sanitizing" the cities was an insufficient solution to complex urban problems. Empowered by the new adulteration laws to impose order and honesty—as well as health-fulness—the sanitarians found themselves more and more relying upon the expertise of the chemical profession.

But the chemists themselves were seldom on firm ground. Despite their positive assertions they were uncertain, unknowledge-able, and insecure. Judges who were obliged to render de-cisions on questions of the healthfulness or acceptability of business practices found themselves listening to contradictory professional testimony, with neither side able to provide convincing proof of its claims. Moreover, businessmen seeking to avoid regulation, or needing expert testimony against competitors, quickly discovered that the services of underpaid public employees were easily purchased. Often professionals retained their public office while working for the very industries they were simultaneously regulating.

Though many of the pharmaceutical and medical professionals were sincerely concerned with the public welfare and with the improvement of their own standards of practice, they too suf-fered from an excess of confidence and an insufficiency of hard knowledge. Moreover, leaders of the pharmacists and physicians were most devoted to establishing their profession's reputability and esteem, and in eliminating the competition of charlatans and amateurs.

But if the chemists, the medical/pharmaceutical professionals, and the public-health spokesmen are not seen here as the saints they are often described as having been, neither were they vil-lains, or merely the corrupt minions of the business interests. Rather, the professionals of this era were trapped in a complex situation of divided loyalties, at a time when codes of ethics and professional pride and dedication were inadequate responses to the temptations of power and to the expanding technology.

Similarly, astute business leaders sought associational power to combat the new commercial giants, such as the railroads, and to respond to the new complexities of the marketplace. Merchant spokesmen quickly came to understand that public anxiety about adulteration and other consumer concerns could be neither ig-nored nor squelched. Rather, they succeeded in shaping and con-trolling the reform movements in ways that they hoped would eliminate the questionable practices of irresponsible merchants and manufacturers, while protecting their own interests. The most modern and responsive leaders of the business community had more difficulty controlling members of their own organizations—making them understand the need for reform—than they did with the reformers.

While business leaders came to agree that the modern marketplace required regulation, they felt that the regulators should tolerate established business practices, including adulterations that had become "sanctioned by usage." In this genesis of governmental regulation business reformers argued that the only way to ensure "legitimate" commercial practices was to establish as the regulators not amateur enthusiasts, but the professionals upon whom they knew they could rely. They believed that only the "monopolist" and the rare immoral entrepreneur need be exposed and eliminated. Ultimately the market could be returned to the natural and immutable laws of competition, and the nation could once again enjoy fair play in its marketplace.

Thus the anti-adulteration movement of the 1880s was dominated by an alliance of certain leaders in business, chemistry, and medicine, whose objectives largely determined the behavior of the sanitarians on the boards of health that enforced the laws that these men had shaped. This study focuses upon the methods and motives of these men, and should not be viewed primarily as a "public health" history. Though it concentrates on one particular issue, it is a history of social and institutional change, an attempt to examine the interactions of a number of important groups in a challenging period of rapid transformation.

Though this study explores events in Washington, D.C., New Jersey, and Massachusetts, it reserves its most detailed examination for New York, where the inspiration for the laws originated, and where "modern" business complexity was greatest and came earliest. The controversies surrounding the federal law of 1906 were played out in New York by 1886; New York was a model for the national problems that culminated in national legislation a generation later.

Acknowledgments

The doctoral dissertation from which this study is adapted began upon the suggestion of Ari Hoogenboom, and my appreciation must be expressed for his continued advice and guidance. I thank Hans Trefousse for his careful reading of the dissertation and his exacting suggestions, and Richard C. Wade for his assistance and his encouragement for the preparation of this revised and abbreviated version. My thanks, also, to Kingsborough Community College for releasing me from some of my teaching duties, and to all the librarians who gave unstintingly of their time and expertise. I wish to express my particular gratitude to Dr. and Mrs. Phil Gorden of Bethesda, Maryland; Julian Aurelius and the Squibb Archives; the Manuscript Library of Columbia University; the Rare Books and Manuscripts Division of the New York Public Library; the Downstate Medical Center Library; the Library of Congress; the New York County Medical Society; the New York Academy of Medicine; and the Massachusetts Historical Society. My thanks also go to Professors Lee Benson, Ernst W. Stieb, and Aaron J. Ihde, and to many others, for responding to my questions.

Abbreviations

AMA	American Medical Association
APhA	American Pharmaceutical Association
APHA	American Public Health Association
ASSA	American Social Science Association
AICP	Association for Improving the Condition of the Poor
NAPAB	National Association for the Prevention of the Adulteration of Butter
NBH	National Board of Health
NBT	National Board of Trade
NWDA	National Wholesale Druggists' Association
NYBT&T	New York Board of Trade and Transportation
NYSPhA	New York State Pharmaceutical Association
SPCA	Society for the Prevention of Cruelty to Animals
USDA	United States Department of Agriculture
U.S.P.	*United States Pharmacopoeia*
WWDA	Western Wholesale Druggists' Association

FAIR PLAY IN THE MARKETPLACE

Some circumstantial evidence is very strong,
as when you find a trout in the milk.

—Henry David Thoreau

1

Intimations of Adulteration

Three generations of reform activity presaged the Pure Food and Drug and the Meat Inspection Acts of 1906. Not only were 190 bills introduced in Congress between 1879 and 1906 to control the proliferation of food and drug adulteration,[1] but on the state level legislative success had come by 1881; within a year three states, led by activists in New York, had passed virtually identical anti-adulteration laws. Yet even these laws represented the culmination of crusades that long antedated legislation, publicity that established remarkably persistent perceptions and misperceptions about poisons and frauds in foods and drugs.

The first man to have an American audience in the effort to strip the mantle of respectability from the purveyors of sophisticated[2] goods was Fredrick Accum, a German pharmacist and chemist living in England. Accum's *Treatise on Adulterations,* published in 1820, quickly went through four editions. A pirated edition was immediately printed in the United States. For the most part, Accum eschewed technical explanations and tests, attempting to warn a broad audience of the prevalence and danger of adulteration; the *Treatise* was a preview of the central arguments concerning adulteration that would endure for the remainder of the century.

---

1. Thomas A. Bailey, "Congressional Opposition to Pure Food Legislation, 1879–1906," *American Journal of Sociology* 36 (July 1930), p. 52.

2. In the terminology of the era "sophisticated" was used almost synonymously with "adulterated." The word suggested the deprivation of "naturalness" or "simplicity."

Accum's main thesis was that the complexity of modern food and drug production, distribution, and sale—the growing separation between producer and consumer—invited fraud and made room for "reprehensible . . . sophistication":

> It is a painful reflection, that the division of labour which has been so instrumental in bringing the manufactures of this country to their present flourishing state, should have also tended to conceal and facilitate the fraudulent practices in question; and that from a correspondent ramification of commerce into a multitude of distinct branches, particularly in the metropolis and the large towns of the empire, the traffic in adulterated commodities should find its way through so many circuitous channels, as to defy the most scrutinising endeavor to trace it to its source.[3]

Accum's most perceptive illustration of this modern process related to the coloring of cheese with annatto, a vegetable agent used by dairymen (and later by the oleomargarine interests) to gild their produce, especially in the winter months, when butter and cheese lack color due to the nature of the cattle feed. Though annatto itself is harmless, it is certainly a "sophistication" when used to improve the appearance of a product. But the annatto was frequently contaminated with red lead, of whose dangers Accum prophetically warned, though lead continued to be used as an ingredient in cosmetics and food colorings for decades.

In Accum's example a mercantile traveler adulterated the dyes, then sold them to a druggist. The druggist, unaware of the existing sophistication, further adulterated the product before selling it to a local merchant, "without any suspicion of the use to which it would be applied." The merchant might contaminate it even further before selling it to a farmer. The farmer would use the now triply adulterated annatto to color his cheese, which he would sell to a dealer in London, who might market it to an innkeeper, who would serve it to a customer.[4] The complexities

3. Fredrick Accum, *A Treatise on Adulterations of Food, and Culinary Poisons* (Philadelphia, 1820), p. 20.
4. Accum, p. 210.

of modern commerce helped to create a situation that would have been exceptional a generation earlier. When tradesmen and customers were neighbors, and anonymity was rare, these casual frauds were far less likely, or so at least Accum believed.

He argued that "almost every commodity which can be classed among either the necessaries or the luxuries of life" was being adulterated "to a most alarming extent in every part of the United Kingdom." He even declared that "there are some substances which are scarcely ever to be procured genuine."[5] These accusations would continually be repeated during the next several decades. Even the specific adulterations singled out by Accum for special consideration were, by and large, the same ones that retained the focus of later critics.

He called attention to the use of alum in bread, but was unable to assess its danger; the debate over alum continued into the twentieth century. Accum accused importers of selling imitation tea leaves; sophisticated teas became the first specific food import prohibited by federal law. Accum warned that ground coffee was frequently adulterated with "pease and beans"; not only was this accusation accurate, but the legal standard for ground coffee eventually established in New York permitted the use of both peas and cereals. Accum warned that mustard was adulterated with flour and colored with turmeric; these sophistications would eventually not only be discovered, but permitted, by the sanitarians. Accum warned that spices were almost universally adulterated; half a century later the experts would not only agree, but throw up their hands in helplessness. Accum also warned of lead in confectionery colors, a deadly practice that later studies confirmed.

Accum failed to deal with only three major foods that later occupied the attention of the sanitarians. But artificial glucose, a sugar manufactured from vegetable starches, and oleomargarine, a butter substitute made from animal fats, had not yet been invented. More puzzling, Accum barely mentioned milk. Yet milk would be regarded by the sanitarians as the most central of all foods, and its adulteration would excite the greatest concern of all.

Accum also introduced other arguments that later became quite common. He regarded "cheapness" as prima facie evidence

5. Accum, pp. 13–14.

of adulteration. After the Civil War both sanitarians and spokes-men for the grocery trade warned that buying the "cheapest" commodity encouraged excessive competition, which induced adulteration. Accum also presented as "proof" of his accusations miscellaneous newspaper and magazine articles whose claims echoed his own, without investigating their truthfulness. He also was willing to identify offenders by name, though he did so spar-ingly. Accum's argument was that such unsought publicity dis-couraged adulterative practices more readily than would the law.

Although Accum devoted far more space to foods than to drugs, he was convinced that "nine-tenths of the most potent drugs and chemical preparations used in pharmacy, are vended in a sophisti-cated state by dealers who would be the last to be suspected." This statement indicates two great weaknesses of Accum's study. He was unable to gauge the actual extent of adulteration with any accuracy and tended—as would those who followed him—to make broad generalizations after studying only a small sample.[6] Second, he relied heavily on "organoleptic" tests—that is, tests of the un-aided five senses. These essentially subjective judgments could be of little assistance to the pharmacist, the grocer, or the consumer, particularly if the adulterator had done his job well. It is true that the *Treatise* was written for the layman. Nonetheless, even though Accum was a thoroughly competent "analyst and industrial chemist,"[7] in this book, at least, his chemical knowledge was largely concealed in generalities.

No discernible action resulted in this country from the alarm Accum raised, and little more was published on the subject for some time. But in 1842 Robert M. Hartley, soon to become secretary of the Association for Improving the Condition of the

6. Accum, p. 23. Ernst Stieb, *Drug Adulteration: Detection and Control in Nineteenth-Century Britain* (Madison, 1966), p. 163, discusses two earlier periodi-cal articles by Accum that dealt with tests for drug adulteration. Stieb, pp. 114–18, notes that Accum's lack of documentation and his quantitative vagueness were typical of the era. Stieb also makes the judgment that, despite the likelihood of exaggeration because of Accum's "zeal as a reformer, we may still infer extensive adulteration (p. 114)."

7. Stieb, p. 165. Frederick A. Filby, *A History of Food Adulteration and Analysis* (London, 1934), p. 19, was more interested in foods than drugs and appears to have been less aware of Accum's pharmaceutical expertise. He argued that Accum "may not rank as an analyst of the first order."

Poor (AICP), wrote a ground-breaking book on the milk supply of large cities. Hartley claimed that increasing quantities of urban milk came from cows kept in confined quarters and fed on "swill," the vegetable residue of distilleries. He argued that it would be difficult to destroy the swill milk business because heavy competition among the distilleries made the sale of these "slops" an important factor in their survival.[8]

Four years later a broader and more exacting study of adulteration was published. Lewis Beck's *Adulterations of Various Substances,* however, was not intended for a general audience. Beck, a chemist at Rutgers College, had no particular theme, presenting simply an alphabetical review of foods and drugs, concentrating on the chemical tests to determine the most "common" sophistications. Though Beck devoted most of his review to drugs and relied heavily upon European authorities,[9] some of his comments on foods filled gaps left by Accum.

On coffee, for example, Beck devoted much of his space to chicory, which would eventually be revealed as the largest single adulterant of ground coffee, but whose use would later be authorized by the health officials in New York. Beck also devoted half a page to adulterations of chicory itself. More important, Beck spent three pages discussing milk. His analysis of the milk situation anticipated the arguments that would be repeated for years: "In large cities, where the consumption of milk is very great, it is seldom exposed for sale without having received some fraudulent addition. Although these adulterants are not always positively injurious, they at least diminish those qualities which render milk so valuable an article of food."[10]

---

8. Robert M. Hartley, *An Historical, Scientific, and Practical Essay on Milk* (New York, 1842), republished in 1850 as *The Cow and the Dairy,* pp. 111–12, estimates that, while there had been 1,129 distilleries in New York State in 1829, only 200 remained in 1842.

The New York Association for Improving the Condition of the Poor was organized in the winter of 1842–1843. It operated on the assumption that there would always be a large substratum of the poor in society and worked to improve their condition without attempting to "lift" them out of poverty.

9. Lewis C. Beck, *Adulterations of Various Substances Used in Medicine and the Arts, with the means of detecting them* (New York, 1846), Preface, which cites only one American source, the *United States Dispensatory,* discussed below.

10. Beck, p. 138.

Beck discussed the instruments available for testing the purity of milk, most of which were designed to measure the specific gravity of liquids, and which theoretically indicated either the addition of water or the removal of cream. But Beck cast doubts upon these tools, especially the one most commonly used, the lactometer. He noted that milk was quite irregular in its specific gravity and that the lactometer itself had been shown to be inaccurate in the measurement of added water. He did not specifically note the accusation later made against this technique for weighing adulteration: since the addition of water reduces specific gravity, while the subtraction of cream increases it, if both operations are performed concurrently, heavily adulterated milk could be produced that defies the lactometer. The debate over the accuracy and value of these instruments would continue into the twentieth century.

Beck reported that the most common adulterations of milk were skimming and dilution, "and the addition of bicarbonate of soda to neutralize its acidity." He also noted that annatto, or other harmless coloring agents, were sometimes added to disguise diluted milk. He dutifully noted reports of more bizarre adulterants, though he affirmed that "there is no doubt that these supposed adulterations have been greatly exaggerated, as most of the substances are easy of detection, and do not after all answer the purpose for which they are said to be employed." Unfortunately, the claims that Beck dismissed were so outrageous that they established themselves firmly in the popular conception of milk adulteration. They would be repeated by knowledgeable experts, most of whom would also dismiss them, yet in the process cement the misconceptions even deeper in the minds of their readers. Thus far-fetched stories persisted that milk was sometimes sophisticated with egg yolks, chalk, plaster of paris, "and even the cerebral matter of the sheep."[11]

At about this time sanitary reformers in New York, inspired by Hartley and Beck, turned their attention to the healthfulness of milk, particularly milk from cattle fed on swill. Early in the century most of the area's milch cows had grazed on open land within the city boundaries, but the rapid growth of population in the metropolis from 1845 to 1860 removed much of this pastur-

11. Beck, pp. 139–40.

age. Though by 1850 neighboring counties had established a thriving dairy industry, they concentrated on butter and cheese production until the 1860s, and though the New York railway net had assumed "modern outlines" by 1850, the system of transporting upstate milk to the city in ten-gallon cans was still in the process of development. For the time being, until the late 1860s, an indeterminate but surely large percentage of the milk supply was "swill."[12]

On June 26, 1847, the *New York Tribune* began an attack on "New York's Augean Stable." When the city government proved loath to act against the dairies, the New York Academy of Medicine organized a committee to investigate conditions. Dr. Augustus K. Gardner was made chairman, and Dr. John H. Griscom, who had recently been removed from his position as New York City Inspector[13] for political reasons, became its most active member. On March 1, 1848, the committee presented its report to the Academy. It cited a deficiency of butter fat, and speculated that distillery milk could cause cholera infantum, a deadly diarrheal disease. But the committee's resolutions—that swill milk was positively harmful and that the authorities should take action against it—were permanently tabled by the Academy.

Whether the majority of the Academy was motivated by a

12. Ulysses P. Hedrick, *A History of Agriculture in the State of New York* (1933; rpt. New York, 1966), p. 364; George R. Taylor, *The Transportation Revolution, 1815–1860* (1951; rpt. New York, 1968), p. 84.

Norman Shaftel, "A History of the Purification of Milk in New York or How Now Brown Cow," *New York State Journal of Medicine,* 58:6 (March 15, 1958), p. 915, believes that the first milk shipment to the city by rail took place in 1841, though regular traffic did not begin until about 1845. John Mullaly, *The Milk Trade in New York and Vicinity* (New York, 1853), pp. 25–30, hoped that the increasing railroad cartage would reduce the substantial sale of swill milk in the city.

13. In 1805 the power to regulate health matters in New York City was transferred from state to city officials. Until 1866 the organization of the city "board of health" underwent a number of changes. See Susan W. Peabody, *Historical Study of Legislation Regarding Public Health in the States of New York and Massachusetts* (Chicago, 1909), pp. 13–18.

In the late 1840s there were several city agencies with overlapping jurisdiction in the health area. The office of City Inspector was created by a law of 1839 and given the power to investigate potential health nuisances. See Duncan R. Jamieson, "Towards a Cleaner New York: John H. Griscom and New York's Public Health, 1830–1870" (Ph.D. diss., Michigan State University, 1971), pp. 193–96.

desire to await even more conclusive evidence or by political considerations, "the net result of their inaction was to strengthen the hands of unscrupulous dealers."[14] Dr. Griscom made a further unsuccessful attempt, at the June meeting, to revive the resolution by changing its wording slightly. But the committee's report was not published officially by the Academy until 1851, and renewed attempts by Griscom and Gardner to have the Academy take a stand on the issue were still being rejected as late as 1857.

In this era pharmacy was essentially an unorganized and unregulated profession. Although three states in the deep South required the licensing of pharmacists, these laws had long been inoperative. A few states theoretically regulated the sale of poisons and abortifacients, but such legislation did not become common until the 1850s, and it is impossible to determine the extent and efficacy of these early efforts. The first national pharmaceutical organization, the American Pharmaceutical Association (APhA), was not organized until 1852, and no parallel state association came into being until after the Civil War. Drug adulteration was reputedly so common that doctors customarily prescribed excessive dosages on the assumption that the medication's strength had been substantially reduced. "The tragedy," John Duffy has explained, "was that occasionally a patient was given a massive dose of highly potent medication which an honest company" had produced.[15]

This was one of the reasons many doctors prepared their own medications; there was no clear distinction between the medical and pharmaceutical professions, and it was as common for pharmacists to prescribe drugs as for doctors to dispense them. Leadership lay within the schools of medicine and pharmacy, but in 1847 there were only four such pharmaceutical schools—the Philadelphia, Massachusetts, New York City, and Maryland colleges of pharmacy. The first national medical organization, the American Medical Association (AMA), had just become offi-

14. John Duffy, *A History of Public Health in New York City,* vol. 1, *1625–1866* (New York, 1968), pp. 429–30.
15. Glenn Sonnedecker, *Kremers and Urdang's History of Pharmacy* (Philadelphia, 1976), pp. 214–15; Duffy, 1, p. 233.

cially operational in May of that year. But no coherent and respected leadership could speak for the profession.

There were two insurmountable obstacles to all attempts to regularize and attain licensure for the medical profession in mid-century. First, there were a number of competing medical theories, each of which generated its own "school" of loyal followers. Since all of these schools were founded on unproven theoretical principles, they continued to coexist; legislatures were understandably reluctant to legitimatize one at the expense of the others. It would be many years before medical science progressed enough to render reliable judgments on their appropriateness and deficiencies. Second, the broad variations in training created schisms even within each school. All professions have their more and less competent practitioners, but nineteenth-century medicine compounded these inequalities, since many "doctors" were merely self-anointed, while others had received the best available training. Even a medical "degree" was a virtually meaningless distinction: each orthodoxy had its own standards, and a proliferation of so-called medical "colleges" debased the diploma.

These problems accelerated, rather than decreased, with time. In New York state, for example, an 1827 licensing law gave control to the medical societies, though it provided exemptions for herbalists and other practitioners. But this law, and an amended version passed three years later, were rarely enforced. Moreover, a general suspicion of all doctors—augmented by the vocal divisions within the profession, and perhaps justified by medicine's general ineffectiveness—helped lead to the repeal of licensing entirely in 1844. For the next thirty years, "the practice of medicine in New York was open to anyone."[16]

If Beck's book on adulterations had helped inspire the activities of Griscom and Gardner, his comments on drug sophistication may also have aroused the pharmacists and physicians to begin lobbying for a federal law to prohibit the importation of adulterated drugs. The direct inspiration for this law came from

16. Duffy, 1: pp. 474–75. See William G. Rothstein, *American Physicians of the Nineteenth Century* (Baltimore, 1972), pp. 76ff., 145, 338; Paul Starr, *The Social Transformation of American Medicine* (New York, 1982), pp. 44–47, 56–59, 88–107; Richard H. Shryock, *Medicine and Society in America, 1660–1860* (New York, 1960), p. 138.

Dr. M. J. Bailey, who in 1846 succeeded in having himself appointed Special Examiner of Drugs at the Port of New York Customs Office, for the purpose of evaluating the quality of the drugs arriving at New York, where, he estimated, three-fourths of all such merchandise entered the country. Most of these crude and processed drugs were imported from England, where members of the British Pharmaceutical Society had already expressed anxiety concerning the quality of the goods handled by English merchants.[17] Bailey contended that the majority of drugs entering the port were adulterated or had deteriorated, and that European drug processors routinely dumped upon their American customers goods that could be sold nowhere else.

Under Bailey's agitation, in 1847 the New York College of Pharmacy and the New York Academy of Medicine appointed committees to confer on the subject of restricting the importation of adulterated and impure drugs. By the next year Bailey had succeeded in having memorials sent to Congress from both organizations, from a number of well-known Washington physicians and apothecaries, and from the AMA. A Select Committee of the House of Representatives, appointed to consider the question, issued a report on June 2, 1848, which served as a forum for Bailey's accusations.[18]

Bailey estimated that more than half the drugs entering the country had been adulterated or were unsatisfactory for other reasons, such as intentional mislabeling or deterioration. He stressed especially that the inexactness of a drug's strength and purity rendered it "less effective and more uncertain in the treatment of disease, and, in some cases, actually dangerous to the patient as well as obviously unjust and greatly embarrassing to the physician."[19]

Bailey placed the blame for adulteration almost wholly upon foreign exporters. He claimed that "but two or three of our regular and otherwise respectable" importers had knowingly ordered

17. *Imported Adulterated Drugs, Medicines, &c.*, 30th Cong., 1st sess., June 2, 1848, H. Rept. 664; Stieb, p. 138.

18. Philip Van Ingen, *The New York Academy of Medicine: Its First 100 Years* (New York, 1949), p. 17; F. W. Nitardy, "Notes on Early Drug Legislation," *Journal of the American Pharmaceutical Association* 23:11 (November 1934), p. 1122.

19. *Imported Adulterated Drugs*, p. 8.

adulterated drugs, and that almost all favored a federal law prohibiting the trade. They were aware, argued Bailey, that their business would improve if they could rely on receiving goods of dependable quality, but they also supported legislation on the grounds of moral "principle." Bailey denied that the domestic manufacturers of drugs would simply adulterate on their own if the trade were stopped. He argued that the separate states could, "if needs be, protect themselves from domestic evils of the kind, by enacting stringent laws" similar to those in operation on the Continent.[20]

Congressman Thomas O. Edwards, a physician and chairman of the Select Committee, laid virtually all the blame for the inadequacies of the medical profession upon "mercenary fraud" that caused discrepancies in the drugs used. Edwards shared Bailey's confidence that the medical profession and the honest importers demanded protection not because of "selfishness, or design of pecuniary advancement," but for humanitarian reasons "and a just professional pride." But he also worried that the public might turn to unqualified practitioners and to substitute remedies, such as the "patent" medicines that were rapidly expanding in this period, if confidence in the medical and pharmaceutical professions was consistently undermined by ineffective drugs.[21]

The legal precedent cited by Edwards is also worth noting. He quoted section 10 of the Tariff Act of 1842, which declared that "all indecent and immoral books and pictures" imported to the United States were "subject to confiscation and destruction." Edwards explained that "the paternal supervision of all good governments is not only needed to protect the morals of the people, but is justly demanded in all that pertains to their health and physical well being." The Secretary of the Treasury concurred, and argued that "the same principle, it is conceived, would justify the prohibition by Congress of the importation of adulterated and deteriorated drugs."[22]

20. Ibid., pp. 13–15.
21. Ibid., pp. 17–18. The so-called "patent" or "proprietary" medicines were not truly patented formulations; only their trademark or brand name was registered. See James H. Young, *The Toadstool Millionaires* (Princeton, 1961).
22. *Imported Adulterated Drugs*, pp. 16, 19, 21–22 (statement of McClintock Young, acting secretary of the treasury).

The bill became law on June 26, 1848, only a few weeks after the report was released. This first federal statute regulating adulteration prohibited the importation of substandard[23] or unsafe drugs, which had to be either reexported or destroyed. Early the next year Edwards reported that the law was working well; though virtually no adulterated drugs had been detected at the customs offices in Philadelphia, Boston, or Baltimore, Bailey had rejected large quantities at the Port of New York. Edwards argued that the law had already proven itself: not only had tons of spurious drugs been seized, but the general quality of drugs received appeared to be improving as exporters responded to the enforcement of the law's provisions. With this law, Edwards felt, Congress had done all it could; it was now up to the states to penalize domestic adulterators. But, he insisted: "No one can believe that adulterations here would be carried to the extent practised by foreigners. It is scarcely presumable that all the druggists will be engaged in a traffic so nefarious. The rivalry of business, the pride of the profession, and the higher and nobler motives of humanity, will be equal to the ingenuity and invention of the dishonest, and will effect its exposure."[24]

Bailey himself reported on the operation of the law a few months later, in an address to the New York Academy of Medicine. He estimated that over 90,000 pounds of drugs destined for the United States had been rejected at the Port of New York alone. Bailey's response to the few "free trade" editorials published in opposition to the law was reminiscent of Accum's complaints about the complexities of modern commerce: "medicines are every where purchased and sold by merchants dealing at the same time in every other description of merchandise, and who do not even profess to have any practical knowledge of the drug trade as a separate pursuit."[25]

Bailey now admitted that "home adulterations" were far more common than previously reported. Although he hoped these ac-

23. The law, 9 Stat. L., 237, set as its standards the various published pharmacopoeias, as discussed below.

24. *Operation of the Law to Prevent the Importation of Adulterated Drugs, &c.,* 30th Cong., 2d sess., January 24, 1849, H. Ex. Doc. 43, p. 8.

25. M. J. Bailey, *Report on the Practical Operation of the Law Relating to the Importation of Adulterated and Spurious Drugs . . . June 6, 1849* (New York, 1849), p. 6.

tivities could be traced to their "guilty source," he did not advocate the passage of state laws for this purpose. Rather, he suggested that the AMA appoint committees representing each of the states, "whose duty it shall be to closely scrutinize powdered drugs, and *all other* medicinal preparations," exposing frauds in the columns of the medical journals. The profession, in other words, should police itself. State laws for this purpose should be the course of "last resort."[26]

If it can safely be assumed that the emphasis Bailey gave to *"all other"* drugs was a subtle reference to patent medicines, his next proposal gains added significance. Bailey urged immediate passage of one type of law: a law that would, as the *American Journal of Pharmacy* expressed it, prohibit "herbalists, grocers, and general store-keepers" from vending drugs.[27] American medical/pharmaceutical professionals were seeking to eliminate the principal threat to their control over the practice of medicine: the ready-made "cures" and nostrums that increasingly took patients away from their care. During the next years pharmaceutical leaders consistently sought laws to remove this competition, always with the promise that their profession could then eliminate adulteration, without further governmental intervention.

One historian of food adulteration has questioned whether adulteration truly increased in the second quarter of the nineteenth century, or whether "the rise of modern chemistry" merely made these frauds "more visible." The great new weapon of analytical chemistry was the microscope, and it was the English physician Arthur Hill Hassall, a member of the Royal College of Surgeons and a recognized authority on the scientific use of the microscope, who first systematically applied this tool to food and drug analysis. In 1850 Hassall became interested in the quality of ground coffee available in London and decided to employ his microscopical expertise to investigate. His paper "On the Adulteration of Coffee" aroused a great deal of public attention because, coincidentally, the Chancellor of the Exchequer, Sir Charles Wood, had just testified in the House of Commons that it was impossible to determine "with any degree

---

26. Ibid., p. 17.
27. Quoted in Bailey, *Report,* p. 18.

of certainty whether a mixture [of coffee] contained chicory or not."[28]

As a result of this publicity Hassall was approached by Thomas Wakley, founder and editor of the medical journal the *Lancet,* the foremost publication of its kind. Wakley proposed forming an "Analytical Sanitary Commission," and offered Hassall the position of chief analyst. Thus began an extensive investigation of food and drug adulteration, published in the *Lancet* between 1851 and 1854 and gathered into the book *Food and Its Adulterations* in 1855; Hassall added material on drugs for a revision two years later, published as *Adulterations Detected.* Hassall's work led directly to the parliamentary investigations of adulteration in 1855 and 1856 and to the Adulteration of Food Act of 1860.

Hassall's microscopical illustrations seemed irrefutable proof of his claim that most foods sold in England were adulterated. But he sometimes made exotic charges on mere hearsay, to which his more verifiable accusations lent credibility. Moreover, Hassall reached conclusions about the vast extent of adulteration that—while they may have been true—he could not really establish, never having conducted a systematic investigation of the scope of adulteration, merely of its nature. Hassall's claims regarding milk, upon which the initial American reform activity in food focused, should serve as a sufficient illustration of his approach.

After reporting on the normal constituents of milk and discussing the use of the lactometer[29] to measure its specific gravity, Hassall noted the weakness of relying on this test alone, much as had Beck. Of the adulterants possibly used to sophisticate milk, Hassall reported that those in *actual* use included water, treacle or other sweeteners, salt, annatto, turmeric, gum tragacanth, bicarbonate of soda, starch, chalk, and "cerebral matter." He reviewed the chemical or microscopical techniques for detecting the presence of each of these ingredients as well as of some "alleged adulterations," such as boiled white carrots.

To what extent had Hassall observed these substances in his own tests? He reported that he had examined twenty-six samples of London milk, twelve of which were geniune and fourteen adulterated. The only adulterant he stated having actually found was "water." Yet, though Hassall had never personally observed chalk, cerebral matter, or starch in milk, he nonetheless asserted that "there is no question but that [they] have been and are occasionally, though rarely, employed." Often he could provide only hearsay evidence, explaining, "There is also good reason for believing . . ." Hassall seems to have made it a practice to name even the most doubtful adulterant, then indicate that its use "is but little probable."[30]

The most bizarre of Hassall's claims was that "cerebral matter"—sheeps' brains—was sometimes used to adulterate milk: "Starch and cerebral matter have been met with at different times by more than one observer. Professor [John T.] Queckett has in his possession some drawings made from samples of adulterated milk, showing the presence of both starch and cerebral matter." Hassall then reproduced Queckett's drawing. At the hearings conducted by the House of Commons on adulteration in 1856, Queckett appears to have been the only witness to testify to having found this substance in milk. Yet even Queckett admitted that he had discovered it in only one instance and that in every other case of milk adulteration since that time he had detected only "the mixture of water with the milk."[31]

At the hearings Hassall not only was the chief witness, but was permitted to both open and close the testimony. "In 999 cases out of 1,000," he testified, "I may state that I have only given to the Committee evidence of which I have distinct personal knowledge, and not from hearsay."[32] But Hassall's testimony was replete with phrases such as "I believe," or "I have never found [a particular adulterant] myself, but there is undoubted evidence of the fact . . ." For all his unquestionable skill with the microscope, and despite the fact that the parliamentary committee found him more than credible, Hassall was an unreliable witness. Yet, for a generation, Hassall's assertions continued to be the

30. Arthur H. Hassall, *Adulterations Detected, or Plain Instructions for the Discovery of Frauds in Food and Medicine*, 2d ed. (London, 1861), pp. 231–32.

31. Ibid., p. 236; *Report from the Select Committee* [of the House of Commons] *on Adulterations of Food, &c., together with the Proceedings of the Committee, Minutes of Evidence* . . . (London, 1856), p. 36.

32. *Report from the Select Committee*, p. 301.

authoritative source upon which American reformers would draw.

In New York at this time milk had suddenly become a burning issue once again. The question of swill milk had never really disappeared, despite the failure of the effort of Drs. Griscom and Gardner, and the newspapers repeatedly ran stories about the intolerable conditions in the "distillery" stables. The *Tribune* asserted that thousands of New York infants died each year because of swill milk, and in 1854 the *Times* blamed it for "the deaths of no fewer than 9,847 children under the age of two." The city inspectors' reports were filled with citizens' complaints about swill dairies and the stench they caused. By 1857 the *Times* was estimating that over two-thirds of all New York City milk came from the distillery stables.[33]

Then, in the spring of 1858, Frank Leslie's *Illustrated Weekly Newspaper* began a campaign against the swill milk industry. Although Leslie's attack had strong elements of "yellow" journalism—the famous illustration (figure 1) shows a distillery cow so weak it had to be suspended from a beam for milking—his accusations were true in their essentials. The campaign, kept up over several issues and supported by both the *Times* and the *Tribune,* finally forced the hand of the city Common Council. But the cursory inspection of Alderman Michael Tuomey, whom, along with Alderman E. Harrison Reed, Leslie would soon accuse of whitewashing the situation, persuaded no one.[34] The public protest against this scandalous "investigation" prompted the Board of Health to appoint a special committee to look into the situation.

But the "Board of Health" at this time consisted merely of the mayor and the Common Council; various aldermen and other city officers were designated "commissioners of health" and were to confer with the mayor on matters related to the public health.[35] Thus the "Select Committee" conducting the June 1858

33. *New York Tribune,* June 6, 1849, January 18, 1853; *New York Times,* March 9, 1854, September 7, 1857; cited in Duffy, 1: pp. 430–31, 438 n. 28.

34. See Duffy, 1: pp. 431–33. Tuomey and Reed brought suit against Leslie for libel, but the grand jury dismissed the charges in October 1858.

35. Laws of 1850, chap. 275.

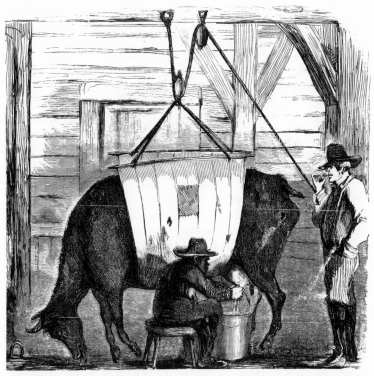

1. A swill stable cow too weak to stand during milking. From *Leslie's Illustrated Weekly Newspaper,* May 15, 1858. The Bettmann Archive, Inc.

investigation on swill milk consisted merely of four aldermen, two of whom were Tuomey and Reed. These two conducted most of the interrogation, and they permitted the attorney for the owner of the largest swill stable unrestricted right of examination; it sometimes appeared that the swill interests were conducting the hearings.

To make matters worse, free access to the hearing room was granted, with the result that hordes of swill stable employees attended daily. The situation became so uncontrolled that Leslie, who was the chief complainant against the stables, and who brought a number of medical and other witnesses to testify in confirmation of his accusations, refused to appear before the committee when called. He sent a letter to the committee, charging that the rowdy mob had "threatened me with personal violence" and "intimidated several of my important witnesses from coming forward."[36] The committee then subpoenaed Leslie, who, now that his protests had been publicly aired in the newspapers, was given more leeway by Tuomey and Reed.

With conditions controlled by those opposed to Leslie, chances for a condemnation of the swill stables were slim. Things were made worse by the repeated insistence of Leslie's witnesses that distillery waste was fatally poisonous, not only to the cattle, but also to children drinking their milk, for such broad claims could not be documented.[37] The more appropriate accusations were directed at the filthy conditions of the stables and the cattle, and the carelessness of the "dairymaids" (predominantly Irish men). Cow droppings and urine, and the unwashed hands of the men, all contaminated the milk. But even these accusations lost effectiveness, for the stable owners had been given advance warning of the "official" investigation and had moved half the cattle out of the stables, which had been cleaned as thoroughly as possible.

Drs. Griscom and Gardner were not very effective witnesses on Leslie's behalf. Griscom admitted that "I am not able to say that I have treated a case of disease contracted directly from swill milk," nor was he able to establish clearly the superiority of "country" milk over swill. Moreover, by testifying that milk with some added water was actually better than pure milk "for very young children," Griscom weakened his credibility, since he could not pinpoint exactly "what proportion" of water was best. Dr. Gardner's testimony was even less persuasive, since it was based, not on a scientific and objective evaluation, but on an emotional appeal. He believed "if God made the milk in a certain way, that it could not be improved upon; and if any milk was totally opposite from the natural milk, God's milk, that it must be totally wrong."[38]

---

36. *Majority and Minority Reports of the Select Committee of the Board of Health, Appointed to Investigate the Character and Condition of the Sources From Which Cows' Milk is Derived, For Sale in the City of New York* (New York, 1858), p. 184.

37. Later investigations conducted by the United States Department of Agriculture established that swill is a satisfactory cattle feed, so long as it is supplemented by other grains.

38. *Majority and Minority Reports,* pp. 97, 107–9, 169–70.

The majority report, signed by Tuomey and Reed, and by Alderman William Tucker, gave the swill stables a clean bill of health, although it recommended increased ventilation and greater stall space for the cattle, since the average of three feet currently provided made it impossible for them to lie down. The minority report, by Alderman Charles H. Haswell, denounced the distillery stables because of their filth, the diseases of the cows, and the careless practices of the milking men. He called for the complete elimination of all such establishments. He also vehemently condemned the practice of slaughtering these cattle for meat after disease had reduced their milk yield below profitability.

But it looked as if Leslie's agitation would have no permanent results. Griscom and Gardner approached the Academy of Medicine once again on June 2, 1858—the very day the public hearings began—in an attempt to win Academy support for the condemnation of swill milk. Their resolution was voted down, 35 to 24. On July 14 the Common Council discussed the reports and records of the hearings and voted to accept the majority report. Mayor Daniel E. Tiemann, however, soon approached the Academy with a request that it investigate the swill milk question further. The report of the committee formed to fulfill this request was presented to the Academy the following March. It condemned both swill milk and the meat of distillery-fed cattle. This time the Academy voted to accept its committee's report. The recommendation to prohibit the sale of swill milk and to institute licensing for all persons involved in milk distribution was sent to the mayor.[39]

When no legal remedy materialized, however, Leslie renewed the attack in his *Weekly,* and other publications joined the battle. An article in the *Knickerbocker,* though merely repeating the worst accusations made by Hassall, and offering no evidence of similar American conditions, concluded that "the practice of adulteration extends to almost every article of food." The *Knickerbocker* claimed that New York milk was "diluted with water and thickened with chalk, and in some instances with sheeps' brains." In contrast, an article in *Hunt's Merchants' Magazine* acknowledged widespread adulteration but—as other business-

39. Duffy, 1: pp. 434–35.

oriented journals would later repeat—placed most of the responsibility upon the "bargain"-hunting consumer.[40]

In 1861 *What We Eat,* an extensive volume on adulteration that gave special attention to American conditions and to the milk problem, was published in Boston. Although most of Thomas Hoskins's statements applied specifically to foods obtained in Massachusetts, he was intimately concerned with the New York milk campaign. He left "to the reader's judgment" the question of whether Aldermen Tuomey and Reed were "open to the suspicion of bribery," and went so far as to suggest that, "unprotected in their dearest rights by the legal authorities," the people of New York "would hardly be condemned by public sentiment" if they should resort to "mob-law." Written at the time that the first English food law was passed, Hoskins's book urged that, in America too, this evil "has become at last so enormous as to call imperatively for governmental interference, to protect the lives and pockets of the public."[41]

Hoskins's greatest concern was for the foods that directly affected children, and he quite properly devoted much attention to the frequently poisonous colorings used in confectionery and to "poisonous milk." Hoskins's treatment of swill milk reflected the general theory of disease prevalent in this period, before the germ theory had been promulgated. The foundations of public health in America were, paradoxically, "based on a structure of erroneous theories": the doctrine of "miasma." It was believed that invisible air-borne poisons emanating from filth, sewers, bodily discharges, and fecal matter directly caused disease. Thus the earliest public health "sanitarians" believed that disease could not develop if the cities were cleared of all contamination. This misconception was serendipitous, for such practices as street cleaning, sealed cartage for "night soil," and the elimination of slaughterhouse refuse, by reducing the breeding ground for

40. *Knickerbocker* 53:4 (May 1859), pp. 515–16; "Adulteration of Groceries in England," *Hunt's Merchants' Magazine* 41:5 (November 1859), p. 252. Though the *Hunt's* article was supposed to deal with British conditions, the journal assumed that the same situation existed in America. *Hunt's* was not particularly interested in milk, since milk was vended door-to-door by itinerant tradesmen, and not sold by the retailers who read this journal.

41. Thomas H. Hoskins, *What We Eat: An Account of the Most Common Adulterations of Food and Drink* (Boston, 1861), pp. 169–170, iii.

germs, helped reduce the urban death rate. Hoskins argued that the miasma of the confined stables affected both the cattle and their milk, making it poisonous. Though this "fine and virulent animal poison . . . like the fatal malaria of swamps" had eluded "the most delicate tests which art has yet been able to employ," Hoskins insisted it must nonetheless exist.[42]

He ridiculed the excuse "that the public demand goods so cheap in price that it is impossible to furnish them of the proper quality," and called for the cooperation of all honest dealers to help suppress the unfair competition of the adulterator. Despite the good intentions of men like Hassall and Leslie, "the efforts of the press alone, in this direction, are an entirely insufficient protection to the public." Publicity merely encourages "a reliance upon the terror of public exposure, rather than upon the law, for protection." But Hoskins held little hope for significant legislation: "In a letter received by me, a few days since, from that most distinguished friend of sanitary science, Dr. John H. Griscom, of New York, he informs me that all attempts to obtain enactments for the suppression of the horrible distillery milk-stables have entirely failed."[43]

Frank Leslie also seems to have temporarily abandoned hope for legislation. At this time he editorialized that the city government refused to take action against the swill stables because the wealthy owners could "buy off the crusade." But Leslie, by 1861, had gained powerful allies in his battle. The Academy of Medicine had taken a stand against swill milk, and the New York Sanitary Association and the AICP were campaigning in Albany.[44] A milk bill now passed the state Senate, though it failed in the Assembly. The New York press kept up its support, hoping for success the following year, and the influential journal the *North American Review* joined the battle with a very extensive article on adulteration.

42. Ibid., pp. 88–89, 94, 95f, 162–64; George Rosen, "Economic and Social Policy in the Development of Public Health," in *From Medical Police to Social Medicine* (New York, 1974), p. 197.

43. Hoskins, pp. 5, 207, iv–v.

44. Duffy, 1: pp. 435–36. The Sanitary Association had been formed in December 1858. It was an organization of physicians and sanitarians concerned with the public health; Dr. Griscom was one of its founders. By 1860 there were 250 active members. Jamieson, p. 232, says that the Association "petered out after the passage of the Metropolitan Health Bill in 1866."

The *Review* took the position that "nothing, we may say, in the whole domain of Nature, has escaped this universal contamination," but reserved its harshest criticism for three "most serious and pernicious" villainies: the sophistication of drugs, milk, and candies. Though the journal stated that "the chief adulteration of milk is with water; the others are of minor importance," it nonetheless mentioned the "traditional" accusations, including "sheeps' brains." It condemned the continuing problem of the swill milk stables. But it reserved its harshest treatment for the use of poisonous confectionery colorings, quoting Dr. Hoskins: "How many children have expired in sudden convulsions, where no one ever suspected the virulent cause in the apparently innocent, gayly-colored sugar-plum, clasped in its little hand, perhaps even in its dying struggles."[45]

The article condemned adulteration, not only for its obvious dangers to health, but also "its immoral influences upon trade,—encouraging fraud, and discouraging the honest trader by a ruinous system of underselling." The *Review* agreed with Hoskins that these evils could not be eliminated by publicity alone and that legislation was needed. But the article raised a problem that would not be overcome in the nineteenth century—nor at the present time, for that matter. Western society had great difficulty treating merchants as common criminals. In contrast to the petty thief, who received harsh punishment, the adulterator was "allowed to violate the law with impunity in his daily dealings, and not only to go unpunished, but to carry about with him, as at present he commonly does, in his intercourse with his fellows, the undeserved reputation of an honest man."[46]

Finally, on April 23, 1862, both houses of the state legislature passed the long-awaited bill prohibiting the adulteration of milk. The new law provided a fifty-dollar fine for the sale of adulterated or unwholesome milk or for maintaining a swill stable. But the law failed to define clearly what constituted an adulteration or to restrict the addition of water. The law was amended two years later to forbid specifically the "addition of water or any substance other than a sufficient quantity of ice to preserve the

45. "The Adulterations of Food," *North American Review* 194 (January 1862), pp. 4, 18–19, 34, 36.
46. Ibid., pp. 38, 9.

milk while on transportation to market" and to define all milk from swill-fed cows as being "impure and unwholesome."[47]

One important loophole remained, however, for though the laws assumed that all those *performing* an adulteration did so intentionally, those who *sold* adulterated milk broke the law only when they did so "knowingly." This question of guilty knowledge would play an important part in the legal battles to come, and set back for a number of years attempts to prosecute adulterators. Moreover, even when "an effective health administration" had been established, in 1866, the sheer number of dairies and milk dealers militated against efficient enforcement of the laws.[48] But at least there was now a legal foundation for the battle against the adulteration of this most vital food.

As criticism of drug adulteration increased in the 1850s, leading pharmacists responded—perhaps defensively—that the problem was centered in flaws within the 1848 drug law. One flaw was identified as the lack of a uniform standard for drugs. Yet even before the founding of the first college of pharmacy in America—the Philadelphia College of Pharmacy (1821)—a group of eleven physicians, each representing a local medical society or school, had met in Washington in an attempt to standardize American pharmacy. They sought to publish a national pharmacopoeia, a book describing drugs and chemicals, with information about their "standard" composition, formulae for preparation, and related information.

A committee was appointed under the leadership of Dr. Lyman Spalding, who had initiated the conference, to draft the manuscript. It was published in December 1820 and was an immediate success, for a second edition was published within two years. Because of "the progressive improvements in medicine," it was understood that this *United States Pharmacopoeia* (U.S.P.) would require periodic revision. Thus the Washington convention voted that in ten years—or sooner, if necessary—a similar convention would be called for this purpose.[49]

47. Laws of 1862, chap. 467; Laws of 1864, chap. 544. See Duffy, 1, p. 436.

48. Duffy, 1: p. 437.

49. James A. Spalding, *The Life of Dr. Lyman Spalding* (Boston, 1916), p. 360; *The Pharmacopoeia of the United States of America* (Boston, 1820), p. 16. The Squibb Archives kindly provided access to the first edition of the U.S.P. as well as to materials relating to APhA and to Dr. Squibb's work.

But when the first revision of the U.S.P. appeared, in 1830, it was almost immediately followed by another, different "first revision," which most pharmacists felt to be a superior version. This variant publication gradually usurped the "official" title of the U.S.P. The editors of this book were Drs. George B. Wood and Franklin Bache, of the Philadelphia College of Pharmacy, who continued to publish revisions of it for the rest of their lives, along with an accompanying volume, *The United States Dispensatory*. The commercial success of the *Dispensatory*, which was an explication of and commentary on the U.S.P., provided the financing for the older book. Thus, with the publication of the first edition of this schismatic revision in 1831, the pharmacists controlled the U.S.P.[50]

By 1851 leading pharmacists, who directed the colleges of pharmacy and represented their profession within the AMA, were dissatisfied with the fact that the law of 1848 sanctioned the use of five different pharmacopoeias, published in the United States and Europe.[51] The federal inspectors could legally choose among varying standards for particular drugs; the U.S.P. was but one guide. The pharmacists wished to establish the U.S.P. as the sole set of standards for the inspectors and as the semiofficial guide for all American druggists. But the AMA, at its 1851 meeting, rejected their proposal. Did this small group of pharmacists, the medical men asked, truly represent the sentiments of the entire profession? Largely because of this disagreement, a group of about twenty pharmacists, representing local societies and colleges of pharmacy, met to form the first national pharmaceutical organization, the American Pharmaceutical Association, in October 1852.

One of the first—and most enduring—problems facing APhA was the question of the proliferation of patent medicines, which

50. Sonnedecker, *History of Pharmacy*, pp. 260–64, 279. Dr. John S. Billings, "A Century of American Medicine, 1776–1876," in *Selected Papers of John Shaw Billings* (n.p., 1965), p. 32, claimed that from "a financial point of view, the *Dispensatory* is the most successful medical book ever published in this country."

51. The United States, Edinburgh, London, French, and German pharmacopoeias. See Glenn Sonnedecker and George Urdang, "Legalization of Drug Standards under State Laws in the United States of America," *Food-Drug-Cosmetic Law Journal* 8:12 (December 1953), p. 744.

the law of 1848 did nothing to regulate. The organization's initial constitution admitted into membership all druggists, but only if they adhered to a "code of ethics" and would "discountenance quackery"—refuse to sell nostrums. But too many practicing druggists depended upon the sale of patent medicines, and within three years this membership requirement was dropped. The new constitution of 1856 compromised by explaining that it was the goal of APhA "to suppress empiricism [quackery] and as much as possible to restrict the dispensing and sale of medicines to regularly educated druggists and apothecaries."[52]

The medical and pharmaceutical leadership consistently placed the blame for a host of problems upon the expanding business of patent and ready-made medications. It will be remembered that Dr. Bailey had advised against state laws regulating drug adulteration, but had sought legislation that would eliminate patent drugs and prevent nonprofessionals such as grocers from vending them. In 1854 Dr. Griscom argued that "the fault" for this proliferation "lies rather with the public which patronizes, and not so much with the tradesman who profits by" the sale of nostrums. Griscom explained that it was the duty of the medical professionals to educate the people away from such "charlatanry."[53]

Similarly, at an 1859 pharmacists' convention, the membership acknowledged its "high duty to purge their profession of the disgrace which their dishonest brethren bring upon it," but laid a central responsibility for such problems upon the patent drugs. As the *North American Review* reminded its readers, however, even if the adulterations were being performed by drug manufacturers, the retail druggists "do not all test, or know how to examine, their drugs, and the fraud passes unsuspected by them." The *Review* estimated that the state of the American drug market "is even worse than in England."[54]

52. Sonnedecker, *History of Pharmacy*, pp. 198–202.

53. John H. Griscom, "Anniversary Discourse, Before the New York Academy of Medicine" (November 22, 1854), reprinted in *Origins of Public Health in America* (New York, 1972), pp. 24–25.

54. "Adulterations in Food and Drugs," *Hunt's Merchants' Magazine* 41:5 (November 1859), p. 254; "The Adulterations of Food," pp. 36–37.

Leaders of APhA responded to this type of criticism by point-ing to an additional flaw in the drug law. In 1858 APhA peti-tioned Congress to improve the system by which inspectors were appointed, arguing that unqualified political spoilsmen were sta-tioned in some of the ports, and that drugs rejected by a qualified inspector were merely reshipped to another port, where a less competent, or more venal, inspector might well pass them on.[55] With the election of President Lincoln, and the opportunity for a fresh start presented by the new Republican administration, a host of New York medical and pharmaceutical societies orga-nized a joint committee to renew these appeals. The leading spokesman for these groups was Dr. Edward R. Squibb, a Brooklyn doctor and pharmaceutical manufacturer who had rap-idly gained a reputation for competence and honesty, and who would later play an important role in the broader battle against adulteration. Squibb argued that the law of 1848, if left "in the hands into which it naturally falls, namely, the political and im-porting interests," would "become almost a dead letter," and even an actual hindrance, discouraging attempts to provide genu-ine deterrence.[56]

In 1860 the AMA had appointed a committee of three men, including Squibb, to investigate the operation of the drug law. Though no report was made, the committee was reappointed in 1863. Similarly, APhA maintained its own interest in the law. In 1862 Dr. Squibb had persuaded APhA to discontinue its Com-mittee on Adulteration and reorganize upon a broader format as the Committee on the Drug Market. Squibb was made chairman of this committee, and his report to APhA the next year was an indictment of the drug market, the government, and the 1848 law. He reported that prices for crude drug supplies had skyrock-eted because of the war and that quality had fallen. But if the war

55. Nitardy, p. 1124; *Proceedings of the American Pharmaceutical Association* 7 (1858), pp. 234, 36; James H. Young, "Drugs and the 1906 Law," in *Safeguard-ing the Public,* ed. John B. Blake (Baltimore, 1970), p. 151. APhA may have decided to act at this time because Bailey's services as drug inspector at the Port of New York ended in 1857. See *Boston Medical and Surgical Journal* 110:11 (March 13, 1884), p. 243.

56. Edward R. Squibb, "The Drug Inspectors and the Profession," correspon-dence marked "To the Editor of the American Medical Times," January 18, 1861, Squibb Archives.

was the immediate instigation for this corruption, there were broader causes: "doubtless the moral tone of the community at large."[57]

Without the effective mediation of the import law, the natural incompatibility between "the drug market" (which sought only profit) and the community (which sought drugs of good quality) had become sharper. The balancing force should be the druggist and the physician. But in these difficult times, Squibb noted sadly, "the magic power of profits" appears to have corrupted "a large majority" of the pharmacists and many of the doctors. Squibb pointed to the natural difficulty of the professional, who had to maintain high ethical standards yet deserved to earn a good living. Squibb was one of the few medical men who freely admitted that, though the professional had an "important duty to his fellow-men," he was still "a merchant."[58]

Squibb prepared a similar report for the AMA committee, but that group never succeeded in agreeing upon a presentation. Always a maverick, and never hesitant to speak out, Squibb blamed the AMA chairman for "procrastination" that had made it impossible to function effectively. Squibb took full responsibility for his comments and presented his views to the AMA, claiming that the law was now an almost complete failure, though it had worked successfully when first instituted, under Dr. Bailey. The failure was due to three things: the appointment of incompetent inspectors at the customhouses; the failure of inspectors to abide by their oath to enforce the law faithfully; and standards adopted by the Treasury Department that were below those set by the U.S.P., and therefore too lenient.[59] The AMA listened to Squibb's "Remarks" politely, but failed to act upon them.

---

57. Nitardy, 1125; William C. Alpers, "History of the American Pharmaceutical Association, Second Decade, 1860–1870," *Journal of the American Pharmaceutical Association* 3 (December 1914), p. 1625; 4 (January 1915), p. 3; Edward R. Squibb, "Report on the Drug Market," *Proceedings of the American Pharmaceutical Association* 12 (1863), p. 193.

58. Squibb, "Report on the Drug Market," pp. 193–95.

59. Edward R. Squibb, "Remarks Upon the Practical Working of the U.S. Drug Law," *Transactions of the American Medical Association* 15 (1865), pp. 142–50. The chairman was Dr. Joseph Carson. The other member of the committee was Dr. Henry Bowditch.

Ernst Stieb notes that when Hassall's articles and books were published in England there was a good deal of antagonism toward his methods. Stieb does not suggest that the British medical and pharmaceutical professions were unaware of the problems of adulteration, but notes that "these problems never seem to have occupied a major place in thought or official action." The movement was maintained, not by the professional organizations, but by individual members of those organizations. On both sides of the Atlantic, many men engaged in the business of medicine saw adulteration as a "natural phenomenon," merely part of free economic competition. On the whole, the professionals preferred to seek a solution in self-regulation rather than in law, except when they could control the administration of the law or when the law enhanced their own authority. Thus, in both nations, "organized pharmacy looked to government action mainly to inspect imported drugs,"[60] and American organizations opposed regulatory legislation except to the extent that regulation would restrict the competition of the amateur and the charlatan.

There was little interest in making the law of 1848 work more effectively. The law existed, and the professions had done their duty in its passage; if the law failed, the government, not the medical and pharmaceutical professions, was responsible for the continuation of adulteration. For similar reasons, in England, drugs were excluded from the act of 1860. The British Pharmaceutical Society had persuaded Parliament that it was perfectly capable of supervising the drug market.

Nonetheless, laws *were* being passed in both countries; the later British adulteration laws, for example, did include pharmaceuticals. In America, the law of 1848, and the New York milk laws, were instances of an increasing tendency to set aside the belief in laissez-faire. Lawrence Friedman notes that by mid-century Americans were slowly moving away from a blind faith in the common law, which emphasized the doctrine of *caveat emptor,* and toward the civil law, which stressed governmental intervention and "paternalism." Increasingly, American courts were finding reasons "to read *express* warranties into a seller's words,"

60. Stieb, pp. 158–59, 144, 154.

and the idea of the implied warranty in commercial transactions was spreading. Nevertheless, Hassall was clearly presumptuous in hoping that traditions would soon be broken, and a belief in *caveat venditor* established.[61]

61. Lawrence M. Friedman, *A History of American Law* (New York, 1973), pp. 232–35, 384–85; Hassall, in *Minutes of Evidence* (1856), p. 4674; see Stieb, p. 105.

2

New York Sanitary Reform: The Exercise of "Autocratic" Power

By mid-century the attention of New Yorkers had been drawn to the problem of food and drug adulteration—especially the question of swill milk—but legislation seemed to promise little in the way of a solution. The responsibility for enforcement of the milk laws of 1862 and 1864 lay in the hands of the same men who vehemently opposed virtually all sanitary reform because it trespassed upon their own political prerogatives. It was unlikely that the reformers' goals would be attained unless supervision of New York's sanitary condition could be wrested from the hands of the political machines, the placemen, and the ignorant. The growing public health movement was in the vanguard of the fight against adulteration. The sanitarians, and the boards of health they helped to create, soon carried the burden of enforcing existing laws and of drafting additional legislation.

The origin of the Metropolitan Board of Health is an oft-told tale[1] that will bear a brief repetition. Concern over epidemic disease—which justifiably continued to be the central issue of health reform for many years—stimulated a number of attempts between 1852 and 1862, spearheaded by the New York Academy of Medicine, to reorganize completely the city's health administration. Each attempt, however, was defeated in the New York

---

1. For an extensive reminiscence of the activities that led to the Board's formation see Stephen Smith, *The City That Was* (1911; rpt. Metuchen, N.J., 1973). The best modern treatment is in John Duffy, *A History of Public Health in New York City,* vol. 1, *1625–1866* (New York, 1968), pp. 540–70.

State Assembly, where legislators feared that the bills would deprive their friends of patronage positions. Then, after the July 1863 New York City draft riots had called attention to the conditions under which the destitute and frustrated rioters had been living, a broad coalition of reformers formed the Citizens' Association, led by Drs. Elisha Harris and Stephen Smith. The Association quickly introduced a new metropolitan health bill into the legislature. At a large meeting on March 30, 1864, the leaders of the Association met with local doctors and organized a Council of Hygiene and a Council of Law. Dorman B. Eaton—now chiefly known for his work in civil service reform—was propitiously selected to head the latter.[2] Eaton suggested that the Council conduct a thorough street-by-street sanitary inspection of the city. After the new health bill had been defeated the Council lent its energies to this inspection, in the summer of 1864.

When the survey had been completed, at the end of the year, it filled seventeen volumes with a remarkable and detailed account of the city's health and social conditions. To make its study more manageable and readable, the Association spent several months condensing the report to one still impressive volume, published in June 1865. Although virtually the entire volume was devoted to the tenement "fever-nests" and public "nuisances" that contributed to epidemic disease, the *Report* did occasionally note the unsanitary condition of meat, and went out of its way to record the existence of swill milk stables. (See figure 2.) The Council reported that food articles exposed in the public markets "may undergo spontaneous deterioration, becoming not only unsuited for their purpose, but absolutely poisonous. . . . such food articles are not unfrequently nefariously adulterated by tradesmen."[3]

Although the Association's health bill was once again stopped in the Assembly by the patronage forces, events were moving toward the ultimate triumph of the reformers. By August of 1865 the newspapers were warning of an approaching cholera epi-

2. Citizens' Association of New York, *Disease and Death in New-York City and its Vicinity* (New York, 1864), p. 15. See John M. Dobson, *Politics in the Gilded Age* (New York, 1972), pp. 79–80: Eaton became federal civil service commissioner in 1873 and "was the logical choice to draft the bill that became the Pendleton Act" (p. 80).

3. *Report of the Council of Hygiene and Public Health of the Citizens' Association,* 2d ed. (1866; rpt. New York, 1970), p. cii.

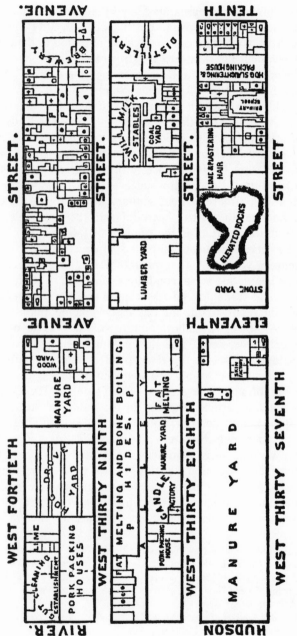

2. Representative sanitary map from *Report of the Council of Hygiene*, p. 266, showing "bone-boiling and swill-milk nuisances" in one neighborhood.

demic; by October and November scattered cases began appearing in this country. The election of Tammany's John T. Hoffman as mayor strengthened the determination of the Association to remove, once and for all, control over sanitary affairs from the hands of the city government, and renewed efforts were directed to Albany. A final push began with the publication, in December, of a lengthy pamphlet that stressed the danger of the approaching epidemic, warning that effective measures could be instituted only if the entire urban area was served by a professional metropolitan health board. The most effective part of the pamphlet was a tour de force: the reformers published the names and occupations of the "health wardens" of the city. These Tammany appointees, theoretically responsible for overseeing the sanitary concerns of New York, were mostly liquor dealers, saloon keepers, or the ne'er-do-well unemployed.[4]

On February 26, 1866, the Metropolitan Board of Health Act became law, giving the state government control over sanitary affairs in an area roughly coinciding with present-day New York City. The new Board usurped all existing agencies, and could call upon the police to carry out its orders and decisions. But the most dramatic fact about the new Board was that it had the authority to create sanitary legislation without consulting either the city or state governments. The man responsible for this remarkable turn of events was Dorman Eaton.

Almost half a century after the creation of the Board, Stephen Smith reflected that he and his associates had felt that, in order for the Board to be effective, it required "autocratic" powers. Smith explained that Eaton, as head of the Council of Law, had prepared the final draft of the bill so as to elevate the Board beyond the interruptions of legislatures and courts. The bill granted it the power to "create ordinances" on its own authority by the simple expedient of publishing them in the city newspapers, whereupon they became part of the health law of the metropolitan district. This was achieved, Smith gloated, through subterfuge. "The language of that portion of the bill conveying these powers was purposely made very technical, in order that only a legal mind could interpret its full meaning, it being be-

4. *Address of the Committee to Promote the Passage of a Metropolitan Health Bill* (New York, 1865).

lieved that the ordinary legislator would not favor the measure if he understood its entire import."[5]

Acting upon the assumption that New York State's legislators were ignorant of legal niceties, Eaton set out to fool them into surrendering legislative power to the Board through obfuscation. Eaton, Smith explained, believed that a health board "should make its own laws, execute its own laws, and sit in judgment on its own acts." Eaton himself, possibly feeling that it would be impolitic, made no claims as broad as these during his lifetime. But he did note that it was essential that the Board be created "possessing powers partly judicial, partly executive and partly legislative," and rejoiced that it was able "to abate the worst classes of nuisances without a resort to the delay and the expense of a jury trial."[6]

In the same year that Stephen Smith published his reminiscences, a commemorative dinner was given to celebrate his service in the cause of public health. Upon this occasion Charles F. Chandler, the first chemist appointed to the original Board and later its president, gave a speech in which he noted that the law of 1866

> conferred powers upon the Board of Health akin to those of martial law. The Board was authorized to make its own laws, and on April 20, 1866, it adopted a sanitary code, embodying sanitary ordinances, rules and regulations, covering everything that affected the public health.
>
> Years afterwards, when the force of these ordinances had been established by numerous judicial decisions, it was suggested that the Shah of Persia should establish a Board of Health, in order to get more power over his subjects.[7]

Perhaps the intervening years had led both Smith and Chandler to gloss over the difficulties of their early work and exaggerate the actual powers they enjoyed. In the area of food and drug

5. Smith, *City That Was*, pp. 44–45.

6. Ibid., p. 171; Dorman B. Eaton, *Sanitary Legislation in England and New York* (New York, 1872), pp. 32, 34.

7. *Stephen Smith, M.D., LL.D. Addresses in Recognition of His Public Services. 1911* (n.p., n.d.), p. 19.

adulteration, at least, the work of the Board was not as smooth as its "autocratic" powers should theoretically have made it.

There has, perhaps, never been a period when the health authorities of New York City were more active than the first two years of the Board's existence. There were so many sanitary problems facing the new Board that it attempted to sweep the city—literally and figuratively—clean. Obviously its first concern was the approaching cholera epidemic, but to combat this threat, from the perspective of pre–germ theory sanitary science, meant war on the broadest scale. The entire crowded, filthy city was seen as a breeding ground for both moral and physical corruption. The two seemed interwoven, for wherever filth existed, disease and death spread among those who lived amid, and caused, the unsanitary conditions. Dirt and disorder were held to be virtually synonymous with disease itself—such chaotic conditions brought on, literally emanated, a host of problems to the public health. The sanitarians saw it as their duty to impose order and cleanliness upon those incapable of keeping their surroundings free of these evils; the sanitarians assumed the responsibility for remediating the chaos of the overflowing urban neighborhoods, as agents of the state. Thus the Board forcibly vacated the worst of the tenement "fever-nests," boarded up cellar apartments, cleaned thousands of water closets, carted thousands of loads of night soil, removed thousands of dead animals from the city streets and alleys, and applied tons of disinfectant. In the view of both the Board and the public, these activities were rewarded with victory over the epidemic; the final estimate was that "only" 1,214 residents died of the disease in 1866. Criticism that had appeared in the newspapers—particularly the Democratic press, suspicious of a Board appointed by a Republican state administration—turned to praise by the fall of the year.[8]

Much of the credit for the determination with which the Board

8. Duffy, 1: pp. 558–59; John Duffy, *A History of Public Health in New York City,* vol. 2, *1866–1966* (New York, 1974), pp. 28–29; Barbara G. Rosenkrantz, *Public Health and the State* (Cambridge, Mass., 1972), pp. 2–3, 9–10, 30–31. Wilson G. Smillie, *Public Health* (New York, 1955), p. 382, estimates that in 1854 twice as many New Yorkers died of the disease; in the great cholera epidemic of 1849 the toll was over 5,000. See *New York Times,* July 5, 1868.

attacked the entire spectrum of sanitary problems must be given to its first president, Jackson S. Schultz. By law, the president could not be a physician; Schultz was the largest leather dealer in the city, a self-made man who had begun his career as a tanner and whose wealth was estimated at close to $2 million.[9] Obviously Schultz and the other members of the Board were swamped with more compelling responsibilities than that of food and drug adulteration. But two sanitary problems that the Board immediately addressed were directly related to the quality of food: the public markets and the slaughterhouse and fat-boiling companies. The Board inspectors identified both as prime suspects for harboring miasmatic disease.

The Board's first annual report noted that, "after securing pure air and general cleanliness, nothing tends so directly to promote the public health as a proper supply of food." The public markets were extensively criticized, and a special report on the largest of them, Washington Market, was included in an appendix. Located roughly where the World Trade Center now stands, Washington Market had been constructed during the War of 1812, but the original brick building was, by mid-century, surrounded by countless wooden stands and wheelless wagons. Most business was conducted from these shabby stalls, and artificial streets and alleys were created by the crazy quilt of permanent and transient merchants. Across the street, in even worse condition, West Washington Market dealt to the wholesale trade. The Board estimated that almost 900 tradesmen, most dealing in foods, were located in the two markets.[10]

Within days of its formation the Board began investigating the markets, after market inspectors seized putrid meat at several locations. After a thorough inspection it was decided to serve the illegal stands that obstructed the public streets with eviction notices, and to maintain limited warfare against the worst sanitary offenders. Meanwhile the Board would investigate the possibility of removing the markets to the upper part of the city. But the

9. Junius H. Browne, *The Great Metropolis, A Mirror of New-York* (Hartford, 1869), pp. 670–71.

10. [First] *Annual Report of the Metropolitan Board of Health. 1866* (New York, 1867), p. 29; *Scribner's Monthly* 14:6 (October 1877), pp. 729–43; *New York Times,* March 24, 1866.

market men were so effectively organized, and apparently paid such substantial contributions to the political coffers, that they soon managed to induce the state legislature to forbid the Board from interfering with their operations before May 1, 1869.[11]

The Board's other major target, the slaughterhouse operators and wholesale butchers, provided the first real legal test of the broad powers granted to the sanitarians. The Board almost immediately declared war against the butchers, though the sanitary complaints dealt with the filth produced in the slaughterhouses, their proximity to residential areas, the ancillary fat-boiling and soap factories, and the practice of driving cattle and other animals through the public streets, rather than with the quality of the meat.

A number of meetings were held with representatives of the Butchers' Hide and Melting Association, who believed that their business could readily be conducted within the city limits without endangering the public health. But Schultz quickly made it clear that a general cleanup was only "a temporary expedient" and that ultimately their "business must be moved to some place remote from the centres of population." The Board set May 1, 1867, as the deadline for this removal. President Schultz had in mind an imitation of the French abattoir system, which eliminated most of the filth of the butchering process and simplified inspection of the meat by concentrating both slaughtering and the rendering of offal in centralized facilities. These would be located near the rivers in order to facilitate the herding of stock and the removal of waste. Temporarily, however, the recommendations were tabled, while the Board awaited a legal ruling on the extent of its power to remove nuisances.[12]

Meanwhile, at a series of mass meetings the butchers raised objections to the Board's proceedings, one of which struck at the

11. [First] *Annual Report, Metropolitan Board*, p. 31; *Second Annual Report of the Metropolitan Board of Health of the State of New York* (New York, 1868), p. 21.

12. *New York Times*, March 13, 1866. The Association was the city's dominant organization of butchers, leather men, and operators of fat-boiling facilities. It was incorporated April 8, 1865, by state legislative action; see Laws of 1865, chap. 330.

New York Times, March 22, 1866; [First] *Annual Report, Metropolitan Board*, p. 34; *Second Annual Report, Metropolitan Board*, p. 289.

heart of the matter: if the Board had the authority to remove the butchers from one part of the city, what power could stop the sanitarians from "issuing another *ukase* a week or a month hence," sending them even further north? Leading Tammany figures harangued the butchers about the excesses of "these phenomena of modern legislation—commissions—institutions which were handling the rights of the people as if they were playthings." The butchers resolved to bypass the city courts and the state legislature, and appeal directly to the state court system.[13]

On November 19, 1867, the state Supreme Court ruled that the Board had exceeded its legal authority and had reached beyond the parameters of the common law; the Board's attempted exercise of "legislative" powers would effect a "revolution."[14] Although the Board would be permitted to enforce sanitary codes within the slaughterhouses, it could not arbitrarily relocate them. Yet government by commission was clearly necessary. The normal legislative processes called for by the court were too slow, too removed from the problems, and too handicapped by politics to respond adequately to the multiplying complexities of urban society. The court was falling back upon a traditional, but inadequate, system. Yet, as the Board noted in its annual report, no final decision had been made.

In New York the "supreme" court is not the highest in the state; the state Court of Appeals is superior, and the entire question was immediately appealed by the Board. On June 18, 1868, the Court of Appeals not only reversed the lower court's decision, but ruled that the Board's "legislative" and quasi-judicial powers—the right to hold hearings and render judgments without going through the regular court system—were unassailable. The Board could both enact and enforce its own codes, as well as assign penalties for their violation, and "there is no right to review this decision by a jury trial or to interfere with its enforcement by injunction." The only course open for those accused by the Board was certiorari, a review by a superior court.[15]

13. *New York Times,* September 3, September 8, September 12, 1867.
14. *New York Times,* November 20, 1867.
15. *New York Times,* July 3, 1868; Susan W. Peabody, *Historical Study of Legislation Regarding Public Health in the States of New York and Massachusetts* (Chicago, 1909), p. 105.

In its first two years of operation the Metropolitan Board dealt with the quality of the food supply only indirectly, through its efforts against the markets and the slaughterhouses. Not until Professor Charles F. Chandler was employed by the Board was adulteration itself attacked. In 1867 Chandler was invited by Elisha Harris, the Registrar of Records, to perform some gratuitous analyses of the city's water supply for the Board. Chandler's work so impressed the Board's physicians, who had not understood the potential importance of chemistry for public health, that the position of Chemist to the Board was created for Chandler at the end of the year.[16]

In 1868 Chandler was authorized to pursue an investigation into "the quality and kinds of burning fluid in common use, and whether any, and if so, what foreign ingredients of an explosive character are added."[17] Kerosene distilled from petroleum, widely used in New York by the 1860s for illumination, was clearly the cause of many explosive fires each year. Yet before Chandler probed into the problem there was little public concern about kerosene safety, the people and the fire department both dismissing such fires as "accidental."

While before the Civil War whale oil was the illuminating fluid of preference, its high price had stimulated a search for cheaper substitutes. A mixture of alcohol and "camphene"—rectified spirits of turpentine—came into common use, despite its volatile nature. After years of accidental fires and explosions caused by this burning fluid, the public came to accept danger as the price paid for using cheaper substances. Chandler was apparently the first scientist to understand that, with kerosene, these risks were avoidable; kerosene, unlike camphene, could be manufactured so as to be perfectly safe when used with care. "Accidents" occurred only when naphtha, benzine, or other light petroleum distillates, selling for much less than pure kerosene, were used to adulterate the fluid.[18]

16. Robert L. Larson, "Charles Frederick Chandler, His Life and Work" (Ph.D. diss., Columbia University, 1950), p. 70.

17. Board resolution, from Emmons Clark to Chandler, November 11, 1868, Chandler Papers.

18. Larson, pp. 78–79; Charles F. Chandler, "Report on Dangerous Kerosene," *Fourth Annual Report of the Metropolitan Board of Health of the State of New York* (New York, 1869), pp. 437–57.

Chandler quickly purchased and tested seventy-eight samples of kerosene from New York City retailers, and found the situation to be even worse than he had suspected: not a single sample was pure kerosene, and some were so adulterated as to be simply naphtha. He submitted his report to the Board on January 11, 1869, and blamed the dangerous situation not only on the greed of the refiners and retailers—all of whom he named in his report—but on the consumers as well. "Consumers should understand that in demanding the cheapest oil they compel the refiners to supply them with a mixture of benzine and kerosene. Competition is irresistible; and if the price is run down below cost, adulteration must follow." Chandler's solution was a demand for legal controls over the manufacture and sale of kerosene.[19]

The report caused a sensation; all the New York papers reported Chandler's findings, and his results were republished throughout the country and in Europe. The Board immediately published a sanitary ordinance forbidding the sale of kerosene that failed to meet safety standards, with the declaration that "there was no excuse for unsafe oil." But when some dealers were arrested for violating the ordinance, the courts threw the cases out with the explanation that illuminating fluids properly lay within the jurisdiction of the fire department, not the Board.[20] Chandler consoled himself with the hope that the publicity he had given to the danger would result in the sale of purer kerosene, but the facts belie any optimism: there were still 98 kerosene fires in the city in 1869, and 157 the following year. Chandler did what he could, publishing a fuller report on the danger in 1871. At that time Colonel Emmons Clark, the secretary of the Board, wrote to Chandler, asking *"what action, if any"* the Board could take.[21] But there would be no new law

19. Chandler, "Report on Dangerous Kerosene," p. 441.

20. Stenographer's Minutes of "Address of Charles F. Chandler to the New York City Medical Society, June 3, 1878," pp. 95–96, Chandler Papers. New York State laws governing burning fluids were Laws of 1865, chap. 773, Laws of 1866, chaps. 872 and 873. On the court decision see *New York Times,* December 31, 1870.

21. Charles F. Chandler, "Report on Petroleum Oil," *First Annual Report of the Board of Health of the Health Department of the City of New York* (New York, 1871), p. 552, notes that kerosene-related fires constituted 11 percent of all

regulating kerosene until 1882, and the hands of the sanitarians were tied.

Until 1869 the Board demonstrated virtually no interest in either the swill milk problem or milk adulteration, merely arresting a few retailers each year for violating the ordinance prohibiting the watering of milk. In its first annual report, the Board was so confident that the distillery stables no longer posed a danger that Colonel Clark could pronounce the situation "almost entirely discontinued in New York." Only in Brooklyn was there a perceptible problem, where, Clark claimed, the Brooklyn Common Council was protecting the swill milk operators through a special ordinance.[22] Indeed, for several years after the passage of the milk laws of 1862 and 1864 there seemed little interest generally in legal activity on the milk issue. The public and the press seemed to acquiesce in the Board's assumption that the problem had been eliminated, and criticism of the milk industry in this period focused, instead, on the accusation that the high prices caused by the war were being maintained artificially. The *Times* believed that the pre-war exposé of the swill stables had all but destroyed "that pernicious branch of the business," and that "the adulteration of milk in this city has its existence more in imagination than in reality."[23]

The truth was that the Board had virtually abdicated its responsibilities in this area, leaving it instead in the hands of Henry Bergh. Bergh, called by one biographer an "angel in top hat," was a genteel reformer who was outraged at the casual cruelty with which the city's animals were treated. On April 10, 1866, he organized the New York Society for the Prevention of Cruelty to

---

fires in the metropolitan area in 1869, and 18 percent in 1870. Chandler also complained (p. 541): "The apathy of the public in regard to this matter is beyond my comprehension."

Clark to Chandler, March 20, 1871, Chandler Papers.

22. [First] *Annual Report, Metropolitan Board*, p. 24.

23. *New York Times*, January 22, August 15, 1865. National Bureau of Economic Research, *Trends in the American Economy in the Nineteenth Century* (Princeton, 1960), pp. 143–44, 169, indicates that although food prices rose slightly less than the average inflation rate during the war, there were substantial increases across the board. Milk prices went up more than 50 percent between 1860 and 1865. The Consumer Price Index for milk dropped slightly by 1866, but there was little further decline until the 1870s.

Animals, becoming its first president. By April 19 he had been invested with the legal power to enforce a new law against such cruelty; the SPCA, though remaining a private organization, was recognized as an arm of the government.[24] Bergh's organization assumed the responsibility for policing the swill stables.

SPCA agents raided seven cow sheds in upper Manhattan in 1866, and the next year brought suit against the owner of a stable on East Fifty-sixth Street. But Bergh's main efforts were directed against the Brooklyn dairies that seemed able to defy the authority of the Metropolitan Board. On February 23, 1867, Bergh decided to make a test case of Morris Phelan, a major Williamsburg stable owner. On the basis of testimony from SPCA witnesses, Phelan was indicted in June, not just for cruelty to animals, but also for the alleged unhealthy nature of the milk produced by his cattle. When the case dragged on for two years without coming to trial, however, Bergh appealed for assistance to George B. Lincoln, the new president of the Board of Health. But Bergh's letter merely drew a strongly sarcastic response from the Brooklyn district attorney, Samuel D. Morris, and the correspondence found its way into the *Herald* and the *Times*. Despite this publicity, Morris continued to refuse to prosecute.[25]

The *Times* followed the SPCA's case against Phelan closely, but it was otherwise virtually silent about milk adulteration for the next two years, reasserting that the "swill-milk nuisance" had been "entirely broken up."[26] The paper recommended that wary consumers protect themselves by using a lactometer, which sold for as little as $1.50 and was an "infallible" instrument for home testing of suspected milk.[27] Thus, as late as the winter of 1868 the battle against milk adulteration had been virtually abandoned. Henry Bergh's efforts had come to naught, the Board was inactive and complacent, the press gave little attention to the question, and the public was apparently sanguine.

24. Zulma Steele, *Angel in Top Hat* (New York, 1942). The SPCA continues to enjoy similar powers today in New York City; it is in charge of dog licensing, uses the fees to maintain animal shelters, and enforces anti-cruelty legislation.

25. Steele, pp. 111–13.

26. *New York Times*, March 8, March 11, March 24, 1867; January 15, February 2, 1868.

27. *New York Times*, August 23, 1868. Earlier articles on the lactometer were published in the August 21, August 25, and September 9, 1865, issues.

The situation rapidly changed, however, because of a campaign initiated by the *New York World*. Beginning on December 17, 1868, the *World*'s exposé of "False Measures and Adulterations" continued intermittently until April 13 of the following year, the most extensive treatment of the subject in the public press in this era. The quality of the exposures is questionable, for the articles dealt more with minor frauds in weights and measures than with adulteration, contained vague and generalized accusations, were more dependent on "established" claims—such as those of Hassall—than upon chemical analysis, and rarely lived up to the expectations aroused by their alarmist headlines. The actual chemical examinations conducted for the paper rarely revealed any unusual or dangerous adulteration—merely chicory in coffee, terra alba (a cheap, inert ingredient used as a "filler") in cream of tartar, and breadstuffs in spices. Thus, for example, the paper claimed that baked horse liver was widely used to adulterate coffee, yet could offer no specific instance of its detection, relying merely on Hassall's statement that this fraud was common.[28]

Yet the impact of the series was clearly great. Throughout the city and the nation other newspapers responded vigorously to the *World*'s assertions. (Indeed, many of the *World* articles were merely reprints of items from other papers that were themselves reprints of earlier *World* stories.) Certainly one immediate consequence of these exposures was reawakened interest in milk adulteration. The *World* began treating this subject on January 19, 1869, and it was at this time that Professor Chandler was asked by Colonel Clark to begin investigating milk for the Board of Health.

Chandler's report, when it was finally submitted the following year, failed to disclose any adulterant except for water, though Chandler nevertheless reviewed seven "traditional" techniques for adulterating milk. This slavish recitation was surely responsible for helping to perpetuate the assumption on the part of the public that chalk, sheep's brains, and other oddities were being employed by devious adulterators, for only a very careful reading would dispel the impression that a wide variety of noxious items were used by the milkmen. Chandler's conclusion that "for every three quarts of pure milk there is added one quart of water" was

28. *New York World,* February 15, 1869.

also deceptive, for it was not based on a random sample of all milk sold in the city, but instead included large quantities known to be adulterated. The report also asserted that cow-stable milk was "in *every* respect poorer than the milk of healthy cows," though Chandler was unable to cite "any specific poison." Though Chandler conceded that New York milk was free from injurious adulterations or disease,[29] the report, by its overall tone, certainly contributed to public outrage concerning milk adulteration.

Armed with Chandler's condemnation of swill milk, which had been publicized as early as April 1869,[30] Henry Bergh stepped up his own campaign against the Brooklyn stables. Although the Brooklyn police did not accept Bergh's recommendation that the "milkmaids" "ought to be hung," they were willing to arrest the offenders en masse. In addition to the employees, several stable owners were arrested and charged with both cruelty to animals and violation of the milk laws. One pleaded guilty, paying a fine of fifty dollars for each offense, while the others were held for trial. At the first court hearing Board President Lincoln came to Brooklyn to lend support to Bergh. After some weeks of delay the trial finally began, with District Attorney Morris still absent. Bergh, as authorized by state law, appeared as the prosecutor, but Justice Buckley refused to accept his right to appear, even after Bergh procured written authorization from Morris. The cases were dismissed. Bergh, however, refused to acknowledge defeat, and he eventually persuaded the Kings County grand jury to indict not only the dairymen, but Justice Buckley as well.[31]

Unfortunately, just as what seemed to be a concerted attack on adulteration was taking place, disaster struck the cause of sanitary reform. Boss William M. Tweed, who had helped achieve

29. Charles F. Chandler, "Report on the Quality of the Milk Supply of the Metropolitan District," *Fourth Annual Report, Metropolitan Board*, pp. 5–6, 12–13. Chandler was frequently remiss in completing important reports; see below, chap. 9 and 10. Much of the milk report was composed by others.

30. *New York Times*, April 13, 1869. The Board declared that, on the basis of Chandler's examination, swill milk was "to be regarded as less healthful and safe for food than milk which has simply been diluted with water, inasmuch as the deficiencies . . . are caused by pathological or unhealthful conditions in the cows that produce such faulty milk."

31. Steele, pp. 115–19; *New York Times*, February 22, 1870.

the Democratic victory in 1869 that had placed Tammany's John T. Hoffman in the New York governor's mansion, demolished the Metropolitan Board of Health. In 1870, arguing for "home rule," Tweed spent an estimated $1 million in bribes to obtain a new charter for the city. Jackson Schultz, now president of the Union League Club, a genteel Republican reform organization, presided over a meeting that sent a special committee, chaired by Horace Greeley, to fight the revision in Albany. But this effort failed, and the city government reorganization replaced metropolitan commissions such as the Board with corrupt municipal departments, whose heads were appointed by the mayor.[32]

In part, the Board was a victim of its own success. Many New Yorkers felt that the Board had already completed its principal public health tasks, now that the city had been partially "sanitized" and the cholera epidemic was a distant memory.[33] Still, it was primarily the political debacle that set back sanitary progress during the Tweed era. The new Health Department had jurisdiction limited principally to Manhattan. Elisha Harris—who had become the Sanitary Superintendent—and Thomas B. Acton, the dedicated police commissioner, both resigned.[34] Professor Chandler stayed on as the Department's chemist, but his duties were seriously diminished. The new health inspectors were the spiritual brothers of the corrupt place-holders the Citizens' Association had worked so hard to eliminate.

Although it would be inexact to say that the new Board was totally derelict in its duties, clearly little was accomplished on any sanitary front during Tweed's brief tenure. As Dorman Eaton lamented, "It is painful to turn . . . to the miserable sanitary methods and the feeble sanitary results which have been the natural consequence of the partisan and dishonest control of our political degradation." The *Times* complained that "the detection of poisonous and dangerous adulterations is nobody's business, and nothing short of some great and general calamity appears capable of arousing public attention." If the press had been san-

32. DeAlva S. Alexander, *A Political History of the State of New York* (1909; rpt. Port Washington, N.Y., 1969), 3: p. 229; William L. Stone, *History of New York City* (New York, 1872), p. 613.

33. Duffy, 2: pp. 48–49.

34. Larson, p. 89.

guine prior to the adoption of the Tweed charter, the *Times* now warned about milk adulteration, the growth of the swill business, the sale of "diseased meat," the watering of canned fruits and vegetables, dangerous kerosene, and the "criminal negligence" of the new Board officials.[35]

The publication, in early 1872, of the long-delayed first annual report of the new Board demonstrated the haphazard manner in which it pursued the city's sanitary work. Chandler's abbreviated report broke little new ground, and his comments mirrored Eaton's pessimism, conveying an air of grudging resignation and disappointment. While he noted, for example, that "it may frequently happen that lead" may contaminate canned vegetables, he failed to pursue the topic, offering merely two brief sentences.[36] The sanitarians, in the Tweed years, were engaged more in holding their own than in aggressive reform.

In 1865, thirteen years after the formation of the American Pharmaceutical Association, whatever local and national control existed over the profession continued to reside within the various colleges of pharmacy; no statewide organizations had yet been formed. Though there were a handful of local laws regulating the practice of pharmacy, none seems to have been enforced at this time.[37] In the state of New York there was little agitation for pharmaceutical reform; deaths by accidental poisoning because of druggist or physician error, for example, were routinely reported along with drownings and household misadventures. But in that year Professor Ferdinand F. Mayer of the New York College of Pharmacy laid the groundwork for the eventual regulation of his profession. The proliferation of small neighborhood drugstores, and of patent medicines, was reducing the College's influence over New York pharmacy. There were many practitioners,

35. Eaton, *Sanitary Legislation*, p. 34; *New York Times*, September 3, 1870, March 7, 1871, August 19, 1871, October 25, 1871.

36. *First Annual Report of the Board of Health*, pp. 312–19.

37. Glenn Sonnedecker, *Kremers and Urdang's History of Pharmacy* (Philadelphia, 1976), pp. 196, 213–14. Sonnedecker, "Controlling Drugs in the Nineteenth Century," in *Safeguarding the Public*, ed. John B. Blake (Baltimore, 1970), pp. 101, 106, indicates that some sort of legislation relating to drug *adulteration* existed in fourteen states before 1865 and in twenty-five states and territories by 1870.

Mayer claimed, "who dispense drugs, without understanding their qualities," and inadequately trained drug clerks were responsible for "many deaths" due to error. Though Mayer could not pinpoint the cure for these problems, he called for a new system of apprenticeship and training.[38]

Perhaps because of this warning, the *Times* began gradually escalating its coverage of both drug adulteration and pharmaceutical error. By the end of 1866 the paper was claiming "that not one half of the drugs used in a majority of the drug-stores in the preparation of physicians' prescriptions are such as they ought to be." The cupidity of the retail druggists was compounded by their "want of sufficient scientific education." The paper issued the most important challenge to professionalism, one that continued to echo within the medical and pharmaceutical communities: many druggists regarded their trade as would "a jobber of dry goods" or "a dealer in hardware. They consider drugs a merchandize, and dealing them out is, in their eyes, not a scientific pursuit."[39]

By 1867 the *Times* was regularly headlining errors made by druggists, not just locally, but all over the nation. Yet ironically—to take one example—an accusation of a fatal oversight in Mobile, Alabama, was surrounded by elaborate advertisements for such products as "Mrs. Winslow's Soothing Syrup," "Phalon and Sons 'Night-Blooming Cereus,' " "Jayne's Expectorant," "Chevalier's Life for the Hair," "Dr. Langley's Root and Herb Bitters," and a full half-column ad for Dr. Von Eisenberg, whose "Aesthetico-Neuralgicon" cured consumption, asthma, and all diseases of the throat, eyes, and ears.[40]

If the *Times* was reflecting a national concern over pharmaceutical safety, then we may understand why the interest of the professionals was renewed at this time. The pharmacists may also have been reacting self-protectively to a growing national political trend. Throughout the nation, state and local political machines were beginning to view the idea of special licensing regulation as an opportunity for bribery and kickbacks. If such legislation was unavoidable, it was understandable that the groups involved would seek to influence the shape of the laws. In 1868 APhA

---

38. *New York Times,* March 18, 1865.
39. *New York Times,* December 27, 1866.
40. *New York Times,* April 24, 1867.

appointed a committee to draft a bill that would regulate the practice of pharmacy and prevent adulteration of drugs. The Association failed to agree upon its committee's report, and did not approve the bill officially, but nevertheless sent copies of the proposal to various state legislatures and encouraged them to act upon it.[41]

In New York, however, Dr. John I. Gray, president of the state Medical Society, argued that the College of Pharmacy was powerless to control adulteration and incompetence, and urged his fellow physicians to seize the initiative for drafting new legislation. With more than ten deaths a year in New York attributed to prescription poisoning, and with pressure increasing for new legislation, in 1869 the Assembly introduced a bill to regulate pharmacy. Though the proposal had not been carefully thought through, it was a first attempt to establish minimum qualifications for the practice of pharmacy in the state.[42] But Governor Hoffman failed to approve the bill, and the incoming Tweed forces then set out to create their own version of the law. Tammany, already in the process of perverting existing institutions to serve patronage purposes, turned its attention to new sources of power and profit.

In January 1871 James Irving, a Tammany lieutenant who would soon be forced to resign from the Assembly,[43] submitted a bill providing for the licensing of druggists' clerks in New York City. The bill was soon amended to apply to all those engaged in pharmacy, proprietor and clerk alike, and to establish a board consisting of "one skilled pharmaceutist, one practical druggist, and two regular physicians." Clearly the Irving law sought to establish a system for reaping licensing fees ($30 per pharmacist),

41. F. W. Nitardy, "Notes on Early Drug Legislation," *Journal of the American Pharmaceutical Association*, 23:11 (November 1934), pp. 1125–26; *Proceedings of the American Pharmaceutical Association* 20 (1872), p. 161.

42. *New York Times*, February 7, 1868, October 11, 1868. David L. Cowen, "America's First Pharmacy Laws," *Journal of the American Pharmaceutical Association* 3: 5 and 6 (May and June 1942), p. 214, and Duffy, 1: pp. 473–74, discuss an abortive 1832 state licensing law that applied to New York City only.

43. Alexander B. Callow, Jr., *The Tweed Ring* (New York, 1965), p. 245, notes that in April 1871 Irving "struck down Smith M. Weed, Republican from Clinton county, on the floor of the Assembly. Even the Ring was powerless in face of public indignation."

while permitting well-paid Tammany appointees the opportunity to dominate the pharmaceutical profession. The very severe penalty of a $500 fine and/or six months imprisonment was established for noncompliance.[44]

Tammany failed to appoint any College of Pharmacy leaders to the examining board, and the new law provided no "grandfathering"; all pharmacists, regardless of training, experience, or prestige, had to appear for examination. Thus the "Irving" law provided an incentive for very active organizing on the part of the New York pharmacists, and apparently for their national society as well. APhA not only objected to the "obnoxious" law, but also, for the first time in eleven years, established a Committee on Adulterations and Sophistications. In twenty-one pages of discussion—the first substantial treatment of adulteration by the profession since the debates over the law of 1848—APhA suddenly awoke to the fact that "Mammon still reigns. . . . Drugs are largely adulterated." The committee placed the onus upon the drug wholesalers, though it suggested that retailers had a responsibility for reforming these culprits by refusing their wares. As for "quack" medicines and cosmetics, APhA's hope was somehow to eliminate them entirely, for "printers' ink and popular credulity" made them a serious threat to the profession.[45]

Though APhA was not yet ready to renew its campaign for regulatory legislation, the New York pharmacists were. After seven organizational meetings (for which the members were, of course, paid), Tweed's examining board, headed by Professor R. Ogden Doremus, began interviewing pharmacists on July 25, 1871. Doremus, though unquestionably a competent chemist, frequently played an obstructionist role in reform efforts. He had been the chief "eminent" expert hired by Aldermen Tuomey and Reed for the purpose of defending the swill milk dairies; his services were for sale to the highest bidder.

44. "An Act to establish a Board for the examination of and licensing Druggists and Prescription Clerks in the city of New York," passed March 28, 1871. A strong bill to regulate the sale of patent medicines was killed in this session by the Tweed forces, Tweed personally submitting remonstrances from over 100 wholesale druggists. See *Journal of the Senate of the State of New York* (Albany, 1871), pp. 322, 452, 457–58.

45. *Proceedings of the American Pharmaceutical Association* 19 (1871), pp. 330–31, 335, 349.

Thirty-two leading New York pharmacists, all of whom were graduates of various colleges of pharmacy, issued a remonstrance against the law, and about 300 other druggists, predominantly German, organized the Druggists' Protective Union. The Union emphasized that the board "was simply another means of serving out Government pap to a few favored individuals," and complained that the examiners' judgments were entirely subjective. Officials of the College of Pharmacy, understandably, argued that a diploma from their institution should be sufficient evidence of proficiency. All agreed that the druggists and druggists' clerks had to lobby in the forthcoming legislature to seek annulment of the law.[46]

Before the new legislature could act upon the law, however, the board of examiners presented its report to the mayor. Even the *Times*, despite its earlier condemnation of the Irving law, was appalled by this evidence of "frightful ignorance." Avoiding all mention of possible bias or insufficiency on the part of the Tammany board, the paper reported that a third of the 1,000 applicants tested had failed and that "not one in twenty" of the others had passed all their examinations on the first trial.[47] This poor showing, whatever the law's inadequacy, surely confirmed the pharmacists' suspicion that simple annulment was now impossible. They apparently accepted the inevitability of regulation and hoped only to acquire a more equitable law.

The Druggists' Union had already met with the Board of Trustees of the College of Pharmacy; a conference committee now completed a draft of a new law. The College presented the bill to the legislature, where it was introduced by State Senator Augustus Weisman, himself a pharmacist and a member of the College. Although their original bill was "disfigured by some amendments," the pharmacists accomplished virtually all they could hope for.[48] The new law, approved by Governor Hoffman on

46. *New York Times*, July 27, July 28, July 30, and August 12, 1871.
47. *New York Times*, January 9, 1872. Dr. Doremus provided more of the failing grades than the other three examiners together.
48. *APhA, Proceedings*, 1872, pp. 163–67. "An Act to regulate the Practice of Pharmacy and the Sale of Poisons in the City and County of New York." APhA argued that the only justifiable regulation should be a diploma from a recognized college of pharmacy before entering practice, and "a strict accountability" once in the business. The Association did not explain what it meant by "accountability."

May 22, 1872, granted to the College of Pharmacy the authority to appoint the new examining board, which consisted of five pharmacists. Although all practicing pharmacists had to be registered, the act grandfathered-in all graduates of colleges of pharmacy with at least four years' experience in the drug business. Practitioners who lacked the diploma had to have passed the examination of the Irving board or that of the new board of examiners. The registration fee was reduced to two dollars.

In addition, the new law required each registered pharmacist to be legally "responsible for the quality of all drugs, chemicals, and medicines he may sell or dispense" except for prepackaged items and patent drugs. A conviction for adulteration was punishable by a fine of $100, and the guilty party could lose his license. The law also enumerated poisons that could not legally be retailed and placed restrictions upon the dispensing of other poisons. Penalties collected under the new law would be turned over to the College of Pharmacy's library fund.

The Tweed takeover had interrupted sanitary progress in New York, but soon Tweed was gone, and no obstacle remained to a direct response to adulteration. Though no general anti-adulteration law existed, the Board of Health provided the instrumentality for sanitary supervision, and the milk laws were ample legal ground for activity in that most crucial arena. Moreover, the power to create ordinances given to the Board by Eaton lent it jurisdiction over virtually any threat to the public health. Of course, the courts had ruled against the Board's kerosene ordinance, but at least Chandler had been able to publicize the problem. Though the Board of Health was not granted jurisdiction over the practice of pharmacy, the new drug law had placed the responsibility for drug purity upon the drug retailers. Now the Board should be able to take action against a broad spectrum of food and drug problems.

3

Charles Frederick Chandler:
Tests of Power

The new state government elected in November
1872 quickly revoked the Tweed charter; by an act of April 30, 1873,
the Board of Health was reorganized for a second time. The Board's
powers were restored to those enjoyed by the Metropolitan Board,
though its jurisdiction continued to be limited to Manhattan. Its key
members were Professor Chandler, the new president, his medical
associate Stephen Smith, and Colonel William P. Prentice, the
Board's counsel. Chandler's intention was to reestablish the power
and respect formerly held by the health authorities. To this end
Chandler attacked those sanitary problems he regarded as the un-
finished business of the old Metropolitan Board.

In the Board's assault upon epidemic disease, the markets,
slaughterhouses, and other "nuisances," there was at first little
time, money, or devotion for the problem of adulteration. The
Board, for example, prepared competitive examinations for those
reapplying for their positions as sanitary inspector and assistant
sanitary inspector. Of the twenty-three questions asked of the
first group, only one question—the last—dealt with adulteration:
"What is the composition of pure cow's milk, and how would you
detect adulterations?" None of the nineteen questions asked of
those reapplying for the job of assistant inspector related to adulteration, nor were new applicants for either job asked such
questions.[1]

In those sanitary contests Chandler chose to enter, probably his
clearest triumph was against the marketmen. It will be remem-

1. *New York Times,* June 18, 1873.

bered that the Metropolitan Board's attack had been cut short when the state legislature forbade any further interference before May 1, 1869; the Tweed Board had virtually ignored the markets. In July Chandler and Smith personally inspected Washington Market, which the Superintendent of Markets and Mayor William F. Havemeyer had been defending. Chandler gave legal notice of his intention to have the wooden stalls destroyed once and for all, whereupon the marketmen sought a restraining injunction on July 23. Colonel Prentice suggested to Chandler that the court would surely issue the injunction the following day and that the Board's last legal opportunity must be taken before 10:00 A.M. Chandler immediately arranged with a house-wrecking firm for the demolition of the stalls, and persuaded the police to provide protection for the sanitarians. The stands were destroyed in a midnight raid upon Washington Market. Under the threat of similar action against the other markets, butchers quickly complied with Board orders.[2]

Chandler, with equal fervor and drama, also succeeded in eradicating the most visible of the city's "stench" nuisances. He had Colonel Prentice annul the contract of the New York Rendering Company, which had been disposing of the city's animal carcasses and offal since 1865 but had violated the terms of its contract by operating within the city limits. All the movable property of the company was forcibly seized and towed over to New Jersey. Similarly, the offal of the slaughterhouses was being rendered on the barge *Algonquin,* in an illegal manner. The owners refused to desist and moved their vessel into the Hudson River, beyond the Board's jurisdiction. Chandler, with questionable legality, arranged for a tugboat to tow the *Algonquin* to Barren (now Ward's) Island at the owners' expense.[3]

An even more difficult target selected by Chandler was the city's meat industry. The most glaring abuses of the slaughter-

2. See manuscript of speech that Chandler gave in 1911 in honor of Dr. Stephen Smith (21 pp., unnumbered), in Chandler Papers; Robert L. Larson, "Charles Frederick Chandler, His Life and Work" (Ph.D. diss., Columbia University, 1950), pp. 99–104; *New York Times,* June 28, July 12, July 17, July 18, July 23, and July 24, 1873.

3. *New York Times,* July 12, August 9, 1873; Larson, pp. 104–5; John Duffy, *A History of Public Health in New York City,* vol. 2, *1866–1966* (New York, 1974), p. 132.

houses had been abated by the Metropolitan Board, and virtually all had been moved north of Fortieth Street. The Tweed Board had offered lip service to centralization, but it had taken no action.[4] Chandler decided that the compromise measures accepted by his predecessors were inadequate. His determination to assault this powerful and entrenched interest may have been encouraged by concurrent alarms raised by members of the humane organizations, upon which he was eager to capitalize.

In 1873 Henry Bergh had turned from his war against cruelty to beasts of burden and the swill stables to the condition of meat animals shipped in railroad cars. He was successful in obtaining federal legislation, put into effect on October 1, 1873, regulating interstate livestock shipment. Bergh's cause was strongly aided by the activities of George T. Angell, founder and president of the Massachusetts SPCA. In 1870 Angell had toured the Chicago stockyards, and published his discoveries in the Illinois press with such effectiveness that he succeeded in founding a sister organization in that state and was assured by the packers of better treatment for the cattle prior to shipment. Angell, like Bergh, argued that inhumane treatment made the meat "not only less nutritious, but actually dangerous."[5]

Early in 1874 Chandler announced his intention to halt the continuing expansion of the slaughtering business, either by the construction of one giant abattoir or by the complete elimination of slaughtering within the city limits. Either measure would, of course, destroy the investments of the more than fifty independent wholesale butchers, and perhaps result in the destruction of even the two large abattoirs built within the city limits at the instigation of the Metropolitan Board. Chandler's abattoir scheme would also violate the promises implicitly made by his predecessors, who had succeeded in moving the butchers uptown with the understanding that they could operate without further molestation. Even Jackson Schultz protested the Board's resolution, accusing Chandler of "a breach of faith."[6]

4. *First Annual Report of the Board of Health of the Health Department of the City of New York* (New York, 1871), p. 143.

5. Zulma Steele, *Angel in Top Hat* (New York, 1942), pp. 103–4. Bergh's bill was the so-called "28-Hour Law," requiring rest and refreshment for livestock after twenty-eight hours in transit.

6. *New York Times,* February 26, March 4, March 11, and March 18, 1874.

Protests notwithstanding, in April the Board proceeded against the butchers by revising the Sanitary Code so as to make their day-to-day operation more difficult. To demonstrate to the slaughterers that he was serious, Chandler had the Board conduct intensive inspections, even though the Board's personnel and finances were limited. In the twenty months from May 1, 1874, to December 31, 1875, the Board made over four *thousand* inspections of slaughterhouses, as well as hundreds of visits to related establishments such as rendering and bone-boiling businesses.[7]

Chandler's war received reinforcement from Angell, who spoke to the American Social Science Association, of which he was a director, in the summer of 1874. Angell condemned the mistreatment of animals in cattle pens, railroads, and slaughterhouses. His speech, filled with graphic and gory descriptions, brought him wide attention in the popular press.[8] In October the Board of Health set July 4, 1876, as the deadline for the abolition of all conventional slaughterhouses. The butchers brought political pressure to bear, and Mayor Havemeyer sent several of the men representing "the slaughtering interest" to Chandler, with letters of introduction. But the legal powers of the Board made it difficult to stop Chandler. In addition, the Board's hand was accidentally strengthened when a number of wild cattle broke loose, tearing and mangling several citizens. Early in 1875 the Board amended the Sanitary Code to provide the legal basis for the abattoir system; conventional slaughterhouses now survived at the sufferance of the Board.[9]

Though Mayor Havemeyer's political opposition ended when he died suddenly in November, the new mayor, William Wickham, quickly allied himself with uptown real estate interests and fought to prevent the construction of Chandler's massive abattoirs. Chan-

7. Sanitary Code of the Board of Health, sec. 55, amended April 28, 1874; *Fifth and Sixth Annual Reports of the Board of Health of the City of New York* (New York, 1876), p. 67.

8. *New York Times,* August 30, 1874; George T. Angell, *Protection of Animals* (Boston, 1874).

9. *Report of the Sanitary Committee of the Board of Health on the Concentration and Regulation of the Business of Slaughtering Animals in the City of New York* (New York, 1874); *New York Times,* September 3, October 11, 1874; Havemeyer to Chandler, July 28, 1874, Chandler Papers; Sanitary Code, sec. 56 (amended January 19, 1875), sec. 60.

dler defended his policies against Tammany's attacks by explaining that slaughtering must not be banished from the island, for only by "examining the animal on foot" could the inspectors detect diseased beasts. And only by concentrating the business in a few central locations could this inspection be conducted effectively: "Now only the foulest varieties of meats can be detected and condemned in the markets, because there are not Inspectors enough to examine all the cattle to be slaughtered."[10]

Though Chandler staved off a Tammany attempt to legislate against the abattoirs,[11] they were never built. Chandler himself later blamed "the influence and misrepresentation of the Roosevelt Hospital people, and other West Side property-owners" for killing his scheme.[12] But Chandler's associates on the Board had already warned him to be satisfied with the new sanitary ordinances, and not push any further. In a letter marked "Private," and signed with a second notation ("This is personal and private"), Colonel Prentice had warned Chandler to halt the Board's involvement in "the butcher business" "for the present": "Meanwhile your Bd. of H has passed its July 4th 76 Resolutions and its Manhattan Market Ordinance and can afford to stop. I judge from what I hear and read, and I write to you because you know that though not a radical I am not timid or a timeserver . . . and the discussion has gone quite as far as the Bd. of H can wish." Board secretary Emmons Clark similarly warned Chandler that he might "agitate the abattoir question very much."[13]

But the warnings came too late. A major economic depression had begun in 1873; as it continued to deepen it contributed to

10. DeAlva S. Alexander, *A Political History of the State of New York* (1909; rpt. Port Washington, N.Y., 1969), 3: pp. 318–19; Seymour J. Mandelbaum, *Boss Tweed's New York* (New York, 1965), pp. 114–15; *New York Times,* April 16, 1875.

11. Tammany's anti-abattoir bill was defeated in the state Assembly, twenty-eight Democrats and twenty-one Republicans voting against it. The bill had received some liberal support because it was believed that the New York Central Railroad wished to construct the proposed abattoir. See *New York Times,* May 3, May 20, 1875.

12. *New York Times,* June 4, 1878. The Chandler Papers contain the full manuscript of Chandler's speech, which the *Times* summarized. See also *Sanitary Engineer,* May 17, 1873.

13. Prentice to Chandler, April 7, 1875, Clark to Chandler, April 30, 1875, Chandler Papers.

broad budget cutbacks, and provided a rationale for Mayor Wickham to cut the Board of Health's budget more deeply and quickly than that of other departments. The Board had been allocated $250,000 in 1872, and for the next few years its budget steadily increased, coinciding with its reorganization and expansion. Yet Chandler's 1876 request of $328,000 was cut down to $220,000, and Tammany also began using a number of irksome ploys to harass Chandler, such as trying to evict the sanitary inspectors from their offices.[14]

The election of a new mayor in 1876 did not help the Board's cause. A tenuously united New York Democratic Party supported Tammany's John Kelly in his choice of Smith Ely to replace Mayor Wickham. Ely was an important hide and leather merchant, whose interests had long been tied to those of the butchers and to the Hide and Melting Association. Even before his election he had written a revealing letter to Mayor Wickham, which Wickham had sent on to Professor Chandler:

> I am considering a proposition to make a further investment in the Hide and Slaughtering business in East 45th St. and I should accept the proposal if I was confident that the Board of Health would not drive the business from that locality. I once lost $20,000 when the business was driven from the 17th Ward to its present location, and I do not want to be caught again.
>
> Please do me the personal favor to talk with your friends in the Board of Health and let me know what probable action will be: whether they will repeal their order or endeavor to enforce it.[15]

While mayor, Ely sent letters instructing Chandler to grant his friends special permits to conduct their slaughtering business outside the boundaries set by the ordinances and codes of the Board. Chandler, already plagued by a drastically reduced budget, asked Ely's Board of Apportionment for an "absolute minimum" of $232,000, explaining that the department could afford only one

14. See *Annual Reports;* Duffy, 2: pp. 72–74.
15. Mandelbaum, pp. 137–39; Ely to Wickham, March 24, 1876, Chandler Papers.

milk inspector for the entire city. The Board received a mere $116,000 for its 1878 appropriation. As a result of the severe budget cuts and mounting political opposition—and perhaps also because many sanitarians felt that the really crucial sanitary problems had been either solved or at least controlled—there was little constructive Board activity after 1874. The decade of Chandler's presidency has been called "the quiet years"; obviously there were still activities on a number of sanitary fronts, but in general the Board seemed "barely able to hold its own." Even a great admirer of Chandler admits that after 1875 the Board's annual reports "contain no new subject-matter of other than formal administrative concern."[16]

The nadir of sanitary reform in postwar New York came in 1878, when the entire Board of Health was indicted for willful neglect of duty.[17] The specific accusation was that the Board had ignored a "stench nuisance" which, Chandler claimed, originated in nearby Brooklyn, rather than within his own jurisdiction. Despite the claims of the Brooklyn Board of Health that "it is not at all probable that [the odors] find their way across the East River," Chandler's accusation was probably correct. In any event, one of the Brooklyn nuisance factories had just been found guilty of violating the sanitary ordinances, and trial was about to begin against several other offenders.[18] Why, then, were the indictments brought against the Board?

Clearly there was broad feeling among the public and the press that for the last several years the Board had been guilty of "inertness, ignorance, and indifference"; the stench nuisance was merely the straw that broke the camel's back. Complaints were raised in the press regarding Chandler's salary of $6,500, and he

16. Notes from Ely to Chandler, Chandler Papers; Duffy, 2: pp. 70, 72; Larson, p. 119; Haven Emerson, "Charles Frederick Chandler, 1836–1925. New York's First Public Health Chemist," *Science* 86:2238 (November 19, 1937), p. 459.

17. Chandler, Edward G. Janeway, the health commissioner, William F. Smith, the president of the Board of Police, and S. Oakley Vanderpoel, the health officer of the Port of New York, were indicted. Emmons Clark, the Board's secretary, was not indicted, and Stephen Smith was no longer a member at that time.

18. *Report of the Board of Health of the City of Brooklyn, 1875–1876* (Brooklyn, 1877), p. 56; *New York Times*, May 25, 1878.

was criticized for devoting insufficient time and attention to his duties as president of the Board.[19] There was justification for this charge, for Chandler held teaching positions at three institutions: the Columbia College School of Mines, the New York College of Pharmacy, and the New York College of Physicians and Surgeons. He was active in several other organizations as well, particularly the American Chemical Society. Chandler appeared frequently as a chemical expert testifying in private court cases, and he permitted his name to be used in testimonials for various products. Receipts in the Chandler papers reveal that his fees from private consulting work exceeded his wages from the Board.

One recent author has speculated that "it is debatable how sincere a reformer Chandler was," noting that after 1883, when Chandler left the Board, he abandoned public health work entirely "and turned exclusively to industrial chemistry. In this work he defended large companies against these same reformers he had formerly led." In 1878 even the medical community was divided on the indictments, many doctors pointing to problems that had received little attention from the Board. Chandler excused the Board's inactivity by citing problems of inadequate manpower and funding, cumbersome laws, and legal restraints. He also claimed that the complaints "emanated from persons who have selfish personal ends to gain," but he never specified which persons or what personal ends. On the day the indictments were presented, "circles friendly" to Chandler claimed a "conspiracy . . . to oust" him from office. The next day Chandler himself claimed that evidence to be used in his defense had been stolen by "burglars."[20]

Chandler presented an elaborate defense of his activities to the New York County Medical Society, speaking for over two and a half hours. But very little of his speech dealt with the stench nuisances; he primarily reviewed the achievements of the Metropolitan and the present boards of health, devoting much time to adulteration. He implied that the Board had virtually eliminated milk adulteration, swill milk, unsafe cosmetics, and dangerous kerosene. In a speech to the Public Health Association of New

19. *New York Times,* May 24, 1878; Larson, p. 123.
20. Margaret W. Rossiter, "The Charles F. Chandler Collection," *Technology and Culture,* 18:2 (April 1977), p. 224; *New York Times,* May 29, June 1, June 2, and June 4, 1878.

York ten days later—apparently his next public appearance—Chandler spoke exclusively on the adulteration question. He argued that the city's milk supply "was in a fair condition" and that though some "deleterious substances had been found in candy," the basic foods consumed in New York were probably unadulterated, though much more money needed to be appropriated before firm conclusions could be reached.[21]

Although for the next several months there was virtually no further public debate on the indictments, behind-the-scenes maneuvering must have taken place; in December the indictments were quashed. Judge Josiah Sutherland, in an exercise of judicial legerdemain, explained that since the Board had the sole authority to declare something a public nuisance, and since it had not done so, the "nuisance" simply did not exist. This had been precisely the argument made by Chandler back in May and June, when he reasoned that "the determination of what constitutes a nuisance was vested in the Board of Health."[22] Judge Sutherland retired from the bench a few days after rendering his decision.

The professional sanitarians had shown consistent interest in only one area of food adulteration: the sophistication of milk. Yet even here it can be argued that that interest had been precipitated by the activities of amateurs like Henry Bergh and by the frequent publicity given to the problem. Although Bergh continued to focus his criticism on the swill stables in Brooklyn, a number of similar establishments surely remained in Manhattan. But Chandler argued that swill milk "is all manufactured on the other side of the River. All that could be done on this side to check it has been done."[23] In reality, Chandler's Board totally failed to pursue investigations into local distillery stables in the period 1875–1878. Rather, the Board's pursuit of pure milk was almost entirely confined to the prosecution of retail milk distributors.

Though chemical analysis could irrefutably determine the pu-

---

21. *New York Times,* June 4, 1878 (manuscript is in Chandler Papers), June 14, 1878; *Sanitary Engineer,* July 1878, p. 163.

22. *New York Times,* December 27, June 1, 1878.

23. *Report of the Board of Health of the City of Brooklyn, 1875–1876,* p. 36; "Address of Charles Frederick Chandler to New York City Medical Society, 6/3/78" (in Chandler Papers), pp. 81–82.

rity of a sample of milk, the Board needed something that could indicate the most common adulterations—skimming and watering—quickly, cheaply, and in the field. Such a device would enable the sanitary inspectors to punish the milkmen not only by prosecution but by confiscating and dumping the alleged impure milk upon discovery, for such was Chandler's interpretation of the 1862 and 1864 milk laws. In his search for a weapon to be used against the adulterators Chandler returned to the lactometer, an instrument he had earlier disparaged.

Chandler had used a "galactometer" for his milk report of 1870 but had not relied upon it; all of the milk he tested was subjected to at least partial chemical analysis. Moreover, in 1871, in an article in the *American Chemist,* a journal he and his brother had just begun publishing, Chandler denounced the lactometer as "a very unreliable guide, as skimming causes the milk to appear better, while watering exerts the opposite effect. By resorting to both forms of fraud at the same time, the normal gravity of the milk may be preserved." Despite this pessimistic conclusion, in 1875 Chandler instructed his inspectors to begin using the lactometer as the standard field test for skimming and watering, in response to increased publicity about milk adulteration. Debate over the lactometer's reliability now became heated.[24]

Chandler sought to establish a legal precedent for this test, which only a conviction for adulteration based exclusively upon the lactometer would accomplish. Yet when the Board managed to obtain a conviction on this basis, the state Supreme Court overturned the ruling on appeal, declaring that the lactometer, when used alone, "furnishes only questionable evidence of adulteration." In this lactometer war R. Ogden Doremus quickly emerged as Chandler's arch opponent. Whether on scientific grounds, for reasons of personal enmity, or simply because he was employed by the milk dealers to represent them in court, Professor Doremus set out to discredit Chandler's tool. For his part, Chandler was now firmly committed to the lactometer and could not admit that some of Doremus's objections were valid without undermining his own position. Chandler finally succeeded, in February 1876, in sustaining a conviction based on the lactometer, but only because he

24. Charles F. Chandler, "Condensed Milk," *American Chemist,* 2:1 (July 1871), p. 26; *New York Times,* March 28, 1875. See below, chap. 9.

presented testimony of an independent chemical analysis that verified the accuracy of the readings.[25]

By this time it was doubly important that Chandler establish the credibility of the lactometer, for the courts were refusing to convict accused adulterators because of the loophole of the 1864 law—that it was illegal only if one "knowingly" sold adulterated milk. How could Chandler prove that dealers "knew" their wares were adulterated? If he persuaded the courts that the lactometer was reliable, he could argue that dealers could no longer plead ignorance or innocence, for they could employ lactometers themselves, *before* selling milk to consumers. Moreover, Chandler had a deadline approaching, for his term of office expired the next spring, and there was little likelihood of reappointment if the milk issue remained unresolved.

Without completely conceding defeat on enforcing the 1864 law, Chandler decided to provide an additional basis for conviction by amending the Sanitary Code. The new ordinance simply declared that (with or without "knowledge") the sale of watered or skimmed milk was illegal. Doremus responded in an address to the New York Medico-Legal Society in April; one of the authorities he cited was Chandler's 1871 denunciation of the lactometer. As the *Herald* commented: "This last quotation, from the pen of Dr. Chandler, who is now so hot an advocate of the efficacy of the lactometer as a scientific instrument, elicited derisive and prolonged laughter. Broad hints were made, in fact it was asserted during the debate . . . that corruption influenced the board in the use of the lactometer."[26]

Undeterred, Chandler waited only long enough for the milk dealers to learn of the new ordinance, then ordered his inspectors to conduct a series of raids, lactometers in hand. More than thirty retailers were arrested that summer; the case selected to be the test of the new ordinance was the People *vs.* Daniel Schrumpf, which came to trial in December. The trial was a battleground for the war between Chandler and Doremus, both men testifying at length on the virtues of the lactometer, for clearly the measuring

25. *New York Times,* December 3, 1875, January 27, January 29, January 31, February 1, February 6, February 17, 1876.

26. Sanitary Code, sec. 186, adopted February, 1876; *New York Herald,* April 6, 1876. See Chandler's response, *Herald,* April 7, 1876.

device was on trial as much as Schrumpf, and with it Chandler's entire approach to the milk problem.

At the trial Professor Doremus frequently made telling points against the lactometer. Professor Chandler apparently told less than the "whole" truth about its reliability, pretending ignorance of some independent scientific literature that cast doubt upon it while being well versed in the studies that defended it. Chandler was, of course, forced to admit having denounced the lactometer in 1871. He three times denied that there was any more accurate test for watering but finally admitted that he had, in an earlier trial, testified that chemical analysis was a "surer test." But he insisted that "my confidence in the lactometer has been increased ten-fold since that case was tried."[27] Chandler's testimony was made even less credible when it was demonstrated that very subjective sensory judgments had to be made by the milk inspectors performing the lactometer tests—for example, they had to evaluate visually the extent to which the milk adhered to the instrument.

The heart of Doremus's argument rested on two propositions: that the mere specific gravity of milk, which the lactometer indeed measures, was useless for determining the purity of the milk; and that healthy cattle could be found whose milk, unquestionably pure and unwatered, tested considerably lower than the standard set by the Board. But Colonel Prentice managed to weaken Doremus's credibility by revealing that, when he went upstate to test a herd of cows in an effort to prove his contention, Doremus was accompanied by representatives from two organizations of milk dealers. Doremus foolishly compounded the implication of collusion by insisting that, at the time, he did not know who the two men were. The defense made an additional error by insisting that the chemical analysis of milk was a simple procedure, which the Board should be forced to follow in all cases of alleged adulteration. But Doremus's courtroom demonstration of chemical analysis took so long and was so clearly a laboratory procedure, impossible to apply in the field, that it certainly helped convince the jury of the justice of Chandler's demand that the Board be allowed to rely upon a simpler test.[28]

27. *The People vs Daniel Schrumpf. Misdemeanor, Adulteration of Milk. Record, Testimony and Proceedings* (New York, 1881), pp. 78, 83.

28. Ibid., pp. 204–6.

Judge Sutherland's behavior must further have inclined the jury to conviction. Sutherland, the same judge who two years later would quash the indictments against Chandler and the Board, consistently overruled defense objections, even when well taken.[29] He refused to permit the defense's most important challenge—a demand that the Board inspectors test a white liquid provided by the defense, to prove the lactometer's accuracy on an unknown substance.[30] Sutherland instructed the jury to acquit Schrumpf on the first count against him—violation of the law of 1864—since it could not be proven that he knew the milk to be watered. But on the charge of violating the Sanitary Code Sutherland's instructions to the jury were clear: guilt did not depend upon prior knowledge; it was irrelevant to what degree the milk was watered; it was irrelevant whether analysis might be a better test than the lactometer. All the jury had to believe, to render a verdict of guilty, was that the lactometer, as used by the Board's inspectors, correctly indicated the presence of added water.

Under these conditions it was almost mandatory that the jury find Schrumpf guilty. In his sentencing Sutherland was quite severe, clearly agreeing with Chandler that this was a precedent-setting case and declaring that unless the Sanitary Code "can be enforced I do not see how the Board of Health is going to protect the public against watered milk."[31] The judge sentenced Schrumpf to a fine of $250 and ten days in jail.

The Doremus family, however, refused to surrender the field; Professor Doremus's son Charles—who had also testified at the trial—decided to beard the lion in his own den. At the March 1, 1877, meeting of the American Chemical Society, which Chandler had helped to found the year before, Professor Henry A. Mott, a close friend of Chandler, presented a paper entitled "Testing Milk for Adulterations." But Mott succeeded merely in preparing the

29. For example, the defense tried to ask the Board's expert witnesses whether the Board's standard of 1.029 specific gravity might not be considered too high, if it could be proven that some healthy cows produced milk below that figure. Judge Sutherland excluded this line of cross-examination.

30. *New York Times,* December 22, 1876, headlined this controversy as "More Scientific Testimony Regarding a Mysterious White Fluid Which the Learned Professors Are Afraid to Pronounce Upon." See also issues for December 19–23 and for December 27–31, 1876.

31. *People vs Schrumpf,* p. 269.

ground for a thorough rebuttal by Doremus, who presented the second paper. "This paper called forth a lively discussion. . . . numerous remarks of a rather personal nature" were made. Doremus repeated the testimony his father had given at the Schrumpf trial, appending additional independent scientific documentation that supported his attack on the lactometer. He noted that since the Schrumpf decision more than forty other milkmen had been convicted of adulteration, without the substantiating evidence of chemical analysis. Though Professor Chandler then presented a paper entitled "On the Use of the Lactometer in Milk Inspection," the Society decided not to print it, or Mott's paper, in its *Proceedings,* possibly to avoid further embarrassment.[32] In April 1878 the state Supreme Court sustained Schrumpf's conviction.

Aside from the milk question, in 1878 little was being written about adulteration, with one major exception, which occupied both the newspapers and the commercial press. In the late 1870s Congress had initiated a debate on the method of taxing sugar imports. The existing tariff was on a sliding scale pegged to the purity of the sugar, which was gauged by its color. This system resulted in a unique practice: the one instance of reverse adulteration. Some importers and exporters colored high-grade sugar to make it appear less pure and thus paid lower duties. Some members of Congress suggested that an instrument called the polariscope be used to determine the actual, rather than the apparent, purity of the sugar.[33] The heated arguments in the press concerning this issue are irrelevant to the present discussion, but it is important to understand that the debate continually brought sugar purity to the public's attention, preparing the ground for an entirely separate controversy.

In October 1878 a large New York sugar refinery, De Castro and Donner, brought suit against a New York sugar wholesaler, Earle and Company, for refusing to pay for sugar sold to it. Earle

32. *Proceedings of the American Chemical Society* 1:4 (March 1, 1877), pp. 226–27.

33. The Treasury Department requested the National Academy of Sciences to conduct a study on the use of polarized light to determine the value of sugar and to prepare a confidential report, "On Artificial Coloring of Sugars to Simulate a Lower Grade" (1876–1879). See *A History of the First Half-Century of the National Academy of Sciences, 1863–1913* (Baltimore, 1913), pp. 204, 264–67.

and Company responded that the sugar had been bleached by De Castro and Donner, using a process employing salts of tin, to appear to be a higher grade than it actually was, and that over the summer it had gradually darkened to its original color. Mr. Earle brought his claims to the attention of the press, which made much of the case because of the sugar tariff controversy, even though one accusation tended to refute the other. After all, this was clearly not a case of reverse adulteration to avoid taxes. To the public, however, the Earle claims apparently seemed one of a piece with the congressional hearings. The accusations spread throughout the nation and began to affect all the New York refiners; if people were suspicious of sugar in general, they were especially suspicious about sugar refined in New York. Wholesalers in other cities began to cancel orders; sales were sharply affected.[34]

The New York Chamber of Commerce, justifiably alarmed, accepted the advice of one of its leading members, Francis B. Thurber, who was head of the city's largest wholesale grocery house. It called upon the Board of Health to investigate the accusations immediately, to "ascertain the facts, and report whether or not adulteration, injurious or otherwise, exists," so that business could return to normal. But the Chamber's effort backfired disastrously. Exactly what happened is not clear, for certainly Chandler had never gone out of his way to make life more difficult for reputable businessmen. In fact, the companies for which he worked as an analytical chemist included at least three of the sugar refiners: Havemeyer and Elder, New York Steam Sugar Refining Company, and Booth and Edgar.[35]

A reasonable assumption is that Chandler was simply careless or perhaps preoccupied with the pending decision on the motion

34. *New York Times,* May 24, 1878, says there were fifteen refineries in New York City; Richard O. Cummings, *The American and His Food* (Chicago, 1940), p. 111, estimates that there were twenty-seven refineries in the nation in 1880. Obviously New York had become the sugar-refining center of the country.

American Grocer, January 16, 1879, p. 195, printed a letter from J. O. Donner in which he claimed that the discoloration of the sugar proved that tin had *not* been used. He also claimed that unadulterated sugars of lower grades, such as that purchased by Earle, will naturally turn darker in warm weather.

35. *New York Times* and *New York Tribune,* December 6, 1878; *American Grocer,* January 2, 1879. See Chandler Papers, folder of work on chemical analysis, and *New York Times,* January 7, 1879.

to quash the indictment against him. In any case, he assigned an assistant, the chemist Dr. P. deP. Ricketts, to conduct the analyses. The examination was completed by December 17 and was sent to the Chamber of Commerce by Secretary Clark on the twenty-fourth, signed by Chandler:

> In several of these sugars we have found tin salts and free acids, probably muriatic, and in two of them artificial glucose. While the amount of tin and acids found in some of these samples were small, yet in one a globule of metal was taken from two ounces of sugar. In any case there is no excuse for the addition of tin salts to sugar. They are used solely for the purpose of defrauding the consumer by deceiving him as to the grade of the sugar; and while in some cases the quantity added may be too small to be injurious, in other cases it may be sufficient to cause derangement of the system.[36]

Not only were these findings exactly the opposite of what the Chamber of Commerce expected, but the entire procedure was questionable, for it was soon revealed that Ricketts had already been hired by Earle and Company to represent it in the suit brought by De Castro and Donner. Moreover, Mr. Earle apparently had provided Ricketts with the samples to be tested. These circumstances cast strong doubts on the validity of the report. Yet Chandler could not very well admit that it was improper for his assistant to accept such outside employment, for Chandler himself wore many hats. Nor could he repudiate the analyses and still save face, both for himself and the Board.

Moreover, as the press quickly noted, Ricketts's report was not only unprofessional but also shamefully inadequate. Even papers normally very friendly to Chandler struck out at him, for a bad situation had been made much worse. The *American Grocer,* the country's largest grocery trade paper, covertly owned by Thurber—who had counted on very different results—said:

> It is a very strange and unsatisfactory report for a Board of Health to make to the public. . . . It alludes to a "globule"

36. *New York Times,* December 25, 1878; *American Grocer,* January 2, 1879, p. 69.

of metal being taken from two ounces of sugar, but neglects to state its size or weight; it may have been as big as an egg or as small as a pin point. It is equally as instructive and explicit where it says, "And while in some cases the quantity added may be too small to be injurious, in other cases it may be sufficient to cause derangement of the system." The public want to know if it *is* sufficient—not that it "may not" or "may be."[37]

The *Sanitary Engineer,* owned by Henry C. Meyer, a friend of Chandler and Thurber's brother-in-law, responded in a similar vein, adding, "It is about time that names were given, so that honest refiners need not rest under a false imputation, but that if wrongly accused they may have an opportunity of proving their innocence."[38] Obviously the business interests of the city could not let things stand as they were, for even if De Castro and Donner was guilty (which it is clear the Chamber of Commerce did not believe), the Board report, by its vagueness, had tarred the entire industry with the same brush.

Things were not made easier by the less sympathetic newspapers, such as the *Tribune.* The *Grocer,* the chief competitor to Thurber's trade paper, not only taunted Thurber to have the Board tell " 'the truth, the whole truth, and nothing but the truth' about the sugar business," but in the same issue published a long report on table syrup by Professor Robert C. Kedzie of the Michigan State Agricultural College. Of seventeen table syrups tested by Kedzie, fifteen had been adulterated with glucose. Kedzie's report was made particularly biting because he stressed that "in making my selections for examination I obtained specimens only from those who are regarded as first-class tradesmen."[39] (See figure 3.)

37. *American Grocer,* January 2, 1879, p. 69.
38. *Sanitary Engineer,* January 1879, p. 33. It may be that it was not widely known that Thurber and Meyer were related by marriage.
39. *Grocer,* January 4, 1879, pp. 5, 7. Kedzie became president of the Michigan State Board of Health, and in 1881 was elected president of the American Public Health Association.
Glucose—now called "corn sweetener"—is a sugar manufactured from starch. In the period under consideration some commentators suspected it of being a poison. See chap. 10 below.

SUGAR.

These prices are those of Thursday morning, Jan. 22, and are liable to change at any moment. All orders will be filled at prices of day when received.

Loaf Sugar, in 7 lb loaves, 18 loaves in box, ℔ lb	—@14
Cut Loaf	10⅛@10¼
Crushed	—@10⅛
Powdered	—@10⅛
Powdered XXX for Confectioners	—@11
Granulated, Standard	9⅝@ 9¾
Granulated, Fine	—@10
Standard A	9⅝@ 9⅝
Steam Refined A	9⅛@ 9¼
Extra C White	8⅞@ 9
Coffee C	8⅜@ 8⅝
Yellow	7⅞@ 8¼
Brown	7⅛@ 7⅜

Sugar packed in bags for frontier trade.

SYRUPS.

OUR STANDARD GRADES.

Riverside Extra White Drips, bbls	90
" " " " half bbls	93
Riverside White Maple Drips, bbls	85
" " " " half bbls	88
Star Drips, bbls	50
Riverside Standard Drips, bbls	49
Thurber's No. 1 Syrup, bbls	44
Thurber's No. 2 Syrup, bbls	41
Thurber's No. 3 Syrup, bbls	36
Thurber's No. 4 Syrup, bbls	—
Common Syrup (in hhds 22), bbls	24

Maple Syrup and Sugar—See column 10.

SYRUP IN SMALL PACKAGES.

Thurber's Brands.	In 10 gall Kegs.	In 5 gall Kegs.	In 5 gall Cans.
Extra White Drips	95	97	101
Riv'side Stand. Drips	55	57	61
No. 1 Syrup	50	52	56
No. 2 Syrup	47	49	53
No. 4 Syrup	—	—	—

All of the above in one gallon cans at 15 cts., and in half-gallon cans at 25 cts. per gallon *over barrel prices*, packed 12 and 24 cans in case. No charge for packages.

MOLASSES.

New Orleans, New Crop, Fancy in bbls	—	@	56
" " Choice in bbls	—	@	54
" " Good in bbls	—	@	51
" " Fair in bbls	47	@	48
" " Sundry Brands	46	@	47
Porto Rico, Ponce in hhds	—	@	—
" Mayaguez in hhds	—	@	—
Demerara in hhds	33	@	35
St. Croix in hhds	—	@	—
Barbadoes in hhds	—	@	—
English Island in hhds	—	@	—
Mixed Molasses, Fancy Ponce in hhds	—	@	39
" Arroyo, in hhds	—	@	36
" English Island in hhds	—	@	33
" Cuba hhds	25	@	28

All the above grades of Mixed Molasses in bbls 2c. per gallon more than hhd prices.

Thurber's Best Porto Rico in bbls	—
Thurber's Fine Porto Rico in bbls	—
Thurber's Good English Island in bbls	—

TEAS.

We were fortunate enough not to believe in the late speculation, and consequently have no Tea bought at high figures to work off upon the trade. Parties ordering good, desirable Teas from us will find them as cheap as they were this time last season.

We do not quote any Teas grading below Medium, as we do not deal in dusty, smoky, weedy or bilgy kinds. We guarantee all Teas bought of us to please the consumer.

OOLONG.

Medium	22	@	25
Superior	30	@	35
Fine	40	@	50
Finest	60	@	75

JAPAN.

Medium	—	@	—
Superior. Crop 1879	—	@	30
Fine, Crop 1879	35	@	45
First Pickings, Fancy April Crop 1879	50	@	55
BASKET FIRED Japans—			
Fine, crop 1879	—	@	40
Finest, crop 1879	—	@	45

GUNPOWDER.

Medium	—	@	35
Superior	38	@	45
Fine	50	@	65
Finest	70	@	1 00

IMPERIAL.

Medium	25	@	30
Superior	33	@	40
Fine	45	@	50
Finest	50	@	60

YOUNG HYSON.

Medium	25	@	30
Superior	32	@	35
Fine	40	@	50
Finest	60	@	80

HYSON.

Medium	—	@	—
Superior	30	@	35
Fine	38	@	43
Finest	45	@	50

TWANKAY.

Medium	—	@	—
Superior	—	@	20

ENGLISH BREAKFAST.

Medium	—	@	—
Superior	30	@	35
Fine	45	@	55
Finest	60	@	75

TEAS IN JARS.

THESE TEAS ARE PACKED IN HALF-GALLON AIR-TIGHT, WIDE-MOUTHED FRUIT JARS, EACH JAR CONTAINING 1 LB. OF TEA.

24 one-pound Jars in case no charge for Jars or Case.

Oolong	℔ lb	50	Retails at	80
Japan	"	50	"	80
English Breakfast	"	50	"	80
Young Hyson	"	60	"	1 00
Gunpowder	"	60	"	1 00

GRAPE SUGAR.

For Brewers', Confectioners' and Wine Manufacturers' Use.

	Per lb
Grape Sugar, Confectioners', in boxes 125 lbs	4⅜
" " in bbls 420 lbs	4⅛
" Brewers' in bbls 420 lbs	4

GLUCOSE.

	Per lb.
Glucose, A, Domestic, in bbls about 600 lbs	5⅛
" B, " " 600 lbs	4⅞
" B, " in 10 gall kegs (kegs free)	6⅞
Imported in casks, about 1000 lbs	6

3. A section of the H. K. and F. B. Thurber and Company price list from *American Grocer,* January 1880. The Thurbers built their reputation on the purity of their merchandise. There is little doubt, however, that retailers purchasing glucose and "grape" sugar from Thurber used them to adulterate table syrup and sugar. Thurber must have been well aware of this activity.

At the next meeting of the Chamber of Commerce Thurber tried to bring the situation under control. He asked the Board of Health to provide the type of information that the press was already demanding, explaining that his "resolution was designed to make the guilty parties known." Actually Thurber, with the aid of the refiners, was trying to clear all the people in the industry and sidestep the difficulty inadvertently created by Chandler. On January 5 Theodore Havemeyer, chief owner of the city's largest refinery and an associate of Thurber's, took two steps to clear the air. After conferring with Chandler, Havemeyer sent $500 to the Chamber of Commerce, so it could pay the Board of Health to investigate all the sugar refineries in the city in a scientific and proper manner. Apparently Chandler and Havemeyer had decided that a sugar man could not simply pay the Board directly; to avoid any appearance of collusion, it was safer to go through Thurber and the Chamber of Commerce. Second, since Chandler himself could not disown Ricketts's report, Havemeyer, in a letter to the *Times,* explained exactly why the original analysis was questionable, and attempted to shift the blame onto Earle by hinting that the sugar may have been tampered with before it was tested.[40]

At the same time Thurber sent a carefully worded letter to J. O. Donner. Superficially the letter was a polite demand for answers to the accusations made against Donner's company. Actually Thurber was simply giving Donner the opportunity to defend himself in public. Both Thurber's letter and Donner's reply were published in Thurber's *American Grocer.* Thurber explained that while the public deserved to know "if injurious adulteration of sugar did exist," the Chamber of Commerce resolutions, "owing to their being hastily and imperfectly written," had not succeeded in drawing out the whole truth. Donner's reply stressed that Ricketts had been "retained by Earle and Co. in a private suit," and that the tests had been "made upon a limited

---

40. *New York Times,* January 3, January 7, 1879. The Havemeyer family controlled at least three New York refineries. Theodore A. and Henry O. Havemeyer were brothers, and partners in Havemeyer and Elder, which later absorbed De Castro and Donner. They were grandnephews of William F. Havemeyer, the former mayor, who had been involved in the sugar business with his brother, Frederick C. Havemeyer, Theodore's grandfather.

number of samples furnished by them from sugars which have now been for seven months in their sole possession."[41] Thus both the Havemeyer letter in the *Times* and the Thurber/Donner letters in *American Grocer* worked cooperatively to resolve the problem.

The final official word came from Chandler on January 21. He implicitly admitted his error in allowing Ricketts's analyses to be published, by advising everyone to ignore his findings: "In the opinion of this Board there is not at present sufficient cause to justify apprehension on the part of the public of ill effects from the use of refined sugar." In view of the content of the Ricketts report to which Chandler had signed his name and the fact that no new tests had been run, Chandler's reversal must be credited to the furor created among the business interests of the city. Hoping to lay the issue to rest, Chandler announced that further analyses would be made "from time to time," but that it would not "be proper to use private funds for this purpose."[42]

Apparently Chandler had decided that the use of "sugar" money, even when supplied through the Chamber of Commerce, might look suspicious, considering how the entire situation had been mishandled. The Board of Health, Chandler explained, would protect the public health, "while by the action which the Chamber of Commerce may think it wise to take the great interests of trade and commerce will be sufficiently guarded."[43] Chandler was inviting the Chamber to spend Havemeyer's $500 for private analyses, if it wished. Having inadvertently enmeshed the Board in private business matters, Chandler now sought to divorce the two interests, at least publicly.

Chandler's "solution" certainly did not satisfy the press. *Sanitary Engineer* called his decision "A Lame and Impotent Conclusion." The *Grocer* noted that the Board's original report to the Chamber of Commerce had "placed both Prof. Chandler and Dr. Ricketts in an unenviable light" which the latest message did little to expunge, and it once again questioned the Board's procedures, objectivity, and honesty. Through either charity or forgetfulness the *Grocer* neglected to remind Chandler of the state-

41. *American Grocer,* January 16, 1879, p. 195.
42. *American Grocer,* January 23, 1879, pp. 249–50.
43. Ibid.

ments he had made before the Public Health Association the previous June. At that time Chandler said he had gathered and tested seventy-five samples of sugar "and had not found a deleterious substance in one." He had even declared "that there existed no substance by which sugar could be adulterated with profit to the person using it."[44]

In the years from 1873 to 1878 Chandler's Board made some notable sanitary progress, but was generally considered unresponsive to the city's health problems. Certainly in terms of food and drug purity the only area Chandler chose to enter was milk adulteration. And here his policy must be considered unrealistic. Though he successfully defended the use of the lactometer—at some cost to his prestige and credibility—his victory was for the purpose of employing this unreliable instrument in a questionable war against the petty tradesmen who delivered milk door to door. Though some of these men were surely guilty of watering their wares, Chandler's one-sided campaign ignored the milk producers and wholesalers, whose dishonesty could be practiced on a far broader scale. He also managed to avoid waging war against the owners of the swill stables by the simple expedient of arguing that they all operated in Brooklyn.

When he became entwined in the sugar controversy, the most charitable appraisal would describe his behavior as careless and unprofessional. His efforts to extricate himself and his Board from this quagmire were complicated by his desire to protect the influential businessmen with whom he regularly dealt, and for whom he often did private work. Indeed, his ethically questionable practice of working for private employers while entrusted with protecting the public by enforcing the sanitary laws, can be argued to have been the cause of the entire contretemps. Ricketts's employment with Earle and Company was not different in its nature from many of Chandler's activities; it was simply a more intimate violation of propriety.

44. *Sanitary Engineer,* February 1879, p. 62; *Grocer,* January 25, 1879, p. 114; *Sanitary Engineer,* July 1878, p. 163. These statements are consistent with the reports on sugar that Chandler made while he was Board chemist, in 1871 and 1873.

4

"Upon Reliable Authority"

The Board of Health's pronouncement that there was no "cause to justify apprehension" may have reassured some New Yorkers about the safety of their sugar, but the entire controversy surely led many others to suspect that there was much more adulteration about than the authorities would reveal, except inadvertently. Moreover, the disclosure of the commercial connections of Chandler and Ricketts may have awakened the suspicion that some scientific experts were more interested in the fees paid them by businessmen than in protecting the public health. Chemists, physicians, and pharmacists were coming to be regarded as mere businessmen, while businessmen were seen as constantly looking for the main chance, eager to cover up one another's missteps. The public was now prepared to believe new revelations about food and drug adulteration. And, in the midst of the sugar controversy, a unique revelation was being presented, by a unique protagonist.

George Thorndike Angell practiced law in Massachusetts until 1868, when he retired "with sufficient capital for his ordinary needs and enough to spare to enable him to contribute largely to the philanthropic enterprises which from now on engaged most of his attention." His work on behalf of animals occupied most of his energies. He was the founder of several state and local SPCAs and president of the American Humane Education Society, which gained fame for publishing *Black Beauty,* considered in its time to have been the animal equivalent of *Uncle Tom's Cabin*. Angell was an intimate of most of the Massachusetts reformers of his time. He was also very active in the American Social Science Association and was a close friend of Frank Sanborn, ASSA's permanent secretary and editor of its *Journal of Social Science*. He was intimate with Benjamin Ware, master of the Massachusetts State Grange, and with George Noyes, who frequently published articles by Angell in his agrarian newspaper, the *Massachusetts Ploughman*. Angell had many powerful friends throughout the nation, for his interest in reform took him on journeys to many states; his influence was taken seriously by politicians and businessmen.[1]

Angell published an autobiography, which he twice updated, reporting on his year-to-year activities on behalf of reform. He was an extraordinarily dedicated and energetic man, intemperate in his enthusiasm. He believed strongly in providence and miracles. In his autobiography Angell repeatedly related perfectly ordinary incidents and coincidences which he attributed to something akin to divine intervention. A highly sympathetic author once commented that "he believed his life was divinely guided." Angell was firmly convinced, not only that he was on the side of the angels, but also that the sinners would stop at nothing to discredit or deter him. He believed, for example, that "every move I made seemed to be watched. I found that among those working against me was a man who had once been tried for murder. I detected him following me in the evening, and was warned by friends that I had better be careful on the streets after dark."[2] There is no way to determine the extent to which these dangers were figments of Angell's imagination, but certainly there is no record that his enemies were reckless enough to assault him physically.

In 1878 Angell discovered the issue of adulteration. He began with a series of articles published in sympathetic newspapers, assaulting a particular brand of ironware which, he claimed, contained soluble lead and was in such wide use "that I had narrowly escaped having my own buckwheat-cakes cooked in a similar utensil. It was clearly my duty to attack it." According to Angell,

1. *Dictionary of American Biography* (New York, 1928), s.v. "George Thorndike Angell"; Thomas L. Haskell, *The Emergence of Professional Social Science* (Urbana, Ill., 1977).

2. George T. Angell, *Autobiographical Sketches and Personal Recollections* (Boston, 1892), especially pp. 2, 15, 62 [1879], 71 [1880]; Sydney H. Coleman, *Humane Society Leaders in America* (Albany, 1924), p. 90.

people by the thousands began returning the cookware to the stores. In response to the insistence of the manufacturer's chemist that the ironware was harmless, Angell obtained a statement from "the Harvard University chemist" (unnamed) that it was *"alive with poison."*[3]

By 1879 Angell had gathered sufficient "evidence" to initiate a broader campaign against adulteration, and once again he sensed the calling that led him to battle. His speech "Public Health Associations" was presented to a sympathetic audience at the annual meeting of the American Social Science Association in Boston, on January 8: "It was in the highest degree sensational. I intended it should be. I wanted to bring on a war of discussion, which should wake the nation."[4] This speech initiated the debates that eventually led to the passage of the first general anti-adulteration laws. Angell began with an attack on the lack of licensing and professional certification for practitioners of medicine and pharmacy, but the bulk of the paper dealt with adulterated food and drugs, poisonous fabrics, and explosive kerosene.

The paper was in typical Angell style, a technique that might best be described as "the multiple half-truth": a mixture of prudent, provable accusations, rash statements by anonymous "experts," unconfirmed newspaper stories, and exaggerated generalizations. His most valid claims were that adulterated and dangerous kerosene was being widely sold and that arsenical and other poisonous coloring matters were being used in fabrics, wallpaper, and colored papers. But many of his other accusations were so broad as to resemble burlesque, if it were not for his deadly seriousness—for Angell was a zealot with no discernible sense of humor:

> Coffee is not only adulterated, but a patent has been taken out for moulding chiccory into the form of coffee berries, and I am told that clay is now moulded, and perhaps flavored with an essence, to represent coffee. . . .
>
> Several mills in New England, and probably many elsewhere, are now engaged in grinding white stone into a fine powder for purposes of adulteration. At some of these mills

3. Angell, *Autobiographical Sketches*, p. 51.
4. Ibid., p. 59.

they grind three grades—soda grade, sugar grade, and flour grade. . . .

I am assured, upon what I believe to be reliable authority, that thousands of gallons of so-called milk have been, and probably are, sold in this city which do not contain one drop of the genuine article.[5]

Angell's claims about adulteration aroused opposition not only from business people, but from sanitarians, chemists, and physicians as well. What most stimulated these antagonists, it is reasonable to assume, was Angell's proposed "remedy," for he argued that anti-adulteration laws could not be enforced by "boards of health." What was needed were voluntary "public health associations" of influential citizens, separate from government, employing "officers who cannot be bribed or removed by outside influence," immune to "combinations of capital and political influences."[6] Angell's contempt for the existing laws and sanitary codes, and for the governmental agencies that helped enact and enforce them, infuriated the professionals he criticized.

Though many newspapers and magazines printed summaries of Angell's speech in their next editions, the story was not immediately ubiquitous. Understandably, the Boston papers gave the fullest coverage, especially the *Herald,* which Angell had used the previous year to initiate his campaign against "poisonous" cookware. In New York, though the *Times* and the *Grocer* printed some of his most outrageous claims, the *Tribune* merely mentioned that an ASSA meeting had taken place, and the *Journal of Commerce* devoted one very brief paragraph to the session. But Angell acted as his own press agent: he sent copies of the speech "very widely over the country to newspapers and others, and then waited the storm."[7]

5. George T. Angell, "Public Health Associations," *Sanitarian* 7 (1879), pp. 126–31. Though ground coffee was commonly heavily adulterated, it is extremely doubtful that coffee *beans* were counterfeited, although poor-quality beans were sometimes "faced"—colored and polished—to make them appear better. See Francis B. Thurber, *Coffee: from Plantation to Cup* (New York, 1881), pp. 20–21, 162–65.

6. Angell, "Public Health Associations," p. 131.

7. *New York Journal of Commerce,* January 16, 1879; Angell, *Autobiographical Sketches,* p. 60.

The "storm" indeed broke. Francis Thurber's *American Grocer,* a weekly, could not cover the story in its issue of January 9, but the following week devoted its entire front page to Angell. Although the story admitted the existence of a small quantity of "harmless" adulteration, and the need for some sort of national legislation, most of the space was used for condemnation of Angell's more extraordinary claims. The speech was called "sensational and unreliable. . . . one feels pity for the man who has to sustain his arguments with such improbabilities . . . calculated to create needless alarm."[8]

The paper repeated the old argument that the public compelled producers and grocers to adulterate through the demand for cheap goods. But this explanation could no longer hold water. Through a combination of factors—the rising efficiency of mass production techniques and new technology, competitive price-cutting, and a series of deflationary depressions—prices, which had begun to drop across the board shortly after the end of the war, continued a steady decline through the 1880s. Chemical, pharmaceutical, and food prices declined as part of this pattern. Even *American Grocer* was forced to admit that present food prices were very low. Thurber therefore suggested "the English law" as the model for American legislation. This proposed law would restrict only "harmful" adulterations but would require the labeling of harmless additives. Thurber would continue to pursue this compromise proposal as the pressure for legislation grew. *American Grocer* hoped that with such a law "the people will be amply protected in health and pocket," while "responsible dealers will be relieved from the annoyance and loss occasioned by exaggerated charges of adulteration."[9]

By this time, however, the *Boston Herald* had decided to reopen the topic; it conducted "interviews with manufacturers and chemists" in order to "unravel" the truth. The *Herald*'s chief witness against Angell was Professor Stephen Sharples, State Assayer of Massachusetts. Although Sharples was polite about Angell's good intentions, he was extremely critical: "In my opinion there is less adulteration in matters of food and medicine at the present time than was ever known before. . . . Most adultera-

8. *American Grocer,* January 16, 1879, p. 189.
9. Ibid.

tions nowadays are harmless extensions, and in no way injurious to health." Sharples refuted all of Angell's claims except his statements about kerosene and arsenical colors, and argued that there was no need for new legislation on adulteration; current laws were "comprehensive enough to serve all purposes, if they are only properly enforced."[10]

This interview provided a perfect opening for Angell: "The battle was on for which I had been two years preparing."[11] He immediately dashed off a letter to the editor of the *Herald,* inviting their reporter to come to his office for the proof of his claims. Thus began a series of articles, running through the end of the month, in which Angell reiterated and expanded all the statements he had made at the ASSA meeting. Although he made Professor Sharples his chief victim, the series essentially accused all those who opposed or disagreed with Angell of being scoundrels, probably in the pay of the adulterators. But a careful reading of the articles clearly reveals that most of the "facts" Angell presented were merely culled from newspaper and magazine clippings and were at best of dubious value and authenticity. Angell also used encyclopedia entries, cited Hassall's outdated material, and took even the wildest claims as gospel. He continually credited anonymous men, who often had been "told" the "truth" by yet another anonymous person.

Nevertheless, Angell was achieving his goal: he was keeping the debate alive. The Boston papers treated him with kid gloves, whatever they may have thought of his claims. The *Springfield Republican* printed a series in his defense, written by his friend Frank Sanborn. The *Massachusetts Ploughman,* owned by his friend George Noyes, actively supported him. And throughout the nation magazines and newspapers either repeated his claims or denounced them. To Angell, denunciation was almost as satisfactory as support, for in either case the whole topic of adulteration was being kept in the public eye.

Perhaps the best index of his success was the publicity given to other stories about adulteration, to satisfy the growing public appetite. *Harper's Weekly,* for example, ran a story that documented merely the presence of alum in some baking powders, yet used the

10. *Boston Herald,* January 17, 1879.
11. Angell, *Autobiographical Sketches,* p. 61.

occasion to declare that "the adulteration of food and drinks has become almost as general as the use of these articles themselves. Scarcely an article used by men in civilized countries has escaped this process." Totally outrageous stories appeared. The *Times* seriously reported that an English manufacturer was caught in the act of producing "coffee" made of equal parts of coffee, chicory, and ground date-stones. A Belgian company was supposedly marketing sewer water as a tooth-wash. The *Times* reported a California plot to sell artificial chicken eggs, and a London "incident" wherein certain sacks of flour were found to be "not flour at all, but [solely] an admixture of plaster of Paris and China clay."[12]

Over the next few months the adulteration question continued to be agitated in the light of the Angell "revelations," not only in the popular press, but in grocery-trade publications as well. The *Grocer* never seriously questioned any of Angell's statements, and several times repeated them. Though the paper argued that adulteration abounded, and that legislation—especially national legislation—was needed, it insisted that no law would be a cure-all; the fault lay partly with the ignorant desire of the consumer for a "bargain." But it was the greedy manufacturer and wholesaler who adulterated: the retail grocer was an innocent victim who merely bought and sold, and who "would gladly cease to traffic in" fraudulent goods.[13]

The *Grocer*'s counterpart, Thurber's *American Grocer*, consistently condemned Angell and all who repeated his claims. While agreeing that there was a need for legislation, particularly on the national level, the paper put the burden for preventing adulteration upon the retailers: "If the retail dealer does not know the quality of the articles he offers for sale, he is in fault; it is a part of his business to inform himself." The paper was also more circumspect concerning the character of any proposed legislation: "What constitutes adulteration must be so defined that a person is not subject to arrest and fine for selling . . . coffee mixed with chicory or peas, or butter or cheese colored artificially." The paper maintained its interest in legislation on the "English"

12. "What We Eat," *Harper's Weekly*, January 25, 1879, p. 74; *New York Times*, February 22, June 28, June 29, February 16, 1879; *Grocer*, February 22, 1879, p. 258.

13. *Grocer*, January 11, 1879, p. 43.

model—prohibiting only specifically dangerous adulterations—and hoped "to see our larger merchants taking an active interest in this matter and taking steps to secure the draft of a law that will meet the exact wants of this difficult case."[14]

Henry Meyer's *Sanitary Engineer* criticized "the readiness of some newspapers to publish the twaddle of any ignoramus provided it looks sensational," and concentrated on ridiculing Angell, suggesting that he was only qualified to arrest "a drunken teamster for abusing his horse." Meyer added that ASSA "had better review papers to be read at their meetings, especially those from men who have no scientific attainments or position."[15] In this attack Meyer had many allies in the sanitary and chemical professions, almost all of whom were as eager to chastise Angell for his effrontery as for his lack of expertise. The paper published critical material from Sharples; H. W. Vaughan, State Assayer of Rhode Island; Professor J. M. Merrick, a well-known Boston chemist and a leader of the Massachusetts College of Pharmacy; Professor Henry Morton, president of the Stevens Institute of Technology; and Professor William Ripley Nichols of the Massachusetts Institute of Technology.

At the height of the controversy over Angell's "Public Health Associations" speech a very different proposal was being made by Dr. Edward R. Squibb. Squibb, who had long been in the forefront of the fight for pure drugs, for radical revision of the *United States Pharmacopoeia,* and for regulation of the practice of pharmacy, had made a number of enemies within the pharmaceutical profession, largely because of his intransigence. But even his opponents recognized and admitted both his professionalism and his dedication. There is little doubt that Squibb was the most respected manufacturing pharmacist in the nation.[16]

14. *American Grocer,* January 23, 1879, p. 253; March 6, 1879, p. 610; March 13, 1879, p. 673.

15. *Sanitary Engineer,* February 1879, pp. 62, 64.

16. C. Lewis Diehl, "Report on Deleterious Adulterations, and Substitutions of Drugs," *NBH Bulletin,* Supplement No. 6 (Washington, D.C., 1880), p. 19, said: "Perhaps no single individual . . . has had more abundant opportunities to observe the various characters and conditions of inferiority in drugs than Dr. Edward R. Squibb, of Brooklyn, and certainly no individual on this side of the Atlantic has given the subject of adulterations more attention than he."

At the annual meeting of the Medical Society of the State of New York, Squibb presented his "Rough Draft of a Proposed Law to Prevent the Adulteration of Food and Medicine and to Create a State Board of Health." The proposal was read to the convention on February 5, 1879, but was dated January 10. Is it significant that the proposal was apparently completed within two days of Angell's speech in Boston? Dr. Squibb did not produce this carefully reasoned document in a matter of hours, but it may indeed be that the publicity surrounding the Angell talk persuaded him that the time was ripe to present a plan upon which he had been working for some months.

In 1878 a blue-ribbon committee had been organized to consider the adulteration problem in New York State; it was "made up of representatives from the New York Academy of Sciences, the New York Academy of Medicine, the New York County Medical Society, the Therapeutical Society, New York College of Pharmacy, New York Medico-legal Society, the Public Health Association, and the American Chemical Society." Squibb was one of the three men appointed to this committee by the New York Academy of Medicine.[17] Though early newspaper coverage of Squibb's "Rough Draft" made it seem the product of the joint committee, there is no evidence that this was the case, even though this idea has shown remarkable persistence.[18] In fact, the joint committee apparently never made any of its deliberations

17. *Transactions of the Medical Society of the State of New York* (Syracuse, 1879), p. 209; "Proceedings of the Council of the New York Academy of Medicine" (manuscript), p. 305 (April 27, 1878); "Minutes of the New York Academy of Medicine" (manuscript), p. 412 (May 2, 1878). The other appointees were Dr. Fordyce Barker, who was elected chairman of the NYAM Council in 1879, and president of the Academy in 1882, and Dr. Willard Parker, who was one of the founders of the Citizens' Association in 1863, and the dean of the New York medical profession.

18. "The Adulteration of Food. A Proposed Act to Punish It," *New York Times,* February 6, 1879. See Carl L. Alsberg, "Progress in Federal Food Control," in *A Half Century of Public Health,* ed. Mazyck P. Ravenel (1921; rpt. New York, 1970), pp. 211–212; F. W. Nitardy, "Notes on Early Drug Legislation," *Journal of the American Pharmaceutical Association* 23 (November 1934), p. 1126; Lawrence G. Blochman, *Doctor Squibb* (New York, 1958), pp. 271–73, not only makes Squibb the "spokesman for a joint committee," but claims that "the Squibb bill was enacted into law by both the New York and New Jersey legislatures, with a few minor changes."

public, and in none of the histories of the member organizations, nor in available proceedings or transactions, is there any discussion of its operation. A reasonable assumption is that Squibb was troubled by the inactivity of the committee to which he had been appointed and decided to act on his own.

After all, he chose to present his paper to the State Medical Society, rather than to any of the organizations directly represented on the committee. In preliminary discussion at the Medical Society meeting Squibb explained that if the society did not wish him to present his paper he would withdraw it, and place it "at the disposition of the Joint Committee having charge of the subject of such a law in the City of New York." Squibb probably chose to act at this time because he felt that the publicity given Angell's paper was dangerous, not only because of its exaggerated claims about adulteration, but also because he felt that Angell's solution—voluntary "public health associations"—was wrongheaded.[19]

Squibb's primary consideration was to prevent, rather than punish, adulteration. To this end he proposed a clear definition of adulteration, arguing that if specific practices were proscribed the potential violator would be forewarned, and hopefully deterred. Second, Squibb sought to eliminate the question of intent from the law. Intentions to defraud "are often entirely wanting in the adulterator, and are always difficult to prove."[20] Since harm is done by adulteration, even when caused by mere carelessness, potential adulterators should be admonished to be cautious. Last, Squibb wished to create a state board of health for the enforcement of the law.

Squibb rejected out-of-hand two alternative enforcement procedures. He did not wish to leave prosecution of adulterators to their victims, "because it has been found that very few persons have either the inclination, time or money to give to such prosecutions." Second, Squibb directly attacked the device proposed by Angell: "Neither has it been proved more effective to place the duty of prosecuting upon institutions or societies, giving them

19. *Transactions of the Medical Society*, p. 209; Edward R. Squibb, *Proposed Legislation on the Adulteration of Food and Medicines* (New York, 1879), preface.
20. *Transactions of the Medical Society*, pp. 26–27.

the fines or other emoluments, in compensation, because in this way the work has rarely if ever been effectively done." A few weeks later Squibb added a more explicit attack, making clear his contempt for the Bostonian: "Without a very careful selection and control of the experts to be used [for enforcement], there would be a liability to fall upon enthusiasts . . . who see offenses everywhere, and so misapply their indiscriminate zeal as to bring up erroneous and unwise and unimportant issues, in which they are repeatedly and very properly beaten, very much to the discredit and injury of the law."[21]

The text of Squibb's proposed act contained, however, weaknesses of both technical and commercial natures. On medicinal adulterations Squibb was on firm ground; the existence of the U.S.P., the use of which he recommended, and the fact that the drugs of that era were "natural" and relatively uncomplicated, permitted simple definitions within the law. Even here, however, one prominent weakness was Squibb's surrender on the question of patent drugs: "In the case of proprietary or private compounds the constituents of which are legally held as secrets, the testimony of the owners of the private formulas shall be accepted as evidence of the character of the compound."[22]

Aside from the patent medicines, a simple standard for pure drugs might have worked, but a similar standard for foods ignored the realities of the marketplace. It was easy enough for Squibb to outlaw alum in baking powder or condemn skimmed milk sold as whole, but such rigid standards would be extremely difficult to apply to coffee, mustard, spices, and a hundred other commonplaces of the grocer's trade. Moreover, Squibb left no room for discretion on the part of his proposed board of health; the draft did not allow for definitions of commercial standards, nor for exemptions or exceptions. Such hard and fast rules would be strongly opposed by business interests of all sorts. These men would also find the penalties suggested by Squibb quite extraordinary: while a first offense could be punished by a $200 fine, each

21. Ibid., p. 211; Squibb, *Proposed Legislation,* pp. 29–30. Squibb may have been thinking of the New York skim milk law passed the previous year. Under this law (Laws of 1878, chap. 220) private citizens could sue milk adulterators, and upon conviction receive half of the penalty imposed.

22. *Transactions of the Medical Society,* p. 215.

succeeding conviction called for imprisonment for six months "with hard labor."[23]

The press reaction to Dr. Squibb's paper was markedly different from the treatment accorded Angell. Though Angell received a "mixed press," he remained newsworthy throughout the rest of 1879. Squibb, whose proposal was far more carefully drawn, was virtually ignored. The *Times* gave the fullest coverage of the New York daily papers but, while consistently courteous, rejected Squibb's entire proposal. The paper's principal objection was to Squibb's suggestion that a state health board be created to fight adulteration: "Our own Board of Health in this City, for instance, has competent jurisdiction to deal with this question in most of its aspects; and yet, even as concerns milk adulteration, one of the simplest of them all, it has lamentably failed." The grocery trade papers had even less to say, and the pharmaceutical and medical press and professional associations paid little attention to Squibb's proposal. Of the more important professional publications and journals, only *New Remedies* gave him any notice, printing two pieces of correspondence relating to the proposal. One letter cautioned about sensationalists like Angell; the second mostly deplored the changing times, reflecting the growing complaint that professionals were becoming mere businessmen: "I found more *haberdashers* in the *drug* business than I had any idea of."[24]

In March Squibb published an expanded version of his proposal, adding also some notes relating to comments in the press. The press criticism to which Squibb responded consisted only of a brief mention in the *Journal of Commerce,* questioning his estimation of the monetary losses to New York because of adulteration, and the *Times* comments already discussed. As of March 4, the date of the revision, these were apparently the only comments in the press—other than strictly reportorial—that Squibb had found.[25] Why was there so little reaction to Squibb's proposal, in contrast to Angell's?

23. Ibid., p. 217.

24. *New York Times,* February 6, February 7, 1879; *Grocer,* February 22, 1879, p. 257; *New Remedies* 8:5 (May 1879), p. 152.

25. Squibb, *Proposed Legislation,* pp. 25–30. (Published as "Putnam's Economic Monograph No. XIV.")

It seems obvious that the popular press was delighted to explore the sensationalism of Angell's claims, while there was little it could do to exploit Squibb's sober recommendations. The trade papers had no choice but to respond to Angell's outrageous claims, which clearly impacted upon the business community, while they could safely give merely polite mention to Squibb. Much of the professional press, on the other hand, tried to ignore members who were rocking the boat. Pharmacists and physicians were busily engaged in cleaning their own houses, and in further professionalizing their occupations, even while perhaps becoming more like "haberdashers."

What of legislative reaction to Squibb's proposals? There was little or no activity in Albany in response to the "Rough Draft." Two bills for a state health board were presented in the Assembly, but both died there, and though a board would be created the following year, it would bear little resemblance to Squibb's conception. One bill on adulteration was introduced on February 17 in the Assembly by Daniel Tallmadge, Squibb's Brooklyn neighbor. It covered only foods, not drugs, and would have prohibited only "unhealthful" adulterations; it therefore more closely resembled the bill suggested by *American Grocer* than that proposed by Squibb. It was referred to the committee on agriculture, where it was quickly and permanently buried.[26]

By the latter part of 1879 the public had been treated to the accusations of George Angell, who was intemperate, inexact, even incompetent as a public health spokesman. But he stood alone against his critics in the professions and the commercial world who did their best to ridicule and condemn him, and he succeeded in publicizing the need for supervision of the marketplace. The one thoughtful proposal of this period, that of Dr. Squibb, was largely ignored, but Squibb had at least proven that a responsible plan to control adulteration could be drafted.

The public was ready for new revelations about adulteration and was beginning to distrust the experts who assured them that the claims of men like Angell should be completely ignored. Though the *Journal of Commerce* condemned the Tallmadge bill, it also noted that "it has never been difficult to hire men pretend-

26. *Journal of the Assembly of the State of New York* (Albany, 1879).

ing to be chemical experts to certify to the purity and harmlessness of food, drink, drugs and cosmetics, in which noxious ingredients lurk."[27]

Since its formation in 1866 the sanitary and medical experts of the Board of Health had been publicizing not only the vast scope of the city's sanitary problems, but also their own competence to apply remediation. It was predictable that public expectations would rise. The old Metropolitan Board, born into "an age of genial corruption and inefficiency," had earned the faith men placed in it and "was held in a public esteem far exceeding that of any other city department."[28] The Tweed takeover had shaken that faith, and the Chandler regime had failed to restore public trust and optimism. The stench scandal, the sugar controversy—so clumsily handled—and the Angell accusations undermined confidence, not just in the Board, but in "experts" in general.

It should not have been surprising that adulteration, even if perhaps one of the lesser sanitary evils, received more than its share of this apprehension and anger. There was something peculiarly personal about adulteration; it was not something that threatened the "community" but something that happened, perhaps daily, to oneself. The sudden ubiquity of canned and packaged foods, "the ready sale of myriad food products brought from all parts of the world by means of ever swifter transportation and improved methods of refrigeration,"[29] was a revolutionary change for the city dweller. But the concurrent concentration of food production and distribution into fewer and fewer hands had begun to take control over quality away from the local grocer, put even honest milkmen at the mercy of the creameries and milk wholesalers, and allowed careless and venal slaughterhouses to distribute to the local butcher the meat one bought.

The postwar assumption of the press that it was largely the pressure of high prices that led grocers to adulterate, and that lower prices would ameliorate the evil, could no longer be posited with prices at a two-decade low and adulteration seemingly

27. *Weekly Journal of Commerce,* February 27, 1879.

28. John Duffy, *A History of Public Health in New York City,* vol. 2, *1866–1966* (New York, 1974), pp. 19, 620.

29. Arthur M. Schlesinger, *The Rise of the City, 1878–1898* (Chicago, 1971), p. 131.

at a new peak. Instead, the press began to react with an excess of moral outrage. Even in the months before Angell's speech condemnation that had once been reserved for the adulterator of milk was being directed at far less serious offenders. The *Nation,* a highly respectable and normally restrained periodical, declared that "for merely pennies . . . a great number of manufacturers and tradespeople are after us . . . . Some of these gentry are satisfied with betraying thousands of the hope of regaining their health . . . others gradually, but directly, systematically, and surely ruin the health of thousands by adulterating their wares with some more or less strong poison . . . still others suffer themselves to be betrayed by their lust of gain into a wholesale slaughter."[30]

By 1879 the public was ready to accept even the most outrageous and improbable accusations. What Angell's speech contributed to this renewed suspicion was not merely a proliferation of charges but also the belief that the guardians of the public health—if not murderously corrupt—were at least failing in their duty. Expert reassurances were suspect, and no accusation of adulteration could be denied; anything was possible. Only new laws and new guardians could mediate between a helpless public and those who were willing to see them poisoned "for merely pennies."

30. *Nation* 26 (February 21, 1878), p. 129.

5

Forging and Using
New Tools

By the late 1870s a number of voluntary medi-
cal, pharmaceutical, scientific, and public health associations and
a network of public and quasi-public agencies had been created in
New York and throughout the nation. Henry Bergh's SPCA had
been granted extraordinary police powers as early as 1866. Philanthropic organizations, such as the Association for Improving
the Condition of the Poor, often exercised substantial political
power. Business organizations like the Chamber of Commerce
and the New York Board of Trade and Transportation now had
dramatic input on issues of public concern. By 1880 local boards
of health had been created in twenty-one New York communities, and statewide health boards existed in the District of Columbia and in nineteen states. The culmination of the professionalization of the public health field—the formation of a National
Board of Health—took place at this time.[1]

Most of these professional voluntary organizations and public
agencies published journals or reports, which not only treated
their own transactions but also served to disseminate research
papers, policy statements, and scientific and social experimentation. These publications also helped build the reputation of both
the organization and the profession, becoming the voices by
which the experts reached out to the public. A specialized public

1. *NBH Bulletin* 47 (May 22, 1880), p. 373; Wilson G. Smillie, *Public Health,
Its Promise for the Future* (New York, 1955), p. 309; Robert D. Leigh, *Federal
Health Administration in the United States* (New York, 1927), pp. 10–12.

press dealing with many of the same issues also came into being during this period.

Though it was Angell's agitation that led to new legislation to control adulteration, the men who shaped that legislation were Francis Thurber, Professor Chandler, Henry Meyer, and Dr. John Shaw Billings. These men, in contrast to Angell, represented the "establishment," and by the late 1870s the established professional organization was in a position to control insurgency and innovation.

Chandler's staunchest supporter was probably Henry C. Meyer. When only eighteen Meyer had enlisted in the cavalry; he emerged from the Civil War with the rank of major, the Congressional Medal of Honor, and a job in his uncle's business, the New York Shot and Lead Company.[2] In 1868 Meyer began his own business in water, gas, and steam supplies, presumably with capital advanced him by his uncle. Although Meyer never had any formal training to prepare him as either a plumber or a sanitarian, his business thrived, and he was soon known and respected as an expert in both fields because of a new plumbing and drainage system he had designed.

At this time an invisible miasmatic "sewer gas" was erroneously believed to be one of the greatest causes of death. Meyer's system vented the sewer gas to the exterior of the building. Francis Thurber, who had married Henry's sister Jeanette in 1869, suggested that he begin "a high-class paper devoted to explaining these matters." With Thurber's assistance and the advice of Watkin T. Jones, editor of *American Grocer,* Meyer set out to publish a monthly paper, at first called *Plumber and Sanitary Engineer.*[3]

Upon Jones's recommendation Meyer hired Charles F. Wingate as editor of his new venture. Although Wingate "at that time had no technical knowledge or any experience in the matters

2. *The National Cyclopaedia of American Biography* (New York, 1936), s. v. "Henry C. Meyer."

3. Henry C. Meyer, *The Story of the Sanitary Engineer* (New York, 1928), pp. 3–6; *New York Times,* July 5, 1907. According to *The National Cyclopaedia,* Meyer named his second son Francis Thurber Meyer.

to be discussed" in a paper devoted to sanitary engineering, he had had editing experience, which Meyer was seeking. Wingate later complained that "I never assumed to be the editor but was content to let Mr. Meyer run the machine as he saw fit . . . and tried to make myself less prominent." But it is an interesting commentary on professionalism in this era that Wingate, after working on Meyer's paper for three years, and with no other training or experience, promoted himself as a "sanitary engineer," and soon built up a profitable consulting practice.[4]

Meyer did not want to create a "house" paper, one that existed merely to "puff" his own company's products; he was interested in sanitary reform projects, and sought the support and cooperation of both sanitarians and his colleagues in the plumbing industry. The paper almost immediately attempted to involve itself in the sanitary reform movement. Meyer published synopses of Board of Health reports, reported on the meetings of a wide variety of public health organizations, and reprinted sanitary information from papers throughout the world. Very quickly Meyer's paper was in contention for leadership in the field. Meyer soon changed its title to *Sanitary Engineer,* though most of his advertising revenue continued to come from the plumbing industry.

It was Meyer's paper that would soon sponsor, in cooperation with business and sanitary leaders, the anti-adulteration bill that became law in New York and other states. The method used to publicize this bill was a nationwide competition for the best draft of such legislation. Meyer had hit upon this "competition" promotion back in 1878, as a technique to increase circulation while advertising his paper's commitment to sanitary reform. The first of these contests was a competition for improving tenement houses.

Meyer quickly realized the potential for publicity in a campaign

4. *Story of the Sanitary Engineer,* p. 8; Wingate to Billings, November 20, 1880, Billings Papers. Wingate had edited two or three periodicals, such as the *Paper Trade Journal* and the *American Stationer.* (See Frank L. Mott, *A History of American Magazines, 1865–1885* [Cambridge, Mass., 1957], p. 291.) In 1880 Wingate tried to promote himself to a vacancy on the New York Board of Health, arguing, "There are many reasons why a sanitary engineer is desirable rather than a medical man" (Wingate to Billings, November 8, 1880, Billings Papers). See also Wingate Papers.

for tenement reform when Wingate, whose relative was the secretary of the AICP, first called his attention to the topic. (It can be assumed that he also saw potential profit in legislating the installation of plumbing in all new tenement construction.) The response to some material on tenements in the first issue of *Sanitary Engineer* was very encouraging, and Meyer decided to go ahead with the project when Daniel W. James and Henry E. Pellew, well-known New York philanthropists, expressed enthusiasm.[5] Over 200 entries were submitted to the paper, competing for the prize money put up by James, Pellew, Robert Gordon, and Thurber. The panel of judges selected by Meyer consisted of Professor Chandler, an architect, a manufacturer, and two ministers.

By 1878 interest in the tenement problem had already resurfaced, and the AICP and the State Charities Aid Association began a special investigation of the situation. A new organization, James Gallatin's Sanitary Reform Association, mobilized public opinion. The Tenement Reform Act of 1879 was the result of this agitation, but the *shape* of that law was determined by the contest run by Henry Meyer, for the law was designed to conform with *Sanitary Engineer*'s rules and prize-winning design.[6]

The terms of the contest required that the "model" tenement be constructed on a lot measuring 25 by 100 feet, because this narrow parcel of land was the standard New York City lot, favored by landlords. A truly healthful apartment house could not, of course, be constructed within these dimensions, but Meyer was more concerned with eliciting the active cooperation of property owners and businessmen than in promoting a radical change in

5. The first issue of *Sanitary Engineer* was published in December 1877. Both James and Pellew were born in England. James arrived in America in 1849, was a merchant, and became a partner in Phelps, Dodge and Company. He was especially interested in the Children's Aid Society. Pellew came to New York in about 1873, married the granddaughter of Chief Justice John Jay, and helped organize the Charity Organization Society.

6. John Duffy, *A History of Public Health in New York City,* vol. 2, *1866–1966* (New York, 1974), pp. 220–29; Seymour J. Mandelbaum, *Boss Tweed's New York* (New York, 1965), points out that Gallatin's board of directors "included many of the wealthiest men in the city" (p. 163). The Association's opponents were "more genuinely middle class," including most of the tenement landlords. In *Story of the Sanitary Engineer,* p. 15, Meyer argued that his contest was the central factor in first creating public interest in tenement reform.

the housing of the poor. By giving such great weight to the desires of the landlords, while claiming simultaneously to improve sanitary conditions, Meyer's contest helped to "sidetrack" the reformers away from more thoroughgoing demands.[7] The AICP reluctantly accepted the winning design, the infamous "dumbbell tenement" of James E. Ware, as an improvement over existing conditions, and when the law was being considered the legislature accepted the terms Meyer had imposed, instead of demanding greater improvements.

Perhaps the harshest critic of Meyer, and of the *Sanitary Engineer* competitions, was Dr. Agrippa Nelson Bell's *Sanitarian,* apparently the earliest American periodical devoted to public health, antedating even the *Reports and Papers* of the American Public Health Association. Bell was a Virginian who had attended Harvard and received an M.D. from Dr. Squibb's alma mater, Jefferson Medical College. Although a neighbor of Squibb, and a fellow member of the select Brooklyn Medical and Surgical Society, Bell engaged in professional and political intrigues that alienated many of his associates, even within the Society. Dr. Squibb, although he claimed to "have no personal enmity against" Bell, felt that Bell's ambitions overreached his medical capabilities. When the Brooklyn Society was reorganized in 1872, Dr. Bell was not included.[8] Shortly thereafter he began publication of the *Sanitarian.*

One of the most important publications of the sanitary movement, Bell's periodical is noteworthy because he often set himself up as an anti-establishment spokesman. It is not at all curious that it was Bell who published George T. Angell's "Public Health Associations" speech in 1879 or that Angell prepared a version specially revised for the *Sanitarian.* There is little doubt that Bell knew Angell's speech would upset his own enemies, and that he delighted in the prospect.[9] Although Bell supported governmen-

7. Duffy, 2: p. 229.

8. This was a professional and social organization, completely separate from the much larger Kings County Medical Society. In the 1860s, when Squibb and Bell belonged to it, membership was limited to twelve, with monthly meetings in the members' homes. See Lawrence G. Blochman, *Doctor Squibb* (New York, 1958), pp. 181–89.

9. See Duffy, 2: pp. 77, 229; *Sanitarian* 7 (1879), pp. 180–81, 8 (1880), p. 225, 11 (1883), pp. 428–29.

tal control over sanitary matters—especially federal control—he apparently saw himself as an opponent of "entrenched" power. He often went out of his way to attack Meyer, Thurber, and other "respectable" reformers. Although somewhat more cordial to Professor Chandler, Bell often viewed him as a tool of the business interests. Thus, though Bell would sympathize with Chandler's failure to secure reappointment to the Board of Health in 1883, he himself supported Chandler's opponent.

The *Sanitarian,* whose position as the leading public health periodical was seriously threatened by Meyer, attacked the tenement competition, justifiably concluding that "the prizes were won by the most ingenious designs for dungeons" and benefited landlords, not tenants. After the 1879 law was passed Bell intensified his criticism. He ridiculed Meyer's dropping the word "Plumber" from the title of his paper and, in an article titled "The Tenement-House Murderers of New York," blamed *Sanitary Engineer* for encouraging the construction of the dumbbell tenements. Bell also accused the AICP of concealing the identity of the owners of the death traps it condemned: "Does it belong to some member of the Association or some member's particular friend?"[10]

By the time Meyer's *Sanitary Engineer* had taken its place in the forefront of the sanitary movement, the *American Grocer* had become an important voice on the adulteration question. "Business" periodicals, many of them with long continuous runs, predate the Revolutionary War. By 1860 a number of papers catered to more specialized aspects of commerce; there were business papers representing the dry goods trade, tobaccos, drugs, and the wine and liquor industry.[11] But, as *American Grocer* observed in its first issue, in 1869, no business press represented the grocery trade.

As part of its first "Prospectus," the paper argued that "this is the day of specialties"; the birth of *American Grocer* represented the "professionalization" of the grocery trade. As part of that sense of professionalism, one of the first targets of the new jour-

10. *Sanitarian* 7 (1879), p. 226, 8 (1880), pp. 183, 225.
11. David P. Forsyth, *The Business Press in America, 1750–1865* (Philadelphia, 1964), p. 277, discusses the early drug press.

nal was the adulterator. Just as those who organized the pharmaceutical, medical, and chemical associations attempted to oust colleagues who gave their trade a bad name, *American Grocer* attacked the adulterator as the scourge of the grocery trade: "Our editorial corps includes some of the best scientific talent in the country, capable of submitting every article of the trade to the test of scientific analysis, enabling us to stand as guardians of the public health, on one hand, and as protectors, on the other, of honest dealers from fraudulent and mischievous imposture."[12]

The founder and first editor of *American Grocer* was W. H. C. Price, a southerner who, after some experience as a wholesale grocer and journalist in Alabama, enlisted in the Confederate army. After the war he came to New York and soon started *American Grocer.* He ran it until 1875, when "circumstances occurred which necessitated either a change in the independent and unbiassed attitude of the paper, or his entire severance from it." The "circumstances" were that the Thurber family, prominent stockholders in the corporation that owned the paper, bought it out completely. There was clearly a conflict between Price and the Thurbers, and he was either fired or forced to resign at that time.[13]

Price immediately started all over again with a new paper, the *Grocer.* With backing from prominent businessmen who were not—it may be assumed—close allies of the Thurbers, Price's new venture was an instant success, and both papers were by 1879 the leaders in their field, engaged in an intense rivalry. Price accused F. B. Thurber of having made *American Grocer* into a "house organ" for his grocery business, using the "Thurber Price List" in each issue as the paper's own "official" price list for wholesale goods. But Price did the same thing in his own paper, using the price list for Frederick H. Leggett, a Thurber competitor, until March 1881. At that time the *Grocer,* while continuing to carry the Leggett prices (now included as an advertisement), added its own "official" prices, separate from Leggett's. This,

12. *American Grocer,* September 15, 1869, p. 16.
13. *Grocer,* October 1, 1881, p. 311. The information about Price comes from obituaries in this issue of *Grocer* and in *American Grocer,* September 29, 1881. Neither paper was specific about the events of 1875. Lee Benson, *Merchants, Farmers, and Railroads* (New York, 1955), pp. 63, 266, indicates that by 1872 the Thurber family "controlled" *American Grocer* and by 1876 owned it outright.

Price argued, made his paper more "independent" than his competitor's.[14]

The conflict between the two papers was most vocal at the Price end. Shortly before his death Price's argument climaxed with a front-page editorial: "Papers that represent certain personal business interests are inevitably shorn of the influence a newspaper should have . . . they cannot come to be regarded as anything else than the mouthpieces of the personal influences behind them." For its part, *American Grocer* ignored its competitor so conspicuously that when it printed Price's obituary it never mentioned the *Grocer* by name, referring to Price's activities since 1875 as "several journalistic enterprises."[15]

This enmity was so strong that the Thurber interests sued Price for copyright infringement, claiming that Price's title was too similar to its own. Only weeks after Price's death the new editor reluctantly reported that the courts had decided in Thurber's favor, and that his paper's new name would henceforth be the *Merchants' Review*. From this time onward, the attacks on *American Grocer* intensified, with the *Merchants' Review* frequently issuing bitter invectives against editor Frank N. Barrett and Thurber, name-calling from which Price had refrained. Regardless of the tone of the criticism, however, many of the accusations seem to have been justified.

The policies of *American Grocer* unquestionably changed after Thurber took over. In the Price years the paper had campaigned vigorously against adulteration, though not always impartially. Price had made a practice of reviewing, one by one, each of the basic grocery trade items: what they should be like in their unadulterated form, and how they might be adulterated or otherwise injured. Though these reports were sometimes a device for promoting specific firms, the information was still probably helpful to the retail grocers. After the change of ownership there were subtle differences. Not only did the paper indeed "puff" Thurber consistently, and frequently act as his spokesman on a number of issues (not all of which were "grocery" topics), but its attitude toward adulteration also changed.

14. *Grocer,* issues for March 1881.

15. *Grocer,* August 6, 1881, p. 119; *American Grocer,* September 29, 1881, p. 708.

The best example of this change is the position taken by Jabez Burns. After the Thurber takeover Burns wrote a series of articles on adulteration for the paper. Later these articles were reprinted in a booklet, the title of which indicates Burns's philosophy on the subject: "The Right and Wrong of Adulteration: The Benefit and Injury of Adulterating: The Use and Abuse of Adulterations . . ." In other words, Burns argued that adulteration was not universally bad; sometimes deception was useful and permissible. He obviously ruled out "poisonous" adulterations, but he discovered many admixtures which he did not consider to be "gross misrepresentation." Burns saw nothing wrong with baking powder that was half flour, or goods artificially colored "to suit taste and standards," or adulterated coffee, tea, or spices: "If I were in the manufacturing business I would willingly put my name on any goods I moved that were not adulterated more than 50 percent . . . I pity the really poor, but you cannot secure for the poor pure goods any more than you can secure residences for all alike on Fifth avenue."[16]

Although *American Grocer* never disavowed these arguments, by 1878 the paper was toning down its approach. It argued for the virtue and commercial necessity of "pure goods" and, while continuing to approve of many of the types of adulteration Burns had advocated, did so without Burns's arrogance. For example, Thurber's "Price List" explained to his retail-grocer subscribers his argument for adulterated coffee:

> There is a large class of consumers to whom pure Ground Coffee is too stimulating; consequently there are many who for this reason do not drink Coffee at all or prefer it diluted with wholesome Farinacous substances. In order to supply the wants of the latter class we grind the finest Roasted Coffees together with wholesome Roasted Grains, Cocoa, Chicory and an article to clear the Coffee. . . . The Costa Rica is a strictly pure Ground Coffee, selected for its fine flavor. The other grades have a large proportion of Coffee

16. Jabez Burns, *The Right and Wrong of Adulteration: The Benefit and Injury of Adulterating: the Use and Abuse of Adulterations . . . being a series of articles on these important subjects, published from time to time in the "American Grocer"* (New York, 1877), pp. 3, 4, 12, 14, 22.

for the price charged, except the Rye Coffee, which has none of the genuine Coffee berry in it. We guarantee these goods to please consumers, or they may be returned at our expense.[17]

These arguments become even more dubious in light of the fact that at this very time Thurber was writing a monumental book on coffee, which warned that "the adulteration of coffee and the vast scale on which it is practised, are well-known facts. . . . the evil still flourishes in the United States, although, so far as I am aware, nothing worse than ground peas, rye, and chicory are used." Thurber also blamed any increase in adulteration on the "foolish demands of the people" and on the high sale of ground coffees, which consumers preferred to whole beans.[18]

Thurber and *American Grocer* defined adulteration differently in different instances, and took no responsibility if retailers sold all his "Farinacous" mixtures as pure coffee. It will be remembered that Thurber also advertised varieties of grape sugar and glucose; presumably it was never his intention for the retail grocer to mix these with Thurber's pure sugar syrups. Thurber was also the exclusive distributor for the largest-selling butter dye, which had "the recommendation of some of the largest creameries and re-workers of butter in the country." But "creameries" were notorious for passing skimmed milk off as whole, and "re-worked" butter was rancid butter that was reprocessed, deodorized, and colored to resemble fresh, using this "perfectly natural color . . . resembling the yellow of the Cowslip and Buttercup."[19] Thurber also became the world's largest distributor of oleomargarine oil, which was used in the manufacture of counterfeit "butter." Such activities make it impossible to accept at face value Thurber's constant declaration that he sold only "pure" goods.

All of this notwithstanding, by 1880 Thurber had become the nation's leading advocate of anti-adulteration legislation; for the next few years *American Grocer* and *Sanitary Engineer* became the organs through which Thurber publicized his campaign. Just

17. Thurber Price List, January 1880.
18. Francis B. Thurber, *Coffee: from Plantation to Cup* (New York, 1881), pp. 162–63, 21.
19. Advertisement in *American Grocer*, January 1880.

as Meyer had influenced the shape of the new tenement law, Thurber, through these two papers, and through a number of organizations that he controlled, would determine the shape—the scope and quality—of adulteration legislation.

By 1880 Francis B. Thurber had become the driving force in a number of important organizations and political/economic movements, but his home base was H. K. and F. B. Thurber and Company, the nation's largest wholesale grocery firm. When he was sixteen Thurber had moved to New York City from upstate, working as a clerk in the warehousing and lighterage firm of Thomas M. Wheeler.[20] In 1864, when Thurber was twenty-two, he had saved enough capital to buy into the firm of Pupke and Thurber, in which his older brother Horace K. Thurber was a partner. By 1866 he had become a full partner himself, and from this time forward the company made rapid strides, for Thurber saw the key to expansion in vertical growth. The firm now entered into the production of many of the items it had previously merely wholesaled.

Thurber introduced a wide variety of new food lines, and the company began its own manufacturing and processing plants. It opened canning plants (at a time when that industry was just beginning), a coffee-processing plant, and its own cigar company; offered a complete line of pharmaceutical supplies; and established offices in England and France. After the company had been reorganized as H. K. and F. B. Thurber and Company, in August 1875, it became one of the largest glucose distributors, and Thurber for a time held a monopoly in oleomargarine, having acquired the American rights from the French company holding the patent. In 1878 it was estimated that the net worth of the Thurber company was at least $1.5 million, and that it was doing over $1 million a month in gross sales. Business seems to have reached a new plateau in 1879, with an October figure of over $2

20. The biographical sketch of Thurber's early career is based on material in Edwards and Critten, *New York's Great Industries* (New York, 1885), p. 112, and *The National Cyclopaedia of American Biography* (New York, 1932), s. v. "Francis B. Thurber." A lighterage company transferred goods from incoming ships. Wheeler became, in 1873, president of the company that purchased *American Grocer*.

million, probably as a result of the steadily increasing sales of oleomargarine in that period.[21] (See figure 4.)

In 1884 Horace Thurber retired, and the company was reorganized as Thurber, Whyland, and Company. The company offered for sale virtually anything that was edible, "while from the firm's laboratory and drug departments come a full line of essences, flavors and syrups." The Thurber "Price List" published in each issue of *American Grocer* often ran to twenty pages of fine type, and much of what was sold was manufactured by, or especially for, the company. The contemporary commercial appraisal of the firm was that "their praise of their own goods is merited because honest; they know whereof they speak."[22]

Despite Thurber's vigorous leadership of his grocery firm, it is apparent that he devoted even more time and energy to other activities. Though the present study cannot detail those activities, some intimation of their nature and scope is important, for Thurber's purposes and philosophy can be assumed to have carried over—at least to some extent—into his position on adulteration. Thurber's best-known "non-grocery" activity was in the anti-monopoly movement, directed against the railroads. In this campaign Thurber used his fertile pen, his influence, wealth, and incredible drive to gain leadership, or at least some degree of control, in an amazing variety of organizations.[23]

These include the American Cheap Transportation Association and its local auxiliary, the New York Cheap Transportation Association. Thurber has been credited with being the leader of the Importers' and Grocers' Board of Trade;[24] he also ran the New

21. *New York Tribune*, January 22, 1878; *American Grocer*, November 6, 1879, p. 1121. It was not until the Civil War that the American canning industry really began to develop, with the invention of a new process for boiling the canned goods; an "automatic" machine for sealing the cans was developed in 1870. See James H. Collins, *The Story of Canned Foods* (New York, 1924), pp.14–32.

22. *American Grocer*, February 7, 1884, p. 9; *New York's Great Industries*, p. 112. For a biographical sketch of Whyland, see *American Grocer*, May 5, 1886, p. 10.

23. See Benson, *Merchants, Farmers, and Railroads*. In addition to a large number of speeches, pamphlets, and articles to which Thurber signed his name, Professor Benson has traced him as being the anonymous author of perhaps hundreds of other important position papers and editorials, often acting as the spokesman for organizations to which he belonged.

24. Benson, p. 267.

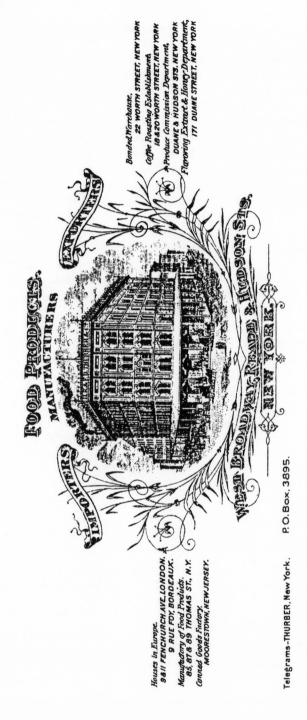

FOOD PRODUCTS,
MANUFACTURERS,
IMPORTERS
EXPORTERS

WEST BROADWAY, READE & HUDSON STS.
NEW YORK.

Bonded Warehouse,
22 WORTH STREET, NEW YORK
Coffee Roasting Establishment,
18 & 20 WORTH STREET, NEW YORK.
Produce Commission Department,
DUANE & HUDSON STS. NEW YORK
Flavoring Extract & Honey Department,
171 DUANE STREET, NEW YORK

Houses in Europe.
9 & 11 FENCHURCH AVE, LONDON.
9 RUE FOY, BORDEAUX.
Manufactory of Food Products,
85, 87 & 89 THOMAS ST., N.Y.
Canned Goods Factory,
MOORESTOWN, NEW JERSEY.

Telegrams—THURBER, New York.   P. O. Box. 3895.

4. Letterhead of H. K. and F. B. Thurber and Company.

York Board of Trade and Transportation, and he assumed the helm of the National Board of Trade immediately upon admission to that organization, in 1875. Thurber controlled the New York Chamber of Commerce, and through his influence there, and in the Board of Trade, instigated the 1879 investigation of New York railroads by Assemblyman William P. Hepburn. Moreover, Thurber's associate Simon Sterne "actually directed the course of the entire proceedings" at the request of the Hepburn committee. Sterne, in effect, was "the state's attorney to prosecute the indictment his co-worker Thurber had drawn up."[25]

In addition, Thurber had great influence in the New York Produce Exchange, apparently bankrolled the New York Farmers' Alliance and was its vice-president, arranged a temporary political union of merchants and farmers in New York in 1878, and was very influential in the New York Dairymen's Association and the International Dairy Fair Association, as well as serving as president of the American Dairymen's Association. All of these activities, and others, engaged Thurber between 1873 and 1880.[26]

What motivated—perhaps "drove" is more appropriate—a man like Thurber? Certainly his reform activities were not simply directed toward personal material gain. The railroads would surely have been willing to grant him favorable rates if he had called off his crusade against them. Although his firm was thriving, despite the depression of the 1870s, Thurber's outside interests kept him from giving full attention to the business. His older brother Horace advised Thurber a number of times to reduce his reform activities because not only the firm, but Thurber's own health, were suffering from his "strenuous regime of mixing groceries with agitation."[27]

25. Benson, p. 134.

26. In January 1881 Thurber became a founder and co-leader (with Peter Cooper) of the National Anti-Monopoly League, the culminating economic reform organization of this period, credited by Benson, pp. 151–52, with being "the major seed-bed for the notions of 'trust-busting' characteristic thereafter of middle-class reform groups in the United States."

27. Benson, p. 124. Benson, p. 280, cites letters from H. K. Thurber to F. B. Thurber dated August 6, 1876, December 25, 1876, and March 1, 1877. Unfortunately, all the Thurber papers have been destroyed by his heirs since being used by Benson (personal communications).

Thurber was not completely altruistic; his activities in the grocery trade were certainly intended to make money, and sometimes, perhaps often, he was not shy about bending the truth in order to promote sales. In some of his reform activities he stood to gain, yet in others he was sure to lose money. Of course the motives of a reformer need not be—as the phrase of the time went—"Simon pure." Part of the answer, for Thurber at least, must rest in his philosophy. It has been speculated that men like Thurber "felt that the traditional structure of American institutions was threatened by a 'vulgar plutocracy,' [and] they received greater satisfaction from thwarting the designs of railroad magnates than they did from more humdrum business activities." In a pamphlet written by Thurber there is perhaps a key to his broader vision, encompassing not only his war against the railroads but adulteration as well: "The American Republic has survived the storms and troubles of a hundred years. Whether or not it will exist for another century will depend largely upon the making and execution of our laws. It is, perhaps, not strange that legislation for the protection of the public interest should have failed to keep pace with the enormous changes which steam, electricity and machinery have wrought."[28]

Thurber, and the reform movements in which he participated, were in this sense basically "conservative." Thurber was attempting to protect certain American traditions and values that were threatened by the rapid changes the society had been undergoing, the most visible of which was the aggregation of capital into large corporations, dominated by the railroads. Thurber explained that "if we would preserve the principles upon which our Government is founded, there must somewhere be lodged a superior power to protect the people." Thurber "persisted in the belief that it was possible to harness the new forces within the framework of an older society."[29]

The necessary device for the reconstruction of American society, Thurber believed, was the law and governmental interven-

---

28. Benson, p. 125; "Some of the Causes of Communism" (1879), quoted in Benson, p. 140.

29. Speech by Thurber, printed in *Report of the Special Committee on Railroad Transportation of the Chamber of Commerce . . . April 7th, 1881*, p. 34; quoted in Benson, p. 161; Benson, p. 177.

tion. "The time for a *laissez faire* policy is past. Our civilization is constantly growing more complex and the forces which now control it must themselves be controlled and directed or disastrous collisions will surely result." For men like Thurber, "to preserve Jeffersonian social ideals amidst the centralizing tendencies of the Communication Revolution, it was necessary to stand Jeffersonian . . . laissez-faire political economy on its head." As Thurber himself put it on another occasion, speaking, aptly enough, to the Thomas Jefferson Club of Brooklyn: "I am opposed to the centralization of power either in the hands of Government or of corporations, but centralization is a *fact* staring us in the face and we must see if we cannot make one form of centralization neutralize the other."[30]

The first centralized public health instrumentality was the National Board of Health, a short-lived but serious commitment of the federal government, constructed from the blueprint of Dr. John Shaw Billings, a remarkably talented man of wide abilities and interests. Billings was graduated from the Medical College of Ohio in 1860, took the examination for the Army Medical Corps (passing first on the list), and served in the field until he suffered a partial paralysis of his left leg. In December 1864 he was transferred to the Surgeon-General's Office.

In addition to handling the routine tasks assigned to him after the war, Billings became an expert microscopist. He designed the Johns Hopkins Hospital, considered to be the model hospital of this era. He was a pioneer in the field of vital statistics, invented the concept of coded cards for data storage, and helped modernize the federal census. He used money left over from a wartime hospital fund to vastly enhance the Surgeon-General's Library, and began publishing the *Index-Catalogue* of its holdings and the monthly *Index Medicus*, which together constitute the premier bibliographic effort of the century.[31]

30. *Our Country, A Paper by F. B. Thurber, Read before the XIX Century Club, New York, November 17, 1885,* p. 28, quoted in Benson, p. 241; Benson, p. 151; *"Democracy and Anti-Monopoly"—An Address by F. B. Thurber before the Thomas Jefferson Club of Brooklyn, April 16, 1883,* p. 15.

31. For more complete biographies see Harry M. Lydenberg, *John Shaw Billings* (Chicago, 1924), and Fielding H. Garrison, *John Shaw Billings, A Memoir* (New York, 1915). For a sketch of his life, in addition to *DAB,* see "The Life

It was to Billings that the Secretary of the Treasury gave the job of redesigning the federal health services. The first permanent national medical service was the Marine Hospital Service, established in 1798 to provide hospital care for members of the merchant marine. But by 1869, after successive epidemics had swept the nation, Secretary George S. Boutwell asked Billings to investigate and report on the operation of the marine hospitals, whose mismanagement had become notorious. Billings reported that "the Regulations of the Treasury Department are a dead letter, each port being more or less a law unto itself." As a result of the Billings report, Congress, which had previously rejected proposals for broader health plans, passed a law reorganizing the Service. It had been Boutwell's intention to have Billings appointed to head the reorganized Service, and had this come about much of the later destructive competition within the public health profession might have been avoided. But the Senate amended the bill so as to rule out a military medical officer from the post, and Dr. John M. Woodworth, a highly competent but politically very active civilian surgeon, was appointed.[32]

The Marine Hospital Service remained the principal federal health agency until 1878, when a savage yellow fever epidemic tested its capabilities. In September a special commission to study the disease was created with private funds, run jointly by Dr. Woodworth and the American Public Health Association. But with only six weeks in which to work before it was due to report to APHA, the commission was doomed to failure. A letter writ-

---

of John Shaw Billings," in Frank B. Rogers, *Selected Papers of John Shaw Billings* (n.p., 1965).

Billings is famous for his work in three separate fields: medicine and public health; bibliographic and library science; and hospital design and administration. See Estelle Brodman, *The Development of Medical Bibliography* (Baltimore, 1954). William F. Poole, *Poole's Index to Periodical Literature* (1882; rpt. Gloucester, Mass., 1963 [see p. vii]) is virtually dedicated to Billings, whom Poole saw as his inspiration. From 1896 to 1913 Billings created the New York Public Library. He was one of the founders of APHA and was on the governing body of the National Academy of Sciences.

32. Leigh, *Federal Health Administration*, pp. 92, 94, 465; Peter W. Bruton, "The National Board of Health" (Ph.D. diss., University of Maryland, 1974), pp. 34–53; Henry I. Bowditch, "The Future Health Council of the Nation," *Transactions of the American Medical Association* 26 (1875), p. 301; James G. Burrow, *AMA, Voice of American Medicine* (Baltimore, 1963), p. 23.

ten by Billings also makes it evident that any consensus was unlikely because of political maneuvering among the sanitary leaders: "I distrust the proposed Yellow Fever Commission under Woodworth—for I distrust him and his motives. But there is no doubt that in consequence of the present epidemic the coming winter will afford an unusually favorable opportunity to secure legislation and funds for promoting Public Hygiene, and that those really interested should try to prevent this enthusiasm from being wasted by being seized on and converted to the benefit of ambitious and scheming medical politicians."[33]

APHA's members were already sharply divided, not only regarding the possible cause of yellow fever and the steps that should be taken to combat it, but also upon what type (if any) of national organization should be formed. APHA finally decided to form a special advisory committee to draw up legislative proposals for the formation of a federally funded national health service. Billings, chairman of the APHA committee assigned to examine the results of the Yellow Fever Commission's work, also headed this special committee.[34]

But on December 10, before the APHA committee had met, Senator L. Q. C. Lamar of Mississippi introduced a bill to establish a bureau of public health. Stephen Smith had drafted this bill for Lamar, acting in concert with Dr. Woodworth. The Lamar bill would have converted the Marine Hospital Service into the new national bureau, enlarging its powers and leaving Woodworth in control. Smith, though the founding father of APHA, was not on its advisory committee, or even on the APHA executive committee, at this time. Though Smith seems to have thought well of Woodworth, the leadership of APHA responded negatively to the bill.[35]

By this time President Hayes had requested Congress to consider legislation for a national sanitary administration, and both houses

33. Billings to Dr. Charles F. Folsom, September 20, 1878, Billings Papers. There were over 100,000 cases of yellow fever in the South, causing 20,000 deaths, during the epidemic of 1878.

34. Bruton, pp. 115–27; "Abstract of the Richmond Meeting," *APHA Reports and Papers* 4 (1878); *New York Times,* October 4, 1878–November 23, 1878.

35. Kathleen F. Cortes, "Democracy in the American Public Health Association: A Historical Analysis" (Ph.D. diss., Columbia University, 1976), p. 81; Nancy R. Bernstein, *The First One Hundred Years, Essays on the History of the American Public Health Association* (n.p., 1972), p. 10.

of Congress responded by forming committees to investigate the yellow fever epidemic. On December 16, 1878, the two congressional committees met jointly and appointed a board of medical experts. Though this board underwent some changes, it consistently remained under the control of Dr. Woodworth. The combined pressure of the Lamar bill and Woodworth's special congressional board forced APHA to act decisively at a time when much of the leadership was hesitant about creating a national board that might supersede the authority of the state boards. After all, most of the APHA leaders were medical men who derived their official power from membership on local or state boards, and they were very conscious of their prerogatives.[36] Largely because of the influence of Billings's APHA advisory committee, the Lamar bill never emerged from committee, and in January 1879 APHA came up with its own bill. Although a variety of bills were proposed in both houses of Congress, it was the APHA bill, drafted by Billings[37] and introduced by Congressman Jonas McGowan of Michigan, that was finally passed into law, on March 3, 1879.

Although the McGowan bill has been heavily criticized for its inadequacies by historians of public health,[38] Billings did not con-

36. Cortes, in table 2-6, indicates that in 1879 95 percent of the leaders were medical men, while only about 70 percent of APHA members were physicians. Tables 2-1 and 2-8 indicate that, in 1879, while only 19 percent of the members held positions on state or local health boards, a majority of the leaders did. Smillie, *Public Health,* p. 305, points out that five of the six members of the APHA executive committee elected for 1879 were "executive officers of state health departments."

37. Billings to Folsom, March 7, 1879, Billings Papers: *"Strictly between you and I* I wrote that McGowan bill literature." This is apparently new information. Bruton, p. 153, says merely that "the bill had been drafted with the assistance of the APHA." Cortes, p. 81, reflecting Leigh, pp. 470–73, says it "was essentially APHA's Advisory and Executive Committee's plan." George Rosen, *A History of Public Health* (New York, 1958), p. 249, and Smillie, p. 332, credit Dorman Eaton with being the author. Mazyck P. Ravenel, "The American Public Health Association, Past, Present, Future," in *A Half Century of Public Health,* ed. Mazyck P. Ravenel (1921; rpt. New York, 1970), p. 31, has Dr. Smith's bill becoming the NBH. Duffy, 2: p. 629, credits Smith and Eaton jointly.

38. The critics have, perhaps, applied hindsight too heavily. See Bruton, p. 154; Cortes, p. 82; Rosen, p. 248; Smillie, p. 466. Some of this criticism reflects Dr. Smith's later reminiscences about the superiority of his own plan. APHA publications in the current century strongly reflect the opinions of Dr. Smith, who is revered as the organization's founder.

sider it to be a compromise, but rather the bill that best reflected APHA's concepts at that time. The National Board of Health (NBH), created by the McGowan bill, avoided the possibility of Woodworth's ascendancy by establishing a board of seven members plus representatives from related federal departments. Members were appointed by the president, but in practice APHA controlled the NBH's membership. Dr. James Cabell, then president of APHA, became president of the NBH, and the real moving force on the Board was Dr. Billings, who became its vice-president. Billings, who has been called "the greatest American physician of his day," was elected to serve as APHA's president for 1880. APHA members dominated both the Board itself and the quarantine inspection force it established.[39]

The primary functions of the Board were to prevent the recurrence of epidemics such as that of the previous year, to obtain information on all matters affecting public health, and to advise federal, state, and local authorities on public health problems. To many APHA leaders the last provision was the most important, and the NBH soon exceeded the congressional mandate of "cooperating" with local boards and set as a major goal the establishment of such boards throughout the nation. From Billings's point of view the only serious defect of the McGowan bill, as passed, was the elimination of the appropriation clause by the Senate. Drs. Cabell and Billings both believed that "the clauses omitted were omitted by the mistake of an engrossing clerk." But whether "by accident or design," the law provided only $50,000 for salaries and expenses. A second act, passed in June, restored the original appropriation request of $500,000 for the operation of the Board, but also attached a four-year limitation to its powers. Congress believed that the NBH was experimental, and many APHA members probably agreed with this position.[40]

39. Smillie, p. 301; Cortes, pp. 82–83. Woodworth's death at this time effectively eliminated the ability of the Marine Hospital Service to influence the new Board, though Dr. John B. Hamilton, Woodworth's successor, would eventually help to destroy the NBH.

40. Billings to Folsom, March 7, 1879, Billings Papers; Leigh, p. 474 (there is some disagreement on the original appropriation discrepancy); Bruton, p. 160; Cortes, pp. 83–87. The Board legally remained in existence until 1893, when legislation was passed terminating it, but in practice ceased to function ten years earlier, when its appropriations were cut.

There are complicated political reasons for the ultimate failure of the NBH—and perhaps the prejudices of the period foredoomed it—but probably the basic flaw was identified quite simply by Dr. Jerome Cochran in a letter to Dr. Billings: "The convenient epidemic of yellow fever did not make its appearance." Billings had identified this central problem of public health in an essay written immediately after passage of the McGowan bill: "Sanitary measures, to be effective, should be carried out at those times when most people see no special cause for anxiety, and often, therefore, appear to involve unnecessary worry and expense. . . . 'If the expected disease does not appear, the warnings are considered to have been a false alarm, and the precautions taken to have been excessive.' "[41]

One of the issues that continued to engage Billings's attention while he served on the NBH was the nature of expertise and professionalism required on boards of health at all levels of government. The dependence of government on the abilities and training of "experts" was beginning to be sharply felt. Government officials eventually came to understand that they must employ their "own" experts, but for the time being civilian professionals, and the voluntary associations they represented (and which represented them) played a vital role. It is clear that the American Public Health Association, the National Academy of Sciences, and to a lesser extent the American Medical Association and the various pharmaceutical associations, were vital to congressional committees and state governments.

In a parallel manner, it has already been seen that, when New York Assemblyman Hepburn decided to conduct hearings on the state's railroads, he was forced to rely on Thurber and his associates on the Chamber of Commerce and the Board of Trade to conduct the investigation, for the state legislature lacked the necessary expertise and information. This delegation of responsibility "to the merchants points up a fundamental problem of the period. . . . Few, if any, 'experts' on the subject could be found who were not closely identified with some interested party." Moreover, as Professor Lee Benson further noted, "even the 'experts'

41. Cochran to Billings, September 10, 1882, Billings Papers; John S. Billings, "Introduction," in *A Treatise on Hygiene and Public Health,* ed. Albert H. Buck (New York, 1879), p. 7.

were inadequately equipped for a task of such complexity."[42]
This assessment would prove as true for the era's professionals as
for its businessmen.

If Thurber pursued a restoration of traditional middle-class values through membership in a wide variety of voluntary associations, men such as Professor Chandler, Dr. Squibb, and leaders
of APHA such as Dr. Billings pursued it through professionalism, through organizations of experts. All these men, in their
different ways and for somewhat different purposes, were reacting to the technological and material changes taking place in
America, changes that made old values seem inconsistent with
the new society. They were trying to formulate appropriate com-
promises between the ideal and the businesslike reality; they
were responding to the new America in terms of the old.[43]

Perhaps even more than Thurber, the businessman-as-
reformer, these health professionals—and men like Meyer who
saw themselves as health professionals—took their cues, built
their reputations, tested their competence, from the associations
of "experts" to which they belonged. More and more in this
period the expert was known by the company he kept. These new
organizations were closely knit, their members few, their alle-
giances strong. When Chandler and a few fellow chemists sent
out invitations to potential members of the new American
Chemical Society in 1876, they could find only 220 men in the
entire country who they felt were qualified to join.[44]

To the new middle-class professional the worst insult was to be
called "amateurish," for this new word "connoted faulty and

42. Benson, p. 133.

43. Everett M. Rogers, *Social Change in Rural Society* (New York, 1960), p.
47, argues: "Cultural lag occurs when technological and material changes take
place more rapidly than non-material changes in social values, attitudes, and
social organization." See also Lawrence M. Friedman and Jack Ladinsky, "Law
and Social Change in the Progressive Era," in *New Perspectives on the American
Past,* ed. Stanley N. Katz and Stanley I. Kutler (Boston, 1969), p. 199: cultural
lag occurred at times "in which issues were collectively defined and alternative
solutions posed." See also Robert H. Wiebe, *The Search For Order, 1877–1920*
(New York, 1967), especially p. 134.

44. Charles A. Browne and Mary E. Weeks, *A History of the American
Chemical Society* (Washington, D. C., 1952), pp. 14–15.

deficient work . . . the pursuit of an activity for amusement and distraction."[45] This was exactly the accusation the professionals tried to fix upon George T. Angell, for men like Angell challenged the esteem, the purpose, the power, the very foundations of professional science and public health. They called him an amateur, a "so-called Sociologist." For if Angell chose to speak through, of necessity to employ, professional organizations such as the American Social Science Association (in contrast to the SPCA or the Humane Society, which the experts would ridicule), he was nonetheless a lone warrior. Although Angell was an old hand at forming and using associational power—witness his activities on behalf of animals—he was still less a "joiner," less the organization man than Chandler or Billings. Angell thrilled in picturing himself as the champion in single combat, opposed by dark and powerful forces, challenging the corrupt power of the professionals and businessmen and the inertia of the merely ignorant. Angell saw himself as a man who, with a few noble and selfless friends, stood as the voice of the people, virtually alone against the corruptionists.

Nor, really, were there such vast differences between the intent of ASSA and of associations of plumbers, chemists, and businessmen. Order meant morality; chaos signified immorality. Men like Meyer felt that professionalism among "sanitary engineers" could not only establish competency in plumbing but also operate to ameliorate the bewildering social problems of tenement life that he and his contemporaries recast in terms of morality. Professionalism among physicians, pharmacists, and chemists could help to restore order to the confusing, modernizing society. Commercial organizations attempted to restore business stability. So too, ASSA attempted to deal with the vast changes taking place. Expertise in the broad field of "social science," of human relationships, was an attempt to understand the entire scope of changing morality and to gain control through science.[46]

45. Burton J. Bledstein, *The Culture of Professionalism* (New York, 1976), p. 31.

46. Thomas L. Haskell, *The Emergence of Professional Social Science* (Urbana, Ill., 1977), pp. 86–87. See also Edward A. Ross, *Sin and Society, An Analysis of Latter-Day Iniquity* (Boston, 1907), especially chap. 1, where Ross discusses the new variety of "sin"—the "impersonal" sin.

Men such as Angell were attempting to confront these new social tendencies and to reconcile them with values that were becoming casualties of modernization. He was trying, more than Chandler, Thurber, Billings, or Meyer, to maintain a grasp on the conventional morality of America's past, and reestablish it once again. Angell saw these other men not just as *symptoms,* but as *agents* of change, conspiring to hasten the collapse of traditional morality while mouthing maxims to disguise their corrupting influence. If Dr. Squibb was, unlike Angell, a true "expert" in the new sense, he too stood apart from men like Thurber, Meyer, Chandler, and Billings. Though he chose to speak through the State Medical Society, he too spoke in the tradition of the independent individual. Though he was a member of several medical and pharmaceutical societies, Squibb was known in the profession as an uncompromising die-hard individualist who stood his ground against all comers. In an older America this had been a noble stance, but in the new society, where the professional assured his status and power through his organizations, Squibb was sometimes a voice in the wilderness.

Nonetheless, all of these men were attempting the same thing: to restore a lost morality. They sought, through publicity and through legislation, to reestablish fair play in the marketplace. But those who succeeded, and thus shaped anti-adulteration legislation to *their* perceptions, were those who had learned best to use the new tools of the new society: the professional organization and the professional publication. In the 1880s the new New York State Board of Health, under Chandler's control, and the new National Board of Health, largely because of Dr. Billings's temporary involvement with Chandler, Thurber, and Meyer, would play a vital role in these efforts.

6

"Without Imposing Unnecessary Burdens upon Commerce"

There is no indication that public health professionals would have taken additional steps toward the regulation of foods and drugs had it not been for the publicity created by amateurs like Angell. Though the newly formed National Board of Health established a standing committee on adulteration on April 3, 1879, the committee neither took specific action nor attempted to evaluate the problem.[1] Similarly, the New York City Board of Health ignored its "legislative" capacity to create ordinances for the control of adulteration. Except for milk and kerosene adulteration—areas of pronounced public concern—little had been done.

Health officials and chemists seemed more interested in reducing public apprehension than in taking direct action—more interested in ridiculing agitators such as Angell than in giving due consideration to their more valid accusations. It is also possible that the ties that had grown between "experts" and businessmen retarded any sweeping legislation that would interfere with commerce. It is not suggested that all health professionals were so dependent upon corporate largess that they feared to anger their wayward employers; the health of American commerce was a legitimate concern for conscientious professionals. Still—for a combination of reasons—the professionals seem to have been unwilling to act.

But by 1880, despite the efforts of the chemists and sanitarians

1. Peter W. Bruton, "The National Board of Health" (Ph.D. diss., University of Maryland, 1974), p. 170; *New York Times,* April 7, 1879.

to refute Angell's accusations, there was a stirring of legislative activity in Washington, an effort that accepted Angell's assertions unquestioningly. In response to this activity Chandler, Billings, and Meyer, following the lead of Francis Thurber and the National Board of Trade, began to prepare legislation of their own—legislation that sought not only to calm public apprehension over adulteration, but to regulate the marketplace with a gentle hand and impose no "unnecessary burdens" upon trade.

The professional appraisal of the adulteration situation as of 1879 is best represented by the chapter on this subject written by Stephen Sharples, Angell's Massachusetts adversary, in Albert Buck's *Treatise on Hygiene*. Sharples's position resembled not the inquietude of Accum and Hassall, but the complacency of *American Grocer* and *Sanitary Engineer*. He cautioned against legislation that was too stringent and against enthusiastic enforcement of the laws, since they would interfere "with the great natural laws of supply and demand." Sharples warned about amateur publicists and "needless alarm." He claimed that many attempts to prosecute alleged adulterators "have arisen more out of malice or mistaken zeal . . . than from any desire to benefit the public."[2]

Sharples differentiated adulteration into the harmful and the merely fraudulent, and argued that adulterations that were "in no way injurious to health" were simply not worth prosecuting, "since the buyer, as a general rule, knows what he is getting. To this class belong such articles as package-coffee, which is generally a compound which contains no coffee . . . mustard diluted with flour and colored with turmeric; the mixture of inferior grades of goods with higher grades of the same material. . . . the sale of oleomargarine or suet butter as genuine butter; and the adulteration of spices with ship-bread." He similarly argued that artificial coloration was not an adulteration at all, and dismissed attempts to prosecute for the use of flour, "terra alba," or glucose in candy. "These were all frauds in their inception, but, sanctioned by usage, they have become difficult to deal with."[3]

---

2. Stephen P. Sharples, "Adulteration of Food," in *A Treatise on Hygiene and Public Health*, ed. Albert H. Buck (New York, 1879), 2: pp. 351, 354.

3. Buck, pp. 355–56. "Ship-bread" is hardtack; Sharples means that harmless grain products and by-products were used to dilute spices.

Sharples also discussed "accidental impurities," concluding that "in this case it would hardly be just to hold the vendor liable to a further degree than is involved in the [confiscation] of his property," even when the "accidental" adulteration is "injurious to health." With this advice Sharples effectively precluded any successful prosecution, for no manufacturer or dealer guilty of adulteration would hesitate to claim lack of responsibility due to accident or error. The only food adulterations Sharples specifically condemned, and urged prosecution for, were poisonous colorings—particularly in candies—and adulterations of milk. Moreover, Sharples concluded, "in the large number of cases" the health officer "will find his purposes served far better by warning the parties privately than he will by bringing the case into court."[4]

If Sharples was indeed representative of sanitary experts in general at this time, what provided, in the words of one writer, "the leaven of revolt"? On January 20, 1879, less than two weeks after Angell had addressed the ASSA convention, Congressman Hendrick B. Wright of Pennsylvania introduced the first federal bill designed primarily to prevent the adulteration of food. Like Assemblyman Tallmadge's bill in the New York legislature, which was introduced a few weeks later, Wright's bill called for prosecution only for manufacturing or selling foods "injurious to the health of persons partaking thereof." Like the Tallmadge bill, the Wright proposal received little attention in the press, and it died in the House Committee on Manufactures.[5]

Nevertheless, the Wright bill was a foretaste of things to come, for in the next sessions of the Congress other bills would be submitted, and these bills would reflect the opinions, not of Sharples, but of George T. Angell. Angell remained the chief agitator for such legislation, and he continued to use his position within ASSA to keep the issue alive. Throughout this period

---

4. Buck, pp. 356–57, 376.
5. F. Leslie Hart, "A History of the Adulteration of Food before 1906," *Food-Drug-Cosmetic Law Journal* 7 (January 1952), p. 14 (Hart deals mainly with Accum and Hassall); *Congressional Record*, 45th Cong., 3d. sess., January 20, 1879, H. R. 5916, p. 575; *New York Times*, May 23, 1879. See Thomas A. Bailey, "Congressional Opposition to Pure Food Legislation, 1879–1906," *American Journal of Sociology* 36 (July 1930), p. 52; Gustavus A. Weber, *The Food, Drug, and Insecticide Administration* (Baltimore, 1928), p. 7.

Angell had the complete trust of Frank Sanborn and other Association leaders. Despite the escalating condemnation heaped upon Angell by the sanitary experts, as late as 1884 Sanborn wrote to Edward Atkinson, in planning an ASSA meeting, that "nobody understands Adulteration of Food better than Mr. George T. Angell."[6]

Angell also continued to use every other opportunity for agitation. Although the Massachusetts State Grange was one of the smallest in the nation, Angell used his friendship with its master, Benjamin Ware, to reach members throughout the country. He used the *Massachusetts Ploughman* to condemn, unlike Sharples, all forms of adulteration, including "careless" or accidental contamination, calling it "hardly less criminal" than intentional adulteration. Angell spoke to a wide variety of groups in 1879, and in September he once again addressed ASSA, though his paper, "The Manufacture and Sale of Poisonous and Dangerously Adulterated Articles," was very similar to his "Public Health Associations" speech. But this time Henry Meyer appeared on the platform with Angell, acting as a spokesman for the professional sanitarians to refute Angell's claims. Meyer explained "that he had investigated previous articles published by Mr. Angell on adulterations, and had tests made, and he could find no such system of general adulteration as reported."[7]

Sanitary Engineer devoted almost two full pages to the ASSA meeting, publishing editorials condemning Angell's speech, the Massachusetts papers that gave credence to it, and the Association itself. The central editorial cited Professor William Ripley Nichols's protest against Angell's comments, and used Sharples's essay in Buck's *Treatise* to refute them. Meyer also published long critical letters from Henry Morton and Sharples. Morton's letter reprinted additional protests against Angell that had been

6. Sanborn to Atkinson, December 22, 1884, Edward Atkinson Papers. The appointment of Angell to speak on the topic for the 1885 meeting was a decision of the ASSA Council, not just of Sanborn.

7. Solon J. Buck, *The Granger Movement, 1870–1880* (Cambridge, Mass., 1913); *Massachusetts Ploughman and New England Journal of Agriculture,* April 22, 1882; George T. Angell, *Autobiographical Sketches and Personal Recollections* (Boston, 1892), p. 62; *American Grocer,* October 2, 1879, pp. 793–94; *Sanitary Engineer,* October 1, 1879, p. 346; *New York Times,* September 11, 1879.

issued after he had presented his "Public Health Associations" speech—by Professors Merrick (now deceased), Vaughan, Chandler, and Charles O. Thompson of the Worcester Free Institute. Thus, much of the leadership of the American chemical profession had aligned itself against Angell.

The crux of Meyer's protest was that Angell, "even though called a 'sociologist,' " was "not an authority on the subject he discusses": "That adulteration does exist we fully admit, and we regret that a paper such as Dr. Sharples' on 'Hygiene and Public Health,' was not read instead of the one so widely published, which reflects upon the honesty of the whole mercantile community." Sharples, in his own letter, went even further toward denying the prevalence of adulteration than he had in his *Treatise* essay, concluding that "our markets are well supplied with good, wholesome food in abundance, and that adulteration so far from being the rule is only exceptional."[8]

American Grocer's editorial on the Angell speech explained that "we desire to build up trade and to encourage the sale of honest products, but this can never be effected by the circulation of wholesale and unfounded alarm and thereby making consumers suspicious of adulteration in everything that is offered for sale." Through the next months both papers continued their attack on Angell, especially when other newspapers reprinted his accusations. A consensus seems to have been reached by *Sanitary Engineer* and *American Grocer,* not only to disparage Angell's comments, but to report with regularity on adulterations, stressing, however, their generally harmless nature. The papers condemned poisonous food colorings and milk adulteration but played down as insignificant the merely fraudulent, though criticizing it as unethical business behavior. Thus *American Grocer* began a series called "Can a Large City Be Supplied With Pure Milk?" and *Sanitary Engineer* started a regular feature page called "Food and Drugs."[9]

Interestingly, the *New York Times* at this point began treating

8. *Sanitary Engineer,* October 1, 1879, p. 352.

9. *American Grocer,* October 2, 1879, p. 793; and see November 20, 1879, p. 1253; March 18, 1880, p. 727; *Sanitary Engineer,* June 15, 1881; and see November 1, 1879, p. 390; November 15, 1879, p. 418; December 1, 1879, p. 5; January 1, 1880, p. 45; February 1, 1880, p. 85; April 1, 1880, p. 170.

adulteration in an identical manner. It is probable that the publication of the highly respected Buck volumes, and the professionals' condemnation of Angell's unsubstantiated claims, inclined the newspaper to reconsider its position. In any case, when the *Times* editorialized on the subject, the paper adopted Sharples's observations, stressing the exaggerations of the public press "when there is but very little cause," and explaining that the vast majority of adulterations "are generally of an innocent character as far as the public health is concerned." The *Times* even argued that "the noises made some six months ago in New-York as to admixture of foreign matters in sugars had no possible foundation." The paper now explained that the public should focus its attention on milk adulteration, and it reported the conclusion of Professor Albert R. Leeds, chief chemical analyst of the New Jersey State Board of Health, that virtually the only poisonous adulterations were in candies and arsenical wallpaper. It also argued that urban food was healthier, and of a better quality, than the food eaten in the countryside; America "may be compared to an immense desert in which some 15 or 20 cities form conspicuous oases."[10]

By the early winter of 1879 the furor over adulteration had generally quieted down. A survey of popular, commercial, and scientific periodicals reveals little material on adulteration in general, although a few specific issues were approached.[11] The New York City Board of Health issued no report on adulteration that year. The American Public Health Association's *Reports and Papers* for 1879 contain no papers on the topic. The *National Board of Health Bulletin,* although it was first issued on June 28 and appeared regularly thereafter, contained virtually nothing on adulteration during the year. Even Dr. Bell's *Sanitarian* printed only one comment on oleomargarine in the second half of the year and nothing else on adulteration.

But amidst this lull, a new storm was brewing. Though the

10. *New York Times,* April 14, April 30, October 26, November 11, 1879. See also *Sanitary Engineer,* December 15, 1879, p. 35. Leeds was the author of "The Adulteration of Food," *Third Annual Report of the New Jersey State Board of Health* (Camden, N. J., 1879), and of similar reports in later annual reports of the Board. The speech was delivered to the New York Academy of Sciences.

11. The purity of milk continued to be discussed, and there was concern over oleomargarine and alum, but these two "adulterations" are considered below.

Wright bill had died in committee, Representative Richard L. T. Beale of Virginia submitted a new bill, similar to Wright's, to the House Committee on Manufactures in the early days of the next session of Congress, and plans were afoot in Washington by the end of the year to introduce additional legislation. Though Angell was ill with severe bronchitis during the winter, he had clearly not given up the fight. For the public health and chemical professionals, and for the businessmen who would be affected by any adulteration legislation, the time to act had come.[12]

Francis Thurber had been abroad in the fall, attending an international dairy fair in London, in his capacity as president of the American Dairymen's Association. When he returned, probably sometime in November, he and Henry Meyer decided to sponsor a contest in *Sanitary Engineer* for a draft of an anti-adulteration law. Thurber was to put up the prize money of $1,000 and enlist the support of the National Board of Trade (NBT) for the competition. As Meyer put it, "it is hoped that the National Board of Trade will be able to propose legislation which will protect the public on the one hand and the honest manufacturer on the other." The rules called for a draft of legislation that would not impose "unnecessary burdens upon commerce."[13]

The National Board of Trade was just recovering from the effects of the great depression of the 1870s. It had been formed in 1868, with a membership of thirty-two local boards of trade, chambers of commerce, and business exchanges. During the depression, however, membership had fallen. Despite the optimism of Frederick Fraley, a Philadelphia merchant and banker and effectively the permanent president of the Board, in December 1879 only seventeen organizations were represented at the annual meeting, four of which had just then been admitted or readmitted to membership. Things had been so bad that the NBT had not even met the previous year, holding only a session of its coun-

12. *Congressional Record*, 46th Cong., 1st sess., May 23, 1879, H.R. 2014, p. 1552, discussed more fully below; Angell, *Autobiographical Sketches*, p. 67.

13. *American Grocer*, November 20, 1879, p. 1253; see Lee Benson, *Merchants, Farmers, and Railroads* (New York, 1955), p. 138. *Sanitary Engineer*, January 1, 1880, p. 45.

cil.[14] Nonetheless, the NBT was the dominant nationwide organization representing the interests of middle-sized business firms. Its central concern since its inception was, and continued to be, transportation—especially attempts to control railroad practices. But the Board was actively engaged in an assortment of battles, each of which attempted in some way to cope with the changing business environment.[15]

Coincidentally, at exactly the time the Board of Trade was about to involve itself in sanitary matters, the new National Board of Health sought the assistance of Thurber and his associates. Dr. Billings was aware that the survival of the NBH was precarious at best, and he sought support from Thurber just when Thurber needed support from reputable national public health figures.[16] One of the central problems of sanitary reform in these formative years was the difficulty of maintaining the "uneasy balance" between health and commerce. Since the accepted practice for controlling the recurring epidemics of yellow fever—which had been the primary reason for the formation of the NBH in the first place—was by quarantine, public health practices regularly ran afoul of business interests, "for a strict quarantine might . . . preserve the health of the populace, but it might also cause commercial stagnation or ruin."[17] A mutuality

14. *Proceedings of the Tenth Annual Meeting of the National Board of Trade, Held in Washington, December, 1879* (Boston, 1880), Introduction. Fraley, a former Pennsylvania state senator, organized the Philadelphia Board of Trade in 1838, became president of the board of Girard College, and helped establish the NBT; he "became its first president and has been reelected each year." (*National Cyclopaedia of American Biography* [New York, 1897], s.v. "Frederick Fraley.") By 1880 membership in the NBT rose to twenty-seven organizations.

15. Benson, *Merchants*, pp. 22–23, 211–12. The NBT prospered over the next years. The National Association of Manufacturers was not formed until 1895, and the national Chamber of Commerce until 1912. James Q. Wilson, *Political Organizations* (New York, 1973), p. 146, points out that it was not in industries controlled by small numbers of large corporations that business associations were stimulated, but rather "in those industries characterized by fragmentation, competition, and localism. . . . Associations formed disproportionately, it appears, in those industries that were unable to achieve control over their resources and markets."

16. Billings to Folsom, December 14, 1879, Billings Papers.

17. Margaret Warner, "Local Control versus National Interest: The Debate over Southern Public Health, 1878–1884," *Journal of Southern History* 50:3 (August 1984), pp. 407–8.

of interests would link the two organizations over the next three years.

Dr. Thomas J. Turner, the Navy's appointee to the Board and its secretary, sent a letter to the NBT, requesting that it join the National Academy of Sciences and the NBH to work on "a plan for a national public health organization." Yet at this very time some members of the NBT, suspicious of the health board's potential interference with commerce, wished to discuss "the propriety of amending, revising, or repealing the Act of Congress, creating a National Board of Health." Thurber made it his business to derail any such attempt, and he had Fraley appoint a special committee to meet with Turner and Billings. Not surprisingly, this committee consisted of Thurber, his associate from New York Ambrose Snow, and George L. Buzby of Philadelphia. Snow was in the shipping and commission business and was an unquestioning supporter of Thurber, who was appointed chairman.[18]

Billings, already serving on *Sanitary Engineer*'s committee to judge entries for a model public school building, was approached to serve on the committee for the adulteration competition. The imminent announcement of his participation in this upcoming competition[19] apparently inspired Billings to have the NBH put together some material on adulteration, which the NBH *Bulletin* was conspicuously lacking. Needing something on short notice, Billings published an article sent by Robert C. Kedzie, which was little more than a survey of the literature of adulteration and showed much internal evidence of haste. Billings, very conscious of its defects, wrote Dr. Folsom that "we have a paper from Kedzie which you would probably put in the wastepaper basket. Don't think we shall however." Though Kedzie's material con-

18. NBT *Proceedings, 1879*, pp. 115, 161–62. For information on Snow, see *Proceedings* of the New York Board of Trade and Transportation (New York, 1883), p. 24.

19. The *New York Times* published the NBT resolution for the organization of "a committee of experts" on December 13, 1879, but the members' names were not yet known. The school competition was Meyer's second contest; the adulteration competition was his third. Billings wrote that Meyer's "prize tenement house plans worked so well that he is going to do the same for School Houses. . . . He is a good man & deserves good counsel for he appreciates it." (Billings to Folsom, October 6, 1879, Billings Papers.)

tained some valuable nutritional information, it was also replete with inane observations and personal philosophy, such as the belief that wheat is "pre-eminently the food of brain-workers." There was little material on adulteration per se, probably constituting less than one page of the *Bulletin,* and most of that was a rehash of Kedzie's earlier research on glucose. Though Kedzie made no attempt to measure the extent of adulteration, his comments were totally compatible with Sharples's conclusion that it was not a serious problem.[20]

Billings also printed a report on drug adulteration by Professor C. Lewis Diehl, which consisted of a review of relevant material published over the years in the *Proceedings* of the American Pharmaceutical Association. Within this self-imposed limit the Diehl report was a competent summary, but little more. Diehl admitted at the outset that he had never "previously given the subject special attention" and that he found the time allotted him "too short to do complete justice to the work." Because of his intimate involvement with APhA Diehl was entirely uncritical of its activities and motives. Whatever improvements had been made in the quality of pharmaceuticals he credited to APhA, and all failures he laid at the door of conniving politicians and the patent medicine clan.[21]

On the whole, Diehl felt "the drug market must be unqualifiedly pronounced to be fair." The drug import law of 1848 had succeeded in removing most adulterated or inferior drugs from the marketplace. The problem was that the public ignorantly demanded "cheap goods," thereby creating "the prime motor to all falsifications and substitutions." Thus, Diehl suggested, two

20. Billings to Folsom, Christmas 1879, Billings Papers; R. C. Kedzie, "The Adulteration and Deterioration of Food," *NBH Bulletin,* Supplement No. 6 (Washington, D.C., 1880), pp. 28–29. (Also published as Appendix D, *Annual Report of the National Board of Health, 1879* [Washington, D. C., 1880].)

21. C. Lewis Diehl, "Report on Deteriorations, Adulterations, and Substitutions of Drugs," NBH *Bulletin,* Supplement No. 6, pp. 1–2. (Also published as Appendix E, *Annual Report of the National Board of Health, 1879* [Washington, D. C., 1880].) Diehl included a summary of the reported general quality of 212 common drugs and chemicals, adapted from APhA *Proceedings* reports. Diehl lived in Louisville, Kentucky, and was a very active member of APhA. He was instrumental in modifying the pharmacy law of Kentucky in order to benefit practicing pharmacists and to hinder the activities of the patent medicine makers and dealers. He was a member of the Kentucky State Board of Pharmacy.

things would operate to eliminate the remaining domestic adulteration: enhancement of the legal authority of APhA; and a system of state laws on the pattern suggested by Dr. Squibb. For the second part of this solution Diehl appended Squibb's "Rough Draft" to his essay.[22]

Although the present study deals with patent medicines only incidentally, it should be pointed out that, like APhA itself, Diehl saw these "secret remedies" as the greatest hindrance to the reformation of American pharmacy. Although he emphasized their medical dangers—ignorant reliance on symptomatic relief, and habit-forming drug dependence—Diehl's basic intention was to make the public more dependent "upon legitimate medicine and less upon the professions of charlatans and mountebanks."[23] Strict state pharmacy laws and laws requiring content labeling of patent medicines, APhA consistently argued, would affect unscrupulous or incompetent druggists who reflected badly upon the profession, and would remove the competition of other merchants, such as neighborhood grocers, who maintained a supply of patent medicines as part of their stock in trade.[24]

The Kedzie and Diehl material, published at about the time *Sanitary Engineer* announced Billings as one of the judges in its contest for a draft adulteration law, established the National Board of Health itself as a participant in this new legislative effort. The weekly NBH *Bulletin* announced and supported the contest, reprinting the NBT resolution and then quoting in its entirety the terms of the contest from *Sanitary Engineer*. The NBT resolution, in addition to specifying that the draft legislation should prevent "injurious" adulterations (nothing was said about the merely fraudulent) "without imposing unnecessary burdens

22. Ibid., pp. 2, 9.

23. Ibid., pp. 20–21. For a treatment of patent medicines, see James H. Young, *The Toadstool Millionaires: A Social History of Patent Medicines in America before Federal Regulation* (Princeton, 1961), and D. L. Dykstra, "Patent and Proprietary Medicines: Regulation Control Prior to 1906" (Ph.D. diss., University of Wisconsin, 1951).

24. *American Grocer* was well aware of this potential threat to retail grocers, and to wholesalers such as Thurber, who maintained his own pharmaceutical department. See May 6, 1880, p. 1177; May 27, 1880, pp. 1366–67; June 10, 1880, p. 1494.

on commerce," also specified that the committee to judge entries should consist of five "experts," including at least one doctor, one chemist, one lawyer, and one merchant. The official announcement in Meyer's paper was more direct about the NBT's concern that "the public mind has of late been considerably agitated by the alleged adulteration of food": "For more than a year we have had frequent occasion to defend the commercial community from wholesale and alarming charges of deleterious food adulteration. We have exposed the absurdity of the sensational statements made by men like Mr. Angell, which in our judgment tended to thwart intelligent and legitimate attempts to correct and control this evil where it does exist."[25]

Two issues later *Sanitary Engineer* published the complete rules of the competition. Entries were to be submitted anonymously, with a code "motto" for identification; judging would take place in October. The committee of experts consisted of Billings, Chandler, Benjamin Williamson, Alpheus H. Hardy, and John A. Gano. Williamson came from a distinguished family, his father having been chancellor, and then governor, of the state of New Jersey. Williamson received a law degree from Princeton and in 1852 was himself appointed chancellor, serving one seven-year term. He then engaged in corporate law, serving as chief counsel for the New Jersey Central and Lehigh Valley railroads, and worked for various other corporations and financial institutions. Hardy was a prominent Boston importer-exporter. He became a partner in his father's firm in 1865, becoming head of the company in 1873. He was president of the Boston Board of Trade. Gano, a Cincinnati businessman, never actually served on the committee.[26]

Even before publication of the complete rules, inquiries from merchant newspapers and news agencies were coming to Meyer, promising to reprint information about the contest; it was also

25. NBH *Bulletin* 1:33 (February 14, 1880), pp. 249–50; NBT *Proceedings, 1879*, p. 162; *Sanitary Engineer*, January 1, 1880, p. 45.

26. *The National Cyclopaedia of American Biography* (New York, 1904), 12: p. 337; *The National Cyclopaedia of American Biography* (New York, 1945), 32: p. 237; *Proceedings of the Eleventh Annual Meeting of the National Board of Trade, Held in Washington, December, 1880* (Boston, 1881), p. 26: "Mr. Gano was in Europe during the summer and autumn, and was, therefore, unable to serve."

reported in the medical press. Even so, Meyer and Thurber felt they were in a race. Congressman Beale's anti-adulteration bill, which had been sitting in the House Committee on Manufactures since May 23, 1879, was now replaced by a new version with a higher likelihood of passage. Whatever the bill's actual prospects, it was clearly being publicized; there was even confusion in the business community, some merchants thinking that the Beale proposal was being supported by the NBT. For example, the New York Board of Trade and Transportation received a communication from the Baltimore Board of Trade, seeking endorsement of the Beale measure. Thurber had the NYBT&T send a letter explaining that it opposed the Beale bill and advising its Baltimore colleagues to wait for the NBT's own forthcoming bill. Thurber also had the NYBT&T appoint a special committee of three, which he chaired, to communicate about the bill with other business groups throughout the nation.[27]

The New York Board of Trade and Transportation was Thurber's most direct and active link to the business community; unlike the NBT, which assembled only once a year, the NYBT&T met monthly. Originally founded as the New York Cheap Transportation Association in 1873, the board had now widened its interests and by the early 1880s had a membership of over a thousand New York state firms and individuals. It maintained communication with dozens of similar organizations in other cities on a regular basis. Unlike Thurber's battle with the railroads, in which the NYBT&T was also his chief vehicle, the adulteration question was not sectional in nature. Public apprehension and pressure for restrictive legislation would affect importers, exporters, and wholesalers throughout the nation equally, and thus Thurber could coordinate this battle more effectively than he could the transportation question, because in the latter case legislation that would benefit one region might harm another.[28]

27. *Congressional Record,* and House of Representatives *Journal,* 46th Cong., 2d. sess., February 25, 1880, H.R. 4738; New York Board of Trade and Transportation *Minutes,* February 1880. See Wingate Papers for correspondence on the contest.

28. Benson, *Merchants,* pp. 60–61, 63–79; New York Board of Trade and Transportation *Minutes* and *Proceedings.* The name change took place at the meeting of September 1877.

Meanwhile, the amended Beale bill was referred to the committee of the whole by the House Committee on Manufactures on March 4, 1880. Beale's original draft had "assumed the right of the general government to legislate in regulating the sale of articles of food and drink for the States." The revised version applied only to the District of Columbia, the territories, and interstate trade, and it would presumably arouse less opposition. The bill not only prohibited the manufacture, importation, or sale of poisonous foods, but also restricted harmless adulterations.[29]

Sanitary Engineer chose to focus its opposition not on the issue of adulteration that was "merely" fraudulent, but instead on two provisions of the bill which were indeed weaknesses. First, the bill incorporated the word "knowingly" in its definitions. As *Sanitary Engineer* pointed out, this clause was "useless . . . except to originate lawyers' fees." Second, the bill provided a complicated system for determining whether a suspected product had indeed been adulterated. Any suspicious customer might demand a sample, to be presented to a chemist for analysis. The New York sugar controversy of 1878–1879 should illustrate the flaw in allowing the accuser to retain possession of an alleged adulteration. Meyer added another objection—extravagant but nonetheless valid: "What a harvest this would open up to bummers and dead beats in general, who would have a right to go around and demand samples from every grocer, butcher, market gardener, etc., in the country!"[30]

Sanitary Engineer objected to the bill's assumption that both fraudulent and harmful adulterations were widespread, since the *Report* of the House Committee lacked the testimony of "chemists or sanitarians of repute." The Committee "had no evidence before them beyond some *ex parte* statements and newspaper clippings, which are in the main false and misleading." What *Sanitary Engineer* failed to note was that the source of these "false and misleading" statements was none other than George T. Angell, and the *Report* indeed copied some of his most outrageous accusations. *American Grocer* was more specific about the

---

29. H.R. 2014 and H.R. 4738; see *Congressional Record*, 46th Cong., 2d sess.; *The Manufacture of Articles of Human Food and Drink*, 46th Cong., 2d sess., February 25, 1880, H. Rept. 346, p. 2.

30. *Sanitary Engineer*, March 15, 1880, p. 151.

"Boston alarmist": "When they disclose that this information comes mainly from such an individual as Angell, it takes away all force from the report."[31]

There were other problems with the Beale bill, particularly since it applied only to food and drink, not to medicines or cosmetics, and neglected to define "adulteration" adequately. But *Sanitary Engineer*'s central objection related to what the paper felt was a cavalier treatment of American business: "If so important a committee, specially charged with looking after the business interest of the country, is willing to report on such a bill as this to Congress with the recommendation that it pass, it is certainly full time for the competition instituted by the National Board of Trade, and in a matter of so much importance it would certainly seem worth while to wait for the results of this competition."[32]

While waiting for the October deadline of their contest, Thurber continued to lobby against the Beale bill and Meyer spent the summer in Europe. Billings, though besieged with NBH problems, was determined that the next annual report of the Board would contain a more appropriate study of adulteration than the Kedzie "wastepaper basket" material, and in the spring he appointed Dr. Charles Smart to conduct a thorough investigation. On June 1, 1880, Dr. Turner sent letters to health boards throughout the country asking them to assist Smart's investigation, and Smart sent out detailed questionnaires.[33]

What seems to have been most on the minds of Meyer and Angell was the approaching annual meeting of the American Social Science Association. At the September 1879 meeting Meyer had confronted Angell by himself. This time practically the entire leadership of the chemical profession would attempt to discredit him, once and for all. Meyer, though he did not return from Europe in time for the meeting, instructed Wingate to publicize the confrontation as much as possible. Angell, having been told that "chemists were to come from various parts of the country to refute my charges, and allay public excitement," spent his

31. Ibid.; H. Rept. 346, p. 3, explains that Angell "has devoted many years to investigations of adulteration of food"; *American Grocer,* March 18, 1880, p. 727.

32. *Sanitary Engineer,* March 15, 1880, p. 151.

33. Copies in Chandler Papers.

entire summer vacation "preparing for the battle at Saratoga," now that "the great adulterating interests, involving many millions of capital, were aroused."[34]

ASSA sent invitations to leading chemists throughout the nation. Professor Samuel W. Johnson would present the main paper on food adulteration, to be followed by remarks limited to ten minutes for each commentator. The Association "hoped that the question will be thoroughly discussed in a fair and scientific spirit."[35] It was well known that Angell would be appearing, and surely many of those invited were eager to confront the man who had consistently attacked the credibility of their profession.

Professor Johnson, the key speaker, exemplified the reputable scientist of this period. He was professor of theoretical and agricultural chemistry at Yale, was the father of the system of agricultural experiment stations run by the states, and had been president of the American Chemical Society in 1878. Although not a man who sought notoriety, he was one of the most influential chemists of his generation.[36] Yet Johnson's lengthy paper clearly reflected the confusion about adulteration in the minds of even the most expert witnesses. It was a peculiar mix: a recitation of oft-told horror stories with the admission that he had never personally witnessed, and had trouble believing, most of them; a warning that adulteration was widespread, yet the assurance that (like Sharples and Leeds) Johnson believed there was little danger inherent in it; and, running through the entire speech, the insistence that the subject was best left to the experts.

Johnson claimed that most of the anguish over adulteration was unjustified. Many so-called adulterants—such as oleomargarine and glucose—were perfectly healthful foods, and the loudest alarms had been raised about adulterations that were either scientifically absurd or simply not true. But the most common adulterations he considered, as had Sharples, merely customary: "certain additions to food that were originally fraudulent and gross

34. Wingate to Billings, September 21, 1880, Billings Papers; *Sanitary Engineer,* September 1, 1880, p. 369; Angell, *Autobiographical Sketches,* pp. 67–68.

35. Form letter from E. W. Cushing, Secretary of the Department of Health of ASSA, May 3, 1880, Chandler Papers.

36. Charles A. Browne and Mary E. Weeks, *A History of the American Chemical Society* (Washington, 1952), pp. 471–72; *Dictionary of American Biography,* s. v. "Samuel W. Johnson."

adulterations, having been practiced without complaint for a long time, have acquired the sanction of use which exempts them from the charge of falsification or even makes them fairly respectable." Into this category fell products such as package coffee, mustard, and spices.[37]

Certain practices Johnson condemned as clearly dangerous to health, especially the use of poisonous coloring in candies, though these activities have "no doubt been oftener the result of ignorance than of intention, for evidently the most depraved candy-maker can have no object to kill his customers outright." He also advised against the use of alum in bread or in baking powders. But overall, Johnson concluded, Americans were not "liable to suffer in purse and health from the adulterations that are now practised upon our food." He cautioned against those enthusiasts who "would have us believe that we are really defrauded and poisoned in a wholly reckless manner." "Only experts" were qualified to evaluate the problem, and "probably the fingers of one hand would suffice for reckoning the number of analysts in the United States, who today are competent" to make such judgments.[38]

In the debate that followed Johnson's paper, Angell, using his position as an ASSA director, "obtained the privilege of both opening and closing the discussion." Angell specifically attacked glucose and oleomargarine at length because he saw Thurber, who was deeply involved in their production and sale, as his chief antagonist. While preparing for this "battle" at Saratoga Springs, Angell wrote: "I knew perfectly well that the great oleomargarine and glucose interests alone could easily raise a million of dollars as a fighting-fund, and would not yield their enormous profits without a struggle." At the time of the ASSA convention Angell was already planning specific accusations against Meyer and Billings and also against Thurber, whom Angell saw as the financial backer of the corruptionist forces.[39]

---

37. *Journal of Social Science* 13, pt. 2 (1881), p. 100. The paper was published in full as "Adulterations of Food," *Good Company* 5:12 (August [sic] 1880), pp. 546–60, but the magazine did not cover the debate that followed.

38. *Journal of Social Science*, pp. 110, 116–17.

39. Angell, *Autobiographical Sketches*, p. 67. See *Adulteration of Food*, 46th Cong., 3d sess., February 4, 1881, H. Rept. 199, discussed in chapter 8 below.

Despite his assertion that much of what he had to say was new, most of Angell's comments and "evidence" had been used by him previously, and the credibility of the two "experts" he cited was weakened by the fact that their expertise was vouched for merely by one another and by an assortment of nonprofessionals, including judges, a humane society leader, a banker, and two merchants. This display could not have impressed the eminent chemists who shared the platform.[40]

In response, Professor William Ripley Nichols defended the purity of glucose and oleomargarine, though noting that they should, indeed, be sold under their own names. He argued that most adulterations were harmless frauds and that, with a few exceptions, "there is no difficulty in obtaining in a state of practical purity all the necessary articles of food and drink by paying a fair price for the same"[41]—which is what Sharples, and now Professor Johnson, had said. But the chief "defense" expert, according to *Sanitary Engineer,* was Professor Ira Remsen.

Remsen reported that he "had tried hard to find samples of deleterious adulterations, but had been surprised to discover how small their number was, and had come to the conclusion that they were not a cause for serious alarm." He ridiculed Angell's two "experts," questioning "the value of evidence furnished by a chemist whose scientific standing had to be vouched for by a county Justice of the Peace." He pronounced that he had never found even a trace of tin in sugar, even if the sugar had indeed been "bleached," and that the tiny trace of tin occasionally found in syrups "was not sufficient . . . to render the syrup a dangerous article of consumption, unless taken into the system by the gallon." Remsen "did not desire to cover up or excuse any adulteration of food now in vogue, but merely to do what he could to allay what must be termed foolish fears."[42]

After some others had spoken (Wingate, interestingly, stressing the need for expert, rather than amateur, testimony), Angell read some additional letters and spoke at length, reiterating

40. Angell, *Autobiographical Sketches,* p. 68; *Journal of Social Science,* p. 123.
41. *Sanitary Engineer,* October 1, 1880, p. 410.
42. Ibid. In the *Times*'s coverage of the debate, September 9, 1880, Remsen is quoted as saying "that a person who should use glucose syrup to the extent of two gallons at one time might be injured by deleterious substances therein."

points he had already made, some of which had been ridiculed by the other speakers, including Johnson himself. There were a few additional comments, Angell's colleague Sanborn, for example, urging that all adulterations be prosecuted, "not overlooked and considered as necessary evils from which the poor must always suffer."[43]

But an interesting light can be thrown upon this debate by examining a letter that Professor Remsen addressed to Dr. Billings the very next day. Remsen, the star chemical witness against Angell in the debates, became one of the best-known names in the history of American chemistry, professor of chemistry and later president of the Johns Hopkins University. A licensed physician as well, Remsen is considered to have been the leader of the modernization of American chemical studies. He would become one of the inventors of saccharin, president of the American Chemical Society, first recipient of the Priestley Medal, and president of the American Association for the Advancement of Science. In 1879, when he founded the *American Chemical Journal,* he was already the nation's foremost expert on water supplies and a member of the National Academy of Sciences. He was noted for refusing to do chemical work for private parties and was held in the highest esteem within the profession.[44]

Remsen wrote to Billings in response to a request Billings had made for "any notes which might be at my disposal regarding adulterations of food," for inclusion in the next NBH supplement. Remsen reported: "As regards the subject of food adulterations, I have very little to say. I have just returned from the Social Science meeting at Saratoga, where a few of us met the great Angell in battle array." He then repeated to Billings the statements he had made regarding tin salts used for bleaching sugar, and glucose adulterations in syrups, but then went on to confess privately:

43. *Journal of Social Science,* p. 135. Among the other chemists speaking were S. A. Lattimore of Rochester, New York, Professor C. R. Fletcher of Boston, Dr. Clifford Mitchell of Chicago, and Dr. Ezra M. Hunt of New Jersey.

44. Browne and Weeks, *American Chemical Society,* p. 478; *Dictionary of American Biography,* s. v. "Ira Remsen." After the passage of the Pure Food and Drug Act of 1906 Remsen became chairman of the Remsen Referee Board, which studied the administration of the law and passed judgments on the purity and adulteration of foodstuffs. See Oscar E. Anderson, Jr., *The Health of a Nation* (Chicago, 1958).

On the other hand the syrups from these sugars were found to contain a minute trace of tin, though not enough, I believe, to cause any injurious effects in the human system. This is only a belief on my part, however. If I had the opportunity I would undertake an exhaustive examination of the whole subject of tin as a possible constituent of articles of food, including the sub-subjects: 1) the occurrence of tin in food; 2) the form in which it occurs; 3) the effect of small doses of tin in various forms taken into the body—In regard to the latter point we really know very little. The authorities do not agree, and all our information may be said to be very indefinite.[45]

In other words, Remsen, though he would later become a renowned expert on the subject of adulteration,[46] had made very positive statements at the convention, when in reality he only *suspected* that they were true, and in fact privately admitted that, with the exception of sugar, he knew little about adulterations of food.

After the ASSA convention Angell began making plans to spend the next months in Washington, in an attempt to have his "evidence sent over the country in the authoritative form of a congressional report." Meanwhile Billings, Meyer, and Chandler arranged to meet in New York after the contest deadline of October 1 had passed, Meyer inviting Dr. and Mrs. Billings to stay over at his home. There were only four entries Meyer thought worthy of consideration for the three prizes to be awarded, and he sent galley copies of the essays and draft acts to the judges. Their correspondence, however, clearly indicates that it was not the choice between the four entries that concerned them, or judges Williamson and Hardy, but rather the official National Board of Trade bills for the proposed state and national legislation. Even before the winners were picked it was apparent that none of the draft bills among the entries were satisfactory and

45. Remsen to Billings, September 10, 1880, Billings Papers.
46. Dr. Harvey W. Wiley, however, came to regard Remsen as a subversive expert. See his *The History of a Crime against the Food Law* (Washington, 1929), pp. 160–204, 230–37; and *An Autobiography* (Indianapolis, 1930), pp. 241–46.

that the judges would have to write their own version of the legislation, drawing from the entries when appropriate and using the contest to validate their actions.[47]

Meyer selected hotel accommodations for the committee meetings, arranged a reception with local reform leaders at the Union League Club, and staged a dinner Tuesday evening at Delmonico's, where local businessmen could meet the judges.[48] The committee met the last week of October, quickly made its selections, and agreed upon a draft report to be published along with the winning essays. Apparently none of the entries, however, impressed at least Chandler. On his galley of the four essays he commented (for the eventual winner): "aludes [sic] to medicines. [The contest was supposed to deal only with foods.] Schedule of definitions does not provide for hair dyes—Pat. meds. contains poisons. Written by an Englishman. Impossible law. I miss the materials he says he gives." For the second prize entry Chandler had less to say: "Argument against adulteration excellent—few facts presented. Law good." For the third-place winner he had no comments at all, and for the honorary-mention fourth essay, only the word "exaggerated."[49]

A letter sent to Billings by Orlando W. Wight, the author of the fourth-place essay, would appear to justify Chandler's reservations about the quality of the entries:

> My essay and draft of law sent to the Committee of award for the best adulteration of food act, were not properly prepared. I made a mistake in time. It was my intention to give the leisure hours of a month to the work. Turning to the announcement in the Sanitary Engineer, for a careful consideration of the requirements, I found that I had only two days time, instead of thirty. In two evenings, after

47. Angell, *Autobiographical Sketches*, p. 69; Billings to Chandler, October 8, 1880, Chandler Papers; Meyer to Billings, October 11, 1880, Billings Papers; Billings to Chandler, October 17, 1880, Chandler Papers.

48. Meyer to Billings, October 23, 1880, Billings Papers; Billings to Chandler, October 24, 1880, Meyer to Chandler, October 22, 1880, Chandler Papers. Arthur M. Schlesinger, *The Rise of the City, 1878–1898* (Chicago, 1971), pp. 107–8, explains that Delmonico's, at Fifth Avenue and Twenty-Sixth Street, served "the best meals in America, at the highest prices."

49. Chandler Papers.

working hard all day, I wrote the essay and drew the bills, which a young lawyer friend of mine, son of the Chief Justice of the State, copied after me and I sent them on: an audacious *tour de force.*[50]

By Wednesday, October 27, the committee's report had been prepared for NBT president Fraley. It, together with the essays, was then printed in full in a twenty-three page supplement to *Sanitary Engineer.*[51] First prize went to Professor George W. Wigner, secretary of the Society of Public Analysts, the English organization founded in 1874 to help prepare "clear definitions of adulteration and standards or limits of purity" to aid in the administration of the British food and drug laws. The other winners were Vernon M. Davis, of New York, and Dr. William H. Newell, who worked for the New Jersey State Board of Health. Also printed were the essay by Dr. Wight, the Health Commissioner of Milwaukee, Wisconsin, and some remarks by Albert B. Prescott, a chemist and physician, and founder of the University of Michigan School of Pharmacy.[52]

It is not difficult to understand why Wigner's winning essay attracted the committee; not only did he provide succinct definitions of food and drug adulterations, but his arguments almost perfectly matched the members' own inclinations. Wigner argued

50. Orlando W. Wight to Billings, November 24, 1880, Billings Papers. Judith W. Leavitt, *The Healthiest City. Milwaukee and the Politics of Health Reform* (Princeton, 1982), p. 49, notes that Wight was a devoted health crusader, though somewhat of a "windbag."

51. *American Grocer* reprinted the committee's report, as well as the Wigner and Davis essays. According to the NBT *Proceedings, 1880,* p. 27, the Supplement was published with the December 1, 1880, issue of *Sanitary Engineer,* but the New York Public Library copy is bound with the 1881 volumes.

52. Ernst W. Stieb, *Drug Adulteration: Detection and Control in Nineteenth-Century Britain* (Madison, 1966), pp. 131–32, explains that Wigner's definition of drug adulteration in his prize essay was essentially the definition that had been adopted by the Society of Public Analysts.

Davis does not appear further in relation to this subject. He probably was Vernon Mansfield Davis, who graduated from Columbia Law School in 1879 and later became a New York judge. Newell would soon play an important part in the legislative efforts of the NBT. Prescott was the author (1875) of the first English-language guide to organic analysis. (See Ernst Stieb, "Drug Control in Britain, 1850–1914," in *Safeguarding the Public,* ed. John B. Blake [Baltimore, 1970], p. 16.)

that there were a "comparatively small number of traders who really carry on dishonest practices," and he attacked "the exaggerated statements which from time to time have been put forward by alarmists." Wigner also stressed the culpability of only those who sold deleterious articles, largely excusing those who dealt in "harmless" fraud. He also implied that the early findings of high amounts of adulteration, by men like Hassall, were based on biased and/or naive assumptions, and he went on to state that now, at least, the most common adulterations had virtually disappeared, with a few exceptions, such as watered milk.[53]

Wigner dismissed most "adulterations"—oleo sold as butter, chicory in coffee, or flour in mustard—as being basically matters of interpretation, commonplaces of the market, or innocuous deception. His only really severe criticism was reserved for the cases of drug adulteration, not merely because of the importance of unadulterated drugs for proper treatment, but because "a chemist and druggist in England is supposed to be an educated man, with special knowledge of his own articles, as shown by his having passed an examination, and he ought to be able to ensure that the goods he sells are up to the standard."[54]

The conclusions of the NBT award committee probably came as no surprise, condemning "the statements which for the last two or three years have from time to time been made with regard to the prevalence in this country of adulterations of food which are dangerous to health and life, and which have created so much agitation in the public mind." Neither Dr. Smart's forthcoming study for the NBH, nor any of the winning essays, the report emphasized, contained evidence of "widespread . . . dangerous adulterations." The only adulterations specifically condemned by the committee as dangerous were the use of poisonous colorings, "as, for instance, in confectionery, and even these are rare," and the watering of milk.[55]

The committee further concluded: "The main objects of legislation upon this subject should be to prevent deception, to furnish to the public authoritative information, and to nullify the operations of ignorant and sensational alarmists, who damage the

53. *Sanitary Engineer,* "Supplement," ii–iii.
54. Ibid.
55. Ibid., p. 1

business interests of the country quite as much as do the evils of which they complain." Thus the committee officially declared war upon Angell. Moreover, even though the original rules of the contest called for essays on the adulteration only of food and drink, the committee now decided that "we are of the opinion that there is much more danger to health and life in this country from adulterated drugs than there is from adulterated food." The committee then laid the groundwork for the draft legislation it was about to prepare: "We do not consider any of the Acts proposed to be satisfactory. In this matter it is much better at first to do too little than too much, and the first steps in such legislation should be tentative and educational in character."[56]

Any national or state law should be administered only by experts, and enforcing agencies should have "a very considerable amount of discretion." Boards of health were invited to define for themselves what constituted an adulteration, and "to exempt any article from the penalties imposed in the Act." Moreover, the committee cautioned against excessive penalties, urging a reliance on the public "exposure of fraudulent practices," and it insisted that no fees should be paid to informants.[57]

With these guidelines, it was doubtful that any but the most audacious manufacturer, wholesaler, or retailer of food or drugs could find much ground for objection in a law based upon the committee report. Meyer, Billings, and Chandler immediately set to work to draft a federal and a state version of the bill. Their deadline was December 15, for Meyer wanted both draft bills ready for submission to the NBT's annual meeting. The approaching battle would determine whether the NBT concept of adulteration legislation or Angell's more restrictive concept would prevail, for by the time the bill supported by Thurber was ready, Angell was already in Washington, lobbying vigorously against his enemies.

56. Ibid.
57. Ibid.

7

Legislative Success
and Failure

Even before Meyer, Billings, and Chandler had drafted the National Board of Trade adulteration bills, opposition was gathering, not only from Angell, but from some of the press as well. The *New York Tribune* accused them of having "knocked most of the powder out of their cartridge" by arguing that no staple articles of food or drink were dangerously adulterated, and it attacked the committee for being chiefly concerned for the "protection of dealers." The *Grocer* reprinted the *Tribune* editorial, and the *Journal of Commerce* accused the committee of "giving aid and comfort to the food adulterators." The *Journal* also condemned the chemists who had confronted Angell at Saratoga: "If these men had been paid for their opinions by the adulterators they could not have defended their employers more ably."[1]

In this atmosphere Meyer, Billings, and Chandler had to appear to be like Caesar's wife; any bill they prepared had to condemn more than just "dangerous" adulterations, or its legislative chances were slight. Billings was assigned the job of drafting federal legislation and Chandler was to write the state bill, while Meyer coordinated their efforts and stayed in touch with Dean Williamson, Alpheus Hardy, and Thurber. On November 10 Billings sent Meyer his rough draft, and asked him to have Chan-

1. *New York Tribune,* November 28, 1880 (Chandler took note of this editorial; he had a clipping in his files); *Grocer,* December 16, 1880; *New York Journal of Commerce,* November 26, 1880.

dler review it before it was sent on to the other judges: "I don't submit it as perfect, but it will do for a beginning."[2]

Two weeks later Chandler sent Billings's draft back to Wingate, making no significant changes, and copies were sent to Williamson and Hardy. Meyer urged Chandler to complete the state bill quickly, before the NBT annual meeting. He noted that Angell had written him that "he proposes 'to push legislation'—It is desirable therefore that we get sensible bills before Congress because if we don't they will likely pass one after his notions." Meyer also kept Billings apprised of events, since Thurber was counting on him as his Washington "connection," both for the upcoming NBT meeting in the capital and for lobbying against Angell.[3]

But meanwhile Hardy and Chandler's colleague Colonel William Prentice—now the counsel for the New York State Board of Health—both found flaws in Billings's draft. Like the Beale bill, which Meyer and Thurber opposed, Billings's draft had included the word "knowingly," and Hardy doubted that the courts could "fix knowledge and intent." Hardy also objected strongly to the enforcement clauses. When Meyer sent this letter on to Chandler, he included a note interpreting Hardy's objection as asking for a delay before the law went into effect, so that "innocent parties" holding adulterated articles "manufactured before the passage of the Act" could legally sell them to consumers.[4] The committee acceded to Hardy's request by providing a ninety-day delay in enforcement.

Prentice, however, found the entire bill legally questionable, suggesting that the legal experts employed by the National Board of Health should "put it into shape." He also suggested that the proposed $50 penalty was "too small for a misdemeanor," and argued that the law should permit citizens to start civil action against offenders.[5] But the legal option of citizen action, which

2. Billings to Meyer, November 10, 1880, Billings Papers.
3. Chandler to Meyer, November 26, 1880, Meyer to Wingate, November 26, 1880, Wingate Papers; Meyer to Chandler, November 27, 1880, Chandler Papers.
4. Hardy to Meyer, November 30, 1880, Meyer to Chandler, December 3, 1880, Chandler Papers.
5. Prentice to Chandler, November 30, 1880, Chandler Papers.

the Beale bill had called for and to which Meyer had already objected, seeing it as an invitation to "bummers and dead beats," was never added.

At this time Billings journeyed to New Orleans to address an American Public Health Association meeting on the relationship between commerce and public health. This topic had suddenly become an urgent public health issue because, during a recent yellow fever epidemic in the South, agents of both the NBH and the newly formed Sanitary Council of the Mississippi Valley had imposed quarantines on shipping, and they were compelled to interfere with business activities in a number of other ways. Billings complained that when times were good the people refused to listen to the sanitarians; only a pestilence could arouse them. "They say to the sanitarian who is warning them: 'Hush, wait a little. Don't make a fuss. You will injure the reputation of the city. You will drive away commerce. We are no worse than our neighbors.' "[6]

Chandler, meanwhile, worked hastily to complete a draft of the state bill, which Meyer hoped to have ready for presentation to the New York state legislature before it completed its session for the year. But Chandler's draft, when it finally reached Meyer, was so inconsistent with Billings's national bill that Meyer failed to submit it at this time, and hurried to Washington to participate in the 1880 NBT annual meeting. Although state food laws, at this time, almost always set specific standards for milk, and often for other food staples, Chandler had decided that all "standards" and specific descriptions should be dropped from the federal bill: "I think those details should be left to the National Board of Health, as it is impossible before hand to get those standards exactly right, & it may be desirable to change them from time to time." Chandler also now supported Prentice's complaints about the $50 penalty being "rather a small one for a maximum."[7]

The most important change made in Billings's original version [see Appendix A] incorporated Chandler's rejection of "stan-

6. Address of Dr. Billings, delivered December 8, 1880, in Billings Papers.
7. Meyer to Chandler, December 12, 1880, Chandler Papers; Chandler to Billings, December 14, 1880, Billings Papers.

dards." Billings's draft had included a vague general definition: "a fair and legitimate standard, ensuring such substance and grade and quality as the consumer may properly expect to obtain under the name by which the article is furnished." This clause could conceivably cause a great deal of inconvenience to manufacturers and dealers, and the version adopted by the NBT eliminated it. Instead, the bill left all interpretations, and all determinations about exemptions, to the NBH. Whether this weakened or strengthened the bill is a matter of opinion, but it seems clear that the decision to omit standards for even the most basic foods created considerable room for negotiation and compromise in enforcement.[8]

But before the NBT could approve the revised Billings draft, Thurber found himself facing a small rebellion. It will be remembered that at the 1879 session of the NBT a committee consisting of Thurber, Ambrose Snow, and George L. Buzby had been appointed to confer with Billings regarding the relations between the two groups; the NBT was especially concerned about the effect of the health board's "bearing upon commercial interests." Speaking for his committee, Thurber now reported favorably, advising complete support for the work Billings had been doing. But some of the sanitary decisions of the NBH now threatened to cause the NBT to cut off its support, justifying the complaint Billings had voiced only a week earlier, in his New Orleans speech.

Because of the tenuous powers granted to the NBH, it could not provide assistance with local public health problems unless a local board initiated the request for aid. In 1880 Baltimore's commissioner of public health, the doctors of the Baltimore quarantine hospital, and the local board of trade asked the NBH for assistance in planning additional quarantine facilities and for advice on improving drainage and sewerage. Clearly the mayor and the local business interests felt they would receive substantial federal monies in return. But although the Board conducted a sanitary survey of the city and offered copious ad-

8. *Proceedings of the Eleventh Annual Meeting of the National Board of Trade, Held in Washington, December 1880* (Boston, 1881); Billings to Chandler, December 15, 1880, Chandler Papers.

vice, no other funds were forthcoming. Moreover, the Board's inspector lacked—to say the least—the quality of diplomacy, and his report, published for the entire nation to see, accused the city of "an alarming degree of indifference or negligence." The report was unnecessarily filled with fanciful descriptions: "The hot sun brings out from the still and polluted waters a terrible stench, just as it breeds maggots in carrion." The inspector described an atmosphere "so poisoned with the malaria that a healthy man's stomach is turned by breathing it."[9]

Now, just a couple of months after the survey was completed, the representatives to the NBT from the Baltimore business community challenged Thurber's motion that the NBT support the National Board of Health in its efforts to secure additional congressional appropriations. Although Meyer and Thurber argued strenuously on behalf of the NBH, there were serious difficulties because of the objections of William S. Young of Baltimore. John P. Wetherill of Philadelphia, normally a Thurber supporter, began to echo Young's concerns, and Thurber was in danger of losing control of his motion. Wetherill was afraid of the extent of power potentially held by the NBH, warning "if such power exists, or if parties not so kindly disposed as the gentlemen now in office were to succeed them, they might make serious and permanent trouble, and put a city like Philadelphia to a great deal of commercial embarrassment."[10]

Thurber, clearly doubtful about having his resolution adopted, called for a postponement until the next day. When the NBT reconvened, Young competely reversed his position, having in the meantime been introduced to Dr. Billings by Thurber and having somehow been persuaded by them that the "National Board of Health will bring about results which must be beneficial to the country at large." Thurber's resolution was adopted, and the NBT could now give its undivided support to the adulteration competition. The competition committee's report was accepted,

9. Peter W. Bruton, "The National Board of Health" (Ph.D. diss., University of Maryland, 1974), pp. 185–88, 287; Margaret Warner, "Local Control versus National Interest: The Debate over Southern Public Health, 1878–1884," *Journal of Southern History* 50:3 (August 1984), p. 414; *Annual Report of the National Board of Health, 1880* (Washington, D.C., 1881), pp. 515–28.

10. NBT *Proceedings, 1880,* p. 48.

and the NBT resolved that it, and its constituent organizations, would work to promote passage of the revised Billings draft.[11]

This national bill [see Appendix B] prohibited the importation or interstate shipment of adulterated foods or drugs, as well as their manufacture or sale in areas under federal jurisdiction. Most of the bill was adapted from two of the prize essays. The first five sections were modified versions of Newell's third-place entry, presumably chosen over Wigner's and Davis's because he dealt at length with protection for the importer and wholesaler, and both Hardy and Thurber were certainly interested in having those protections incorporated. The very important section 8, on definitions of adulteration, was taken largely from Wigner's winning draft, in place of Billings's original material. But the committee established the National Board of Health as the central enforcement agency for the law, rather than the state boards, as all three winning essays had recommended.

The committee also made the crucial decision to allow the NBH to exempt "certain articles or preparations," and resolved that the law would "not apply to mixtures or compounds *recognized* as ordinary articles of food, provided that the same are not injurious to health and that the articles are distinctly labelled as a mixture, stating the components of the mixture." This was apparently a compromise measure, exempting very large numbers of common food products from prosecution, yet requiring some degree of content labeling. This provision was further enhanced by section 9, which made it the "duty" of the NBH to declare "lists of articles, mixtures, or compounds" to be exempted—perhaps without the labeling required by the previous section. Section 9 also permitted the NBH to "fix the limits of variability permissible in any article or compound"—a very broad discretionary power.

While Meyer organized a lobbying effort on behalf of the federal bill, Chandler continued to struggle with revisions of the state version, which, by prohibiting the manufacture or sale of adulterated foods or drugs within a state, would fill the gap left

11. Ibid., pp. 79, 83. Interestingly, in its next annual report the NBH carefully explained why it could not provide additional financial assistance, and it gratuitously complimented Baltimore's "full equipment of quarantine machinery." See *Annual Report of the National Board of Health, 1881* (Washington, D.C., 1882), pp. 11–12.

by the federal bill. A month later Chandler finally completed his draft, incorporating some additional suggestions from Billings. Chandler's final version [see Appendix C], despite all the time he had taken to complete it, was basically the same as Billings's national bill, with the obvious differences called for by the fact that it was limited to the state level.[12]

The definitions of adulteration are identical (taken from Wigner), and Chandler gave to the State Board of Health the same power of declaring exemptions that Billings had given to the NBH. He also, like Billings, exempted "mixtures or compounds recognized as ordinary articles of food," which would, of course, allow the state board to decide which foods were "ordinary." Although Chandler's bill, even more than Billings's, made very specific provision for the gathering of suspected samples by the inspectors appointed under the law, he too was careful to make no provision for "bummers and dead beats" to collect samples on their own. The penalties assigned were similar to those of the national bill: a fine of $50 for a first conviction and a maximum of $100 for subsequent offenses. Chandler's bill, despite his letter to Billings urging harsher sentences, did not call for imprisonment. There seems to have been only one substantive difference between the bills: Chandler omitted the word "knowingly." As in his enforcement of the New York milk laws, Chandler felt that only the illegal act itself should be proven, not knowledge of illegality.

While Thurber, Meyer, Billings, and Chandler began mustering support for both their bills, opponents were also busy, either attacking the NBT/NBH proposals or promoting their own versions of legislation. The *Tribune* attacked the limited scope of the NBT federal bill, arguing that a broader interpretation of constitutional powers would allow the government to "strike squarely at the manufacture and sale of fraudulent and injurious articles" rather than merely prohibiting their interstate transportation.[13] Soon both the *Tribune* and the *Journal of Commerce* were directing their most vicious attacks against oleomargarine and against

---

12. Meyer to Chandler, December 19, 1880, Chandler Papers; Meyer to Billings, January 17, 1881, Billings Papers; see Laws of 1881, chap. 407.

13. *New York Tribune*, January 22, 1881.

Thurber, the largest oleo distributor. These attacks coincided with a New York state investigation of the industry in 1881 and intimated that Thurber's proposed legislation was camouflage for continuing oleomargarine production and sale.

The *Tribune* suggested that the public would "like to know" whether Thurber

> was long largely engaged in selling oleomargarine for butter, fraudulently concealing its real character; whether he used his position as president of the Dairymen's Association to deceive his customers into the belief that they were buying real butter, while he did what he could to destroy the business of the dairymen; whether he pretended to be a temperance man, while one of the main elements of his business was the manufacture of bogus brandy and whiskey out of crude alcohol and flavoring extracts; whether he has since been largely engaged in the manufacture of a bogus honey out of glucose.

The paper accused Thurber of merely posing "as the disinterested friend of the people and public-spirited philanthropist" in order "to advertise his groceries." The *Journal of Commerce* reserved its harshest criticism for the scientists, such as Chandler, who received payment from the oleomargarine manufacturers for the use of their names in advertising testifying to oleo's purity and wholesomeness.[14]

Dr. Bell's *Sanitarian,* surprisingly, had little to say about either bill, merely reporting on them factually. It may be speculated that Bell, previously Meyer's outspoken opponent and Angell's supporter, refrained from criticism out of gratitude to Billings. It was an unwritten policy of the NBH to obtain the support of sanitarians by securing appointments for prominent local public health officials, and Billings had obtained Bell's appointment, in 1879, as one of the district sanitary inspectors.[15] Nevertheless,

14. *New York Tribune,* April 7, 1881; *Journal of Commerce,* March 25, 1881. The oleomargarine question is discussed below, chap. 11.

15. Bruton, pp. 178–79. See *Sanitarian* 10 (1882), pp. 237–38; 11 (1883), pp. 188–89. It should be noted that Bell was later dismissed because of some impolitic remarks he made concerning "filth" in the South; see Bruton, pp. 239–40.

this reluctance to render judgments on the bills seems to have been the pattern in much of the professional press.

One major exception was *New Remedies,* which ran a series of editorials and debates on the NBT bill. Though officially edited by Dr. Frederick A. Castle, *New Remedies* seems to have been run primarily by Dr. Charles Rice, the associate editor. Rice, a man of many talents, was a philologist and Sanskrit scholar as well as a noted chemist. He was superintendent of the pharmacy department of Bellevue Hospital, New York, first vice-president of APhA, and chairman of the APhA committee to revise the *U.S. Pharmacopoeia* from 1880 to his death in 1901. He has been called "the creator of the modern American pharmacopeia."[16] *New Remedies* was the most important pharmaceutical trade journal of the period, the unofficial voice of the American Pharmaceutical Association.

It was important that Meyer gain APhA's support, though the pronouncement of the NBT committee that there was more to be feared of from adulterated drugs than from foods may certainly have started any such effort off on the wrong foot. On December 31 Meyer managed to secure a verbal commitment from Rice to support the NBT federal bill "on the assurance that it was not intended that the National Board of Health should *interfere with standards made by any National Pharmacopoeia.*" Meyer wrote Billings that, though "the Quack Medicine Interest may oppose" the bill, "I think now the Pharmacists will be satisfied."[17]

Rice also promised to seek the support of Dr. John M. Maisch, the most important man in APhA at that time. Maisch had been manager of the U.S. Army Laboratory during the Civil War and then became professor and later dean of the Philadelphia College of Pharmacy, where he served until his death. He was, in 1881, writing the important *Manual of Organic Materia Medica,* became APhA's permanent secretary, was its chief official expert

16. Glenn Sonnedecker, *Kremers and Urdang's History of Pharmacy* (Philadelphia, 1976), p. 196. Sonnedecker considers Rice and John M. Maisch the "two German immigrants who exerted the greatest influence on the development of American pharmacy."

17. Meyer to Billings, January 1, 1881, Billings Papers.

on pharmaceutical adulterations, and was editor of the *American Journal of Pharmacy* from 1871 until his death in 1893.

In the February issue of *New Remedies* Rice gave the NBT bill reserved approval, on the condition that it "will have first been so modified by general criticism as to reduce to a minimum the opportunities for an inefficient discharge of duty by the inspectors, and evasion of its true intent by dealers." The meaning of this sentence, considered in the light of the conversation between Rice and Meyer, was that APhA would not give unequivocal support to the bill until it was amended so that the *United States Pharmacopoeia* and APhA—which controlled the U.S.P.—were recognized as the undisputed authorities for all drug formulae, by which adulterations could be judged. Meyer had anticipated this response and had written to Billings in January, requesting him to respond in the *Sanitary Engineer* to criticisms of the bill, and to point out in his editorial that suggestions for "good amendments" to the bill "will have the consideration of the Comm. having it in charge." He also asked Billings to see Maisch in Philadelphia, explaining that "a half hour's talk I am sure will satisfy them and do much good."[18]

But in the February issue of *New Remedies* Rice also published a letter from an anonymous correspondent who submitted a substitute bill, which the journal printed side by side with the NBT bill for purposes of comparison. Correspondent "O.O."—almost certainly Oscar Oldberg, a prominent member of APhA—raised many objections to the NBT bill, but almost all of them hinged upon one idea: the danger that in the administration of the law the experts of APhA might not be called upon to judge what is, and what is not, an adulteration. Though Oldberg expressed confidence in the NBH, he insisted that the bill should "require the Board to consult the chemists and pharmacists," and even insisted that all NBH food and drug inspectors pass an examination "conducted by a Board of Experts consisting of three chemists and two pharmacists" approved by the "Colleges of Medicine and Pharmacy." Billings's *Sanitary Engineer* editorial was a direct attempt to satisfy the Oldberg/Rice demand. Billings explained

18. *New Remedies* 10:2 (February 1881), p. 33; Meyer to Billings, January 12, January 19, 1881, Billings Papers.

that "we have no doubt that the National Board of Health would necessarily proceed to form a commission and Board of such experts."[19]

Another response to Oldberg's criticism appeared in the next issue of *New Remedies,* signed "W. H. N." This correspondent was almost certainly William H. Newell, who not only was the author of the third-place essay in the NBT contest, but by this time had been employed by Meyer as a troubleshooter and lobbyist on behalf of the National Board of Trade adulteration bills. Months earlier Newell had written to Billings requesting information on drug adulteration: "We expect some antagonism from the drug trade particularly and wish to combat it with all the statistics possible."[20]

Though Newell's *New Remedies* letter was basically conciliatory, he noted that the NBT bill had already been endorsed "by the members of the National Board of Trade, the Chamber of Commerce, Produce Exchange, and every wholesale druggist in the city of New York." He explained that the bill was now "in the hands of a committee appointed by the President of the National Board of Trade, composed of Henry C. Meyer, Esq., of New York; John P. Wetherill, Esq., of Philadelphia, and Richard D. Fisher, Esq., of Baltimore." This committee was perfectly willing to consider "any amendment or objection . . . if it is deemed proper and desirable." But Newell's most important concession, reflecting Billings's *Sanitary Engineer* editorial, was: "I am assured that the National Board of Health will select public analysts . . . from among the number reported to them as properly qualified, by a committee of experts appointed by the different colleges of medicine and pharmacy."[21]

In the next month's issue, while *New Remedies* refrained from editorializing directly, Rice published a response from Oldberg, wherein he repeated his insistence that the final version of the bill must explicitly state the qualifications of all examiners and ana-

19. *New Remedies* 10:2, pp. 59–61; *Sanitary Engineer,* February 15, 1881, p. 130. Oldberg had been on the staff of the Marine Hospital Service and on the faculty of the National College of Pharmacy; in 1881 he took a job with Schieffelin and Company, a major drug manufacturer.

20. Newell to Billings, December 24, 1880, Billings Papers.

21. *New Remedies* 10:3 (March 1881), p. 87.

lysts. Oldberg—and perhaps Rice—was explaining that the compromise offered by Newell and Billings was insufficient. APhA was unwilling to depend upon the goodwill of the NBH; a specific commitment to defer to the pharmaceutical profession would need to be written into the bill before APhA could lend its full support.[22]

Though Meyer and Billings had been concentrating on their federal bill, passage of the state version was by no means a certainty. Chandler's bill had received endorsements from the New York drug manufacturers, sugar refiners, and commercial associations, but these were not in themselves enough to get the legislation through Albany. Public interest had begun to rise—but from Meyer's viewpoint perhaps dangerously so. The situation threatened to get beyond the control of the NBT interests, for other, more specific, adulteration bills had been proposed, stimulated by a State Assembly investigation of oleomargarine. The press began to awaken to the topic: after the scarcity of stories and editorials on adulteration during the previous months, there was a virtual explosion of material. In the first six months of 1881 the *New York Times* ran over sixty items related to adulteration, not counting stories about the NBT bills themselves.[23]

Perhaps the greatest curiosity about the state legislative effort is the fact that the "New York" bill was passed in New Jersey several days before it was even introduced in the New York Senate. It had always been intended that the first test of the Chandler version of the bill would be in Albany. But Newell had been working with the NBT legislative committee (Meyer, Wetherill, and Fisher) since December, and he obtained a copy of Chandler's bill as soon as revisions had been completed. From New Jersey he reported to Billings in triumph:

> I have the honor of informing you that I procured the introduction into our State legislature of the Bill which I mail you today. You will see, with some few additions, that it is

22. *New Remedies* 10:4 (April 1881), pp. 115–16.
23. Each month in this period there were more items on the topic than usual; *Times* coverage peaked in March, when twenty-four stories appeared.

a facsimile of the draft of a State Bill which you were so kind as to furnish me with.

We kept the matter very quiet so that there would be as little public attention called to it as possible & thereby we aroused but little opposition. At the latter part of the session the bill was rushed through successfully.

Newell sent a similar note to Chandler, adding: "New Jersey now may be congratulated as being the pioneer state in this movement. I trust that you may be as successful in your State."[24]

The tactic of surprise, however, was unlikely to work in New York. On March 30 Senator William W. Astor introduced the Chandler bill, now approved by the NBT Executive Council, in the New York state Senate. It received no initial opposition and was referred to Senator Benjamin Williams's Committee on Public Health, where it sat for a few weeks while Meyer rallied support for it. Perhaps the greatest danger it faced was the fact that six separate oleomargarine bills, a bill to regulate the practice of pharmacy, and a bill to control patent medicines (the latter two bills supported by the New York State Pharmaceutical Association and by a large group of physicians) were in competition with it. The NBT not only supported its own bill but also opposed the others, particularly the oleo bills, which challenged substantial business interests in which Thurber had hundreds of thousands of dollars invested.[25]

Meyer bivouacked in Albany, but realized that he needed support from professional groups beyond those he had already tapped, particularly in light of the competing bills. He wrote Dr. Billings for help in obtaining the assistance of prominent public health spokesmen, although, for reasons that will become clear, Meyer specifically excluded Elisha Harris from his list. Billings apparently acted immediately, for Stephen Smith replied in a letter dated only two days after Meyer's request: "I will give it all the aid I can—there should have been some preliminary work done in the profession of the State to have rendered its passage

24. Newell to Billings, March 29, 1881, Billings Papers; Newell to Chandler, March 29, 1881, Chandler Papers.

25. *Journal of the Senate of the State of New York, 104th Session* (Albany, 1881), pp. 312, 456, 895. The NBT bill was Senate Bill #317.

easy—It is extremely difficult (& generally a very thankless task) to gain the support of members to a bill that don't specially interest them."[26]

Meyer also asked Billings to send him some copies of Dr. Diehl's report on drug adulteration. Presumably, therefore, he was trying to persuade medical representatives to support the NBT legislation rather than the Pharmaceutical Association's bill, because he did not ask for copies of the NBH report on *food* adulteration by Dr. Smart, which was already available. While Meyer lobbied in the Senate, Chandler was at work on a similar mission, for a note in Colonel Prentice's handwriting indicates that Chandler had persuaded Assemblyman William S. Andrews, who had introduced the pharmacists' bill back in February, to "substitute the bill of the National Board of Trade. I think Mr. [Thomas G.] Alvord will introduce it, for he knows Chandler." Prentice set out to have copies of the bill printed up for Andrews and Alvord.[27]

On May 3 Senator Williams's Committee on Public Health reported in favor of the NBT bill, and two days later the Assembly substituted it for the pharmacists' bill. But Meyer believed that the bill would have difficulty in the Assembly, and he wrote Billings with some interesting revelations about the legislative process:

> I have just returned from Albany having last night had a final hearing before the Assembly Committee on Public Health. . . . The truth is most of the Committee are too ignorant to understand it and one man (Dr. [Isaac I.] Hayes) on it who might influence them was partly drunk last night and asked absurd questions—He afterwards changed his *tune* when he learned *you had* had a hand in drawing the bill and informed me he was under you in the Army. . . . Dr. Harris I am sorry to say is of no use to me

26. Meyer to Billings, April 7, 1881, Smith to Billings, April 9, 1881, Billings Papers.

27. Meyer to Billings, n.d., Billings Papers; note in Chandler Papers, n.d., no signature. Billings noted on Meyer's card that he sent NBH *Bulletin* Supplement No. 6 to Meyer on April 18, 1881. The Smart report on food adulteration was published January 1, 1881 and is discussed below, chap. 8. There is, of course, no evidence that Meyer did not already have copies of the Smart report with him.

and acts and talks as though it could not possibly pass—
Erastus Brooks who is an influential member of the Assembly and also a member of the State Board of Health is helping me all he can. . . .

P. S. I was advised by Chandler not to set Harris to work, for as he saw he would be apt—well I'll tell you when I see you.[28]

Chandler had warned about Elisha Harris because the two men did not see eye-to-eye about the operation of the new State Board of Health. Harris consistently gave the public health his first priority, while Chandler tended to compromise in favor of the commercial interests. Chandler would later complain that "it was absolutely impossible for me to do business with such a meddlesome old granny." Meyer soon began to have trouble of his own with Harris: "From certain indications I infer that Dr. Harris does not like it that I have put the commercial interest to the front in urging the bill at Albany. . . . The fact is that he is a well meaning old fool and I fear would be more of a hindrance than help to me."[29]

The state Senate passed the bill on May 10, with no dissenting votes, and on May 19 the Assembly sent it on to Governor Alonzo Cornell, who found one legal problem. Newell explained to Chandler that Cornell favored the bill but wanted it to have a specific appropriation. "I therefore had it returned with message from Governor, and amended in the Senate . . . with the $10,000 appropriation." Now the amended bill had to be repassed by the Assembly, where Newell feared opposition would coalesce. He asked Chandler what minimum amount "would serve to carry out this law" if he had to negotiate over money.[30]

But Newell's anxiety turned out to be misplaced; the full

28. Senate *Journal* (1881), p. 580, 583; *Journal of the Assembly of the State of New York, 104th Session* (Albany, 1881), p. 1080; Meyer to Billings, May 5, 1881, Billings Papers.

29. Chandler to Dr. Edward M. Moore, president of the State Board of Health, August 28, 1883, Chandler Papers; Meyer to Billings, May 9, 1881, Billings Papers.

30. Newell to Chandler, May 21, 1881, Chandler Papers. The original bill had called for an allotment of the money, but had failed to appropriate it from the state treasury. See the last sentence of section 5, Appendix C.

$10,000 was appropriated. Newell may have been magnifying the difficulties, and his role in solving them, to impress Chandler. Although Newell had been appointed to the council of analysts and chemists in New Jersey, after passage of the bill there, his position apparently paid no regular salary. He had discussed with both Harris and Meyer the possibility of getting a similar job in New York and later wrote Chandler about it.[31] Nonetheless there was unquestionably *some* last-minute confusion about the bill which Newell helped to rectify. Meyer wrote to Chandler, just before leaving for Albany, that he had sent Newell to ask Cornell to sign the bill but that the governor "wanted to take time to consider it and also to hear those that might oppose it. . . . Will you dictate a letter to him & mail it tonight urging it and indicating the policy of the Board to be conservative and cautious in executing it?"[32]

On June 2, 1881, the NBT bill became law in New York State. In all of the votes cast in the legislature there was never any significant opposition to the bill, nor did Governor Cornell express any anxiety, except about the appropriation clause. Whether this is a measure of the successful lobbying of Meyer, Chandler, and Newell in Albany, or whether their concern was overstated, is impossible to tell, especially since the real legislative battles were fought in the public health committees, of which no records were kept.

It might be speculated, however, that members of the legislature—particularly those from dairy counties—went along with the NBT bill only because they *also* passed two anti-oleomargarine bills which, had they been signed by the governor, would have

31. Newell had, according to this letter, been *promised* a position and was very annoyed that Chandler did not follow through with his appointment. In effect, he also threatened to renege on his commitment to work for the NBT bill in Washington if Chandler didn't keep his promise: "I also desired this official position in New York State because it would give me more prominence in my intercourse with members of Congress next session should I determine on going on to Washington to work in favor of the National Bill, as the most of its friends desire me so to do." (Newell to Chandler, July 8, 1881, Chandler Papers.)

32. Meyer to Chandler, May 25, 1881, Chandler Papers. Meyer also wrote to Billings: "I shall rely on [Newell] to work it through Congress and should be glad if he can get something to do under our State Bd. as in Jersey he gets no pay." (Meyer to Billings, June 1, 1881, Billings Papers.)

imposed strict responsibilities upon the State Board of Health in its enforcement of the adulteration law. Cornell's veto of these bills and the failure of the two pharmacy bills were to some extent additional triumphs of the commercial interests that had supported the NBT legislation.[33]

Although it was the intention of the National Board of Trade to promote passage of legislation modeled upon Chandler's bill in all of the states, it seems to have succeeded in only three. After the easy victory in New Jersey, thanks to Newell's tactic of surprise, and in New York, because of an intensive lobbying campaign, the NBT seems to have been able to follow through with a victory only in the state of Massachusetts. Jesse P. Battershall's 1887 survey of food and drug laws indicates that there were general adulteration laws in only these states at the time of publication. There were indeed many laws in many states related to adulteration, but they concerned only specific products—usually dairy products, and particularly oleomargarine.[34] This—plus the fact that the victory in Massachusetts was quite narrow—indicates that the NBT effort collapsed after 1882.

The Massachusetts State Board of Health, Lunacy, and Charity, under the control of Stephen Sharples in 1882–1883, not only published Sharples's chapter on adulteration from the Buck book *Hygiene and Public Health* as a supplement to its annual report, but also officially recommended a law on the model of that passed in New York. Adhering to Sharples's perspective, the Board noted:

33. Cornell's veto of the two oleo bills is discussed below, chap. 11; the two pharmacy bills are discussed in chap. 8.

34. *Food Adulteration and Its Detection* (New York, 1887).

Massachusetts State Board of Health, A Brief History of Its Organization and Its Work, 1869–1912 (Boston, 1912), p. 48, says that the NBT bill was also passed in the state of Michigan. In *Report of the Industrial Commission on Agriculture* 11 (Washington, 1901), p. 110, F. B. Thurber testified that the NBT's "draft is the foundation of the regulation of food in New York, Ohio, Illinois, New Jersey, Massachusetts, and other States. Most of the States have made variations in their provisions, but the definitions are largely those which the committee outlined." The present study suggests that Thurber's claim was too broad; not the NBT bill, but its *definitions of adulteration,* adapted from Wigner's prize essay, were widely adopted.

As many of the prominent articles of commerce, though they may be said to be adulterated, are quite harmless, and in some cases useful, it should be left to the discretion of some competent authority to relieve such articles from the fines imposed by this bill. The honest and persistent exposing of fraudulent practices will generally have an effect upon public opinion fully equal to any penalty imposed by the courts, and will in the end prove as effective in making such practices unprofitable.[35]

The Massachusetts law, as finally adopted, was based upon the NBT bill but was somewhat stronger than its New York and New Jersey counterparts, probably because of the lobbying efforts of George T. Angell. There is some confusion about the legislation, since Angell claimed responsibility for its creation, but there seems to be no question that it was Angell who managed to secure broad support for *some* sort of anti-adulteration bill in Massachusetts and who persuaded hundreds of grocers and a number of prominent citizens, particularly from the Boston area, to send in petitions he had drawn up.[36]

Angell apparently accepted the NBT bill as the basic instrument for his own campaign against adulteration on the state level. Perhaps he felt that, with some additions and modifications, the Thurber bill was the best that could be achieved at that time. He noted in a letter to the *Ploughman* that the time had come to act, and that New York and New Jersey had already passed "stringent laws." Whether through Angell's efforts or not, the Massachusetts law added cosmetics and some other items to its list of affected articles, imposed imprisonment for those knowingly purveying adulterated goods that were unwholesome or injurious, and established poison regulations for the state.[37]

---

35. S. P. Sharples, "Adulteration of Food," *Supplement to 4th Annual Report, Massachusetts Department of Health* (Boston, 1883); *Third Annual Report of the State Board of Health, Lunacy, and Charity of Massachusetts, January, 1882* (Boston, 1882), p. xlvi–xlvii.

36. George T. Angell, *Autobiographical Sketches and Personal Recollections* (Boston, 1892), pp. 76–77.

37. *Massachusetts Ploughman and New England Journal of Agriculture*, February 25, 1882. Ernst Stieb, *Drug Adulteration: Detection and Control in Nineteenth-*

The voting pattern in the Massachusetts legislature was very different from that in New York. Dairy and other rural counties gave very little support to the bill. Perhaps this may be explained by the fact that in Massachusetts—in contrast to New York—the legislature did *not* pass anti-oleomargarine bills at this time. Rural representatives may therefore have been more skeptical about the intent of the state version of the NBT bill. Figure 5 shows the narrowness of the victory. The bill received well under half of the possible votes to be cast; it passed only because of large numbers of abstentions. It can be speculated that members from rural counties disliked the bill but failed to oppose it actively because the alternative was to have no adulteration law at all.

All but nine of the votes cast in favor of the bill came from the five counties immediately in and around Boston. The vote was even more skewed than the map shows, because the residence information given in the House of Representatives *Journal* indicates that members voting in favor, from Essex, Middlesex, Norfolk, and Plymouth counties, tended to be those living closest to Boston. In Middlesex County, for example, of the twenty-two representatives living in areas that are today part of Greater Boston, seventeen voted in favor of the bill; of the eighteen Middlesex representatives living outside that area, only one voted for the bill. In Massachusetts, the NBT bill was a Boston bill. From the petitions sent to the legislature in its support, it seems to have been the bill of the Boston grocers.[38]

Century Britain (Madison, 1966), p. 282, n. 21, correctly notes that the Massachusetts definition of "drug" apparently combined that of Wigner with that of Dr. E. R. Squibb in his "Rough Draft" of 1879. In *Transactions of the Medical Society of the State of New York* (Syracuse, 1879), p. 214, Squibb included antiseptics, disinfectants, and cosmetics—anything, other than food, "used for the preservation of health, or for the relief or cure of disease in man or animals."

38. Source of residence information was the Appendix to the *Journal of the House of Representatives of the Commonwealth of Massachusetts, Session of 1882* (Boston, 1882). See also *Journal of the Senate of the Commonwealth of Massachusetts, Session of 1882* (Boston, 1882), p. 410.

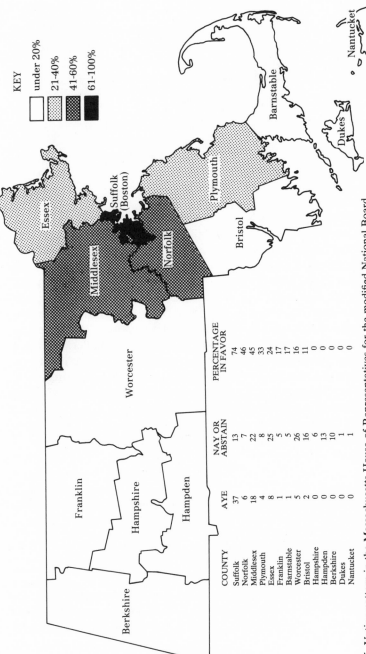

COUNTY	AYE	NAY OR ABSTAIN	PERCENTAGE IN FAVOR
Suffolk	37	13	74
Norfolk	6	7	46
Middlesex	18	22	45
Plymouth	4	8	33
Essex	8	25	24
Franklin	1	5	17
Barnstable	1	5	17
Worcester	5	26	16
Bristol	2	16	11
Hampshire	0	6	0
Hampden	0	13	0
Berkshire	0	10	0
Dukes	0	1	0
Nantucket	0	1	0

KEY

under 20%

21-40%

41-60%

61-100%

5. Voting pattern in the Massachusetts House of Representatives for the modified National Board of Trade anti-adulteration bill, 1882.

8

Legislative Failure
and Success

O_f all the bills related to adulteration before
the legislators in Albany during the 1881 session, only the National Board of Trade bill became law. But the pharmacy bills,
though they failed at this time, reflected long-range changes taking place within the drug market. Not only were the pharmaceutical associations strengthening their control over the profession,
but the drug manufacturers and wholesalers were also emerging
as powers to be reckoned with. Professor Chandler, who was
about to assume responsibility for interpreting and enforcing the
new law, would have to decide whether he wished to tread into
this area at all, or leave regulation of pharmacy to the pharmacists and concentrate upon food adulteration.

For his part, Henry Meyer had to mend fences with these
groups, for he needed their support to promote the passage of
the federal version of the NBT bill. In Albany, Meyer had had
the backing of New York business organizations, the endorsement of local sanitary authorities, and the qualified support of
the pharmaceutical associations. In Washington, even though Dr.
Billings and other public health leaders lent some assistance, he
was more on his own. Moreover, he had to contend with the
presence of George T. Angell.

Angell was spending the winter of 1880–1881 in Washington,
lobbying to revive interest in the Beale bill, which had been favorably reported by the Committee on Manufactures on March 4 but
which had been dormant since then. Angell was aware that Newell
was lobbying in opposition to him and believed that "the oleomargarine and glucose rings" had "fixed" the Washington papers and

the Associated Press. It was at this time that he thought he was being followed by "a man who had once been tried for murder." A hearing scheduled with Beale's committee was canceled for lack of a quorum, and Angell at "the close of 1880 . . . had found no man who was willing to do battle against the great political and financial power of adulteration."[1]

Billings, meanwhile, was doing what he could, not only to support the NBT endeavor, but to cast doubts upon Angell's sensational claims. He had Dr. Charles Smart's report on adulteration published as Supplement No. 11 to the NBH *Bulletin* on January 1, 1881. The Smart report was intended to be much more comprehensive and reliable than last year's "wastepaper basket" report of Dr. Kedzie, and Smart had been gathering food samples and professional opinions from various local health officials since June. Though this "official" NBH report found ample evidence of adulteration in many common products, its conclusions and recommendations were completely compatible with those of Drs. Sharples, Leeds, and Johnson.

Smart reported that, though legislation was needed, there was absolutely no cause for alarm. Goods purchased from reputable dealers were rarely adulterated, and only "the poor and ignorant" were exposed to fraudulent goods on an every day basis. Most foods were not adulterated at all, though a few, such as spices and "package" coffee, were universal deceptions. More important, with few exceptions, "the adulterations cannot be considered as deleterious. They affect the pocket of the individual rather than his health, so that, to use the words of the committee appointed by the National Board of Trade," the problem was merely one of fraud rather than "a sanitary" consideration.[2]

Smart denounced "sensational writing" and claimed that the most common and important foods—including tea, lard, loose coffee, sugar, and flour—were rarely sophisticated. There were some serious problems, of course. Alum, though not necessarily deleterious, "should be suppressed," and yellow candies were

1. George T. Angell, *Autobiographical Sketches and Personal Recollections* (Boston, 1892), pp. 70–71.
2. Dr. Charles Smart, "Report of an Investigation to Determine the Prevalence of Adulteration in Food Supplies," *National Board of Health Bulletin*, Supplement No. 11 (January 1, 1881), p. 1.

frequently colored with lead chromate. But these were the only adulterations Smart discovered to be potentially dangerous.[3] The key to the Smart report, therefore, is that it was in complete accord with the NBT report, from which Smart quoted. It was an endorsement of Dr. Billings's draft legislation even before that bill had been submitted to Congress.

Meyer, of course, made preparations to present the bill when Congress reconvened after the Christmas break. He sent Richard Fisher and John Wetherill of the NBT committee to confer with Billings and to prepare to appear before the Commerce Committee of the House of Representatives. But before they could act word leaked out that Congressman Beale was about to ask "for a suspension of the rules" in order to have his own bill acted on. Meyer dashed off a letter requesting Billings to have Fisher ask the NBT's friends in the House to "be on the look out," and stop Beale: "Delay might be urged on the ground that the bill prepared by experts under direction of the Natl Bd of Trade should be carefully considered before decisive action on either measure was taken."[4]

Meyer also mentioned that the *Nation* was about to support their efforts to stop any attempt Beale might make. The *Nation* was an independent Republican journal that was acquiring a reputation as the country's leading reform publication. The editorial appeared a few days later. It repeated Meyer's old bugbear that Beale's bill provided a "harvest" for "bummers and dead beats" by "persistent calling for samples," and it rejected the bill in toto as showing "not a vestige of scientific or legal sense." In contrast, the journal praised the NBT bill as "a very guarded measure . . . simple and perspicuous in every part."[5] Whether this timely editorial had any effect upon Beale cannot be known but Beale's alleged attempt to revive his bill never took place.

Perhaps because of the final collapse of the Beale bill, Angell decided at this time to take action of his own. Beale had twice

3. Watered milk would have been included in Smart's list, but milk was not among the foods tested, since it was assumed that milk was commonly adulterated. See NBH form letter dated June 7, 1880, from Smart: "Wines, liquors, and dairy produce are not included in this investigation as their status is believed to be understood." (Chandler Papers.)

4. Meyer to Billings, January 1, 1881, January 21, 1881, Billings Papers.

5. *Nation*, 32:813 (January 27, 1881), p. 52.

granted him additional appointments to appear before the House Committee on Manufactures, but both times, as in 1880, no quorum appeared. He then tried the House Committee on Agriculture, with the same result. As Angell viewed the situation those committees would never give him a hearing, because "the lobbyists were too active" in preventing it. But Angell had met Casey Young, chairman of the House Committee on Epidemic Diseases, back in 1878 while lobbying for a different purpose. Angell felt that the "Southern men" on that committee "were not afraid of the political influence of either glucose or oleomargarine."[6]

Whether Angell's analysis of the situation was correct or not, Young allowed him to draft a completely new bill on the adulteration question, which Young presented to the House on January 24, 1881. A very simple bill of only fifteen lines, the Young measure was Angell's rejection of the reassuring conclusions reached by NBH Supplement No. 11 and the NBT report. It asked for the appointment of a commission of "three persons learned in chemistry and sanitary science, to investigate and report upon the adulteration of food."[7]

A week later the NBT bill was finally submitted to the House of Representatives. The man selected by Meyer to introduce it was Congressman Joseph R. Hawley, a conservative Republican who had been a major-general in the Civil War and then governor of Connecticut. He seemed a strange bedfellow for Meyer's efforts, for in 1880 Hawley had questioned the National Board of Health's administrative abilities and "its penchant to waste money." Hawley believed that "health was a local responsibility and the federal government should help only in emergency situations." But Hawley had written to Meyer on April 23, 1880, in response to the *Sanitary Engineer* contest, remarking on his own interest in adulteration questions and adding that he was "glad to see them in such good hands."[8]

The bill was sent to the Committee on Commerce rather than to

6. Angell, *Autobiographical Sketches,* p. 72.

7. "A Bill Authorizing the President to appoint a commission to examine and report upon the adulteration of food," 46th Cong., 3d sess., January 24, 1881, H. R. 7005.

8. Peter W. Bruton, "The National Board of Health" (Ph.D. diss., University of Maryland, 1974), pp. 252–53; Wingate Papers.

Beale's committee. In addition, a sudden flood of petitions in favor of an adulteration law arrived in Congress to support the NBT bill. Fifteen petitions were reported in the House and six in the Senate, from a wide variety of boards of trade, chambers of commerce, and produce exchanges. But Angell's response to Hawley's bill came a few days later—the report of Young's committee, which consisted of a brief introduction by Young, and twenty pages of "evidence" supplied by Angell, evidence that attacked not only the NBH/NBT conclusions about the general harmlessness of adulteration, but also Thurber, Meyer, and Billings.

Young's introduction, reflecting Angell's testimony, completely contradicted Sharples, Leeds, Johnson, Smart, and the NBT report. His committee (in just over one week) had concluded, in its "investigation" of "the injurious and poisonous compounds used in the preparation of food substances . . . that the adulteration of articles used in the everyday diet of vast numbers of people has grown to and is now practiced to such an extent as to seriously endanger the public health."[9]

Angell's evidence consisted of a repetition of his 1879 testimony plus some interesting new comments. Through selective quotation he twisted the Smart report, the NBT contest, and Professor Johnson's speech so that they seemed to support his own contentions. Angell continued with a wide assortment of miscellaneous citations from professional reports, anonymous correspondents, and newspaper stories—often his own stories, although he seldom mentioned their source. He claimed that glucose was manufactured from "rags" and "sawdust," and that oleomargarine was unfit to eat despite the "certificates" from the "paid chemists" who testified to its wholesomeness. "A great glucose or oleomargarine ring, making millions of dollars, can easily afford to furnish all the chemists in the country carefully-prepared samples of their commodities, and pay the highest prices for analyses and certificates." Among the items Angell cited as having been found in oleo under microscopic analysis were tapeworms, cockroach parts, sheep blood, yeast, fungi, parasitic eggs, and tallow.

He then proceeded to attack the Hawley/NBT bill, while giving some support to the Beale measure, "which seems a good one so

9. *Adulteration of Food,* 46th Cong., 3d sess., February 4, 1881, H. Rept. 199, p. 1.

far as it goes." He attacked all his opponents in a manner worth
quoting at some length, for despite Angell's own wildly improbable claims, his analysis of his opponents' arguments was basically correct:

Last year a great oleomargarine seller in New York City . . .
who is also . . . an influential member of the National Board
of Trade, offered through that board [a] $1,000 prize for the
best essays on adulteration. The affair was managed by a
paper in New York City, said to be owned by a dealer in
plumbers' materials of that city, and called the Plumber and
Sanitary Engineer, which paper has published so much to
disparage and denounce my humble efforts that I have come
to look upon it as the organ of those gentlemen whose opinions do not agree with my own. A high officer . . . of the
National Board of Health is a regular contributor to that
paper, and probably through its influence was made chairman of its committee of award on these prizes. The report of
that committee . . . sets forth, among other things:

1st. That none of our staple articles of food or drink are
so adulterated as to be dangerous.

2d. That one of the main objects of legislation should
be to nullify the operations of ignorant and sensational
alarmists.

3d. That adulterated drugs are more dangerous than
adulterated foods.

4th. That it is much better to do too little than too much.

5th. That it would be unwise to attempt to secure uniform State laws.

6th. That the law should not attempt to define in detail
what is adulteration.

7th. That the Board of Health should have power to exempt any article from the penalties.

8th. That care should be taken not to make penalties
excessive.

9th. That under no circumstances should fees or moieties
be allowed informers.

And the bill now before Congress, urged and pushed by
this Plumber and Sanitary Engineer man . . . seems to be
drawn in strict compliance with the above recommendations.

Angell then concluded that since Billings, as one of the NBT judges, had expressed the opinion that "none of our staple articles of food or drink are dangerously adulterated," the investigation of adulteration must be taken away from the National Board of Health, and "put into the hands of an independent committee or commission."[10]

Meyer responded by having *Sanitary Engineer* attack the Young bill, in addition to Beale's, and by pledging to avoid all future mention of Angell. "I have decided not to print Angells name in our paper and have an idea he would be more annoyed at being ignored than anything else." From this time on, neither Meyer's paper nor Thurber's *American Grocer* appear to have referred to Angell.[11] Meyer left the Washington problems in Billings's hands, while he lobbied in Albany; when they both left the country for the summer—Billings attending an international medical conference in London, and Meyer accompanying him—neither the Beale, Young, nor NBT bills had been passed. Meyer determined to try again during the next session of Congress.

The final word, for the time being, belonged to Albert Leeds. Speaking to the American Chemical Society on June 3, he reiterated the "official" position of the professionals: virtually no dangerous adulterations existed. Without mentioning him by name, Leeds devoted much of his paper to an attack on Angell, but blamed the professionals for having "left the field in the possession of scientific demagogues and pseudo chemists." Because of such "sensational literature . . . there is a vast deal of misinformation passing for exact science . . . an impression which requires correction." Leeds called upon all true professional scientists to support the search for the truth, and "to control and shape the laws now under consideration."[12]

With the seating of the Forty-seventh Congress Meyer and Billings once again took to the attack. Since General Hawley had

10. Ibid., pp. 14, 15, 17–19.

11. *Sanitary Engineer,* February 15, 1881, p. 130; Meyer to Billings, February 21, 1881, Billings Papers. Similar sentiments were repeated by Meyer in another letter dated March 1, 1881. *American Grocer* respected this prohibition until February 22, 1883, p. 390, when it briefly mentioned "the notorious Boston Angell," at a time when agitation was stirring once again.

12. *Journal of the American Chemical Society,* 3 (1881), pp. 60, 62; *New York Times,* June 4, 1881.

been elected to the Senate, they selected Roswell P. Flower, a wealthy New York Democrat who had just been elected to the House, as their standard-bearer. Flower introduced the NBT bill on December 16, 1881, and it was once again sent to the Committee on Commerce.

At this point Billings decided to draw the American Public Health Association directly into the fray, drafting a circular for the current president, Dr. Kedzie, to send out under his own name. In the guise of a questionnaire, Billings sought to stir up the membership to support the NBT bill:

> If you approve the general features of the bill will you *at once* write to the members of Congress from your State to urge them to enact the bill into a law?
>
> The work of the Association in the past has largely been to disseminate information and to mould public opinion. . . .
>
> It seems to me that it is time that some of the results of the eight years' beneficent work of our Association should become operative through the form of law.[13]

While Billings continued to lobby in the capital, Meyer tried to contend with new attacks in both the professional and the popular press. One of the first editorials in Dr. Squibb's new journal, *An Ephemeris of the Materia Medica,* was directed against the NBT proposal. Although neither Billings nor Chandler could have, publicly at least, objected to Squibb's desire to *prevent,* rather than to *punish,* adulteration, their bills were designed to give a great deal of discretionary authority to the experts administering the law, whether within the NBH or the state boards. But Squibb argued that only specific definitions of food adulteration could act to discourage adulterators from choosing to run the risk of prosecution. Squibb also drew attention to the "very large opening for the escape of defendants" created by the clause excusing "mixtures or compounds recognized as ordinary articles of food." He consistently stressed that it was fraud that must be prevented, not just injurious adulterations, for the latter were

13. Kedzie to Billings, January 5, 1982, Billings Papers (letter confirms receipt of Billings's draft of the circular, and Kedzie's willingness to print it under his own name); printed memorandum from Kedzie, dated January 5, 1882.

usually the result of accident, not intent. In conclusion, not surprisingly, Squibb recommended his own proposal of 1879 over the current NBT bill.[14]

Charles Dana's *New York Sun* also editorialized against the NBT bill. Dana was a conservative critic of Gilded Age politics, one of a new breed of newspapermen who tried to remain independent of partisan loyalties; he was more concerned about reform (and circulation) than about serving party interests. Startled by this unexpected attack, Meyer called on Dana to "see if it was done with his knowledge." But Dana, who had also begun criticizing the National Board of Health and opposing any extension of its tenure, told Meyer that "the policy of the paper was 'to go for' any national legislation that would make more officers, or tend to 'centralization.' "[15]

Meyer and Billings continued to develop their lobbying strategy, as part of which they divided up a list of the members of the Commerce Committee between them. Meyer also hurriedly sent Newell back to Washington "to try to educe Horr to make the report and leave out the reference to liquors." Roswell G. Horr, chairman of the Committee, had apparently decided to include alcoholic beverages in the bill by specific reference, and Meyer understood that this would merely bring a new and powerful interest into opposition: "I only heard about an hour before I left [Washington] that Horr wanted something about whiskey. I think it impolitic to call the liquor people's attention to the measure which any reference to beer or liquor will do—they are well organized and with little trouble can quietly sit upon us."[16]

14. *An Ephemeris of the Materia Medica, Pharmacy, Therapeutics, and Collateral Information* 1:1 (January 1882), pp. 21, 24–29. Squibb wrote Billings (January 5, 1882, Billings Papers) that while the NBT state adulteration bill was "in its passage" he had had time only to criticize it "verbally, and that without effect. But when this U.S. Law was prepared I felt a very strong desire to criticize it, as it was so much like the others, and would be a model for so many states."

15. Meyer to Billings, February 1, 1882, Billings Papers. See Edwin Emery, *The Press and America* (Englewood Cliffs, N.J., 1972), pp. 260ff.; Alan Trachtenberg, *The Incorporation of America* (New York, 1982), pp. 123–25.

16. Meyer to Billings, February 1, 1882, February 3, 1882, undated, and February 13, 1882, Billings Papers. Apparently Meyer intended that the proposed law apply to liquors, but wished to avoid calling this to public attention.

On March 3 Newell reported that Horr's Committee had unanimously approved an amended version of the NBT bill and would report it to the House the next day. But the substitute bill was drastically watered down, when compared to the NBT's original version. Though it retained the general definitions of adulteration from Wigner's essay, the revised bill dropped all provisions regarding manufacture, sale, and interstate shipment of these foods and drugs. Pleading reluctance to interfere with commerce, Horr's committee opted to regulate only the importation of foreign goods. Horr argued that, by setting this limited example, state governments would be encouraged to regulate where the federal authorities refused to tread.[17]

If Meyer, Newell, and Billings were dismayed by this radical surgery, they did not discuss it in their correspondence. Instead, Newell immediately began lobbying in the Senate to persuade members of its Commerce Committee "to report favorably on House of Representatives Bill as amended." But, while Newell continued doing the job for which he had been hired, the others now seemed to be merely going through the motions.[18] Meyer and Billings could not have been satisfied with the substitute measure, which would only have rendered their efforts absurd. Thurber had never sought so emasculated a bill. What the NBT had been after was not merely a paper tiger, but a reasonable, moderate, effective law. Thurber wanted to empower responsible professional sanitarians to hound the corrupt business competitor, yet leave space for the normal give and take of everyday trade while silencing the anxieties of a consuming public that had been aroused by men such as Angell and by the exaggerations—and true revelations—of the press.

Meyer sent one last letter to Billings regarding lobbying efforts, but unlike his earlier messages it was confused, and filled with doubts and contradictions. Meyer ended this letter by simply say-

17. Newell to Billings, March 3, 1882, Billings Papers (bills H.R. 4789 and H.R. 1080); *Adulterated Food and Drugs,* 47th Cong., 1st sess., March 4, 1882, H. Rept. 634.
18. Newell to Billings, March 7, 1882, Congressman Thomas H. Herndon to Billings, March 10, 1882, Dr. D. W. Hand to Billings, March 28, 1882, Billings Papers.

ing that he would "do nothing until I hear from you."[19] There is no evidence that Meyer continued his lobbying activities after sending this letter to Billings.

As for Billings, he soon submitted his resignation from the National Board of Health. Congress had been delaying renewed appropriations for the Board; in June its powers were sharply curtailed and its appropriations cut to the bone. An emergency fund of $100,000 was created to serve in the event of an epidemic, but it was turned over to President Chester A. Arthur rather than to the Board. In July the Board was forced to terminate its quarantine inspection service for lack of funds. By the time it was ready to resume this function, on a reduced scale, the Marine Hospital Service had usurped it. When a yellow fever epidemic began in August, the emergency funds were turned over to the Marine Hospital Service rather than to the Board. By the end of the month all ongoing scientific investigations had been suspended and the weekly *Bulletin* had shut down. Though legally the NBH continued to exist, it had effectively been destroyed.

Billings stayed on in the surgeon-general's office, and his connections with the American Public Health Association remained strong, but he was no longer involved with the National Board of Trade or any coordinated movement for adulteration legislation. Meyer, who had written him at least seventy-four letters since 1879, apparently did not write again, except for one letter almost three years later. The joint NBH/NBT legislative effort had ended.

In July 1881, after the NBT bill had become law in New York, Dr. Rice printed a letter from Meyer, thanking *New Remedies* for its "valuable aid" and specifically expressing indebtedness to ten wholesale drug manufacturers and distributors and nine sugar refiners.[20] The refineries had a special interest in the legislation for, as will be seen, accusations about sugar adulteration had been revived, and the New York sugar industry was once again in troubled waters. The active support of the New York drug com-

19. Meyer to Billings, April 4, 1882, Billings Papers. A year earlier Meyer might have hoped for support from the Senate, where New York's Roscoe Conkling was chairman of the Commerce Committee. But Conkling had made a dramatic resignation from the Senate in May 1881. For additional information on Conkling, see below, chap. 11.

20. *New Remedies* 10:7 (July 1881), p. 208.

panies was evidence of their increasing importance, and the rapid evolution of modern pharmacy.

It has already been mentioned that it had once been quite common for doctors to run their own dispensaries, while apothecaries often engaged in a limited practice of medicine. In addition, even in the colonial period, the availability of patent medicines made it possible for general stores to compete with both professions by carrying a broad selection of "pharmaceutical" aids. But in the period before the Civil War the medical and pharmaceutical professions had begun to separate and specialize, putting the prescription and the preparation of drugs into separate hands. The city was the cutting edge of this movement; the more highly trained urban physicians lobbied for legislation to keep pharmacists from engaging in diagnosis, and the better-educated urban pharmacists sought to eliminate the competition of both the incompetent untrained "druggist" and the general merchant.

Lending urgency to this movement was the growing importance of pharmaceutical manufacturing. The pharmaceutical market was rapidly shifting from a reliance on the formulations of the individual druggist to the prepackaged preparations of the manufacturer. While there were only about ten pharmaceutical manufacturers in the entire nation prior to the Civil War, by 1880 there were almost one hundred. Manufacturers, using mass-production techniques and new processes, not only developed novel and potent drugs that were otherwise unobtainable, but also could offer the pharmacist standard remedies in greater uniformity of dosage, strength, and reliability than he could produce for himself—and at a competitive price; the "industrialization" of pharmacy "was almost inevitable." In addition, the number of proprietary manufacturers continued to increase at an even faster pace. To bring order to this growing competition, with its wide fluctuations in pricing, quality, and variety, wholesalers were at this very time organizing a national trade association, which would begin operating in 1882.[21]

21. See David L. Cowen, "The Role of the Pharmaceutical Industry," in *Safeguarding the Public,* ed. John B. Blake (Baltimore, 1970), pp. 72–74; William H. Becker, "The Wholesalers of Hardware and Drugs, 1870–1900" (Ph.D. diss., The Johns Hopkins University, 1969), pp. 160, 171; F. E. Bogart et al., *A History of the National Wholesale Druggists' Association from Its Organization to Nineteen-twenty-four* (New York, 1924), pp. 24–27.

Paradoxically, while these developments increased the public's estimation of pharmacy as a science, they threatened the professional esteem of the individual druggist, for both the competent and the incompetent could deal equally well in preparations already manufactured and packaged for their use. As one prominent New York pharmacist complained in 1883, the preparation of pharmaceuticals had passed "into other hands" to such an extent in the previous fifty years "that many so-called pharmacists do not, and could not, properly manufacture the simplest of their preparations." Dr. Squibb—a manufacturer who was conspicuously absent from Meyer's list—saw that the average physician and pharmacist (particularly those located in towns and rural areas) were becoming virtual middlemen and distributors for the manufactured preparations sold through the traveling salesmen employed by the pharmaceutical houses: "The merchant, as such, follows his business to make money by it, and the dealers in medicines are no exception to the rule. Medical supplies are to them simply merchandise, and are dealt in very much as railroad supplies, groceries, and dry goods are, and the invariable and inevitable law of trade is to favor the articles upon which most money is to be made."[22]

L. F. Kebler, "The Good Work of the Western Wholesale Drug Association (1876–1882) for Honest Drugs," *Journal of the American Pharmaceutical Association,* 15:4 (April 1926), pp. 293–97, argues that the WWDA, the forerunner of the National Wholesale Druggists' Association, was particularly outraged by the poor quality and broad adulteration of drugs in the western market, and that it set out to elevate standards. It should be noted, however, that the WWDA laid the lion's share of the blame upon the ineffectiveness of the 1848 import law, and was loath to consider whether its own members were equally guilty.

22. *Proceedings of the New York State Pharmaceutical Association* 5 (1883), p. 19, statement of Albert B. Huested, president of NYSPhA that year (obviously, competency remained important, for a qualified pharmacist is expected to interpret and, to some degree, monitor the physician's instructions); Edward R. Squibb, "The Relations of Physicians to their Medical Supplies," in *Transactions of the New York State Medical Association for the Year 1886* (Concord, N.H., 1887), 3:89.

Squibb did not deny that benefits could derive from large-scale pharmaceutical manufacture. He indicated in his own *Squibb Trade List,* August 1, 1861, that high-quality mass production could supply "a class of standard preparations . . . accessible to all," replacing the haphazard quality control faced by physicians dealing with a succession of local druggists, or by druggists buying from an assortment of importers and distributors.

Though the pharmaceutical manufacturers, especially McKesson and Robbins, and Schieffelin and Company, had given strong support to Meyer's legislative efforts, Dr. Squibb considered many of the "reform" activities of competing firms to be self-seeking behavior. He wrote to Dr. Billings, for example, that Parke, Davis and Company had "simply taken up" the anti-adulteration movement "as a high-toned advertisement to bring in money." As for the American Pharmaceutical Association, at its 1881 annual meeting it accepted the reality of the NBT law as having been passed in New York and New Jersey, and as seemingly well on its way in the Congress. Dr. Maisch, however, warned that the Association must remain circumspect: APhA's candid reports on adulteration, though they had succeeded "in directing attention to adulterated articles and in preventing or exposing fraud," were being cited "as proof of the inferior or sophisticated condition of the great bulk of the drugs in the American market."[23]

Meyer, for his part, proceeded to mend fences with APhA. In the very next issue of *Sanitary Engineer* he published a long exposition on the "Comparative Purity of Drugs," which was essentially an apologia for the pharmacists. Inasmuch as the law was about to be put into effect, he explained, it was important "to carefully avoid any exaggerations or sensational statements" about "the inferior quality of the medicines sold in this country." Prepared drugs—especially powdered drugs—were the most heavily adulterated. Meyer laid the blame not on the pharmacists, who were portrayed as being equally victimized, but upon his recent allies, the wholesale dealers, and upon the federal government's lax enforcement of the 1848 drug import law.[24]

In his next issue Meyer began a celebration of the pharmaceutical associations. Besides reporting on the work they were doing to investigate adulteration, Meyer cheerfully listed all the state associations and stressed that "the new health law . . . is the ally of the pharmacist." He chiefly hailed the "importance" of APhA, which "has done vigorous and loyal work." By August Meyer was explaining that in a recent—and highly publicized—case of druggist

23. Meyer to Billings, February 2, 1881, Squibb to Billings, December 23, 1881, Billings Papers; *Proceedings of the American Pharmaceutical Association* 29 (1881), pp. 377–78.

24. *Sanitary Engineer,* June 15, 1881, pp. 330–31.

error, not the druggist, but the doctor, had probably been at fault. He noted "the negligent writing of physicians, and the general want of any accompanying directions as to the administration of the remedy." Meyer went on to congratulate the New York druggists on the pharmacy laws for New York City (1872) and Brooklyn (1879), stressing the quality of the profession under the supervision of the Boards of Pharmacy, and he now urged passage of the statewide law desired by the druggists.[25]

The key to much of the new interest in legislation may well have been the growing public concern over adulteration. Here was an issue that threatened both the medical and pharmaceutical professions. The newspapers not only made a career of attacking incompetent physicians and pharmacists, but anticipated one conclusion of the NBT committee: adulterated drugs were more dangerous than adulterated foods. Dr. Billings warned the students graduating from Bellevue Hospital that they ignored the adulteration question at their own peril: "Unless you can depend upon getting what you call for in your prescription what success can you hope for? and yet unless you know what apothecary is to fill that prescription, you cannot rely upon it." Although Billings felt that the rural practitioner was in more danger of relying upon incompetent druggists than the urban physician, the warning was clear: if the prescription does not work, the doctor will be blamed at least as much as the druggist.[26]

If physicians warned against incompetence in pharmacy, pharmacists were perfectly willing to include the doctors in their own catalog of accusation. Dr. Maisch, in a well-publicized speech to the American Public Health Association, had laid the blame for drug adulteration on three factors: the inadequacies of the 1848 drug importation law; irresponsible manufacturers of patent medicines; and the lack of responsiveness of the medical societies, which, he claimed, had refused to cooperate with the anti-adulteration efforts of the American Pharmaceutical Association.[27]

25. *Sanitary Engineer,* July 1, 1881, p. 354; August 1, 1881, p. 402.
26. John S. Billings, "Address to the Graduating Class of Bellevue Hospital Medical College" (delivered March 15, 1882), in Frank B. Rogers, *Selected Papers of John Shaw Billings* (n.p., 1965), p. 143.
27. *New York Times,* November 14, 1874.

Thus, both the medical and pharmaceutical professions realized that they could be made to bear the blame for ineffective or dangerous drugs.

But while these accusations constituted a threat to APhA's desire to regularize the profession, the Association could turn the adulteration issue into an asset by demonstrating concerned involvement. For eleven years APhA had virtually ignored the entire subject, then, beginning with the session of 1871, each issue of the *Proceedings* carried a report of the new Committee on Adulterations and Sophistications. But these reports were designed for the trade, not the general public, and concentrated on technical information on specific medicinal supplies. Throughout this period APhA made no attempt to evaluate the actual extent of adulteration in the marketplace.[28]

By 1881, when agitation over the NBT bills and publication of the Diehl report in the NBH *Bulletin* brought the subject before the public eye, APhA became more responsive. The organization accepted for discussion at the following year's meeting a challenging question on the purity of powdered drugs, the form of medication most notoriously susceptible to sophistication. The eight-page response by C. B. Allaire of Illinois was, at first glance, anything but sanguine: it reported that fully 46 percent of the samples tested "were sufficiently adulterated that detection was easy." Moreover, Allaire noted that "these examinations were not made from suspected samples or with the intention of making an unfavorable showing."[29]

Considering these results, Allaire's comments and conclusions are interesting: any druggist wishing "powdered drugs of absolute purity and prime quality" could easily obtain them by paying an appropriate price. He declared that virtually all wholesalers and processors were honest and reputable and "that the present large percentage of adulterated goods in the market, is the result of a

28. See *Proceedings of the American Pharmaceutical Association* 22 (1874), p. 305, and APhA *Proceedings* 24 (1876), p. 403.

29. *Proceedings of the American Pharmaceutical Association* 30 (1882), p. 578. Allaire's estimates were based on the examination of *one* stock of drugs, from the supplies of a *single* Illinois pharmacist, and thus were virtually worthless, since he attempted to draw broad conclusions from this limited sample. He did report on samples tested by other pharmacists in other states, but his table of results—a report on 416 samples—was based only on the single source.

wide-spread demand for cheap goods."[30] Allaire concluded that legislation was incapable of curing adulteration. There were only two effective steps: better training within the profession, so that pharmacists could detect (and, presumably, reject) adulterations more readily; and a willingness to pay higher prices for quality supplies.

These same sentiments were repeated in the discussion that followed Allaire's paper. Dr. Maisch, after insisting that the adulteration situation was certainly no worse than it had been "thirty or forty years ago," strongly suggested that pharmacists should hesitate before rushing into print with revelations about adulteration, because so few of them were really experienced enough to form positive judgments. Even Dr. Squibb, Maisch pointed out, "hesitates to make such results public." James Richardson, of the Western Wholesale Druggists' Association, condemned the growing practice of price-cutting, and hinted that if retailers were only willing to pay decent prices to the wholesalers, they would be entitled to raise their own charges in turn, and receive "a just and honorable compensation." By the following year APhA's report on adulteration was insisting that pharmacists should be held responsible only if they *knowingly* sold adulterated goods, and it effectively precluded prosecution by explaining that "it is folly to ask that all pharmacists should be able to test the articles entering their doors."[31]

---

30. Ibid., p. 576. The depression of the 1870s had accelerated the decline of wholesale drug prices already begun by the expansion of the industry. Becker, p. 175, provides the following chart, taken from U.S. Department of Commerce figures:

Wholesale Price Index for Drugs and Chemicals
(1910–1914 = 100)

1855	178	1875	149
1860	175	1880	120
1865	300	1885	100
1870	199	1890	90

31. APhA *Proceedings* (1882), pp. 655–56; APhA *Proceedings* (1883), p. 363. The Western Wholesale Druggists' Association, founded in 1876, became the present National Wholesale Druggists' Association in 1882. The organization was founded specifically to overcome "excessive and unmercantile competition" (Sonnedecker, p. 323). See Becker, pp. 189–93; Henry Assael, ed., *The Politics of Distributive Trade Associations: A Study in Conflict Resolution* (Hempstead, N.Y., 1967), p. 28.

New York pharmacists demonstrated concern over adulteration and professionalization that paralleled the activities of their national organization. Though it was the medical profession that had first initiated legislation to regularize the two professions, urban pharmacists had come to share an interest in licensing. New York state had finally enacted a physicians' licensing law on May 11, 1874, which put the responsibility for enforcement exactly where the medical profession wanted it: with the county medical societies. But the continuing divisions within the medical profession doomed the law to compromise and concession; no effective physicians' licensing was created by the state in this period.[32]

The pharmacists of New York City had stood together in 1872 and succeeded in replacing the "Irving" law imposed upon them the previous year, but then once again they went their separate ways. Having defeated the type of law Dr. Maisch called "rulings of the general government where they oppress the true liberty of those engaged in business,"[33] New York druggists were apparently willing to allow further activity regarding both drug adulteration and the regulation of the practice of pharmacy to lie in the hands of their national organization. They waited until 1879 to form their own association.

The specific event leading to the formation of the New York State Pharmaceutical Association (NYSPhA) appears to be the recommendation for a law governing the sale of drugs and poisons in Brooklyn, by the newly formed Kings County Pharmaceutical Society. This organization was closely affiliated with the Kings County Medical Society and even published its *Proceedings* in the larger organization's journal. The bill was proposed by the Brooklyn pharmacists in November 1877 and was "in the main a copy of the law enacted for the city of New York in 1872," but with one interesting difference. While one of the main objections the New York pharmacists had had to the 1871 "Irving" law was the participation of physicians on the pharmacists' licensing

32. John Duffy, *A History of Public Health in New York City,* vol. 2, *1866– 1966* (New York, 1974), p. 178; and see William G. Rothstein, *American Physicians of the Nineteenth Century* (Baltimore, 1972).

33. *American Journal of Pharmacy* 52 (1880), p. 382; quoted in Glenn Sonnedecker, *Kremers and Urdang's History of Pharmacy* (Philadelphia, 1976), p. 196.

board, the Brooklyn bill intentionally proposed such a joint endeavor.[34]

Although physicians had sometimes sought to establish joint boards,[35] in this period it was quite unusual, if not unique, for pharmacists to have initiated such a plan by their own design. A possible solution to this enigma may lie in the fact that Dr. Squibb was extremely active in both Brooklyn organizations. At this time Squibb had just suffered a sharp rebuff in his attempts to involve the medical profession in the process by which the U.S.P. was to be revised.[36] His ideas were rejected not only by his fellow pharmacists, but by the American Medical Association as well. Although no direct evidence can be found to substantiate the contention that the Brooklyn bill was Squibb's brainchild, and although Squibb himself was not on the drafting committee, the nature of the proposal and its timing, as well as Squibb's interest in both adulteration and regulation, and his dual membership in both the medical and pharmaceutical professions, are suggestive.

Whether or not Squibb had been involved in the proposal, regulation of the profession was certainly the most heated topic discussed by NYSPhA. Meeting for the first time in May 1879, while the Brooklyn bill was before the legislature, the Association appointed a committee to draft a bill of its own. But the pharmacists quickly divided on an issue that was fundamental to the state of the profession at that time: the differences between rural and urban pharmacy. Most of the improvements in pharmaceutical training and practice had been largely confined to urban areas. Dr. Maisch had pointed out that rural pharmacy had changed but little since the turn of the century, with physicians "compelled to dispense medicines and carry them in suitable forms in their saddle bags." As one rural New York pharmacist later pleaded: "The demands made upon the country druggists, are not equal to those in our large cities. . . . we ought to have

34. *Proceedings of the American Pharmaceutical Association* 27 (1879), pp. 659, 663–66. See *Proceedings of the Medical Society of the County of Kings,* 2:10 (December 1877), pp. 294–97, for the original draft of the bill.

35. Sonnedecker, pp. 189–95.

36. See below at nn. 47–49.

the privilege, and the right . . . [to] not be measured by the standard that is used in New York [City]."[37]

The rural representatives chiefly objected to legislation relating to adulteration, and enough of the urban members—who made up the majority—joined to create a deadlock. But at the second session of NYSPhA, in 1880, upstate urban members succeeded in drafting a statewide bill very much like the New York City law of 1872. It imposed strict conditions upon those wishing to begin a pharmaceutical practice but grandfathered-in all existing druggists, and covered the entire state except for New York and Kings counties, both of which now had their own laws. The proposed state licensing board was to be composed of members of the Association, and one section of the bill prohibited adulteration. But the pharmacists vigorously debated protection for the innocent druggist who inadvertently sold sophisticated drugs: P. W. Bedford, that year's president, insisted that only those *"knowingly"* selling adulterated drugs should be punished. Once this loophole had been accepted, the proposed bill was finally approved for submission to the state legislature in 1881.[38]

With the bill undergoing the amendment process in the state Senate, debate continued in the NYSPhA session of 1881, the chief complaints continuing to come from the rural minority. The Association finally endorsed the amended bill, but it died in the state Assembly, and the NYSPhA law was not enacted until 1884. The law, as finally passed, put control over the practice of pharmacy firmly in the hands of the Association. NYSPhA was not fully satisfied, however, because the law provided a good deal of leeway for merchants and grocers who sold patent medicines or "the usual domestic remedies" put up by legitimate pharmaceutical manufacturers; also, doctors could supply "their pa-

37. *Proceedings of the New York State Pharmaceutical Association* 1 (1879), p. 60; *American Journal of Pharmacy* 44 (1872), p. 137, quoted in Sonnedecker, p. 216; statements of Mr. Tozier, of Brockport, N.Y., in *Proceedings of the New York State Pharmaceutical Association* 3 (1881), pp. 33–34, 45–46.

38. *Proceedings of the New York State Pharmaceutical Association* 2 (1880), pp. 19, 140. An analysis of the membership roll reveals that the vast majority came from upstate; of the 122 whose names appeared, only 6 came from New York City and 4 from Brooklyn. Nevertheless, the membership was primarily urban, most members coming from smaller cities like Buffalo, Utica, and Syracuse.

tients with such articles as they may deem proper." The 1884 law contained no section dealing with drug adulteration.[39]

The other state pharmacy bill of 1881 dealt with patent medicines, and was virtually confiscatory in nature. The bill would have required complete ingredient labeling of proprietary drugs, including proportional quantities, and would have set up a special board with the power to inspect manufacturing facilities and to deny certification, without which no proprietary drug could be sold. To add insult to injury, the manufacturers would have to pay the commissioners for the time spent investigating their products. Similar bills had been submitted to earlier legislatures and, like them, this patent-medicine bill was accompanied by endorsements from a large number of eminent New York physicians and pharmacists.

But the Assembly Committee on Public Health rejected the bill less than a month later, an annoying setback for the pharmacists, who had long been attempting to make the nostrum manufacturers the scapegoats on the drug adulteration question. Professor James H. Young notes that state formula disclosure bills, promoted by physicians and pharmacists, became common in the 1880s. And it is probably not coincidence that the nostrum makers formed the Proprietary Medicine Manufacturers and Dealers Association at this time. Publication of the Diehl report, the passage of the NBT state bills (though they did not prohibit nostrums), and the New York patent-medicine bill, all coming in 1880–1881, may well have influenced the proprietary manufacturers to join in self-defense.[40]

Although 1881 long antedates the time when the nostrum

39. *Proceedings, NYSPhA,* 1881; Albert B. Huested (Chairman), "Report of the Legislative Committee," *Proceedings of the New York State Pharmaceutical Association* 6 (1884), p. 51; New York State Pharmacy Law of 1884, published in *Proceedings of the American Pharmaceutical Association* 32 (1884), p. 371. Although the 1884 bill passed both houses comfortably, two companion bills died in the state Senate. These bills would have (1) forbidden the sale of drugs by non-professionals such as grocers, and (2) prohibited retail druggists from selling "wines and liquors." See New York State Assembly and Senate *Journals,* 1884.

40. James H. Young, *The Toadstool Millionaires* (Princeton, 1961), p. 228. Young, pp. 106–8, citing several histories of the Proprietary Association, explains that it was formed to fight a special federal tax on patent medicines that had been initiated in 1861. This was indeed a primary early goal of the Association, which succeeded in having the tax repealed in 1883, as Professor Young notes. This

makers held an iron hand upon much of the press, certainly patent-medicine advertising was becoming ubiquitous. It is ironic that the proprietaries were reaching these new heights in both sales and advertising at exactly the time that the medical profession acquired the knowledge to prove that the nostrums were dangerous and inefficacious. One reason it was difficult to attack the nostrums effectively was that they camouflaged themselves with the jargon of legitimacy. The nostrums pretended to be part of this new age of medical discovery, and appropriated quotations—and misquotations—from medical authorities for their own purposes.[41]

A letter in Dr. Billings's files is a good example of these practices. Lambert and Company, manufacturers of the new product Listerine, informed Billings that they had selected a quotation of his "to form the *introduction* for our pamphlet" describing their nostrum. Lambert also explained the source of their trade name with unconscious satire: "It was difficult to find a strictly scientific name for the preparation, owing to the number of ingredients, and as Mr. Lister's name is so inseparably connected with 'antisepticism,' we deemed that the one selected would define its character, as well as confide its nature to the knowledge of the profession."[42]

In 1884 APhA appointed a committee to prepare model legislation on proprietary drugs, which was presented at the next year's session. Resembling the failed New York bill of 1881, the draft called for registration of the formulae of all patent medicines, and content labeling of the active ingredients. APhA recommended that such laws be passed, not only by Congress, but in

---

explication, however, does not explain adequately why the Association was formed at this particular time, especially since the tax had been in existence for twenty years. See also *New York Times,* March 11, 1881.

41. Young, pp. 211-22, 157, 169. See *Scribner's Monthly* 22:2 (June 1881), pp. 304–6.

At the turn of the century the proprietaries employed a "red clause" in advertising contracts in order to coerce newspapers, which had become dependent upon nostrum advertising, to lobby against restrictive legislation.

42. Lambert and Company, St. Louis, Missouri, to Billings, May 29, 1882, Billings Papers. Although recent studies indicate that Listerine can help reduce plaque, for more than a century Listerine was a solution "discovered before the problem." It was originally touted as a general antiseptic and dandruff treatment. See *Consumer Reports* 49:5 (March 1984), pp. 143–45.

every state. The committee stressed that druggists felt compelled to carry nostrums because they believed that otherwise the public would simply buy them from less competent merchants, such as grocers.[43]

Pharmacists argued that it was really the patent drugs that caused price-cutting—which in turn encouraged adulteration—since the public paid relatively low prices for the nostrums, which cost almost nothing to manufacture. In contrast, the legitimate druggist, in addition to his business overhead, had to pay high prices for quality ingredients for officinal drugs. But an ignorant public simply assumed that, because he charged more for his own preparations than for patent drugs, the pharmacist was profiteering. Thus both APhA and NYSPhA argued that the nostrums were now the single greatest obstacle to victory over adulteration.[44]

The grocery trade understandably saw the legislative efforts of the pharmacists as a selfish attempt to reserve the sale of profitable "over-the-counter" drugs to their own profession. *American Grocer* ran a number of articles specifically attacking these efforts between 1880 and 1883: "it rightfully belongs to the grocer to add such merchandise to his stock. Heretofore the objection has been urged with force that drugs should only be sold by persons educated to the business. This no longer holds good, except where prescriptions are to be compounded, because of the new method of compounding standard remedies and putting them up with full directions as to their use."[45]

American Grocer's parallel criticism that the druggists were themselves "encroaching" upon the grocer's territory was echoed by Dr. Albert B. Huested of NYSPhA, who found it impossible to explain "how it is that we have come to include, even in cities and

43. *Proceedings of the American Pharmaceutical Association* 33 (1885), pp. 394–96; see Young, p. 208. The committee was made up of Charles Rice, Frederick Hoffmann, and Albert B. Prescott. Prescott's "Remarks" had been published in the *Sanitary Engineer* competition "Supplement." Hoffmann had been an analyst for the New York State Board of Health (see below, chap.10), was on the faculty of the New York College of Pharmacy, and a member of the APhA U.S.P. revision committee.

44. *Proceedings of the New York State Pharmaceutical Association* 7 (1885), p. 32.

45. *American Grocer,* December 21, 1882, p. 1353; and see (especially) issues of May 6, 1880, p. 1177; May 27, 1880, pp. 1366–67; June 10, 1880, p. 1494.

populous districts, nick-nacks of all sorts . . . even teas, coffees, knives, razors, pocket-books, stationery, cigars. . . . They are certainly not medicines, nor do they require pharmaceutical skill to handle." The *Grocer,* reacting to the renewal of discussion on the subject in 1884, responded bitterly, that "When a man gets ten cents for a grain of salt that costs two cents a pound, and sells a glass of soda at a thousand per cent. profit, he don't seem to be suffering for 'protection' so much as his customers do."[46]

Drs. Squibb and Billings agreed that, with the passage of the NBT bill in New Jersey and New York, the *United States Pharmacopoeia* had taken on new significance. After all, in both states officinal drugs were now to be legally judged in "strength, quality, or purity" by the standards of this unofficial directory. For this reason Squibb felt that it was now more important than ever that APhA's control over the U.S.P. be reduced, with "two or three strong representative medical men" influencing the Committee of Revision.[47] Ideally, Squibb wanted the AMA to take over responsibility for the decennial revisions.

Squibb, because of his concern about adulteration and high standards for the profession, had first initiated his one-man campaign to alter the manner by which the U.S.P. was revised in 1876. Squibb addressed a wide variety of medical and pharmaceutical societies and participated in a pamphlet war for his cause, but virtually the entire pharmaceutical profession rose up in indignation. Horatio C. Wood, Dr. George Wood's nephew, called Squibb's objections "a misunderstanding so groundless . . . that it is monstrous." Dr. Alfred B. Taylor, a leading Philadelphia pharmacist and first treasurer of APhA, accused Squibb of planning "a *coup d'etat.*"[48] The AMA reacted in a more subdued but similar manner, giving Squibb little time to present his arguments. He noted in his journal: "My entire subject of the Pharmacopoeia was

46. NYSPhA *Proceedings* (1883), p. 18; *Grocer,* May 9, 1884, p. 835.

47. Squibb to Billings, December 23, 1881, Billings Papers.

48. See Lawrence G. Blochman, *Doctor Squibb* (New York, 1958), pp. 266–69. Dr. Squibb circulated, at his own expense, reprints of his arguments, and those of his opponents, during the conflict. The final version, titled "The American Medical Association and the Pharmacopoeia," consists of 157 pages. This material was made available by the Squibb Archives. Wood's comment is found on p. 61 of the pamphlet and Taylor's on p. 68.

indefinitely postponed without hearing the whole of my paper, and thus I was sat down upon very hard."[49]

After his defeat Squibb participated in APhA revision conferences as an invited guest, though not elected as a delegate. After the publication of the 1882 revision he admitted gladly: "As a whole . . . it seems to be by far the best Pharmacopoeia of the time." It may have been Squibb's influence, and also the new significance of the U.S.P. under the NBT laws, that encouraged the APhA Committee of Revision, led by Dr. Charles Rice, to make some radical departures in this sixth revision. The new U.S.P. placed much less emphasis on the outworn notion that the community pharmacy was a place of pharmaceutical manufacture. Instead it provided the druggist with better guides by which to judge the quality of the medicinal supplies and products he purchased from manufacturers and wholesalers, and with many new tests for establishing the purity of drugs.[50]

Interestingly, however, while the revision was nearing completion some of Squibb's opponents privately sought to put the stamp of legality upon the U.S.P., and to broaden its base. Dr. Maisch, though he had attacked Squibb's plan vehemently and was a member of the Committee of Revision, wrote Billings, urging the federal government to take a hand in "the revision of the U.S. Pharmacopoeia." He stressed the need to create a truly "authoritative medical lawbook for the entire country," a uniform standard. Three days later he wrote again, emphasizing that "at present the U.S. Pharmacopoeia is a voluntary production of a fraction of the medical and pharmaceutical professions," and that the nation needed a better system.[51]

49. From Squibb journals; quoted by Blochman, p. 270. Squibb's criticisms were not ignored by all AMA members. Later that year the Medical Society of the County of New York, to which Squibb did not even, apparently, belong, heard a report from its committee on the pharmacopoeia, "that the present *United States Pharmacopoeia* is a work of inferior merit, and in need of radical revision." The next year the committee suggested "a departure from its present plan, or an enlargement of its scope." See "Minutes of the Medical Society of the County of New York" (manuscript), October 17, 1877, October 28, 1878.

50. *An Ephemeris* 1:7 (January 1883), p. 201; Sonnedecker, pp. 266–67.

51. "AMA and the Pharmacopoeia," p. 100; Maisch to Billings, May 29, 1882, June 1, 1882, Billings Papers. In addition to Rice and Maisch, the committee included Frederick Hoffmann, P. W. Bedford of NYSPhA, C. Lewis Diehl, and ten others.

Dr. Isaac M. Hays of Philadelphia, publisher of the respected *Medical News and Library,* to which Billings often contributed, had declared that Squibb's plan "is neither admissable in law nor justifiable in morals." Yet when Hays received a similar letter from Maisch, he too wrote Billings, supporting Maisch's arguments:

> The present "Pharmacopeia" simply bears the authority of custom while such a book should bear the stamp of the "Government," for it is the very essence from which other volumes are to draw their authority.
>
> The [1870] convention for the revision of the U.S. Pharmacopeia was manipulated in the most disgraceful if not corrupt manner—and the committee of revision then appointed is notable for the absence of names of note and standing from the Medical profession. . . . The production of a work such as the Pharmacopeia in incompetent and corrupt hands is to say the least a public misfortune.[52]

When, however, a bill was introduced in the House of Representatives in January 1884, for the federal government to "Prepare and Publish a National Pharmacopoeia for the United States," the medical and pharmaceutical professions rose to oppose it. One suggestion was perhaps typical of the sentiment within both groups: "Resolved . . . That all necessary legal authority which the present Pharmacopoeia does not now possess can easily be given it."[53] But indeed, this is exactly what was already happening, for as other states followed the lead of New Jersey and New York in passing adulteration laws—even when those laws varied widely from the original NBT plan—the new laws used the U.S.P. to set the standards by which adulterations of officinal drugs were judged. Dr. Rice's excellent revision made enforcement of the new state laws potentially more efficient and secure.

To what extent would that potentiality be realized? The NBT law intentionally avoided providing definitions of "purity" for

---

52. *The Medical News and Library* (May 1877), p. 72; see Squibb, "AMA and the Pharmacopoeia," p. 105; Hays to Billings, May 30, 1882, Billings Papers.
53. *Boston Medical and Surgical Journal* 110:12 (March 20, 1884), p. 275.

even the most common *foods*. But since the law adopted the U.S.P. as its official guide to *drug* purity and quality, the health authorities were provided with a ready-made standard by which to judge every officinal medicinal formula and ingredient. Meanwhile the pharmaceutical profession argued that it was capable of regulating itself. In the area of food, of course, no parallel organization existed. The sanitarians would have to decide if they were willing—at least through inaction—to entrust the pharmacists with such self-regulation, or choose to supervise the drug market themselves.

9

Enforcement:
An Uneven Hand

The activities of the druggists and the pharmaceutical manufacturers, the businessmen, chemists, and sanitarians, can be linked together through what may at first seem an irrelevant event. On June 7, 1881, a new law, supported by Henry Meyer, was passed for New York City and Brooklyn. This law called for the licensing of plumbers and for the inspection of their work by the State Board of Health. The *Times* commented, when the bill was first contemplated, that an ignorant and careless population needed protection from its own folly: "To any thoughtful person it is amazing that people in general are so wholly indifferent to the commonest sanitary observances. . . . As for the mass, they go on heedlessly contaminating their homes, buying and using impure milk, unwholesome meat and vegetables, and adulterated food."[1]

In this turbulent and challenging era the tempting new concept of government *in loco parentis* was beginning to emerge. The *Times* editorialized, after the plumbers' bill became law, that "it is not enough that a paternal Government should protect [citizens] against criminals, lottery ticket sellers, and three-card monte men—it must intervene in their dealings with artisans and tradesmen to avert the consequences of their own incompetence."[2]

Nor was it merely chance that so many of these new laws and

---

1. *New York Times,* November 14, 1880. The licensing legislation was Laws of 1881, chap. 450.

2. *New York Times,* June 12, 1881. See John A. Garraty, *The New Commonwealth, 1877–1890* (New York, 1968), pp. 208–19.

licensing provisions were couched in terms of the public health. This plea was the common thread that bound embalmers, barbers, veterinarians, plumbers—and even the horseshoers of Illinois—as well as doctors and druggists. Thus Meyer was reflecting a national trend when he renamed his newspaper; plumbers seeking legislation claimed that their occupation was "no longer merely a trade. Its importance and value in relation to health . . . have elevated it to a profession." The editor of Chicago's *Sanitary News* (another plumbers' trade weekly) explained that incompetent plumbers could "do more damage to health and life" than ignorant physicians or pharmacists. As Lawrence Friedman has explained, "The health argument . . . was needed to enroll neutrals in the legislature, and convince judges that some public interest was at stake," even if the real motivation was economic.[3]

In general, "professionals" were eager to assume their responsibilities as guardians of their specialized trade, whether it was pharmacy, medicine, or plumbing. In the same issue of *Sanitary Engineer* that announced the passage of the Plumbing Inspection Law, Meyer celebrated the success of the New York adulteration bill. He believed that "if the new law is efficiently enforced" by the professionals of the State Board of Health, not only would the public health be protected, but "the food products and pharmaceutical preparations made and sold in this State will command a premium over those of States where similar laws do not exist or are not enforced."[4]

If Friedman is correct in saying that, in this era, "business generally welcomed state control, provided the control was not unfriendly, and provided it carried with it protection for their little citadels of privilege," the same was true for the professionals. Regulation was not so much imposed *upon* both groups as it

3. Burton J. Bledstein, *The Culture of Professionalism* (New York, 1976), pp. 34–35, in part citing Barbara G. Rosenkrantz, "Cart before Horse," *Journal of the History of Medicine and Allied Sciences* 29 (January 1974), p. 60; Lawrence Friedman, *A History of American Law* (New York, 1973), pp. 399–400. For a discussion of common economic factors of groups seeking licensing, see Friedman, "Freedom of Contract and Occupational Licensing, 1890–1910: A Legal and Social Study," *California Law Review* 53 (May 1965); Paul Starr, *The Social Transformation of American Medicine* (New York, 1982), pp. 102–4.

4. *Sanitary Engineer,* June 15, 1881, p. 325.

was urged *by* them. While publicity may have helped inspire reform, certainly businessmen like Thurber did more than ride a wave of popular protest. They sought to guide and direct; in Professor Leed's words, "to control and shape the laws." In an age of technological innovation and reckless competition, augmented by a rapidly expanding transportation and communication network, businessmen sought to regularize the marketplace. Like the insurance promoters discussed by H. Roger Grant, men such as Thurber felt they "could generate business if they drove out dishonest promoters."[5]

But if the professionals were equally concerned about establishing their prerogatives, and also turned to government for protection and legitimization, the businessmen were eager to turn this to their own advantage, to use the professional as an instrument for legitimizing commercial activities. Nor was money the sole inducement used, for the professional and the businessman needed one another and served one another. If, as Robert Wiebe has said, the professionals were seeking to control the new fields of science and were trying to bring order out of chaos by bureaucratizing society, it was often through an alliance with men like Thurber.[6]

The "Thurbers" were more willing to entrust themselves to regulation, because the professionals took pride in their skills and qualifications; the regulators were reliable and predictable. But this alliance carried with it a great potential danger, for professionals were becoming more dependent upon those whom they helped to regulate, and they were often pitted against one another in defense of corporate clients. And if the professional came to depend upon the businessman, as the businessman needed him in turn, only professional pride operated to prevent their association from becoming an unholy alliance. More and more, society was coming to depend upon the professional, yet expected the professions to regulate themselves, once granted the fiat of occupational licensing. This was the challenge and temptation that Chandler faced, in his administration of the New York adulteration law he had helped to write.

---

5. Friedman, *A History of American Law,* p. 397; H. Roger Grant, *Insurance Reform* (Ames, Iowa, 1979), p. 3.

6. See Robert H. Wiebe, *The Search for Order, 1877–1920* (New York, 1967).

The instrument through which the sanitarians could now supervise the salubrity of New York was the State Board of Health, created on May 18, 1880. As president of the New York City Board of Health, Chandler automatically became a member of the new board. But if Chandler and the other members, which included Dr. Edward M. Moore (as president), Erastus Brooks, and Elisha Harris (its secretary), showed any sudden interest in adulteration, the records do not show it. Within two weeks they had met for organizational purposes and soon had established permanent committees covering a broad range of sanitary concerns, but not adulteration.[7]

After a full year of operation the Board had still taken no initiative on this problem; its first *Annual Report* barely mentioned adulteration. The *Report* was trying to lay broad foundations for governmental intervention against sanitary evils considered far more important than the quality of food; its pages were devoted to "sewer gas" and—more appropriately—epidemic disease. Though the Board acknowledged its responsibility "to prevent adulterations in food and drugs," this would be accomplished by empowering and encouraging local governments to act against threats to "the general health of the people."[8]

All local boards of health in the state had long been empowered to pass ordinances to protect the public hygiene. Moreover, there existed a number of state and local laws specifically directed at the adulteration question. In addition, the Board's *Manual* specified relevant court decisions to aid local prosecutors in litigation. Yet despite these long-established legal powers, apparently no new ordinances related to adulteration were passed by either the State or local boards of health, nor were any prosecutions begun, by the State or New York City boards, before the passage of the NBT law.[9]

---

7. *New York Times*, May 30, 1880, June 10, 1880; see *Sanitary Engineer*, July 15, 1880, p. 317, for an abstract of Stephen Smith's explanation of the process by which the law was put through the legislature.

8. *First Annual Report of the State Board of Health of New York* (Albany, 1881), pp. 82–83.

9. State Board of Health of New York, *Duties and Procedures of Local Boards of Health and their officers* (Publication No. 27, n.d.), p. 3; *Manual of the State Board of Health of New York* (Albany, 1880), p. 9. See also Laws of 1850, chap. 324; Laws of 1870, chap. 559.

An orchestrated assault upon the adulteration of food, drugs, and kerosene, however, began with a fanfare soon after Governor Alonzo Cornell signed into law the bill drafted by Chandler.[10] At its June 1881 meeting the Board discussed its responsibilities under the new law, and placed all work connected with it under the jurisdiction of a Sanitary Committee, headed by Professor Chandler. Whether this interest stemmed merely from the Board's legal obligation under the new law, or whether Chandler and the other members were indeed eager to exercise their new powers, the eventual result was the publication of what must be considered the most comprehensive American examination of adulteration to that time.

The Board's press releases explained that Chandler's Sanitary Committee was dividing up the various foods and drugs into a dozen different groups and assigning them to special analysts, in order to present a complete report the following year. Eight chemists were hired to complete the tests, while three inspectors were employed to gather samples. But while the analyses were being made there was no State Board enforcement of the new law. This meant that for two and a half years after its formation the State Board of Health took no direct steps to reduce adulteration, other than the preparation of its report. Chandler and Harris later defended this delay, claiming that it was necessary "to ascertain the nature and extent of the various adulterations found in articles sold within the State, and to determine the best methods for detecting them under the law; also to secure the necessary data by which to fix the standards of purity."[11]

Though their explanation might be suitable for some types of adulteration—mustard, for example, where certain modes of sophistication might well prove acceptable—it surely was insufficient for others, such as yellow confectionery, which was, according to every study to that date, dangerously contaminated with

10. See Elisha Harris, "Report of the Sanitary Committee," *Second Annual Report of the State Board of Health of New York* (Albany, 1882). Kerosene adulteration is discussed below, chap. 10. Chandler and other members of the Board consistently included references to illuminating oil—though obviously neither a food nor drug—in their attack on adulteration, and they worked to acquire additional legislation for its regulation.

11. *Second Annual Report*, N.Y., pp. 17–18.

chromate of lead. Meyer, who published a preliminary abstract of the Committee's findings in a special Supplement to *Sanitary Engineer,* responded to criticism of the Board's apparent "neglect in enforcing the provisions of the Act" by applauding the delay in initiating prosecution. A "systematic" examination was necessary, he argued, to offset the "many conflicting statements" that had excited "the public mind on this subject," and he cautioned against "undue haste in enforcing the law."[12]

The final version of the *Report* openly admitted that the Board's intent was to avoid inflicting excessive restrictions upon commerce. Meyer insisted that "it is essential that while the protection of the public health is to be first considered, the commercial interests be as little interfered with as possible." What, therefore, was Chandler's interpretation of Meyer's 1881 promise to Governor Cornell that it will be "the policy of the Board to be conservative and cautious in executing" the new law? Perhaps a clue to Chandler's attitude lies in some rough notes, in his handwriting, which indicate that he felt a *show* of strength and concern to be more important than actual enforcement:

> The Public expects the State B of H to do something under this law. . . . Seems necessary for reputation of the State Board that something should be done[.] Few prosecutions will be necessary . . . Publication of dealers in adulterated goods. Therefore first thing to be done is to arrange for analysis and publication[.] San. Eng. will publish everything we wish. The slips will be gladly taken by the daily press.

Another note similarly indicates that the "publication of names and of dealers—very few prosecutions" should satisfy public expectations.[13]

Whether or not Chandler was using the preparation of the twelve reports as a delaying tactic, work proceeded on the examinations, though not as smoothly as the published results would imply. A "Supplementary Report on Sugars" was added,

12. *Sanitary Engineer* "Supplement," March 30, 1882, p. 377.
13. *Second Annual Report,* N.Y., p. 500; *Sanitary Engineer* "Supplement," March 30, 1882, p. 337; notes, n.d., and March 16, 1882, Chandler Papers.

delaying completion of the *Report* by two months, because the original examination of glucose and sugar by Dr. W. H. Pitt was blatantly inadequate. A second chemist, Dr. W. G. Tucker, was privately considered by Chandler to be incapable of conducting certain analyses. Letters from a third analyst, Professor S. A. Lattimore of the University of Rochester, indicate that he too was out of his depth. Though Lattimore had been given a relatively easy assignment, he reported that he was having difficulty using the microscope for analysis, in organizing a reference library, and in getting pure spices for the purpose of comparison.[14] Lattimore's comments about the way he was gathering materials should also provide food for thought about the entire study: "During my recent visit with a number of large importers and manufacturers in New York, most of whom I found deeply interested in the success of the present effort to suppress adulteration, I was unexpectedly successful in arranging for samples of interest and importance, including samples of the adulterating materials themselves."[15]

Leaving aside the obvious questions about why the manufacturers should have happened to have such "samples" on hand, it must be understood that one of the central issues facing the Board was whether to prosecute retailers, rather than wholesalers and manufacturers. Not only would the former approach have immediate results, since it would be easy to find violators, but the Board would avoid antagonizing influential and apparently cooperative businessmen. After all, Lattimore's positive encounter with the large dealers was only a faint reflection of Chandler's intimate ties with wholesalers and manufacturers. From the very beginning there existed a tendency to rely upon these men for assistance and advice; there was a likelihood that the Board would come to echo their prejudices and perceptions.

To test the intentions behind the adulteration law and the consequences of its passage, it is obviously necessary to examine and

14. Chandler privately marked Pitt's report "not suitable for publication"; Chandler's notes on Tucker's report; Lattimore to Chandler, July 13, December 10, 1881, Chandler Papers.
15. Lattimore to Chandler, December 10, 1881, Chandler Papers.

evaluate the enforcement procedures in the three states where the NBT bill had become law. The present study deals with a representative group of commodities, and concentrates upon the activities of the New York Board, but the reports and legal actions of all three state boards,[16] through 1886, will be examined, beginning with the most fundamental of foods, milk.

As one author has succinctly noted, in this era "milk was a public health disaster area." But coincidentally, just at this time the professional literature on milk began to increase dramatically. This proliferation of material on milk may have been stimulated, in part, by the studies undertaken in the states in which new adulteration laws were passed, but it multiplied for unrelated medical reasons. In 1881, Dr. Ernest Hart of England published the first statistics on milk-related epidemics, initiating studies linking milk to typhoid fever, scarlet fever, and diphtheria. In that same year Robert Koch in Germany discovered how to cultivate bacteria in solid culture media, laying the foundation for the examination of milk bacteria. Thus at just the time that the state boards were beginning to enforce the adulteration laws, milk had once again come to public attention.[17]

The experts in all three states agreed on two things. "It is absolutely necessary," explained William K. Newton, the New Jersey Milk Inspector, that milk, more than any other food, "should be easily obtained in a pure state, unadulterated, and free from the germs of disease. There is, however, no one article of food that is so frequently adulterated or sold in an impure state." Massachusetts's Stephen Sharples similarly insisted that "injurious adulteration is by no means common," with the exception of "the single article of milk. Professor Chandler agreed with his colleagues; while he had stressed the *fraudulent* practices of

16. In addition to the reports of the New York, New Jersey, and Massachusetts boards, the reports of the Brooklyn and Boston boards were examined.

17. Stuart Galishoff, *Safeguarding the Public Health* (Westport, Conn., 1975), p. 81; Charles E. North, "Milk and Its Relation to Public Health," in *A Half Century of Public Health,* ed. Mazyck P. Ravenel (1921; rpt. New York, 1970), pp. 237, 243–44. North notes, p. 237, that between 1839, when the first scientific article on milk appeared, and 1879, "only thirteen writers felt it worth while to write scientific or medical articles on this subject." See John Duffy, *A History of Public Health in New York City,* vol. 2, *1866–1966* (New York, 1974), p. 133.

skimming and watering in his 1870 report on milk, he now emphasized that these activities were *deleterious,* reducing the nourishment received by infants and the elderly.[18]

There is no paradox in the fact that this most essential food was the one most commonly adulterated. Milk was very easy to sophisticate and passed through many hands on its way to the consumer; milk adulteration also remained difficult to detect, especially because "pure milk varies in its composition in a very marked degree, making it impossible to establish a standard of purity." Attempts to remedy this situation antedate the NBT bill; all three states had milk laws on their statute books long before 1881, and all three had already established measuring systems to determine milk adulteration.[19]

While the New Jersey laws did not at first specify a test for purity, Dr. Newton accepted Professor Chandler's "New York standard" lactometer, although he argued, in his report for 1880, that the minimum specific gravity used in New York—1.029—"is many degrees too low, and admits of watering from five to ten per cent." By the next year, after passage of the general adulteration law, Newton had fixed 1.030 as the state standard, but he concluded that each county in the state must be judged separately, since his tests had determined that the milk produced in different sections varied in quality. Newton also complained that the courts were often unwilling to accept the lactometer reading alone, and he therefore made chemical analyses as well, "in case

18. William K. Newton, "Our Milk Supply," in *Fourth Annual Report of the Board of Health of the State of New Jersey* (Camden, N.J., 1881), p. 209; Stephen P. Sharples, "Adulteration of Food," in *Fourth Annual Report of the State Board of Health, Lunacy, and Charity of Massachusetts. Supplement for 1882–1883* (Boston, 1883), p. 6; Charles F. Chandler, "Report of the Sanitary Committee of the State Board of Health on the Adulteration of Food and Drugs," in *Second Annual Report,* N.Y., p. 503.

For an excellent treatment of related—and more important—health problems of milk, see Judith W. Leavitt, *The Healthiest City* (Princeton, 1982), pp. 156–89.

19. Chandler, "Report of the Sanitary Committee," p. 502; James A. Tobey, *The Legal Aspects of Milk Control* (Chicago, 1936), pp. 1–3, notes that the first U.S. milk law prohibiting adulteration was a Massachusetts act of 1856. The first court decision on this law (1860) ruled that prior knowledge was necessary for conviction. A Massachusetts law of 1864 made milk adulteration a crime regardless of the dealer's knowledge or ignorance. See also Duffy, 2: pp. 427–37.

any dispute should arise." In 1882 the New Jersey Milk Law set the state standard at 12 percent milk solids, necessitating a chemical test for purity.[20]

In Massachusetts, the State Board rejected the lactometer; in imitation of the English authorities, Massachusetts employed the method advocated by J. Alfred Wanklyn, who had condemned the lactometer as "a most untrustworthy instrument." According to Sharples, the Wanklyn test, which was an abbreviated chemical analysis, was accurate enough for the purpose of detecting adulteration, yet far quicker than "the very elaborate analyses that were made some twenty or thirty years ago." Thus Massachusetts law specified that the only legal test for prosecution was a measurement of the total solids in the milk. But the state adopted a standard (13 percent total solids) even higher than that used in England, a standard that Sharples felt was too high, since tests conducted on unquestionably pure milk had sometimes resulted in significantly lower amounts of solids.[21] In Massachusetts, therefore, the Board used a great deal of discretion in enforcing the law.[22]

---

20. Newton, "Our Milk Supply," p. 216; William K. Newton, "Report of the Milk Inspector," in *Fifth Annual Report of the Board of Health of the State of New Jersey* (Mount Holly, N.J., 1881), pp. 116, 120.

21. Alfred Wanklyn, *Milk-Analysis, A Practical Treatise on the Examination of Milk* (New York, 1874), p. 13; *Fourth Annual Report,* Mass., pp. 39–40, 44; Stephen P. Sharples, "Specimens of Milk From the Vicinity of Boston," *Proceedings of the American Academy of Arts and Sciences,* n.s. 3, w.s. 11 (May 1875–May 1876), pp. 149ff.; n.s. 4, w.s. 12 (May 1876–May 1877), pp. 102–3. Sharples argued that the Massachusetts standard should be set at 12.5 percent.

In *Third Annual Report of the State Board of Health, Lunacy, and Charity of Massachusetts. Supplement* ((Boston, 1882), pp. 40–42, Sharples discussed this topic further, declaring that the Massachusetts law, "like all other attempts to measure the purity of milk by a single standard, is open to grave objections."

22. *Massachusetts State Board of Health: A Brief History of Its Organization and Its Work, 1869–1912* (Boston, 1912), p. 50, reports that the findings of the Massachusetts milk inspectors were as follows:

1883	50 percent adulterated
1884	58 percent adulterated
1885	44 percent adulterated
1886	42 percent adulterated.

(The figures in the annual reports vary slightly from those given here.) These unusually high numbers are the result of an impossibly high standard. In actual

When Chandler divided the dozen food and drug groups among the New York analysts in 1881, he retained "milk fresh and condensed" for himself. Presumably because of its importance, and because of the continuing interest in milk purity, the 1882 *Annual Report* gave this topic first priority. Yet, bewilderingly, except for a brief summary of Chandler's "examination," no other material on milk is to be found in the 200 pages of the *Report*. This one-page summary was printed, as were the other eleven summaries, preceding the bulk of the *Report*. On the page where the twelve actual reports were to begin, a footnote explained, "This report is printed after the reports on the other groups." But it was not, and a closing note appended to the *Report* merely indicates that "the urgency" of Chandler's duties caused his report on milk to be delayed.[23]

Chandler's summary was mostly a rehash of old material, defending both the use of the lactometer and the current legal minimum specific gravity of 1.029. Chandler mentioned new studies, conducted by Charles E. Munsell, one of his graduate students at the School of Mines, but the *Report* printed nothing of them. It cannot be determined exactly why Chandler's and Munsell's full report was not included. Chandler's private notes on the progress of the twelve reports indicate only that it was being "held for revision." Yet in the next year's *Annual Report* the Chandler/Munsell material was still missing. A note from Chandler to Dr. Harris at this time simply says, "Regret that I have not been able to finish my milk report."[24]

Amazingly, in its place was a simple resolution of the Board of Health, concluding that, because of the prevalence of milk adulteration and the importance of milk as a food, and because

---

practice, only milk testing below 11.5 percent solids served as a basis for prosecution. See statement of Dr. Charles Harrington, chemist for the Massachusetts State Board of Health, *Boston Medical and Surgical Journal* 110:11 (March 13, 1884), p. 255.

23. *Second Annual Report,* N.Y., pp. 509, 704.

24. Robert L. Larson, "Charles Frederick Chandler, His Life and Work" (Ph.D. diss., Columbia University, 1950), p. 144; note, n.d., Chandler to Harris, March 15, 1883, Chandler Papers.

> the perishable nature of milk makes it impossible for the State Board, through its inspector and milk analysts, to take charge of this subject, therefore,
>
> Resolved, That the attention of the local boards of health be called to this matter in the hope that some system of inspection may be adopted by them to remedy the existing evil.

Munsell's study was not published until 1884, by which time Chandler was no longer a member of the city or state boards.[25]

A possible explanation for the absence of the milk material may be the fact that Chandler's use of the lactometer was once again under fire. Chandler's own milk inspectors privately continued to question its value, since it could be outwitted through the established technique of concurrently skimming and watering, and because of the necessity of rigid temperature control of the milk being tested. Then in June 1881 Professor Leeds, an old associate of Chandler's and now Newton's colleague, gave a paper before Chandler's own American Chemical Society in which he condemned the lactometer's foibles, even explaining that New Jersey adulterators jokingly called milk that had been both skimmed and watered "New York milk." Dr. Charles A. Doremus gleefully noted in a letter to the *Times* that Leeds's statements, as well as the increasing demand of the courts for "an analysis as evidence of the adulteration," vindicated the objections his father had once raised against the lactometer.[26] Furthermore, Newton's rejection of Chandler's 1.029 specific gravity standard opened the door to additional criticism, while the Mas-

25. *Third Annual Report of the State Board of Health of New York* (printed as *Assembly Document Number 110,* 1883), p. 100; C. E. Munsell, "Milk, Fresh and Condensed," in *Fourth Annual Report of the State Board of Health of New York* (printed as *Assembly Document Number 89,* 1884), pp. 269–311.

26. J. Blake White to Chandler, December 1878, pp. 31–35, Chandler Papers; *Journal of the American Chemical Society* 3 (1881), pp. 60–62; *New York Times,* June 6, June 11, 1881.

The lactometer was calibrated for testing milk solely at a temperature of 60°F. Since specific gravity varies irregularly with temperature, even a slight variation from the "normal" 60° would throw off the reading. At the Schrumpf trial Chandler and the sanitary inspectors were unable to calculate the actual specific gravity when the temperature varied from that norm. Interestingly, the *Journal,* in its abstract of Leed's speech, failed to mention his challenge to the lactometer. Professor Chandler, in 1881, was president of the American Chemical Society.

sachusetts Board, of course, had rejected the lactometer itself except as a handy, if unreliable, tool.[27]

In the years between the Schrumpf decision of 1876 and passage of the NBT bill, relatively little attention had been paid to milk adulteration in New York. The sanitarians had suffered a setback in 1878, when the state legislature passed a law "to prevent deception in the sale of milk," a thinly disguised attempt to protect dealers in skimmed milk from Chandler's prosecution. The law provided for the labeling of all cans containing "skimmed milk" and so at first might have seemed directed against adulteration. But the key to the law is the fact that it permitted the sale of skimmed milk at all. In addition, the Senate had cooperated with the milk interests by requiring only a painted "marking" (rather than "stamping") of the identifying words and by reducing the size of the required lettering to one inch. This created a situation in which the city's Sanitary Code and the state law were in direct conflict. Chandler's inspectors continued to destroy all skimmed milk found entering the city, marked or not.[28]

27. The Massachusetts legislature acted with more determination upon the milk question than its counterparts in either New York or New Jersey. In addition to its rigorous testing requirement and unreasonable "purity" standard, it legislated that the bulk of the Board's funds go to preventing and prosecuting milk adulteration. The original appropriation of $3,000 made in 1882 was raised to $5,000 the next year, with the proviso that two-fifths "should be expended in enforcing the milk law"; in 1884 the appropriation was raised to $10,000, with three-fifths devoted to milk.

In New York, the state standard eventually adopted was fat content, measured by a "gravimetric or weighing method." See George L. Flanders, "Accurate Determination of the Amount of Fat in Milk," (three-page pamphlet, August 3, 1909), p. 2; Raymond A. Pearson, *Facts about Milk* (Washington, D.C., 1906), pp. 19–20.

Debate about the accuracy of the lactometer continued until the report by R. H. Shaw and C. H. Eckles, *The Estimation of Total Solids in Milk by Use of Formulas,* USDA *Bulletin 134* (Washington, D.C., 1911), pp. 15–16; the lactometer can result in discrepancies as great as "one per cent of total solids calculated" by weighing, and is therefore unreliable. On the debate at the time of the publication of the *Second Annual Report* see also John Morris, *Milk: Its Adulterations, Analysis, Etc.* (pamphlet, Maryland Academy of Sciences, 1882), p. 2.

28. Laws of 1878, chap. 220; *Journal of the Senate of the State of New York, 1878* (Albany, 1878), pp. 442–43; *Fourth Annual Report,* N.Y., p. 308. The bill passed both houses of the legislature virtually without opposition. *American*

The decision that Board policy was not affected by the new law—an interpretation the courts permitted—led the skimmed milk interests to attempt to override the Code through passage of a state law specifically legalizing its sale. In May 1882 such a bill passed the state Senate, and Chandler organized a campaign to defeat it before it could become law. Beyond getting the support of the friendly press, he worked with William Newton on the wording of a public letter strongly opposing the bill, and he had the City Health Department publish its own "letter," claiming that the bill would "certainly" lead to an increase in infant mortality. Chandler induced Edward G. Janeway, a noted health authority, to support this contention. Janeway predicted that the law would "be the death-knell of five hundred children a year, at least."[29]

But perhaps Chandler's greatest coup was in obtaining support from James Gallatin's Sanitary Reform Society, the premier reform organization in the state. The Society's flyer, which condemned the bill as an attempt "to legalize fraud in milk," was signed by such social, economic, and political notables as Gallatin, F. B. Thurber, James A. Roosevelt, Joseph W. Drexel, Morris K. Jesup, James W. Pinchot, William E. Dodge, Jr., and Henry E. Pellew. The next year, after this bill had been defeated, Chandler found himself facing another effort to legalize skimmed milk—the fifth attempt in as many years. Once again Chandler mobilized the opposition, including Elbridge Gerry's Society for the Prevention of Cruelty to Children. This time the bill failed to get past even the Committee on General Laws, to which it had been referred.[30]

Grocer ran a number of routine items on milk throughout the period. It should be remembered that milk was not a large part of the grocer's business, since it was mostly sold door-to-door, scooped out of cans. (Some early experiments were made at this time in selling milk in glass jars. See *New York Times,* February 28, 1881; *American Grocer,* October 30, 1879, p. 1053.)

29. *Sanitary Engineer,* May 25, 1882, pp. 533, 540; Newton to Chandler, April 24, 1882, printed letter from "Health Department, 301 Mott Street," dated May 23, 1882, "Letter from E. G. Janeway, Late Commissioner of Health and Chairman of the Committee on Hygiene of the County Medical Society," dated May 23, 1882, Chandler Papers. Janeway was professor of pathological anatomy at Bellevue and a noted diagnostician and consultant.

30. Untitled letter from the Sanitary Reform Society, Chandler to Gerry, March 5, 1882, Chandler Papers. See Larson, *Chandler,* pp. 153–55.

Chandler's second effort in relation to milk adulteration dealt with interstate cooperation, in an attempt to prevent the shipment of skimmed milk into the city. Chandler's success in this endeavor was made possible because of three things: his friendship with Newton, the New Jersey Milk Inspector; the growing cohesiveness of the dairy farmers; and cooperation from the railroads. The farmers and the railroads were both acting, understandably, from economic rather than humanitarian motives. On February 24, 1881, the Orange County Producers' Milk Association, the largest of the dairy-farmer organizations, had been formed in an attempt to control prices by regulating the supply of milk.[31] William P. Richardson of the Erie Railroad was elected its president, and by 1883 the Association represented approximately 700 dairy farmers.

The railroads had been under fire from Thurber's Cheap Transportation Association and other business organizations under his influence. Thurber also utilized his position as president of the New York Dairymen's Association to recruit farmer support for the reduction of freight rates. With the threat of rate-regulation legislation in the state legislature, the Erie had "voluntarily" reduced milk rates slightly, and began to evince interest in improving its public posture. Thus when Chandler approached Richardson with a proposal to get the company's cooperation in derailing the traffic in skimmed milk, he eagerly accepted.[32]

The skimmed milk was being shipped from creameries upstate, through New Jersey, to evade Chandler's inspectors. Chandler decided that the Board had two apparent choices: either attempt to prosecute the producers "in their own villages" with the doubtful cooperation of local authorities, or "put inspectors on the Erie trains at night and examine every can of milk that is put on the trains." Richardson advised sending a representative of the Board to see whether Newton would help them implement

31. *New York Times,* February 25, 1881.
32. Lee Benson, *Merchants, Farmers, and Railroads* (New York, 1955). At about the same time Richardson had made the same proposal to an organization of dairy farmers, along with several other concessions for their convenience. See *New York Times,* December 27, 1882. On efforts to legislate special freight rates for milk see *New York Times,* March 20, April 2, June 20, 1879.

the second alternative, and Chandler sent Inspector Munsell. "You and Mr. Richardson should meet in Patterson, in Dr. Newton's offices, so that the whole work might be carried on jointly by the New Jersey officers, the New York State officers, and the New York City Board."[33]

Newton "deputized" Munsell a New Jersey inspector to lend legal authority to his activities, and soon did the same for Inspector Edward W. Martin at Chandler's request; Munsell and Martin were now officials of three separate health departments. The program was believed to be a great success. Munsell and Martin reported that their efforts, "to which the aid given to the inspectors by the railroads was of the greatest importance," were effective in preventing city dealers from receiving skimmed milk, which in turn discouraged the shippers from sending it to New York. "The result was that the sale of at least 40,000 quarts of adulterated milk daily was prevented," Chandler claimed.[34]

Chandler's third effort in relation to milk was in the area of prosecution. The figures presented by Munsell in the 1884 *Annual Report* suggest that there was a growing incidence of centralized corporate adulteration, undeterred by any actions of the Board. There had even come into existence a sort of adulterators' union. Mirroring the organization of the Orange County Producers' Association, the creameries and larger milk dealers had formed the New York Milk Exchange Limited, an attempt to control the industry through blatant price-fixing. According to the by-laws of the Exchange, members would hold fast, under threat of disciplinary action, both in the rates paid to farmers and in the prices charged to consumers. Unspoken, but ill-concealed, were the Exchange's activities in the skimming business.[35]

33. Chandler to J. Blake White, January 31, 1883, Chandler to Munsell, January 31, 1883, Chandler Papers.

34. Chandler to Newton, February 8, 1883, Chandler Papers; *Fourth Annual Report,* N.Y., p. 268.

35. By-Laws of the New York Milk Exchange Limited, Chandler Papers. See also Larson, p. 150. Chandler reported in *Sanitary Engineer* "Supplement," March 30, 1882, that "so openly are these frauds practiced that 'creameries' have been established in many localities; the names and locations of seventy-three of such establishments being known to the writers, of which sixty-three are known to send skimmed milk to New York City, all of which is sold as whole milk on its arrival." Chandler may have known their locations, but he never brought suit against any of the creameries.

Despite these developments, there is nothing to indicate that any of the men leading the creamery operations were prosecuted. Only unimportant dealers, carters, and employees were arrested. The arrest records of the 1880s for the sale of adulterated milk are not significantly different, in any manner, from the records of the city health board, before the State Board had been formed. Yet the Board's interstate operation had almost immediately netted some very big fish indeed. It was discovered by Munsell and Newton that the New York Dairy Company was deeply involved in the shipment of adulterated milk.

New York Dairy was a "model" milk company organized for the purpose of providing the city with unquestionably pure milk at reasonable prices and owned by some of the most noted reform and philanthropic leaders of New York. One of the directors was Henry E. Pellew, a leader of the Sanitary Reform Society who had signed the Society's flyer condemning the skimmed-milk bill the previous year, a leader of the tenement-reform movement and the Charity Organization Society, and president of the Association for Improving the Condition of the Poor. Another director was Cornelius R. Agnew, a noted New York doctor, a sanitary reform leader, and a close associate of Chandler. Chandler was put in the embarrassing position of having to write to Pellew, "I find myself placed in a very disagreeable predicament with regard to you and several of my other friends."[36]

Pellew's and Agnew's sales agent, R. R. Stone, was caught shipping skimmed milk to a New York distributor. When the inspectors seized the company's records they discovered that this operation had been going on since at least August 1881 and involved the president and the treasurer of the company—Alex Campbell and Walter Stillman—as well. Obviously Chandler wished to avoid prosecuting his friends, yet he was obligated to

36. Chandler to Pellew, February 13, 1883, Chandler Papers. Present at the original meeting setting up the cooperative, according to the *New York Tribune,* September 24, 1879, but perhaps no longer involved in its operation by 1883, were fifty civic leaders, including John Jay (Pellew's brother-in-law, and organizer of the company), Senator William H. Robertson, Manton Marble's father Joel, and other rural gentry. Pellew and Agnew, and their associates in similar reform organizations, represent "the men of breeding and intelligence, of taste and substance" who were the enlightened upper-middle-class liberals of John G. Sproat, *The Best Men* (London, 1968); see p. 7.

do something to stop the company's traffic in adulteration. He continued in his letter to Pellew:

> I write to you in order that you may bring this matter to the attention of your fellow directors, as I am confident that no one of you would ever have countenanced any such deliberate violation of the law as your agent has practiced. . . . It will be extremely disagreeable to be compelled to have your agent indicted, but you can understand that we cannot make fish of one and flesh of another. At the same time if your Company forbids the illegal traffic in skimmed milk by its agents, and arrays itself on the side of the farmers and honest milk, and your agent withdraws from the organization which we are engaged in fighting, we should feel that there was nothing to be gained by prosecuting Stone and Campbell.[37]

Pellew quickly responded to Chandler's letter, denying that he and Agnew had any active part in running the company. "I am very much obliged to you for writing in so friendly a manner and in giving me such timely notice: Please wait a little longer." Pellew promised that, although he personally saw nothing wrong with skimmed milk, he would straighten things out. The very next day he mailed Chandler identical "confessions" from Stone, Campbell, and Stillman.[38]

Chandler communicated with his own agents, in an effort to keep the discovery quiet. He wrote to Dr. J. Blake White, the chief city milk inspector:

> I didn't think it would be just to have these gentlemen paraded in the newspapers as guilty of selling skimmed milk in New York, so I wrote to them . . . and they have assured me that it was without their knowledge and shall never happen again.

37. Chandler to Pellew, February 13, 1883, Chandler Papers.
38. Pellew to Chandler, February 13, February 14 (two letters), Chandler Papers. Chandler partially agreed with Pellew about skimmed milk: "I do not believe that skimmed milk is unwholesome or without nutritive properties. That is not the issue. I consider it a fraud to sell skimmed milk for whole milk, and I consider it unwholesome to make the chief article of diet of an infant to consist of skimmed milk." See Chandler to Pellew, February 14, 1883, Chandler Papers.

I do not propose, therefore, to have any action taken against this company at the present time, either under the City or the State law. . . .

I would also suggest that care should be taken that the newspaper reporters learn nothing whatever with regard to this case. Many of them would take the greatest delight in making an excuse for throwing mud at some of the best and most philanthropic of our citizens.

Chandler sent similar letters that same day to Inspectors Martin and Munsell.[39]

W. P. Richardson, however, was dissatisfied with Chandler's solution. Richardson's idea of patrolling the trains had borne fruit within a week of its initiation, yet Chandler was throwing away an ironclad case. He urged that the people running New York Dairy receive "the punishment they richly deserve." Richardson correctly pointed out that this was the first case that could be made against the producers of skimmed milk, not just the dealers. Speaking for the railroads and the farmers, Richardson insisted that the case be "pushed to the full extent of the law." Richardson also argued that the farmers would want to see the case publicized and urged Chandler to release the information to the press.[40]

But Chandler answered Richardson to the effect that Pellew, Agnew, and the other directors were honorable men "who have always been ready to give their time and their money for benevolent and philanthropic objects." He refused to have them "humiliated through the newspapers because their agent, without their knowledge or consent, has been sending skim milk to New York City." Chandler noted Pellew's pledge to clean house: "Now this is a bloodless victory and I think is sufficient." He refused to prosecute Stone, because doing so would drag Pellew and Agnew into the picture. He even sent Pellew copies of Rich-

---

39. Chandler to White, February 14, 1883, Chandler to Martin, February 14, 1883, Chandler to Munsell, February 14, 1883, Chandler Papers. Martin responded: "I have not said a word about the N.Y.D. Ass. to anyone and of course shall not, now anyway." (Martin to Chandler, February 15, 1883, Chandler Papers.)

40. Richardson to Chandler, February 14, 1883, Chandler Papers.

ardson's letter and his own reply, as well as copies of his letters to White, Munsell, and Martin.[41]

Setting aside the question of Chandler's friendship with Pellew and Agnew, his sincerity may still be examined. How successful could his pure milk campaign be if he continued to prosecute only the milk dealers, and not the producers? Did a similar pattern become evident in Chandler's prosecution of other kinds of food adulteration? The peculiarity of his position was magnified by the fact that, only a few days after the Pellew affair, the *New York Tribune* began a series on the milk trade and the inspection system aboard the trains. A public relations coup could have been created if Chandler had pursued the prosecution of the dairy company officials and had released the information to the press.[42]

Instead, he wrote to Munsell for information to give the newspaper, pleading, "I have run dry of material. Unless you can give me something I don't know what to tell the reporter the next time he calls." Similarly, he had written to Richardson for "some ammunition. . . . Now we must keep the ball moving." In light of his reluctance to pursue the producers, Chandler's letter to Dr. White a few weeks later also takes on an uncomfortable coloration: "Catch as many milk dealers as you can, who are selling watered and skimmed milk, and show them no mercy. They are a set of villains and I only wish we could get them all into the penitentiary at once."[43]

The retail grocers very quickly came to suspect that the Board's enforcement of the adulteration law would concentrate on themselves, rather than on the manufacturers and wholesalers. The New York City retailers formed a protective union shortly after the Board's preliminary report on foods and drugs was published. It was obvious that, even with the best of intentions, the Board would find it easier to inculpate retailers than to trace the more

41. Chandler to Richardson, February 16, 1883, Chandler to Pellew, February 16, 1883, Pellew to Chandler, February 16, 1883, Chandler Papers.

42. The *Tribune* ran a major interview with Chandler on February 21, 1883, with followups for the next two issues. A final story on the train-board inspections, including an interview with Richardson, was run on February 25, 1883, but by then the story was played out, with no new information forthcoming.

43. Chandler to Munsell, February 23, 1883, Chandler to Richardson, February 21, 1883, Chandler to White, March 13, 1883, Chandler Papers.

remote origins of adulteration. Moreover, anxiety among the retailers must have been aroused when Chandler reported in his summary that the Board was temporarily ignoring all of the "numerous applications" for clarification of the provision of the law relating to "mixtures and compounds recognized as ordinary articles of food" and refusing, for the meantime, to rule on special exemptions and exceptions.[44]

A number of reasons, beyond fear of the law, induced the small businessmen to form the New York Retail Grocers' Union on May 18, 1882. Although some of these reasons involved the establishment of a grocers' library, better information on deadbeats, legislation against itinerant peddlers, and an "intelligence bureau" to provide a blacklist of clerks "detected in wrong doing," the primary objective was to achieve equity—"equal trade rights"—with the manufacturers and wholesalers. One of the first accomplishments of the Union was the establishment of a Roll of Honor, rapidly signed by the important wholesalers, pledging to abstain from selling at retail. This early success surely encouraged the grocers to believe that they could similarly persuade the Board to enforce the adulteration law with an even hand.[45]

The Board's preliminary report stimulated speculation among the retailers as to what allowances would be made on an assortment of the most fundamental grocery items. Professor Lattimore, for example, reported that he had found 112 of the 180 tested samples of mustard and spices to be adulterated, although with "harmless" articles. It was common knowledge that spices were universally adulterated, and mustard was openly sophisticated, at least in a technical sense. Pure mustard is simply the ground contents of the black or white mustard seed. The best mustard is a mix of both kinds, with much of the natural oil removed, improving the "keeping qualities" of the product. The common mustard sold in stores was usually thinned with flour and then colored with turmeric to restore its natural yellow.[46]

44. *Second Annual Report,* N.Y., p. 509; *Sanitary Engineer* "Supplement," March 30, 1882.

45. "New York Retail Grocers' Union" (four-page booklet, n.d.). Philadelphia, Baltimore, and New England had similar associations operating by 1881; see *Grocer,* July 30, 1881, p. 96.

46. *Second Annual Report,* N.Y., p. 505; *Report of the Commissioner of Agriculture for the Year 1886* (Washington, D.C., 1886), pp. 298–99.

It is clear that even respectable manufacturers and dealers regarded the use of flour in mustard as an attempt to satisfy the public taste, not to cheat the public pocket. F. B. Thurber, for example, had been accused in 1880 of using artificial coloring in his mustard. Such coloring, the retail accuser assumed, "showed that the same had been adulterated, else why should there be turmeric or other coloring matter? Genuine mustard does not need coloring." Thurber responded that some manufacturers used "an arsenical preparation—a deadly poison" for coloring, while his mustard division used only turmeric, "a harmless vegetable coloring." This reply left the central question unanswered: was there flour in "Thurber's Best"? Undoubtedly, because the retailer was correct—had the mustard not been diluted, there would be no need for added coloring. But it was also assumed that even "simon-pure" wholesale mustard would be thinned by the retailer. Professor Chandler, in his first public statement after the Board met to discuss the newly passed adulteration act had said: "Some substances are never sold unadulterated. Table mustard, for instance, is always mixed with flour, the pure mustard being too strong for use; this is a legitimate adulteration."[47]

With this disclaimer, the retailers could be fairly sure that when the Board finally released its list of exemptions and acceptable admixtures, mustard mixed with flour would be included. But how much mustard to how much flour? And Chandler had not specified any other commodities. Lattimore had found nineteen of twenty-one samples of ground coffee to contain adulterants, "chiefly chicory and beans."[48] The grocers suspected that chicory in coffee would be pronounced legal, but once again, the conditions of certification were unknown. Would spices be regarded by the Board as "ordinary articles of food" in their diluted form? It was expected that the exemption list would be released quickly.

After all, how could such a fundamentally new law be executed without first establishing and announcing standards? It would be as if the first automobile regulations had simply outlawed "speeding" without specifying the legal limits for roads or streets. The highly respected *Sanitary Record* of England had pronounced the New York law superior to the British law exactly because it could

47. *American Grocer,* March 4, 1880, p. 602; *Grocer,* July 2, 1881, p. 4.
48. *Second Annual Report,* N.Y., p. 506.

avoid "all those foolish squabbles as to the desirability or otherwise of selling mustard containing ten per cent. of farina, and pepper containing two per cent. of sand, which have so disgraced our own national administration of the Sale of Food and Drugs Act." Yet in New York months went by not only without prosecution but without the publication of exemptions.[49]

The grocers awaited the delayed *Second Annual Report*, for in it further clues might be found as to the Board's eventual policy. When it finally appeared, its most prominent feature, from the grocers' point of view, was probably Lattimore's argument that, since it would be difficult to establish "whether a definitely fixed proportion had been exceeded or not," it would be simpler to "prohibit the manufacture and sale of all mixtures, with possibly a few exceptions." Moreover, Lattimore specifically condemned coffee/chicory mixtures, and he implied that no spices should be adulterated in any manner, and mustard only to the extent that excess oils could be removed.[50]

Yet rather than first set Board policy on any of these grocery items, Chandler decided at this point to establish a test case against the retailers. He recruited his old associate Colonel Prentice to act as the Board's prosecutor and they immediately initiated suits against five men for selling adulterated cream of tartar. In all, during the month of December, fifteen retailers were arrested on that charge, plus two for selling adulterated coffee, four for selling mustard mixed with flour, and one for selling adulterated precipitated sulphur.[51]

The Board's test case was selected from those accused of adulterating cream of tartar with "terra alba," a harmless filler usually made of gypsum or kaolin. For the Board's *Report*, Dr. E. G. Love had been assigned the food group that included flours, cereals, and baking products. Of all the 283 assorted samples he tested, only 37 were found to be adulterated, and the creams of tartar were by far the most commonly fraudulent; 16 of the 24

49. "Repression of Adulteration in America," *Sanitary Record* 3 n.s. (September 15, 1881), p. 98. See also *Third Annual Report,* Mass. (January 1882), p. xlvii.

50. *Second Annual Report,* N.Y., p. 595.

51. Chandler to Harris, December 7, 1882, Chandler Papers; *Third Annual Report,* N.Y., p. 99. One tartar case was dropped because of the grocer's illness, two grocers were twice charged with selling adulterated tartar, and the same two were also charged with selling adulterated mustard.

samples tested were adulterated, since "its comparatively high price renders it an article of very general adulteration."[52]

The test case was chosen from among the cream-of-tartar arrests partly because terra alba lent itself to simple analysis and would make for a clear presentation in court, and because Colonel Prentice was seeking a conviction without complications related to the healthfulness of the product. In addition, cream of tartar was felt by Prentice to have an advantage over the mustard or coffee cases because it was sold by druggists as well as grocers and was therefore listed in the *United States Pharmacopoeia.* Prentice calculated that if the retailer was charged with selling an adulterated drug, rather than an adulterated grocery item, it would be easier to prove that an established standard had been violated. After all, the law specified that officinal drugs must conform to the U.S.P. definition, while no official standard existed for cream of tartar as a food.

The case selected was that of Henry Fulle, whose cream of tartar tested out as being 92 percent gypsum, with the remainder tartaric acid, a cheaper and more acidic substitute for the genuine ingredient. Predictably, both *Sanitary Engineer* and *American Grocer* applauded the arrests, reminding the retailers that they had had ample time to learn about the law. *Sanitary Engineer* conceded that it "was doubtless true" that the retailers did not know their products were adulterated, and urged that the Board clarify the law by issuing a list of exemptions and standards "at the earliest possible moment." Still, both papers left unresolved the obvious question: "Would it not have been better to have commenced with the manufacturers of impure articles of food, rather than with the retailer?"[53]

The Grocers' Union conducted a stormy meeting three days after the arrests were made, one of the speakers declaring that "there was hardly a groceryman who understood how to adulterate such an article as cream of tartar, a proof of the grocer's innocence and helplessness in the matter." The animated discussion that followed was all in this vein: that the retail grocer was at

52. *Second Annual Report,* N.Y., pp. 559–73. See Chandler to Tucker, January 23, 1883, Chandler Papers, on the term "terra alba" misused by Dr. Love.

53. *American Grocer,* November 21, 1882, p. 1354; *Sanitary Engineer,* December 14, 1882, p. 30; *American Grocer,* December 14, 1882, p. 1296.

the mercy of both the wholesaler and the Board. Although it was agreed at this meeting that all manufacturers and wholesalers should follow the "house of Thurber" example of affixing guarantees of purity upon their products,[54] the retailers soon took a less charitable attitude toward Thurber and other wholesalers.

Thurber had been a welcome guest at a recent meeting of the Union, insisting that "there is no competition so objectionable as an unfair or dishonest one," and urging the cooperation of all legitimate businessmen in enforcing the adulteration law. But at a meeting of the Union soon after the arrests the members took a much stronger position regarding the culpability of the manufacturers and wholesalers: "If any arrests are to be made, they ought to be arrested." Veritable war was declared against the wholesalers, and Thurber was not exempted. "I understand," said the principal speaker, "that Mr. Thurber refused to give . . . a guarantee when a member of this Union wanted to buy a new brand of his spices. I am also informed that a very prominent wholesale house in this city had engineered this whole adulteration law, and is pushing it at present in actually furnishing the State Board of Health with names and addresses, whom and where to arrest!"[55] Although the accusation almost certainly went too far, it clearly was Thurber's "wholesale house" to which the retailer was referring.

The *German-American Grocer*, edited by John Fredericks and described as "the official organ of the New York Retail Grocers' Union," continued to record the anger and determination of the retailers. After all, by the end of December at least eight members of the Union were among those arrested. The retailers decided to hire an attorney to defend all members brought up on charges of "selling impure goods," although this resolution was cautiously amended to read "which said member has purchased in good faith as being pure, paying a fair price for them." Meanwhile *Sanitary Engineer* disingenuously denied that the Board's policy was "a persecution of the retail grocers": "It does seem a little hard that the grocer who supposes the goods he sells to be pure, should be prosecuted before the manufacturer who fraudu-

---

54. *American Grocer*, December 14, 1882, p. 1296.

55. *Sanitary Engineer*, September 21, 1882, p. 328; *German-American Grocer*, December 30, 1882, p. 3687. The speaker was Mr. M. Hahn.

lently adulterates the goods. At the same time such a course seems quite unavoidable."[56]

This argument was obviously rejected by the grocers. A typical response was an anonymous letter in the *German-American Grocer,* by correspondent "H.F.," who, it may be assumed, was Henry Fulle, whose court date was now set. "H.F." justifiably complained: "If that is the proper interpretation of the adulteration law, a more ridiculous law could hardly be imagined." The next issue of the paper reported that a committee of the Union had brought their complaint to Professor Chandler, who argued that the Board had found it "impracticable to pursue any other course than the one adopted." In this unenviable situation the retailers' "own" newspaper, Thurber's *American Grocer,* was cold comfort, repeating, at the very time the trial began, that "to avoid trouble under the new law simply requires that retailers shall sell pure food. Otherwise they invite arrest and have no one but themselves to blame."[57]

Yet on the first day of the trial Henry T. Atwater, the Union's lawyer, was accompanied by two attorneys hired by a coalition of manufacturers and wholesalers—a coalition that presumably did *not* include Thurber.[58] Chandler commented, in a letter to Harris, that he and Prentice had "found some of the best counsel in the State retained by the manufacturers to defend the retail dealers." The *German-American Grocer* strongly objected to this situation, feeling that the members coming up for trial had given "the wholesalers and manufacturers a chance to smuggle themselves into this trial, and through their able attorneys, [ex-] Judges Beach and Flammer, to divert the real issue into a question of unconstitutionality of the law in question." Fredericks wanted the cases "tried on their own merits. If the wholesalers want to fight the law, let them do so; but the retailers ought not to be mixed up with such a course, which naturally creates the

56. *Sanitary Engineer,* December 28, 1882, p. 78; *German-American Grocer,* December 30, 1882, p. 3687.

57. *German-American Grocer,* December 30, 1882, p. 3688; January 6, 1883, n.p.; *American Grocer,* January 4, 1883, p. 8.

58. It is not possible to determine the membership of this coalition. Fulle bought the cream of tartar from James E. Armstrong, and presumably Armstrong and other wholesalers who would be named by the defendants hired the lawyers to assist Atwater, with Fulle's permission.

impression that manufacturers, wholesalers and retailers combined together to defeat the law, which, so far as the latter are concerned, is not the case, as they want to sell only pure goods."[59]

After a postponement, so that the three attorneys could confer, the Fulle case took two more days to be heard. On the basis that he had sold an adulterated drug, Fulle was convicted and fined ten dollars. At the trial, however, counsel Beach had argued that "he represented a large number of merchants who had applied for and had long been in constant expectation of information and instruction from the State and local Boards of Health concerning their right to sell cream of tartar, but such had never been received."[60] Surely the Board now had to issue pronouncements on standards and exemptions, for by Prentice's own reasoning, until such standards were set the Board would be obliged to continue prosecuting only adulterators of U.S.P. pharmaceuticals.

By this time Chandler was also under fire from members of his own Board. He wrote a defensive letter to Elisha Harris: "We have not fined the milkmen $35,000 in the last ten years without acquiring a great deal of experience in this kind of litigation, and we have learned that it is impossible to reach the wholesale dealers except through the retailers." Seeking additional support, Chandler also wrote to Meyer at this time, complaining that *Sanitary Engineer* had not devoted enough space to the Fulle trial.[61]

At its January meeting the Board finally agreed upon a short list of exemptions and standards. The Board would permit a coffee/chicory mix as long as at least half was coffee and no other substances were added, and it allowed a similar mix of mustard and flour, forbidding "any coloring matter." In both cases the product had to be properly labeled as to both contents and proportions. The Board also fixed a standard for vinegar. But having made these three rulings, "the Board deems it inexpedient at present to authorize any other mixture or fix any other stan-

59. Chandler to Harris, January 4, 1883, Chandler Papers; *German-American Grocer,* January 6, 1883, n.p.

60. *New York Times,* January 9, 1883, January 10, 1883.

61. Chandler to Harris, January 25, 1883, Chandler to Meyer, January 27, 1883, Chandler Papers.

dards." Chandler had asked for greater latitude from his colleagues but was outvoted.[62]

There was an immediate and angry response from both retailers and wholesalers, complaining about the labeling restrictions and the lack of exemption for many other standard food items. But it was the support of "the best and most honorable manufacturers of food products"—presumably including F. B. Thurber—that Chandler worried about, not that of the retailers. Chandler brought the matter to Board President Moore:

> if we insist upon the position we have taken in the matter it will array in opposition to us the very persons who secured the passage of the law. As I am almost the only member of the Board who comes in contact with the manufacturers, it is very difficult for the other members of the Board to realize the conditions surrounding the question. I think it would be extremely desirable to hold a session in New York and make arrangements to have the manufacturers come before the Board and state their case themselves. . . . I think we should keep the meeting private as otherwise the reporters would get hold of it and these manufacturers would be paraded in the newspapers as adulterators.[63]

With Moore's approval, Chandler planned the meeting for February 24. He wrote to Harris that four of the analysts would be present and explained to Moore that he wanted members of the Board to hear "the arguments of the business men." It was Chandler's difficult chore to sway the Board members and analysts to a more probusiness position so as to retain the support of Thurber and the other large manufacturers, and still make a show of force in regard to the law. "I think if we can manage the exemptions clause of the law so as to secure the cooperation of those manufacturers who appear to be willing to aid us, we shall have no difficulty in making a success of the whole movement."[64]

62. *American Grocer,* February 1, 1883, p. 225; *Sanitary Engineer,* February 1, 1883, p. 200.

63. Chandler to Moore, February 5, 1883, Chandler Papers.

64. Chandler to Harris, February 20, 1883, Chandler to Moore, February 20, 1883, Chandler Papers.

Now that Chandler had established the power of the Board by making an example of some of the retailers, he had to establish his supremacy over his sanitarian colleagues on the Board itself. Meyer cooperated by editorializing against the excessive restrictions—the "needless interference with trade"—of the Board's unilateral decisions on exemptions. He urged more permissive standards, cautioning that the Board should "avoid unnecessary antagonisms." Presumably he was reflecting not only Chandler's position but Thurber's as well.[65]

Despite the confidentiality planned for the new meeting, Chandler sent notice of the event to Meyer, asking him to print it in *Sanitary Engineer*. Elisha Harris questioned this decision, but Chandler responded that, since the *Sanitary Engineer* "makes a specialty of this sort of thing," the notice "would reach the proper persons." Yet he repeated that reporters must not be admitted and urged that Harris "leave the whole matter to me." He sent Meyer a package of invitations to distribute "where they will do the most good," and he hired a private stenographer to take verbatim minutes but keep them secret "till they are wanted . . . although there might not be anything which is particularly secret."[66]

Chandler decided to keep the more controversial food products out of the discussion entirely. Former senator Roscoe Conkling, who had been hired to protect the interests of Thurber's oleomargarine company, asked Chandler whether standards for this product would be discussed at the meeting. Chandler, well aware of the special problems of the Commercial Manufacturing Company, decided that such arguments "would be ruled out of order." Chandler felt that this first, delicate meeting was not the place to push the demands of the company, although Chandler too had been in the pay of Commercial Manufacturing for some time.[67]

Although "newspaper representatives were excluded" from the

65. *Sanitary Engineer,* February 8, 1883, p. 225.
66. Chandler to Harris, February 20, 1883 (second letter for that date), Chandler to Meyer, February 21, 1883, Chandler to James W. Tooley, February 23, 1883, Chandler Papers.
67. Chandler to Conkling, February 23, 1883, Chandler Papers. See chap. 11 below on Conkling and oleomargarine.

meeting, John Fredericks gained admission as a representative of the New York and the Brooklyn retailers' associations.[68] The representatives of *American Grocer* and *Sanitary Engineer* were not, apparently, considered "newspaper" people at all, and both journals presented full coverage of the meeting. The manufacturers and wholesalers invited to the meeting were asked to vote on certain key questions, and then the Board met and passed new resolutions, taking their opinions into consideration.

The coffee standard was amended to allow chicory, peas, or cereal as diluents as long as half the mixture consisted of coffee. The mustard standard was amended so as to allow turmeric coloring, and the minimum percentage of mustard was reduced to 40 percent. In both cases, content labeling would be required, but only the percentage of the main ingredient, i.e., the coffee or the mustard, need be given. One month later the governor, as required by law, approved the resolutions.[69] Even though the full Board ruled on only these two products, Chandler had established himself and the wholesalers as the stewards of the law, forcing the sanitarians to acquiesce to their judgment.

From the retailers' point of view the most important achievement of the meeting was a concession from the Board: "We were successful in exacting from the State Board of Health the unanimous consent that in the future it would prosecute the wholesale merchants from whom adulterated goods are bought, instead of the retailers, providing the latter are willing to furnish the evidence, and were acting in good faith."[70] The value of this concession is debatable. The law explicitly instructed the Board to investigate, obtain samples, and bring charges in cases of suspected adulteration. Yet here the retailers would be obliged to do the Board's work for it. Also, how might the Board weigh the "good faith" of the complaining retailer? In any event, whatever the sincerity of the commitment at this time, the Board never honored its pledge.

But if the retailers were unable to sway Chandler from his path, the court system now challenged either his wisdom or his

68. *German-American Grocer,* March 3, 1883, p. 3831.
69. Notes in Chandler Papers; *Sanitary Engineer,* March 1, 1883, p. 300; *American Grocer,* March 1, 1883, p. 445; *Sanitary Engineer,* April 5, 1883, p. 421.
70. *German-American Grocer,* March 3, 1883, p. 3831.

honesty. On February 23 Judge Cowing of the Court of General Sessions reversed the conviction of Henry Fulle and ordered a new trial. This decision was based on a technicality. While the Board had brought charges against Fulle for having sold the cream of tartar as an adulterated *drug,* Fulle's original attorney— Atwater, who had been hired by the Grocers' Union—had argued that Fulle had clearly sold the tartar as a *food.* Judge Cowing accepted this appeal, and also found that it had not been proven that Fulle had "criminal intent." But Cowing had gone much further: "if the State Board of Health really desires to put a stop to the practice of food adulteration and clear the worthless and deleterious stuff from the market, the proper course to take is to prosecute the manufacturers directly and not allow them to escape while the retail dealers, who are the minor offenders, are very indifferently and weakly attacked."[71]

The Cowing decision had repercussions within the Board. Harris, who had been critical of Chandler's policy, now redoubled his protests. Chandler responded, arguing with a strange lack of logic, "Just as the physician and surgeon are liable to be sued for mal practice, so the retailer is liable to be punished for neglecting to supply honest articles to his customers" even if "he bought the goods supposing them to be pure." Professor Chandler continued to insist that his policy of prosecuting the retailers was correct: "No other plan is at all feasible." A month later Chandler was still being criticized by Harris, who had apparently persuaded Erastus Brooks that something was wrong with Chandler's strategy. Chandler once again responded that his success in prosecuting milk dealers justified the same approach for retail grocers. He insisted that "we can not get evidence against the wholesale dealer," and he expressed the hope that "you and Mr. Brooks will realize that in a new enterprise of this kind we have to make haste slowly."[72]

Meanwhile, some of the other retailers who had been indicted in December were brought to trial. They pleaded guilty, paying a nominal fine of ten dollars. The State Board, during the entire tenure of Professor Chandler—until November 1883—had a rec-

71. *New York Tribune,* February 24, 1883; *New York Times,* February 24, 1883.
72. Chandler to Harris, March 2, 1883, April 12, 1883, Chandler Papers.

ord of indicting a total of twenty retailers for violation of the Food and Drug Act. All the indictments were made in the one month of December 1882. Only five men were tried and convicted. Ironically, the "crimes" of four of them were decriminalized after their indictment by the Board's announcement of new standards for mustard and coffee. In addition, in all of 1883, the Board inspectors had only six dealers indicted for selling adulterated milk. No food manufacturer or wholesaler, nor any milk processor, was arrested.[73]

73. *Sanitary Engineer,* March 1, 1883, p. 300; *Fourth Annual Report,* N.Y., pp. 260, 267–68. The figure given in this 1884 report—eight convictions—has been adjusted to account for multiple charges against the same defendants. Fulle's conviction, which was ultimately reversed, is also counted in the *Report,* but subtracted in the present study.

10

Enforcement: One Man's Poison

By the time Chandler left office, in November 1883, and began to work more intensively for the interests of private corporations, not only the popular press but leaders in the sanitary movement were reassessing the question of enforcement. Chandler's friend Newton, in a speech to the American Public Health Association, confessed his disillusionment:

> I am afraid that we place too much trust in laws themselves. Some people with whom I have talked on this subject seemed to labor under the delusion that the moment a law is placed on the statute-books a moral revolution takes place, and that the end sought for would be attained without more trouble. I once had great faith in laws myself. . . . But one hour on the witness stand . . . dispelled the delusion, and I came to the conclusion that there was no such a thing as justice any more.
>
> With this experience in mind, I would say that the only way to prove the value of our food laws is to enforce them more vigorously.[1]

When F. B. Thurber reviewed Newton's speech in his new newspaper, *Justice,* he ignored this sense of disenchantment, merely stating, "Dr. Newton is right in his conclusion that the only way to test the value of our food laws is to enforce them

1. William K. Newton, "The Sanitary Control of the Food Supply," *Public Health Papers and Reports* 9 (1883), p. 157.

vigorously."[2] The remainder of Thurber's two columns repeatedly stressed the harmlessness of adulteration, and attacked sensationalism. While this perspective may once have been effective, it rang hollow three years after the passage of the National Board of Trade law.

Was prosecution the key to stopping adulteration, or had Chandler been right in his private memo that "few prosecutions will be necessary"? Involved in this question is the motivation of the experts empowered to enforce the new laws. Chandler's activities and behavior were surely not unique. When he began working for the old Metropolitan Board of Health he apparently worked without compensation for the first few months; when the position of chemist to the Board was created for Chandler in 1867, his pay was $2,000. Unhappy with this amount, Chandler sought an increase, but was informed by Dr. Harris in no uncertain terms that "the salary of the Chemist *is fixed.*" In 1883, as president of the Health Department and an officer of the State Board, Chandler's annual pay had risen to a very respectable $6,500.[3]

His teaching pay probably added about as much again to his income.[4] It is doubtful, however, that Chandler kept his three teaching positions, or that he fought so vigorously for the presidency of the Board, both in 1873 and 1883, simply for the remuneration. Men of Chandler's training and ambition sought such positions partly, no doubt, out of a sense of public responsibility, but also for prestige, and because such positions enhanced the opportunity for private consulting work. The reputability bestowed upon Chandler by his titles surely facilitated his success in obtaining hundreds of such jobs, for which he was very well paid.

2. *Justice,* October 18, 1884, p. 7.

3. Robert L. Larson, "Charles Frederick Chandler, His Life and Work" (Ph.D. diss., Columbia University, 1950), pp. 68, 70; Harris to Chandler, May 20, 1869, Chandler Papers.

4. *New York Herald,* May 13, 1881, at a time when there was once again much criticism of the Board's inactivity, claimed that Chandler was receiving $10,000 a year from Columbia. This was probably an exaggeration, since the *Herald* was complaining that Chandler was being paid too much for his Board post, and devoting too little time to it. The Office of the Secretary of Columbia University was unable to confirm this figure, but said (personal communication) that it was possible that Chandler had received that much. Chandler worked gratuitously at the College of Pharmacy.

A recent periodical article describing the historical value of the Chandler collection at Columbia University stresses that: "Chandler's life-style was essentially that of the New York City clubman at the turn of the century. . . . In addition, the collection also contains the household bills and receipts for Chandler's two homes in Manhattan . . . and his summer home at Westhampton, Long Island. The collection, therefore, gives important details of the costs and problems of living the affluent life in a New York brownstone between 1880 and 1925."[5] The funds for this "affluent life" did not come from Chandler's more public occupations. At a time when an unskilled worker was earning less than $400 annually, when the wages of skilled craftsmen were about $2 a day, and an urban physician in general practice typically received $1,000 to $2,000 in fees each year, one contemporary estimate of Chandler's annual income from private consultation alone was $25,000.[6]

It took great care to thread the narrow path between private consultation and public service, especially when the majority of the companies employing Chandler were involved in manufacturing the very items that Chandler had been appointed to supervise and regulate. The polite rivalry that later developed between Chandler and Dr. Harvey W. Wiley, which repeatedly pitted the two men against each other regarding enforcement of the Pure Food and Drug Act of 1906,[7] was ethically unimpeachable. After 1883 Chandler was free to advise corporations resisting regulation. But, while he was president of the Health Department, how disinterested could Chandler have been in rendering judgments on products he had been paid to endorse, or for which he testified in court cases?

Yet Chandler sometimes roundly condemned chemists who allowed their names to be used for product endorsements. For example, he sent a very interesting reprimand to Jesse P. Battershall, the United States customs analyst for the Port of New York:

5. Margaret W. Rossiter, "The Charles F. Chandler Collection," *Technology and Culture* 18:2 (April 1977), p. 223.

6. *Historical Statistics of the United States* (Washington, 1975), pp. 165–67; Paul Starr, *The Social Transformation of American Medicine* (New York, 1982), pp. 84–85; *Truth,* May 1, 1883. See Larson, pp. 135–36.

7. Larson, pp. 226ff., especially p. 229.

I have been dreadfully mortified to see your name attached to a certificate for porous plasters. How could you do such an imprudent thing? It will prejudice every chemist in the country against you. One of the plaster men came to me and I declined, under any circumstances, to give such a certificate, and when he asked me to recommend somebody else I told him that no respectable chemist would give him such a certificate, unless he was dreadfully pressed for money.

Two or three certificates of that kind will ruin your reputation.[8]

In this era each of the new professions developed a "code of ethics," not to restrict the profitability of the profession, but to lend it a certain dignity. The new professions disdained mere materialism, and they replaced commercial advertising with "degrees, diplomas, and honorary awards."[9] From Chandler's perspective, if the professional chemist was employed to perform a legitimate task, such as the chemical analysis of a product, his testimony—the technical results of his investigation—became the property of his employer. Battershall had committed the sin of allowing his name to be used without the specific employment of his technical skills. Chandler did not consider this a respectable use of a professional's training, expertise, and reputation.

In this genesis of professionalism, new to American society in the postwar period, many naive errors of judgment and many ethical difficulties must have arisen: the Chandler/Ricketts sugar imbroglio is but one example. Dr. Squibb had warned of the dependence of medical men upon their pharmaceutical suppliers; in 1883 Professor Leeds similarly warned sanitarians that, since businessmen could pay more than government for professional services, "most of the so-called chemical experts . . . are desirous of being in the employ of the manufacturers and not of the state," in suits brought under the new adulteration laws.

Leeds also repeated what Newton had said: what was needed now was not "information concerning facts, or the passage of

8. Chandler to Battershall, May 23, 1883, Chandler Papers.
9. Burton J. Bledstein, *The Culture of Professionalism* (New York, 1976), pp. 95–96.

new laws," but enforcement. To accomplish this, Leeds urged "the appointment in each state of a public analyst of high professional attainments, undoubted honesty, and secure of honorable pay."[10] But surely this is what the people of New York thought they already *had*.

Certainly, if any food item apart from milk required prompt and rigorous supervision, it was confectionery. Sharples had declared, "No article of food is so liable to be injuriously adulterated as candy." Dr. Smart, in the *National Board of Health Bulletin* Supplement No. 11, had not only reviewed prior investigations of candy colorings but also conducted tests of his own. All the studies agreed that confectionery was frequently colored with dangerous materials, most commonly chromate of lead in yellow-colored candies. Dr. Pitt had also examined candies, for his part of the New York State Board of Health's 1882 *Report,* and had found seven of the ten yellow samples tested similarly contaminated.[11]

In view of the obvious danger presented by candy adulterated with lead coloring, the lack of concern on the part of the Board is most peculiar. Pitt's few lines in his report merely confirmed the presence of this poison. Dr. Colby's "Supplementary Report on Sugars," printed to ameliorate the inadequacies of Pitt's work, never mentioned confectionery. The 1883 Board *Report* reveals that only one sample of candy was purchased and tested in all of the previous year. (It was found to be unadulterated.) Harris's introductory remarks in this *Report* emphasized the tartar, mustard, and coffee cases that the Board had brought to court, claiming, peculiarly, that these "were instances of dangerous substitutions and frauds." Nor can this lack of concern about poisoned candy be explained away by Harris's plea for additional funds for the administration of the adulteration law,

10. Albert R. Leeds, "The Adulteration of Foods," *Public Health Papers and Reports* 9 (1883), p. 170.

11. Stephen P. Sharples, "Adulteration of Food," in *A Treatise on Hygiene and Public Health,* ed. Albert H. Buck (New York, 1879), 2: p. 363; Charles Smart, "Report of an Investigation to Determine the Prevalence of Adulteration . . ." in NBH *Bulletin,* Supplement No. 11 (Washington, D.C., January 1, 1881), p. 5; "Report of the Sanitary Committee," in *Second Annual Report of the State Board of Health of New York* (Albany, 1882), p. 601.

when one considers that the Board did make 286 purchases, including 33 additional samples of cream of tartar, in that year. Similarly, in 1884, despite the continuing lack of funds, a number of miscellaneous samples were purchased for testing, but no candies were included.[12]

Surprisingly, the authorities in both New Jersey and Massachusetts seem to have been similarly unimpressed with the need to investigate candies. The Board reports for New Jersey, from 1880 to 1885, completely ignored candy adulterations. In Massachusetts Dr. Edward S. Wood, the new analyst of food for the Board, simply dismissed the problem, stating that "poisonous colors are not now, so far as I can learn, commonly found in candies." Yet Wood gave no statistics and did not report on samples tested. Later *Reports* virtually ignored confectionery. Of the 119 prosecutions initiated by the Massachusetts Board between December 1, 1884, and May 31, 1886, only 3 were for selling adulterated candies.[13]

The Brooklyn Board, by its own admission, performed virtually no work relating to food adulteration beyond routine milk and meat inspections prior to 1884. The next year, however, the Brooklyn Board began a broad range of inspections, seeking evidence of *"injurious adulterations."* The Board inspector found one candy manufacturer using dye adulterated with chrome yellow. He confiscated the contaminated dye, but no suit was brought against the manufacturer upon his promise of future caution. The addresses of five retailers selling the candy (whose names were apparently supplied by the manufacturer) were published. But the *Report* several times stressed that this adulteration was unusual, and that the supply of candy was generally perfectly safe. The next year the Brooklyn Board inspected 183

12. *Third Annual Report of the State Board of Health of New York* (printed as *Assembly Document Number 110*, 1883), pp. 97, 36, 62; *Fourth Annual Report of the State Board of Health of New York* (printed as *Assembly Document Number 89*, 1884), p. 256. In 1883, more samples of cream of tartar were bought than any other item, presumably to lend credence to the Fulle prosecution. As the Board surely expected, most of the samples were adulterated.

13. *Fifth Annual Report of the State Board of Health, Lunacy, and Charity of Massachusetts. Supplement* (Boston, 1884), p. 128; *Seventh Annual Report of the State Board of Health, Lunacy, and Charity of Massachusetts. Supplement* (Boston, 1886), pp. 71, 87.

confectionery stores, but the *Report* provided no statistics on candy adulteration.[14]

The only intense campaign against chromate of lead in candies was conducted by the New York City Board, under its new chief sanitary inspector, Cyrus Edson. Edson was the son of Mayor Franklin Edson, and his appointment had been a blatantly political move, followed by considerable noise in the press. It may be that Edson needed to prove he was serious about the job, for in 1884 the Board destroyed 72,700 pounds of adulterated confectionery, which may well have been the inspiration for the sudden, though brief, activity of its sister board in Brooklyn.

Sanitary Engineer congratulated Edson upon his work but complained about the Board's refusal to publish the names of the offenders. Such publication would protect "the honest manufacturers" from being tarred with the same brush. *American Grocer* added a comment from "one of the leading manufacturers" to the effect that the guilty parties were surely "ignorant" of the injurious nature of their colorings. Though this observation was reminiscent of Professor Johnson's remark that no candy maker would desire "to kill his customers outright," it is of little assistance in explaining why, with these few exceptions, there was such slight concern about confectionery, considering that this was almost certainly the most common example of poisonous food adulteration to be found.[15]

The furor over the possibility of sugar bleached with tin acids that had hit the city by storm in 1878–1879 had pretty much died down by the end of the year. The reassurances by Chandler, and the efforts of Thurber and Havemeyer, may not have completely

14. *Annual Report of the Department of Health of the City of Brooklyn, 1884* [–1885] (Brooklyn, 1885), pp. 57, 66, 69, 74–75, 135–38; *Annual Report of the Department of Health of the City of Brooklyn for the Year 1886* (Brooklyn, 1887), p. 24.

15. Jesse P. Battershall, *Food Adulteration and Its Detection* (New York, 1887), p. 6; *Sanitary Engineer*, January 1, 1885, p. 104; *American Grocer*, January 1, 1885, p. 14. John Duffy, *A History of Public Health in New York City*, vol. 2, *1866–1966* (New York, 1974), p. 77, cites the non-reappointment of Chandler in 1883 as "the advent of politicization" of the Health Department. General Alexander Shaler took Chandler's place as president, while Edson was appointed as part of a "package deal."

cleared the air of the "discovery" by Dr. Ricketts of "tin" in De Castro and Donner's sugar. Still, the *Times* could deny, in October, that there had been any "possible foundation" for the excitement and could declare, "In sugars, adulterations of any kind are exceedingly rare."[16]

By 1880, however, a new alarm was being raised, concerning the possible presence of granulated glucose—what is today called "corn sweetener"—in cane sugars. Dr. Kedzie, it will be recalled, had found a majority of the syrups he tested, in 1874, to be adulterated with glucose. Dr. Leed's November 1879 speech to the Academy of Sciences had repeated Kedzie's conclusion, and Kedzie himself reprinted his findings in the NBH *Bulletin* Supplement No. 6, published in early 1880. Both Kedzie and Leeds, it is true, categorically denied that white granulated sugars could be so adulterated without its being obvious to the merest tyro. But Kedzie had admitted that "adulteration by glucose is more feasible" in brown sugars.[17] Both Kedzie and Leeds, however, insisted that glucose was perfectly harmless.

But by the beginning of 1880 Angell's accusations had been well circulated: not only was even the whitest sugar adulterated with glucose, but glucose was a rank poison. Some foundation had inadvertently been laid for these claims by Sharples. He had said, in his chapter in Buck's book, "The glucose itself is harmless; it is only its impurities that are to be feared."[18] Angell, in addition to claiming that glucose was commonly made from rags and sawdust, stated that the sulphuric acid used to convert starch to glucose sugar could sometimes leave a deadly residue. Although these claims were denied by most chemists, there was really no way for them to be sure, for no comprehensive study of glucose had ever been undertaken.

Then, in April, claims of widespread adulteration of sugar with glucose were made, not by either Angell or the chemists, but by four of the largest New York sugar refiners themselves. They announced that current rumors of the sale of this "new process" sugar were true, though they were not personally involved. But

16. *New York Times,* October 26, 1879.
17. Robert C. Kedzie, "The Adulteration and Deterioration of Food," NBH *Bulletin,* Supplement No. 6 (Washington, D.C., 1880), p. 32.
18. Buck, *Treatise on Hygiene,* p. 363.

the refiners warned that unless this trade was prohibited they would have to participate in the fraud. New technology had created the basis for a tremendous expansion of the sugar industry in the 1870s. New entrepreneurs entered the business, and soon price competition and production capacity that exceeded demand ate away profit margins. Several manufacturers attempted to form a pool at this very time, but these cooperative arrangements were unwieldy and were doomed to collapse. The large New York refiners, faced with a very heavy investment in plant and equipment, could not cut back production. They warned that they could not profitably compete with the adulterators and called for protective "legislation in every State."[19] It was this new sugar scandal that would lead the New York sugar interests to support so wholeheartedly Meyer's lobbying activities in Albany in 1881.

At the height of the controversy a reporter from the *Evening Post* interviewed a number of sugar merchants, and quoted Professor Chandler at some length. Chandler noted the chemical fact that we all "eat glucose with every mouthful we take; every bit of starchy food we take turns into glucose." In reality, of course, Chandler was twisting the facts; he was trying to establish that glucose was a harmless and "natural" food, but in the process he ignored the substantial difference between the commercial processing of corn to produce glucose and the natural digestive processes.[20]

Yet he might safely have made this claim and his additional statement that there was no cause to fear sulphuric acid in glucose, but he foolishly added, with dry wit, "So long as the mixers only put one part of glucose to five parts of sugar there need be no trouble. When they get to mixing one part of sugar to five parts of glucose it may be time for some one to protest."[21] Readers could legitimately wonder how effectively the new State

19. *Grocer,* April 9, 1880, pp. 509–10; Glenn Porter, *The Rise of Big Business, 1860–1910* (New York, 1973), pp. 66–68, citing Alfred Eichner, *Emergence of Oligopoly: Sugar Refining as a Case Study* (Baltimore, 1969); see *American Grocer,* April 8, 1880, p. 925. The sugar refiners formed a trust in 1887, and reorganized as the American Sugar Refining Company in 1891.

20. *Grocer,* December 30, 1880, p. 838; and see *New York Times,* December 30, 1880.

21. Ibid.

Board would protect the health, if not the pockets, of the people. The public might have been further upset had it known that Chandler was privately employed by three of the New York sugar refiners.

The state legislature, in response to the demands of the refiners, passed a bill to prevent fraud in sugar and syrup at about the same time it passed the NBT adulteration bill. But Governor Cornell vetoed it, partly because of some uneven wording, but basically because the bill was made "unnecessary" by passage of the general law. Still, by this time the people had received new reassurances about glucose from other sources. The U.S. Department of Agriculture reported glucose to be "perfectly healthy." The NBH *Bulletin* Supplement No. 11, by Charles Smart, testified to some adulteration of dark sugars, but affirmed that none of the samples tested "show any free sulphuric acidity or excess of iron or lime. They are indeed a wholesome article of food."[22]

Dr. Pitt, to whom Chandler had assigned the sugars for the extensive State Board *Annual Report,* devoted four pages to an explanation of the nature of glucose and the processes followed in three glucose factories in Buffalo, New York. Pitt's report tended to support the assertions of Harvey Wiley, who warned of the possibility of contamination in glucose, which he felt was being manufactured in "immense quantities."[23] An editorial in *Science* had contrasted the opinions of Leeds and Wiley, Wiley contending that adulterations of sugar must exist on a large scale because of the sheer extent of glucose manufacture. Leeds, addressing the American Chemical Society, had stated that he

22. *American Grocer,* April 14, 1881, p. 845; *New York Times,* July 13, 1881; *Report of the Commissioner of Agriculture for the Years 1881 and 1882* (Washington, D.C., 1882), p. 544; NBH *Bulletin,* Supplement No. 11, p. 3. Smart may have been the first chemist to explain that a form of glucose, or "reducing sugar," occurs naturally in syrup and molasses.

23. Harvey W. Wiley, "Glucose and Grape-Sugar," *Popular Science Monthly* 19 (June 1881), pp. 251–57, notes that use of sulphurous acid in bleaching would be dangerous, creating free sulphuric acid in the finished product. But Wiley noted that he had never found a sample of this kind, and he declared the glucose of the marketplace "wholesome." H. W. Wiley, "Mixed Sugars," *Proceedings of the American Association for the Advancement of Science, 30th Meeting* (August 1881), pp. 61–64, estimated production at 1,500 barrels a day, and warned about fraudulent sale by retailers. See also Oscar E. Anderson, *The Health of a Nation* (Chicago, 1958), p. 22.

failed to find such extensive adulteration. *Science* responded: "We believe that Professor Leeds reported correctly on the samples as he found them; but, if Professor Wiley is correct, the former must have been very fortunate, or, perhaps, unfortunate, in the selection of his samples."[24]

Pitt concluded that "physiologically considered, glucose, pure and uncontaminated with other compounds, is certainly a good and wholesome food." He then devoted a total of only one page to sugar, maple syrup, honey, and confectionery. The small amounts of glucose present in his samples could be accounted for by natural causes. But Pitt tested only fifteen samples of sugar. Professor Colby's supplementary report, prepared on short notice upon Chandler's request, was a more direct attempt to respond to the growing public concern over the actual status of sugar. Colby tested 116 samples of commercial sugars and concluded that "the sugars now in the market are free from the long list of insoluble mineral matter alleged to be used in former times" and from any contamination by "organic impurities." Several of the white sugars had been bleached, but with harmless ultramarine; Colby never even mentioned the possibility of tin acids being used for this purpose.[25]

All forty-nine samples of white sugar were pure, but four of the sixty-seven brown sugars had been adulterated with glucose. This finding led Colby to claim that "the use of glucose as an adulterant is practiced to a considerable extent," a peculiar conclusion to reach on the basis of 6 percent adulteration among the brown sugars tested. Moreover, the consecutive numbers for these four samples of brown sugar would indicate that they came from the same source. If this is true—and the normal sampling technique followed in this period would indicate that it was—Colby's *actual* finding was that *one* merchant had added glucose to his cheap varieties of dark sugar.

Yet Colby went on to state very positively that "these so called 'mixed sugars' are sold in the wholesale market under certain trade names, such as 'New Process Sugar,' . . . which signify to

24. *Science: A Weekly Record of Scientific Progress,* June 18, 1881, p. 281.
25. *Second Annual Report,* N.Y., pp. 596, 600–1. Pitt found one of the three syrups to contain artificial glucose, one of the three honeys similarly adulterated, and candy widely adulterated with glucose.

the purchaser their character. They are, however, usually disposed of in the retail trade as pure sugars. As most of these 'mixed sugars' are sent to the country, they are rarely to be found in the hands of retail city grocers." Colby was saying that the very fact that he was unable to find greater frequency of adulteration in New York City merely indicated that the adulterated sugars were sold in vast quantities elsewhere in the state. "Absence of evidence is not evidence of absence," but Colby made it into evidence of presence, as if he had been instructed that it was a "given" that glucose adulteration was very common—but only among dark sugars! Colby stressed not only that white sugars were completely unadulterated but also that the glucose present in the dark sugars was "not a question of a deleterious adulteration; but one of fraud."[26]

But there still had been no definitive study of glucose, and a bill was now pending before Congress "to tax and regulate" its manufacture and sale. Thus, at the very time that Colby was preparing his supplementary report, Chandler was being commissioned to participate in a federal study of corn sweetener. On April 27 the commissioner of the Office of Internal Revenue had written to the president of the National Academy of Sciences requesting an investigation of glucose by the Academy. In light of the pending bill, the government was interested not only in glucose's sweetening properties, but also, and especially, in "its deleterious effects when used as an article of food or drink."[27]

In addition to Chandler, the original committee members included Ira Remsen and George F. Barker, of the Academy. Barker, a noted chemist and physicist, was a professor at the University of Pennsylvania. There is no indication that he had any predisposition regarding glucose. Remsen, however, had written about the subject to Dr. Billings a year and a half earlier, after returning from his confrontation with Angell at the American Social Science Association meeting. At that time he wrote, "I know simply that glucose is now largely used in syrups and to

26. Ibid., pp. 604, 605, 607.
27. 47th Cong., 1st sess., January 16, 1882, H. R. 3170; Green B. Raum to William B. Rogers, April 27, 1882, copy in Chandler Papers. The bill initially proposed a tax of ten cents per pound or one dollar per gallon (in liquid form) on glucose.

some extent in sugars themselves."[28] Thus, though more concerned about the possibility of tin salts in bleached sugar, Remsen was apparently predisposed to regard glucose as an undesirable—though not necessarily an unhealthy—adulterant.

As for Chandler, he had just been hired by G. H. Nichols and Company, manufacturers of glucose, to testify on behalf of their product at hearings conducted by the House Ways and Means Committee, which was studying the glucose regulation bill. He was also approached by F. B. Thurber, probably the city's largest wholesale distributor of glucose, to use the facilities of either the city or the state boards to investigate arguments against discriminatory taxation of glucose. Thurber wanted Chandler to quash the allegations about its unwholesomeness, though he "would with pleasure join in the demand for restrictive legislation" if Chandler found that the accusations were justified.[29] (See figure 6.)

The final version of the Academy committee's *Report* contained a history of the industry, a study of the varieties of glucose manufactured, and an examination of the product's healthfulness. The *Report* completely exonerated glucose from any suspicion of being deleterious. It noted that "the manufacture of sugar from starch is a long-established industry, scientifically valuable and commercially important; second, that the processes which it employs at the present time are unobjectionable in their character, and leave the product uncontaminated; third, that the starch-sugar thus made and sent into commerce is of exceptional purity and uniformity of composition, and contains no injurious substances." Even "when taken in large quantities" there was no cause for worry.[30]

This glowing report ignored the fact that carelessness in the neutralization of the acid used in its manufacture *could* produce a

28. Remsen to Billings, September 10, 1880, Billings Papers.

29. G. H. Nichols to Chandler, March 2, 1882, F. B. Thurber to Chandler, April 27, 1882, Chandler Papers.

30. *Report on Glucose, Prepared by the National Academy of Sciences* (Washington, D.C., 1884), pp. 31–32. See also *A History of the First Half-Century of the National Academy of Sciences, 1863–1913* (Baltimore, 1913), pp. 293–94. The final report was not submitted until January 12, 1884; see Barker to Chandler, January 7, 1884, Remsen to Chandler, January 10, 1884, Chandler Papers, blaming Chandler for this delay. See Larson, "Chandler," pp. 202–3. Walter Evans had by this time replaced Raum as commissioner of internal revenue. The report was also signed by William H. Brewer and Wolcott Gibbs.

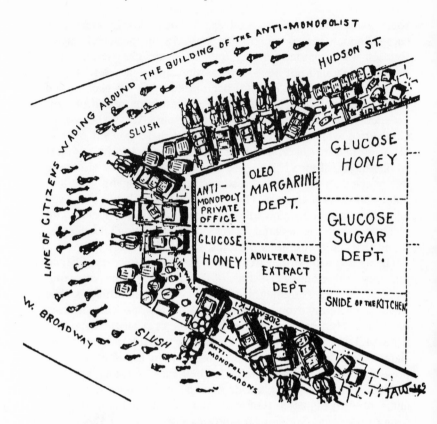

6. "The Home of the Anti-Monopolist." If this cartoon is compared with the Thurber letterhead in illustration 4, it becomes obvious that Thurber was the "anti-monopolist" in question. The cartoon reflects Thurber's notoriety, since neither the cartoonist nor the magazine identifies him by name. Such publicity probably influenced Thurber's "anti-adulteration" activities. From *Judge* 1:23 (April 1, 1881), p. 11.

harmful batch of glucose (especially since there was no legal regulation of production techniques), and that the clandestine substitution of glucose for cane sugar is a fraud. At best, glucose is about 60 percent as sweet as sugar. The "commercial" argument against restricting its manufacture or use could apply just as well to outrageously criminal activities—after all, money is invested, and people are employed, in a variety of antisocial activities. Yet after the preliminary report of the committee was issued on September 18, 1882, and glucose received this overwhelming endorsement from the Academy's elite committee of experts, no reputable chemist could very well object to the use of glucose, or to the committee's conclusions, without threatening his professional standing.

Consider, for example, William Newton. Newton made the point that ten pounds of glucose were manufactured per capita each year: "We naturally ask, What becomes of it? No one ever heard of a person asking for the substance at a grocery store; yet it is sold and consumed somewhere." Newton quoted Dr. Squibb's sarcastic comment that glucose "marks the progress of the age." He was aware that production errors could result in harmful contamination. He noted that when the New Jersey legislature tried to restrict its sale, Governor Ludlow vetoed the bill because glucose manufacture could be a boon to the "utilization of the corn crop." Ludlow reasoned: "Scientists of acknowledged ability and integrity have declared it to be a healthful article of food, and there is no reason why the result of its mixture with cane sugar should be marked 'adulterated,' as if it were a debasement or pollution." Yet, despite these observations, Newton concluded "that glucose may be considered a harmless article of food. As to the use of this article as an adulterant, I hold that it does not come under the jurisdiction of health officers."[31]

Dr. Leeds had recently denied the extensiveness of the glucose industry as an excuse for inaction against its use as an adulterant. Leeds now argued that the "extensive manufacture" of glucose had caused improvements in its scientific evaluation. Though Leeds noted its wide use "admixed" with other products, he chose not to label it an adulterant. Professor William H. Brewer of Yale, president of the Board of Health of New Haven and an added member of the Academy committee, presented a paper that treated glucose as a natural product in its own right, a "perfectly legitimate and honest" substance, used for fruit jellies, confectionery, canning, syrups, and beer. He categorized glucose as an "adulterant" only when used ("to a less extent than many have claimed") in cane sugar.[32] In line with this reasoning, the

31. Newton, "Sanitary Control," pp. 160–61.
32. Leeds, "Adulteration of Foods," p. 167; William H. Brewer, "Glucose in Its Sanitary Aspects," *Public Health Papers and Reports* 10 (1884), pp. 100–5.

third, fourth, and fifth *Annual Report*s of the New York State Board of Health never even mention glucose as an adulterant.

There was apparently only one chemist who chose to disagree with the Academy's conclusions. Dr. Edward S. Wood, Massachusetts analyst of food, while admitting the wholesomeness of glucose "when properly and carefully manufactured," noted that "when carelessly made it may . . . rightly be considered a dangerous article to be taken into the system." Wood warned that "disturbances of the digestion" would result if all the acid used in processing was not removed, and he pointed out the hazard of "the contaminations which are ordinarily present in commercial sulphuric acid." Wood tested four samples of commercial glucose. Three were "perfectly pure and wholesome," but the fourth "contained a very large amount of free sulphuric acid, and moreover, a large trace of arsenic."[33]

Alum—aluminum sulfate—is an astringent used from time immemorial by bakers to whiten and improve the texture of their goods. But for home baking in antebellum America alum was avoided. Homemakers purchased two separate powders, one an alkali, and the other a weak acid; the chemical combination of the two produced a gas that made dough porous. But the difficulty of achieving the correct proportion of the two ingredients with such home "chemistry" led to the establishment of companies that manufactured ready-mixed powders. In an age prior to the introduction of packaged breads most Americans still baked their own, even in urban areas where bakery shops offering home delivery were beginning to proliferate; the sale of baking ingredients was of significant commercial importance. The first company to produce the mixture on a large scale appears to have been the Royal Baking Powder Company, established in 1867. Royal used a combination of cream of tartar and bicarbonate of soda as the acid and alkali. This combination of ingredients could not be patented, and other companies soon manufactured the same product.

With the rising price of cream of tartar, however, a number of companies substituted alum; by 1879 the comparative wholesale prices were thirty cents per pound for pure cream of tartar, while alum sold for only three cents a pound. But in postwar America

33. *Fifth Annual Report,* Mass., pp. 127–28.

there was, at first, no agitation concerning the manufacture of alum baking powders. In fact, when the New York City Board of Health reported on bicarbonate of soda, cream of tartar, and the baking powder mixtures, in 1873, the only adulterations discovered involved flour and terra alba in some of the sodas and tartars.

The inspector, Elwyn Waller, dutifully reported that alum was traditionally "mentioned" as an adulterant of cream of tartar, but was "not detected in the samples purchased in this city."[34] Waller never discussed the possibility that the soda-tartar mixtures were adulterated with alum. Considering that studies conducted only a few years later would disclose that the overwhelming majority of the baking powders were alum mixes, it is difficult to credit Waller's statements, but perhaps the price differential had not, in 1872–1873, become significant enough to drive manufacturers to adulterate their product.

By 1879, however, a furor had arisen over the use of alum in baking powder. Virtually every chemist and sanitarian now agreed that commercial alum powders were irritants that could upset the mucous membranes of the stomach and intestines. In a short period of time an extensive literature on the subject had appeared. Both the Brooklyn and New York City boards of health had ruled alum deleterious. Waller had publicly condemned the product. Dr. Willard Parker, a respected surgical and sanitary pioneer, Dr. Alonzo Clark, president of the College of Physicians and Surgeons, Dr. William A. Hammond, former surgeon-general of the United States, Dr. E. A. Parkes, famous author of the first public hygiene manual, Dr. Lewis A. Sayre, founder of Bellevue Hospital Medical College, and a score of other leading medical and chemical experts had all publicly testified to the danger of alum.

Perhaps one of the inspirations for this aroused reaction was the fact that the great German chemist Baron von Liebig had conducted experiments indicating that alum was deleterious. But certainly the immediate cause of the furor was the publication, in the November 16, 1878, issue of *Scientific American* of an article by Dr. Henry A. Mott that drew attention to the prolif-

34. *Third Annual Report of the Board of Health of the Health Department of the City of New York, 1872–1873* (New York, 1873), pp. 292–94.

eration of alum baking powders, and called the substance an outright poison. What was not immediately apparent was that, in writing this article, Mott had been the employee of the Royal Baking Powder Company, and was paid by the company to discredit its competitors.

Mott exemplified the professional out for the main chance. Having once held a minor federal post, he liked to be called a "Government chemist." His business card tells his story well:

> DR. H. A. MOTT,
> Analytical and Consulting Chemist,
> Expert in Patent Cases,
> Scientific Investigation Conducted
> Chemical Advice to Manufacturing
> Establishments by the Year
> Analysis of Portable [sic] Waters and Articles of Commerce
>
> Office, 10 Spruce Street

Mott reported that most of the forty-two baking powders he had tested were adulterated with alum. He praised only the Royal powder by name, while providing analyses of four "deleterious" competitors. He rather disingenuously explained: "I do not mean by signalizing the Royal Baking Powder, that it is the only properly made powder on the market, as there may be others equally as good. I simply introduce it as I had to select one, and thought the one I had used in my kitchen for years, and which had always proved satisfactory, would be the best illustration."[35]

Scientific American was soon filled with responses to Mott's article. The manufacturers of Dooley's powder—one of those attacked by Mott—claimed that his analysis had been incorrect. The editors, evidently trying to get out from under a libelous situation, supported this protest: "Those who know the gentlemen in question will not need to be told that they would not be guilty of making and selling for public consumption an article either adulterated or injurious. The whole matter, indeed, seems,

---

35. Card in Chandler Papers; Henry A. Mott, "The Deleterious Use of Alum in Bread and Baking Powders—Alum Being Substituted For Cream of Tartar," *Scientific American* 39:20 (November 16, 1878), p. 308. Royal was an old hand at placing subtle advertising; see *American Grocer*, May 9, 1870, p. 191.

on examination, to resolve itself into a rivalry between different methods of producing baking powders; and in lauding one form, at the expense of another equally wholesome, Dr. Mott, we fear, lays his communication justly open to . . . criticism." Dr. R. O. Doremus, having been paid by Dooley's to analyze their product, was not quite so ready to assert that alum was an "equally wholesome" ingredient; he simply certified that Dooley's contained no alum "or any other deleterious substance."[36]

In the following issue of the magazine another manufacturer sarcastically expressed the hope that Mott's "services have been liberally requited" by Royal. "Professor Mott, in attempting to prove a fraud in food, had perpetrated a fraud in facts." Mott responded that he could not list all the healthful powders "and have my name on every baking powder can in the country, as I have been asked to do by a large number of manufacturers already." But, despite Mott's protests, it is clear that the trap that awaited all professionals in this commercializing society had been sprung, and Royal's strategy had backfired, because their chemist's objectivity was in question.[37]

Over the next few years, as this baking-powder war escalated, disinterested chemical and sanitarian evaluation of the poisonous nature of alum was exceedingly circumspect. Since the rules of governmental employment in this era did not prohibit potential conflicts of interest, few government chemists hesitated to undertake private commissions, either for Royal or for its competitors. In this instance the experts not directly employed by either side apparently believed that discretion was the better part of valor—or ethics. Their treatment of the entire alum question was typified by the conclusion of the Massachusetts State Board of Health: "Much has been written on each side of the question, without any very definite results having been arrived at."[38]

36. *Scientific American* 39:23 (December 7, 1878), p. 353.

37. *Scientific American* 39:24 (December 14, 1878), p. 376; *Scientific American* 39:26 (December 28, 1878), p. 404.

38. *Fourth Annual Report of the State Board of Health, Lunacy, and Charity of Massachusetts; Supplement* [July 1882] (Boston, 1883), p. 74. See also NBH Bulletin Supplement No. 11, p. 4; *Annual Report of the Commissioner of Agriculture for the Year 1878* (Washington, D.C., 1879), p. 135; Leeds, "Adulteration of Foods," p. 167.

After the publication of Mott's analyses, some alum powder companies hired Dr. R. O. Doremus and food "expert" Jabez Burns to present counter-arguments. Doremus, who now decided that alum was not, after all, deleterious, prepared a booklet in its defense, which he distributed to chemists, professional societies, and editors. At this point Royal decided that it required experts more prestigious than Mott (who continued in their employ, however), and asked him to hire his friend Professor Chandler to perform services for the company. Mott informed Chandler that Professor Henry Morton, president of the Stevens Institute of Technology, was already working for Royal. Mott wrote, "I am authorized by the Royal Baking Powder Co. to direct you to procure at once a can of Dooley's Baking Powder and submit the same to a quantitative analysis." Receipts in the Chandler papers indicate that in 1878–1879 he several times received checks from Royal for analytical work.[39]

Though Chandler soon began to receive requests from alum powder companies for analyses and/or testimonials on behalf of their products, there is no indication that Chandler was working both sides of the street. But a letter from one of these alum companies raised a particularly interesting point. Chandler had immediately responded to Mott's request, and sent Royal his analysis of Dooley and Brothers' powder. Royal's new advertisement cited Chandler's analysis, using his title "President of the New York City Board of Health" in their text. Dooley complained that "Royal Baking Powder Company advertise that their powder has the endorsement of the Board of Health—Will you please inform us if such is the fact."[40]

Considering the strongly worded letter that Chandler would sent to Dr. Battershall in 1883, this question should be examined: Where is the line between the expert's allowing his name and title to be used in an advertisement, and his being paid for an outright endorsement, if both achieve the same objective? As Dooley's letter indicated, to the public there was no distinction between the two practices. In 1883 Chandler judged that so long as the expert was "really" being paid for the use of his professional

39. Two letters from Mott to Chandler, November 18, 1878, Chandler Papers. For Burns's defense of alum, see *Grocer*, September 13, 1879, p. 374.
40. Dooley and Brothers to Chandler, November 26, 1878, Chandler Papers.

skills, there was no violation of ethics. But it is obvious that Chandler understood he was huckstering his title, not his analytical skills, because he charged Royal $250 for each of the analyses he conducted for them. This was ten times the going rate for a routine analysis by a qualified chemist.

Meanwhile, Mott was conducting an elaborate experiment on alum, this time with the open support of Royal. Mott fed alum to dogs, and then performed partial vivisection upon them to test the effects of their food. Mott read his paper before the American Chemical Society on January 8, and it was then published as an article in the February 7, 1880, issue of *Scientific American*. The experiment caused a sensation and was reported in most major newspapers and in a cross section of the professional press. It was certainly the most highly publicized food experiment of its time, unsurpassed until Professor Wiley conducted his famous "poison-squad" experiments of 1902–1907.[41]

Mott's experiment convinced the press that alum was an outright poison; the *Tribune* editorialized that it was "the most dangerous adulteration that a community has to guard against."[42] But from a scientific standpoint Mott's findings are questionable. Most of his observations were highly subjective and unaccompanied by quantitative support. Moreover, the amount of alum fed to the dogs far exceeded any conceivable normal intake. Their diet consisted exclusively of biscuits made from one quart of sifted flour, two cups of water, one tablespoon of butter, and a disproportionate twenty teaspoons of alum.

Nevertheless, Mott now put together a new sixty-page booklet that reviewed every previous scientific statement that threw doubt upon alum's healthfulness, plus an account of his "vivisection" experiment. This booklet was then widely distributed by

41. For example, *New York Times,* March 6, 1880; *American Grocer,* April 15, 1880, p. 987; *Sanitarian* 8 (1880), pp. 263–70. Wiley fed suspected "poisons"— questionable foods—to volunteers while continually monitoring their health. See Anderson, pp. 148–52; Harvey W. Wiley, *The History of a Crime Against the Food Law* (Washington, D.C., 1929), pp. 57–77, explains that "alum in any form should not be used in human food." Harvey W. Wiley, *An Autobiography,* (Indianapolis, 1930), p. 264–66, 268, gives an account of his difficulties in enforcing the law of 1906, particularly in opposition to Professor Ira Remsen's Referee Board, especially on the alum question.

42. *New York Tribune,* March 5, 1880.

Royal. In response, Jabez Burns published a scurrilous attack in his Chicago trade-paper, the *Spice Mill,* accusing Mott and Royal of trying to "dupe" the American public. Mott was accused of having been "bribed" to print his reports, and Royal of attempting to destroy competition by a "libelous and unprincipled" method of business. Mott was "a mercenary, unscrupulous individual" who endeavored to gull the public "by professing comprehensive scientific learning."[43]

With support from Royal, Mott decided to bring charges of slander against Burns. But Royal wanted the trial to be not just a civil suit, but also a testimonial for its product. To this end, while Burns hired Professor Doremus to support his own statements, Royal employed Chandler, Morton, Dr. Samuel W. Johnson of Yale, and Professor Joseph H. Raymond, Sanitary Superintendent of Brooklyn, to speak on the truthfulness of Mott's claims against alum. Undoubtedly the testimony of Chandler and the other experts was instrumental in the decision. Chandler testified "emphatically" that alum was "injurious," and "liable to produce serious disturbances of the liver of the individual making use of such powders." Morton, Johnson, and Raymond were just as "emphatic" as Chandler.[44]

The *Grocer* editorialized that the people must "trust the conscientious and disinterested testimony, based on careful experiments, of such men as Professor Chandler, Morton, and others." Yet there is no indication that any of the four had ever themselves conducted experiments upon the harmfulness of alum. Moreover, Chandler and Morton, at least, had been in the pay of Royal for a minimum of two years, and Mott had promised to share any award he received from the trial with Chandler and, presumably, the other witnesses. "Mott got the verdict for 8000 [dollars] in ½ hour," Colonel Prentice gleefully wrote Chandler.[45]

If one seeks a truly "disinterested" contemporary discussion of

---

43. Henry A. Mott, Jr., *The Effect of Alum Upon the Human System, When Used in Baking Powders: Elaborate Experiments Upon Living Dogs: Researches Made Under the Auspices of the ROYAL BAKING POWDER COMPANY* (New York, 1880); *Grocer,* May 28, 1880, pp. 766–67.

44. *Grocer,* December 9, 1880, p. 775.

45. Ibid.; Mott to Chandler, n.d., Prentice to Chandler, November 15, 1880, Chandler Papers.

alum, one of the very few places to turn is to the New York State Board of Health *Second Annual Report,* where Dr. E. G. Love was assigned the food group that included "the alum question." In 1881 Dr. Love, shortly before he was hired as one of the Board chemists, wrote to *Sanitary Engineer:* "I am not now nor ever have been interested in any brand of Baking Powder; that, as an analytical chemist, I have merely analyzed such products as were submitted to me, or as I was requested to buy, without a thought as to whether the results of such analyses would please the parties for whom they were made."[46]

Love's report was the most thorough objective review of the evidence regarding alum to that date. He explored every possible aspect of the question, summarizing and evaluating the scientific testimony of nineteen different chemists and food experts, as well as the legal status of alum in European countries. He responded to negative findings and opinions on alum by explaining that "Most or all of these opinions seem to be based on theoretical grounds, and I do not find that any systematic experiments have been made to settle the question." He concluded that "at the present time there does not seem sufficient evidence as to the injurious effects of alum upon the human system to warrant legislation against it."[47] It is significant, considering the thoroughness of Love's review of the literature, that he never once mentioned Dr. Mott's questionable vivisection experiment.

Neither the successful conclusion of the trial against Burns nor Love's report, which contradicted Chandler's testimony, ended Chandler's relationship with the Royal Company. J. C. Hoagland, president of Royal, asked Chandler to testify in a suit against Cleveland Brothers of Albany, who had alleged that Royal's powder was deleterious. The Cleveland ad quoted James F. Babcock, State Assayer of Massachusetts: "Cleveland's contains only pure and unobjectionable materials, while the Royal contains Ammonia, a drug derived from disgusting sources, powerful in its action upon the system, and unfit to enter into the composition of human food. The adulteration of the Royal Baking Powder with Ammonia is in my opinion nothing less than a crime against the public health." The ad also contained an en-

46. *Sanitary Engineer,* April 1, 1881, p. 204.
47. *Second Annual Report,* N.Y., pp. 567, 573.

dorsement from R. O. Doremus, implying that the Royal powder was not only unwholesome, but short-weighted.[48]

Using Professors Morton and Chandler, Royal prepared to do battle with Cleveland Brothers. Hoagland wrote to Chandler, accepting his fee request of $250, and adding: "Noting your suggestion as to the fact of your aversion to figuring in advertisements, I beg to say that this is no part of an advertising scheme. It is simply this: the competitors referred to, have sought through the aid of Prof. Doremus and some other chemists of that ilk to create an unjustifiable prejudice against the Royal Baking Powder on account of the insignificant amount of ammonia which we have seen fit to employ as an ingredient."[49]

While Royal's attorneys prepared the libel suit, Hoagland published an ad in response to Cleveland's. He accused Cleveland Brothers and seventeen other companies of being "most largely adulterated" with lime or alum. The ad included testimonials by Mott, William McMurtrie, "chief chemist, United States Department of Agriculture," Morton, and even E. G. Love, who had apparently decided it was time he got in on a good thing, despite the protestations of disinterest in his 1881 letter to *Sanitary Engineer* and the clean bill of health he had given alum in his report in 1882.[50]

The ad also used Chandler's name, indicating that he not only testified as to the healthfulness of Royal, but joined in the accusation against the other eighteen companies. Cleveland Brothers wrote Chandler that "we cannot but believe that the use of your name by the Royal Baking Powder Co. in the manner indicated above is wholly unauthorized. Will you kindly let us hear from you on the subject." Yet two months later Royal used Chandler's

48. J. C. Hoagland to Chandler, October 25, 1884, Chandler Papers; newspaper ad, clipping in Chandler Papers. Babcock's letter quoted in the ad was dated August 14, 1884; Doremus's was dated July 11, 1884. Doremus had made a similar endorsement for Dr. Price's Cream Baking Powder on May 24, 1884; see Chandler Papers.

According to testimony in the *Report of the Industrial Commission on Agriculture* 11 (Washington, D.C., 1901), pp. 117–24, Royal later merged with two other tartar baking powder companies, Price and Cleveland, to form a virtual monopoly of this product.

49. Hoagland to Chandler, October 31, 1884, Chandler Papers.

50. Newspaper ad dated December 12, 1884, Chandler Papers.

name again, this time to condemn all baking powders but Royal's, noting that it had been tested by the New York State Board of Health, thereby implying that the Board itself gave similar endorsement.[51]

A few days earlier Hoagland had written to Chandler, once again getting clearance for the use of his name.[52] Apparently Chandler did not object, despite his "aversion to figuring in advertisements." By his reasoning, he had performed chemical analyses for Royal, which entitled them to use his name. This, he apparently felt, kept him from being like Doremus and "chemists of that ilk." There is no record that he responded to the query from Cleveland Brothers.

Except for oleomargarine, which is discussed below in a chapter by itself because of the complexity of the issues involved, there are few other foods of this era that warrant extended consideration, whether regarded from the basis of deleteriousness or of fraud. Though, by the standards first employed under the new state laws, many foods were technically adulterated, for most foods enforcement quickly came to follow the practices of the marketplace. Not only were most of the prosecutions initiated by Chandler in December 1882 made irrelevant by the rules adopted shortly thereafter, but by the actual practices of the New York, New Jersey, and Massachusetts boards, the varieties of foods in use were almost universally accepted. Although most of the analysts stopped short of accusing the fathers of the movement— such as Accum and Hassall—of outright fabrication, they denied that most of the "traditional" adulterations existed any longer. And though the sanitarians found many frauds in current usage, they were generally content to issue a verbal rebuke rather than proceed to legal action.

Of the other "food" items, a few words should be said concerning alcoholic beverages. The sanitarians suspected widespread adulteration, especially watering, but found it difficult to deal with this as a serious problem. It seemed incongruous for reformers to urge a strengthening of the alcoholic content of li-

51. Cleveland Brothers to Chandler, December 15, 1884, newspaper ad dated February 5, 1885, Chandler Papers.
52. Hoagland to Chandler, January 27, 1885, Chandler Papers.

quors. Dr. F. E. Engelhardt, to whom was assigned "wines, beers, spirits and cordials" for the 1882 *Report,* argued, "It is evident that the worst and most injurious ingredient in our so-called strong or distilled liquors is the alcohol itself."[53]

Canned food was another item suspected of being deleterious. But Professor Lattimore found no evidence of adulteration or of harmful qualities in canned fruits and vegetables, and Professor A. H. Chester similarly gave his approval to canned meats, so far as the canning process was concerned. But Chester warned, "The scraps and bits that formerly went into the manufacture of fertilizers are undoubtedly often used up in this way," even though he presented no evidence to substantiate his claims. He warned especially about canned pork because of the danger of trichinosis.[54]

No amount of reassurance, however, was enough to convince the public about the safety of this relatively new process, and accusations continually surfaced about poisoning from canned foods. The grocery press responded vehemently to these claims, because commercial canning was proving to be a boon to the business, both wholesale and retail. *American Grocer,* for example, made canned goods information a regular feature and consistently attacked unsubstantiated stories about canned food poisoning, challenging newspapers to verify rumors about tinware "poisonings."[55]

After one such suspected case had created unwanted publicity about canned vegetables, a committee of the New York Mercantile Exchange drafted a bill "prohibiting the sale of canned goods under fictitious labels." Though *American Grocer* attacked this bill as an attempt to "make it difficult for the packers of other states to sell their goods in this market," in actuality the bill would restrict Thurber's production of private-label goods of varied quality and price, which had become a very important part of his company's business. His paper decried the publicity surrounding the measure, which had "raised a cry against the whole-

53. *Second Annual Report,* N.Y., p. 634. Engelhardt did find traces of fusel oil—the result of insufficient distillation—in some brandies and recommended a law regulating its removal. His analysis of lager beers revealed that their average alcohol content was only 2.781 percent.

54. Ibid., p. 557.

55. *New York Herald,* December 24, 1882, December 25, 1882; *American Grocer,* December 28, 1882, p. 7.

someness of canned goods . . . needlessly alarming consumers."
But *American Grocer*'s argument that competition between can-
ners made the law unnecessary was rather thin, for how could a
manufacturer be held "responsible for the quality of goods he
sells" if the can labels were anonymous? The canning bill was
signed into law, to take effect on January 1, 1886. It required that
can labels bear the name and address of the producer "or the
name of the wholesale dealer in this State who sells or offers the
same for sale."[56]

The lack of attention paid to the adulteration of drugs is surprising, even considering the generally haphazard enforcement of
the NBT law in the three states in which it had been passed. The
most active of the three was Massachusetts, which finally appointed an inspector of drugs a year after the law went into
effect. Dr. Bennett F. Davenport's first report found 41.67 percent of the 680 drug samples examined to have been adulterated.
Despite this large number of adulterations, only seven cases were
brought to court, five of them successfully. There was little improvement the next year, the adulteration rate remaining at 36.8
percent. Yet only one new prosecution was initiated, and again
only one more the following year. Of course, an 1884 amendment
to the Massachusetts law required that 60 percent of the monies
spent by the Health Department be devoted to the inspection and
analysis of milk. Nonetheless it is interesting that, while the food
analyst received a salary of $1,500, the drug analyst—whose work
was more exacting—was paid only $1,000 a year.[57]

For the first year under the new law in the state of New Jersey,
the Board pleaded inability to evaluate drugs because of the mea-
ger appropriation of $500. Little was done the following year,
aside from some milk analysis and a report on infant foods, since

56. *Grocer,* April 11, 1884, p. 661; *American Grocer,* May 14, 1885, p. 9; Laws
of 1885, chap. 269. The canned tomatoes in question were Thurber's. See Mitchell Okun, "Fair Play in the Marketplace" (Ph.D. diss., City University of New
York, 1983), pp. 353–58.

57. *Fifth Annual Report,* Mass. (July 1884), pp. 153, 173–74; *Sixth Annual
Report of the State Board of Health, Lunacy, and Charity of Massachusetts* (Bos-
ton, 1885), pp. li, 112; *Seventh Annual Report,* Mass., p. 87; Newton, "Sanitary
Control," p. 153. It should be noted that there is some discrepancy in the Mas-
sachusetts *Reports* as to how many drug samples were actually analyzed; see
Seventh Annual Report, p. 66.

the legislature failed to appropriate *any* additional funds for the enforcement of the law, and the analysts had to make do with the small amount left over from 1881. Finally, in 1883, an annual appropriation of $1,000 was made, but apparently none of this was applied to drug analysis over the next three years.[58]

In New York, where $10,000 was initially appropriated for the enforcement of the new law, considerable attention was paid to drugs in the *Annual Report* of 1882. Although Dr. Frederick Hoffmann, to whom the drugs were assigned by Chandler, failed to analyze any compound drug preparations, he did examine 659 samples of crude vegetable drugs, pharmaceutical chemicals, and powdered drugs. Hoffmann found a fairly large percentage to be either "adulterated" or "deteriorated," especially among the powdered drugs, but it is impossible to judge the extent of intentional adulteration from his report since many of the specimens he condemned were clearly deficient only because of aging or improper storage. Although Hoffmann did not test proprietary drugs, he went out of his way to condemn them.[59] This is understandable, since Hoffman was a leader of APhA and became a member of its committee recommending full content labeling of patent medicines. The next year the number of samples analyzed by the Board had dropped to seventy-five, and in 1883 to forty-two. *None* of the prosecutions initiated by the State Board in this entire period was for drug adulteration.

The present study can only speculate as to the reasons for the neglect of enforcement in the area of drugs. Certainly this era saw a tremendous increase in the number of patent medicines produced and sold. Though many of these proprietaries were merely variations of standard prescription drugs, by the 1880s they constituted a majority of the medicines purchased in this

58. *Fifth Annual Report of the Board of Health of the State of New Jersey* (Mount Holly, N.J., 1881), pp. 112–13; *Sixth Annual Report of the Board of Health of the State of New Jersey* (Woodbury, N.J., 1882), p. 31; *Seventh Annual Report of the Board of Health of the State of New Jersey* (Woodbury, N.J., 1883); *Eighth Annual Report of the Board of Health of the State of New Jersey* (Trenton, 1884); *Ninth Annual Report of the Board of Health of the State of New Jersey* (Trenton, 1885).

59. *Second Annual Report,* N.Y., pp. 687–96; *Third Annual Report,* N.Y., p. 97; *Fourth Annual Report,* N.Y., p. 257.

country.[60] Yet in all three states the NBT laws failed to provide for regulation of non-officinal, over-the-counter medicines. Only those drugs and drug ingredients included in the *United States Pharmacopoeia* were covered, and so the proprietaries remained outside the direct jurisdiction of the boards.

There may also have been an understanding on the part of the board analysts that the responsibility for policing the "legitimate" drug trade should lie within the profession itself. In this era the pharmaceutical associations were emerging as strong advocates, not only of honesty in the trade, but of internal regulation, aided by laws shaped by themselves. Apparently all the board chemists appointed to examine the drug market were members of the professional associations, and leaders of the local colleges of pharmacy. In addition, the explanation was frequently offered that the public demanded cheap medicines. Faced with the rivalry of the proprietaries, it is possible that many pharmacists acquiesced in the adulteration alternative as the only means of coping with the competition.[61]

Aside from food and drugs, three related items fell under the jurisdiction of the health authorities, either because of their interpretation of the National Board of Trade law or because of additional legislation. These were decorative papers and fabrics, cosmetics, and kerosene.

Considering that it was widely authenticated that poisonous coloring materials were commonly used in clothing and paper goods, it is noteworthy that the authorities did virtually nothing except issue public warnings. A typical treatment was that of the Massachusetts Board:

> The most dangerous article that enters into every-day use is paper colored with pigments of which arsenic forms a component part.

60. James H. Young, *The Toadstool Millionaires* (Princeton, 1961), pp. 106–10; William H. Becker, "The Wholesalers of Hardware and Drugs, 1870–1900" (Ph.D. diss., The Johns Hopkins University, 1969), p. 178.

61. Similar patterns of neglect occurred in England; see Ernst W. Stieb, *Drug Adulteration: Detection and Control in Nineteenth-Century Britain* (Madison, 1966), pp. 118–19, 153.

This paper is met with in great abundance. The bright green glazed paper boxes used so freely in fancy-goods stores are always covered with paper of this kind. Car and theatre tickets are printed on it, and it is quite freely used as a wall-paper. It has even been met with as a covering for lozenges.

There is no good reason for its use, except that it is cheap. It should be condemned whenever met with.

Dr. Frank W. Draper had warned of these dangers as early as the Massachusetts report for 1871. Yet a law prohibiting arsenical coloring did not go into effect in that state until 1900.[62]

While serving as chemist to the Metropolitan Board of Health, Chandler had been active in the war against poisonous cosmetics. In 1870 he tested a number of hair remedies. Finding most of them to be heavily contaminated with lead, Chandler published a list, giving brand names and quantity of lead detected. Only two were found to be uncontaminated, one of which was Dr. I. J. O'Brien's "Restorer America." But Chandler reported to Colonel Emmons Clark, then secretary of the Board, that he had been duped. His sample had been purchased "from a druggist on 8th Avenue," upon the direction of Mr. O'Brien. But a second bottle, bought "at Macy's on 6th Avenue corner of 14th Street . . . is one of the most dangerous of the poisonous hair restorers. . . . And I have reason to believe that I was imposed upon by the druggist of whom I purchased the [first] sample."[63]

Chandler grimly entered into a war with O'Brien, sending special notices to the press about the great danger of this product, which claimed to be "the greatest discovery of this century for restoring the original color of the hair. . . . Removes Dandruff, Prevents The Hair From Falling Off." O'Brien sent an indignant

---

62. *Fourth Annual Report,* Mass., p. 75; *The Massachusetts State Board of Health, A Brief History of Its Organization and Its Work, 1869–1912* (Boston, 1912), p. 47.

63. "Report on Dangerous Cosmetics," *Fourth Annual Report of the Metropolitan Board of Health* (New York, 1870), p. 5; Chandler to Clark, April 9, 1870, Chandler Papers. Chandler reported on skin lotions and powders, and on enamels as well. In the *Report* he called only one hair tonic safe, but later added a second to his list.

letter to Colonel Clark, protesting being "wickedly and maliciously" singled out by Chandler and complaining that the lead content of several other preparations was as bad as, or worse than, his own. Moreover, he insisted that lead was not harmful, even when swallowed.[64]

But the number of such nostrums merely multiplied faster than Chandler could examine and condemn them, many of the manufacturers even having the effrontery to write Chandler for endorsements. The manufacturers also found a clever method of using Chandler's condemnation for their own purposes: they republished his 1870 list, merely leaving out their own product, as a public warning against buying competing brands. As Dr. Haven Emerson later noted, "the health officer is at the mercy of the consuming public," and Chandler soon abandoned his efforts "to save a beauty-mad generation" from its own folly.[65] The State Board, after its formation, did not include cosmetics in the category of drugs, and the New Jersey and Massachusetts boards similarly ignored these poisons, even though in the latter state they were specifically included in the law.

It will be remembered that a menace far deadlier than any of the food or drug adulterations was the adulteration of kerosene with naphtha or other light petroleum distillates. These adulterations were sometimes so volatile that a nearby stove could set them afire or even cause an explosion. Hundreds of deaths could be traced to fires caused by sophisticated kerosene. The early efforts of the New York City Board had had some positive impact upon this problem, yet kerosene fires continued to occur regularly, and Chandler urged legislation that would give the new State Board authority to move on this hazard. In New York City, still the only place in the state with any law controlling kerosene,

64. Advertisement copy; O'Brien to Clark, April 15, 1870, Chandler Papers. *New York Times,* January 6, 1870, reported three deaths attributed to "the use of Laird's Bloom of Youth" hair dye. It is noteworthy that not until 1985 did the Food and Drug Administration finally decide to attempt to ban non-prescription hair restorers.

65. Letters in Chandler Papers; speech given by Chandler, June 3, 1878, to New York Medical Society, p. 90 of stenographic minutes, Chandler Papers; Haven Emerson, "Charles Frederick Chandler," *Science* 86 (November 19, 1937), p. 457.

the fire commissioners reported that in 1880, of 1,783 fires, fully 103 were proven to have begun by kerosene lamps—and 54 were classified as "explosions."[66]

In 1881 Chandler successfully lobbied for a bill to regulate kerosene statewide and to take jurisdiction away from the Fire Department in New York City, but Governor Cornell issued a veto of the measure. His veto message clearly explained that he wished to avoid "hampering trade," but Cornell's reasoning was bizarre. He argued, "It can hardly be maintained that safe oils must be inspected simply because unsafe oils are sometimes manufactured and offered for sale. . . . the inspection of oils ought to be confined to such as are fairly presumed to be dangerous." As Dr. Love objected, "No one would think it necessary to inspect safe burning oils, but how are the safe oils to be protected and the unsafe ones condemned, except by a system of inspection?"[67]

A modified version of the law was finally passed in June of the following year, giving jurisdiction to the State Board, except for the city of New York. The Board urged that the city fire commissioners adopt the Board instrument for measuring kerosene safety, but a year later noted that they had not received any response to their resolution. The law allowed for the appointment of only one oil inspector for the entire state; in his first year of testing, the Board's inspector discovered that only 32 of 236 samples met the standard set by the law.[68] On December 21, 1882, the Board initiated its test case, in an incident at Batavia, New York, in which a kerosene explosion caused one death and destroyed a house. The local justice of the peace refused to indict the oil dealer, and conviction was not obtained until the Board took the case to a grand jury.[69]

---

66. Arthur H. Elliott, "Report on the Methods and Apparatus for Testing Inflammable Oils," New York State Board of Health *Report #45* (Albany, 1882).

67. *Grocer,* July 2, 1881, p. 4; Alonzo B. Cornell, veto message to state Assembly; E. G. Love, letter to the editor, *Sanitary Engineer,* August 1, 1881, p. 399.

68. *Third Annual Report,* N.Y., p. 96; Laws of 1882, chap. 292; *New York Times,* February 18, 1883. A similar law went into effect in New Jersey in July 1883, though at first there was no provision for a paid state inspector. No indication was found in the Massachusetts *Reports* of this period that a comparable law existed in that state.

69. *American Grocer,* December 28, 1882, p. 1408; *Third Annual Report,* N.Y., p. 96; Larson, p. 149.

Chandler's enforcement of the new law, however, was complicated by the fact that he had been receiving private payments for analyzing oil samples for dealers, and because of his connections with Standard Oil, a major supplier to the New York wholesalers. The situation came to a boil when a Pottsdam dealer, George W. Bonney, refused to accept delivery of four carloads of oil ordered from Standard. Bonney had had the shipment tested by the state inspector, Dr. W. G. Tucker, and received notification from Dr. Harris that the oil failed to meet the state standard. Chandler reprimanded Bonney for allowing Tucker to test the oil, claiming that Tucker "did not know how to use the instrument of the State Board of Health, he didn't use it properly, & the results which he obtained were not correct. . . . it was a very unfortunate circumstance that you should have sent the samples of oil to Albany, & I never have been able to understand why you did it, particularly as I had been testing oils for you from time to time. . . . The blunder was entirely on your part. You knew that the whole business was in my hands."[70]

Chandler then sent a letter to Thomson McGowan of Standard Oil, expressing regret for the inconvenience, and sent him a copy of the letter written to Bonney. He explained to Harris that Bonney's continued refusal to accept delivery of the oil could well result in a suit for payment, which would make public the opposite findings of his and Tucker's analyses and "put the State Board of Health in a most mortifying position—a house divided against itself." Chandler sent Harris a copy of the letter to Bonney—but *not* a copy of the letter sent to McGowan.[71]

A month later the issue was still unresolved. Chandler wrote Bonney, affirming his determination that Board members would no longer "enter into any entangling alliances with any business man . . . as we should if we received fees from him." Chandler explained, "The law never contemplated providing chemists to make analyses and tests for private parties for the convenience of their business. You might as well expect that H. K. Thurber should send samples of all the groceries he buys to me to be analysed." Yet six months later Bonney was still writing to Chan-

70. Chandler to George W. Bonney, December 8, 1882, Chandler Papers.
71. Chandler to Thomson McGowan, December 8, 1882, Chandler to Harris, December 8, 1882, Chandler Papers.

dler for assistance. Chandler repeated the Board's new resolution: "The only safe policy for us to pursue was not to act as umpires between the buyers and sellers of oil."[72] At this very time, of course, Chandler was still receiving fees from sugar, glucose, oleomargarine, and baking powder manufacturers.

When Professor Leeds warned that chemists might eschew public service for the monetary rewards offered by private employers fighting regulation, he did not contemplate the problems created when chemists served both masters simultaneously. If there was but slight interest in carrying out the law—as demonstrated both by deficient legislative appropriations and by the casual attitude of the experts entrusted with enforcement—the work was further complicated by these ethical questions.

There is no reason to doubt that Chandler's concern about kerosene safety was genuine, but even here his own commercial involvement jeopardized his performance. Perhaps the acid test—to see whether there was, in Newton's words, "such a thing as justice any more"—was oleomargarine, the most complicated and controversial "adulteration," which eventually involved virtually every leading chemical expert in the nation.

72. Chandler to Bonney, January 19, 1883, June 9, 1883, Chandler Papers.

11

Oleomargarine:
Intimations of *The Jungle*

No food generated more acrimony and excitement than oleomargarine, which in this era was produced from the fatty residue that slaughterhouses normally sent to be rendered into candle tallow and soap.[1] Oleo was invented in 1869 by a Frenchman, Hippolyte Mège, in response to a prize offered by Napoleon III for a substitute for butter. Mège patented his product in a number of European countries and in 1871 sold his patent rights to various investors. On December 30, 1873, the Mège process was patented in the United States, initiating a debate about both its wholesomeness and its legitimacy that culminated in the first federal law regulating a domestic food.

Since the controversy over oleo was complicated by the rapid appearance of a multitude of imitators, it is important to understand the basic process by which the Mège product was manufactured. The patent called for the use of the "caul" fat of cattle—the "choicest" fat surrounding the stomach. This fat had to be processed immediately after slaughtering, while the animal heat still remained. This material was then washed and cooled in ice water, put through a grinding machine, and melted at a temperature that had to remain below 120°F. The oil was extracted, and

1. "Oleomargarine" was originally intended by its inventor to mean "beef fat oil." Though vegetable oils were sometimes added to oleo in this era, purely vegetable margarine is a twentieth-century product. Until the Margarine Act of 1950 took effect, all butter substitutes were legally designated "oleomargarine." See Johannes H. van Stuyvenberg, ed., *Margarine: An Economic, Social and Scientific History, 1869–1969* (Liverpool, 1969); Sjert F. Riepina, *The Story of Margarine* (Washington, D.C., 1970).

the residue of tissue and fiber was sent to the tallow works. After extended heating at low temperatures the stearine, the solid portion of the fat, was isolated by hydraulic pressure and rejected. The remaining oil—now called oleomargarine oil—was churned with fresh milk at a ratio of eighty pounds of milk to five hundred pounds of oil, along with salt, and annatto for color. The Mège patent allowed for no other ingredients.[2]

Although it is not possible to date precisely the establishment of the first oleo factory in this country, an imitator of Mège had established at least one plant by 1873. Mège's patentee, the United States Dairy Company, began operation, in New York, in early 1876. The central manufacturing arm for U.S. Dairy was the Commercial Manufacturing Company, Consolidated, and its exclusive wholesale distributor was H. K. and F. B. Thurber and Company. It is likely that Francis Thurber had a controlling interest in U.S. Dairy; although Thurber disavowed ownership of Commercial Manufacturing, he never testified about possible ownership of the parent company. Whether or not Thurber directly owned either company, his control of oleo distribution tied him intimately to the product; the *Tribune,* which opposed his political activities, dubbed him "Oleomargarine Thurber."[3]

The butter interests were justifiably alarmed by the rapid expansion of oleo manufacture because it was virtually impossible to distinguish between the two products by sensory examination. The butter producers rejected Thurber's proposal that oleo be displayed at the International Dairy Fair of 1878 as "an insult to dairymen," but when samples were smuggled in disguised as butter the experts of the New York Butter and Cheese Exchange

---

2. *Testimony Taken Before the Assembly Committee on Public Health in the Matter of the Investigation into the Subject of the Manufacture and Sale of Oleomargarine and Lard-Cheese.* New York *Assembly Document No. 000* [?] (1881), pp. 153ff.

This report was obviously intended to become part of the regular Assembly records, but it was never included as part of the state documents for 1881; it appears that the only extant copy is in the Chandler Papers in the Columbia University Rare Book and Manuscript Library. This document will be referred to henceforth as the "Fenner report."

3. *New York Journal of Commerce,* April 21, 1874; Lee Benson, *Merchants, Farmers, and Railroads* (New York, 1955), pp. 171–72.

were unable to identify the counterfeit product.[4] Even chemists could identify oleo only after elaborate tests, and there is good reason to suspect that oleo mixed with butter could defy any microscopical or chemical test known in this era.[5]

This analytical difficulty led some chemists—such as Professor Chandler, who became one of the strongest oleo advocates—to argue that the Mège product was simply butter produced by a method superior to that of the milch cow and the dairy. Once again, however, Chandler's objectivity must be brought into question, for as early as 1876 he was receiving substantial sums of money from both U.S. Dairy and Commercial Manufacturing for testimony against those who infringed upon the Mège patent. He was receiving a regular retainer of $500 a year to guarantee his availability in future patent suits, as well as a variety of fees for his chemical work for the two companies.[6]

Another chemist who was wholeheartedly supportive of Mège oleo was Henry Mott. Although Mott had performed yeoman's service for the Royal Baking Powder Company, he had an even greater loyalty to Commercial Manufacturing, perhaps because he was the brother-in-law of James Wilson, the vice-president and manager of the company. Right after the factory began operation, Mott published an elaborate description of the processes employed, along with a half-dozen flattering illustrations, in two issues of the *Scientific American Supplement*. This was then revised into booklet form, not just as a celebration of oleomargarine, but as an advertisement for Commercial Manufacturing.

4. *New York Times*, November 27, 1878; Fenner report, p. 163. Thurber and Company traditionally had the largest and most spectacular display of butter and cheese at the annual fairs. See *New York Times*, December 2, 1878.

5. Otto Hehner and Arthur Angell, *Butter, Its Analysis and Adulterations*, 2d ed. (London, 1877), p. 50; Thomas Taylor, "Oleomargarine Under the Microscope," *Scientific American* 38 (June 15, 1878), p. 374; Thomas Taylor, "Oleomargarine and Butter," *American Quarterly Microscopical Journal* 1:4 (July 1879), p. 294; Peter Collier, "Report of the Chemist," in *Report of the Commissioner of Agriculture for the Year 1879* (Washington, D.C. 1880), p. 77.

6. U.S. Dairy to Chandler, March 22, 1876, Dickerson and Beaman to Chandler, July 28, 1876, October 18, 1876, U.S. Dairy to Chandler, November 11, 1876, May 29, 1877, Commercial Manufacturing to Chandler, January 24, 1878, Chandler Papers; Robert L. Larson, "Charles Frederick Chandler, His Life and Work" (Ph.D. diss., Columbia University, 1950), pp. 218–19.

Mott disparaged other manufacturers' products as poor imitations that "in no way resembled butter."[7]

Mott managed to keep oleo in the public eye. Chandler, whose scientific approval of the Mège product was cited by Mott, invited him to address the American Chemical Society. This paper became the pretext for another story in *Scientific American*. Though the magazine regretted the duplicity of those selling oleo as butter, it concluded that "if people cannot distinguish the made from the natural product, and if the former is, as reported by Professor Chandler, actually more healthful than the average cow butter sold, it would be difficult to prove any damages save to the moral sense."[8]

Meanwhile, with relatively little fanfare, the state legislature of New York acted upon the prodding of the dairymen by passing a law in 1877 "to prevent deception in sales of butter." This act was straightforward and simple—and proved impossible to enforce. It required that oleo manufacturers "distinctly and durably stamp, brand or mark upon every tub" an identification of the contents, and that retailers present a slip of paper with the printed word "oleo-margarin" with every sale of the product.[9] Only an army of inspectors and chemists could have enforced the law, since the grocers scooped out and weighed retail purchases of both butter and oleo from large wholesale tubs.

Coincidental with a renewed discussion of oleo at the 1878 annual convention of the American Dairymen's Association, the New York Senate began an inquiry as to the efficacy of the branding law. In response to the Senate's request, Professor Chandler issued a brief official report of the Board, in which he claimed that oleo was "a good and wholesome article of food,"

---

7. *Scientific American Supplement,* Nos. 48 and 49 (1876); Henry A. Mott, *Complete History and Process of Manufacture of Artificial Butter* (New York, 1876), pp. 3, 27.

8. Henry A. Mott, "Manufacture of Artificial Butter," *Proceedings of the American Chemical Society* 1:3 (November 2, 1876), pp. 154–59; "Artificial Butter," *Scientific American* 35:22 (November 25, 1876), p. 337. Another treatment of the same material appeared in *Scientific American* 36:11 (March 17, 1877), p. 168, which cited Chandler's "experiments" to show that the Mège process, followed with precision, was the *only* successful method of manufacturing oleo: "it is chemically butter." See also *American Dairyman* 2:17 (January 17, 1878).

9. *Laws of 1877,* chap. 415.

and "That no legislation is necessary to prevent its imposition upon the public as pure butter, the product of the dairy, additional to the law of 1877." But these reassurances were meaningless to the dairymen; oleo had already captured a substantial share of the "butter" export market, and no one knew to what extent oleo was being sold domestically, whether under its own name or disguised as butter. A second attempt by Thurber to have the dairymen openly accept an oleo display at the next annual dairy fair was defeated.[10]

Thus by 1879 sharp lines were being drawn on the oleo issue, and its opponents, hesitating to ask for restrictive legislation on strictly economic grounds, tried to establish oleo's unwholesomeness. As long as Mège oleo dominated the market, however, there was little chance of success; while it is possible that Mège oleo harbored an array of dangerous bacteria, no scientific expertise was available to prove it to be harmful, and no testimony was ever presented that proved carelessness, or deviation from the patented process, at the Commercial plant. Even chemists who were probably independent of the Company testified as to oleo's wholesomeness. Stephen Sharples concluded that because it was sold as butter, oleo was one of those foods that had been "frauds in their inception" but which, by 1879, had been "sanctioned by usage."[11]

Nonetheless, a number of dairymen and amateur chemists and microscopists continued to issue unsubstantiated charges about oleo, all of which were brought into focus in 1879 by George T. Angell's infamous "Public Health Associations" speech. Though his comments about this "butter" made from "horse fat, fat from bones, and fat such as is principally used for making candles" added no new facts to the controversy, it succeeded in pulling together the accusations and fears concerning oleo and in raising public concern.[12]

The grocery press, which had addressed oleo only in passing

10. *New York Times,* January 9, 1878; letter from Board of Health, February 8, 1878, Chandler Papers; *Sanitarian,* 7 (1879), p. 510.
11. Stephen P. Sharples, "Adulteration of Food," in *A Treatise on Hygiene and Public Health,* ed. Albert H. Buck (New York, 1879), 2: p. 356.
12. George T. Angell, "Public Health Associations," *Sanitarian* 7 (1879), p. 128.

before this time, now began to deal with it at some length. The *Grocer* began its attack in February, reprinting a lengthy speech by farm leader Joseph H. Reall. Reall placed the blame for the disastrous losses of the dairy industry in 1878—when prices for butter and cheese fell below the cost of production—upon overproduction and oleomargarine. The chief responsibility for the increased use of oleo was laid upon Mott and other "humbugs," and upon dairy organizations which had sold themselves "for one consideration or another." Reall especially singled out the American Dairymen's Association, which had been "prostituted to discussions of patent rights and selfish schemes." Though neither Reall nor the *Grocer* mentioned him by name, Francis Thurber was president of the American Dairymen's Association.[13]

By the end of 1879 the dairymen and butter merchants had organized the National Association for the Prevention of the Adulteration of Butter (NAPAB), which was headquartered in New York and led by Reall, Washington Winsor (president of the Butter, Cheese, and Egg Exchange), and attorney T. Mortimer Seaver. The Association's premise was that if the retailers were compelled to sell oleo as oleo, no consumer would buy it; oleo had become a threat to their livelihood only because it was disguised as butter. Thurber was singled out as "more largely interested in the manufacture and sale of oleomargarine than any other person in the community." NAPAB adopted a resolution to raise $5,000 "to prosecute offenders" who violated the New York law of 1877.[14]

The Association's efforts in this direction, however, were quickly disappointed, for in a trial of five food dealers charged with selling oleo as butter, held only a few weeks later, the butter "experts" were unable to agree on whether the chief exhibit was a cheap grade of "Western" butter or oleomargarine. The very next day NAPAB called a general meeting of the Association. Horace Thurber, who had been invited to the meeting, argued that sooner or later every butter merchant would be compelled to sell oleo because of its value as a product. In response, Seaver

13. *Grocer,* February 15, 1879, pp. 222–23. Reall was the secretary of the American Agricultural Society, editor and publisher of the *Agricultural Review,* and author of *Dairying and Dairy Improvements* (New York, 1882).

14. *New York Times,* December 6, 1879.

blamed Thurber and Company for keeping this "swindle" from being "driven from the market."[15]

Following this meeting the Thurbers attempted to bolster the image of oleo. On January 29, 1880, the *Produce Exchange Bulletin* reported on a visit to the Commercial Manufacturing factory in a manner Thurber's *American Grocer* categorized as "written in a disinterested and independent spirit." Although it cannot be established that the Thurbers "placed" this article, certainly their influence in the Produce Exchange was powerful, and the article was anything but "disinterested." It lauded the manufacturing process as "a beautiful sight" and waxed poetic about its "neatness and cleanliness." *American Grocer* added the comment that, since "oleomargarine is handled by the Thurbers," the public was afforded "a very sufficient guarantee of the cleanliness and wholesomeness of the article." Thurber also succeeded in persuading the president of the New York State Dairymen's Association to testify "that oleomargarine is a perfectly legitimate product when sold as oleomargarine," and that it had not injured the farmers of New York.[16]

Although the *Grocer* never published any advertisements from Thurber and Company, it now began advertising competing brands of oleo, thus acknowledging the legitimacy of the product. But the tide was beginning to turn against oleo, for it was at this time that Congressman Beale's anti-adulteration bill was approved by the House Committee on Manufactures. Beale's report on food, issued on February 25, 1880, included oleo as one of its chief targets. Like the bulk of the accusations and "facts" presented by Beale, his material on oleo came directly from George T. Angell, who claimed that oleo carried "the fungi, living organisms, and eggs resembling those of the tape-worm."[17] Similarly, the dairy interests were stirring up activity in Albany, and the state Senate Committee on Agriculture made plans to begin hearings on the need for additional legislation.

15. *New York Times,* January 10, 1880, January 14, 1880; Fenner report, p. 211.

16. *American Grocer,* February 5, 1880, pp. 334–35; *Grocer,* February 7, 1880, p. 187; February 14, 1880, p. 221. The New York State Dairy Association president, Mancelia Folsom, soon turned against oleo.

17. *The Manufacture of Articles of Human Food and Drink,* 46th Cong., 2d sess., February 25, 1880, H. Rept. 346, p. 3.

In response to these threats, U.S. Dairy and Commercial Manufacturing developed the strategy of assembling a panel of scientific experts to testify to the wholesomeness of their product. Conveniently, Congressman Morgan R. Wise of Pennsylvania, chairman of the House Committee on Manufactures, now wrote to Chandler requesting information about oleomargarine. Although no evidence exists to prove that Wise was prompted to make this request, it certainly seems strange that, at this crucial moment, he would think of contacting Chandler—whose support of oleo was well known—rather than consulting the chemists of the Department of Agriculture. Chandler, for his part, was already at work assembling the panel of experts, in anticipation of Wise's request.

On February 27 Mott had sent Chandler a letter arranging for the two of them to meet at the Commercial factory, to set things up for inspection. That same day the attorneys for U.S. Dairy sent Chandler a note promising that a check to cover his professional services was on its way. Within a couple of weeks whatever arrangements Mott and Chandler were making at the factory were apparently completed, but as Mott explained, U.S. Dairy needed some stopgap material from Chandler immediately:

> U.S. Dairy wants you to write *between now and Wednesday*—your opinion of oleo[margarine] Butter, as regards its purity and wholesomeness, and also the value of the Mège discovery as supplying a want, especially among those who can not afford to buy the best products of the creamery.
>
> The object of the congregation of scientific men is to get an *individual opinion* from each one in their own language after they have made such examinations as they may deem proper. Your thoroughly understanding the subject can give us one now—as we need it in Albany whether you go there or not—we also need it in Washington.[18]

Mott had hoped that Chandler would have something ready for him by the next morning. When nothing was immediately forth-

---

18. Mott to Chandler, February 27, 1880, Charles D. Deshler (attorney for U.S. Dairy) to Chandler, February 27, 1880, Mott to Chandler, March 14, 1880, Chandler Papers. The scientific experts began inspecting the Commercial factory in mid-March.

coming, he wrote again, urging speed and instructing Chandler that Commercial's James Wilson "would like you to bring in the words the 'Mège Discovery,' that it is essentially identical to Butter, contains less of volatile fats which decompose and make dairy butter rancid." The next day Wilson himself wrote Chandler, hoping "that you will not allow the interests of this great company to suffer before the public, by our resting under the ban and imputation, that our Butter is not pure."[19]

Chandler had already assembled the "congregation of scientific men," and had begun his "official" investigation in the name of the Board of Health. But events were militating against the company, and Wilson sent off a desperate letter to Chandler:

> I am astounded beyond expression at the indifference you manifest on matters vital to our interests. You have in your hands all the certificates of the party [of scientists] called here at a vast expense of money and [the certificates] have been called for from Washington, by letter. I delegated a special messenger to take them on last night, expecting to obtain them from you through Dr. Mott also your own written views, but you block me at every point. My party could not go on to Washington, but had to remain over. I beg to say that we do not think, we are deserving of such a lack of interest in our affairs from your hands.[20]

Chandler immediately sent his evaluation to Wise, although two of the scientists brought to New York by the company had not yet completed their "investigation." The eight visiting experts were a distinguished group, with an emphasis on chemists well known to informed agriculturalists. They represented a cross section of the most reputable professionals in the country.[21] But all the reports might have been written by an identical hand, stress-

19. Mott to Chandler, March 15, 1880, Wilson to Chandler, March 16, 1880, Chandler Papers.

20. Wilson to Chandler, [?] 27, 1880, Chandler Papers.

21. The eight scientists:

J. W. S. Arnold, professor of physiology and histology for the Medical Department of New York University, considered to be one of the nation's foremost microscopists.

Wilbur O. Atwater, perhaps the most famous agricultural chemist in American

ing the points urged by Wilson, and in virtually identical language. Each of the men briefly explained that oleo, as produced by the Commercial Company under the Mège patent, was not only as good as, but better than, butter.

Wilson was so delighted with the results of his strategy that he put together the testimonials, along with engravings of comparative microscopic views, the signatures of 165 "members of the New York Produce Exchange" who testified to recognizing oleo as being "a pure and wholesome article of food, and of value to commerce," and some other comments and illustrations, and published the whole package as a fourteen-page booklet. Wilson also published this material as an advertisement in various journals, such as *American Grocer* and *Sanitary Engineer*. He then commissioned Mott to revise his 1876 pamphlet on oleo, incorporating the new testimonials. Mott's new booklet noted that U.S. Dairy now had factories operating at full capacity in eleven cities.[22]

---

history, set up the first state agricultural station; he later designed the calorimeter and discovered the caloric value of foods.

George F. Barker, of the University of Pennsylvania, was on the National Academy of Sciences' glucose committee; a well-known consultant and editor of scientific periodicals.

G. C. Caldwell was, in 1880, a member of the chemical laboratory at Cornell; he soon became one of the chemists working for the new New York State Board of Health.

Charles A. Goessman was professor of chemistry at the Massachusetts Agricultural College from 1868 until his death in 1907. In 1883 he was appointed one of the two milk analysts for the Massachusetts State Board of Health.

Samuel W. Johnson will be remembered as the chief speaker at the ASSA meeting of 1880, where he attempted to refute Angell's contentions. In 1880 he was at the Sheffield Scientific School of Yale College, serving as professor of theoretical and agricultural chemistry and as director of the Connecticut Agricultural Experiment Station. He had already written his two classic volumes on agriculture, *How Crops Grow* (1868) and *How Crops Feed* (1870).

Henry Morton, who has been seen as one of the chief opponents of G. T. Angell, was the first president of the Stevens Institute of Technology, serving from 1870 until his death in 1902. Morton is best known for his work in mechanical engineering but was also a research chemist.

Charles P. Williams was a chemist, formerly director of the School of Mines, State University of Missouri.

22. Commercial Manufacturing Company, "Oleomargarine Butter: The New Article of Commerce" (New York, 1880); Henry A. Mott, *The Production of Oleomargarine and Oleomargarine Butter: As Manufactured By the Commercial Manufacturing Co., Consolidated* (New York, 1880), p. 16.

Meanwhile debate over oleo continued in Washington. Members of the National Association for the Prevention of the Adulteration of Butter, spearheaded by Reall (who had now replaced Thurber as president of the International Dairy Fair Association), decided to send a delegation to the capital to lobby in favor of legislation. This decision was inspired by the announcement that Commercial Manufacturing was to host a banquet at Delmonico's for the members of the congressional committees interested in the oleo question.[23] This time neither Thurber brother was invited to the NAPAB meeting. Though Francis Thurber had managed to coordinate the activities of New York businessmen and farmers in the "antimonopoly" war against the railroads, it is clear that by this time his own oleo monopoly had seriously jeopardized his relations with members of both groups. In the battle over oleo no quarter was being given.

Members of the House Committee on Agriculture were already in the city, inspecting the Commercial factory. On the evening of April 9, the same day the butter men met, the dinner was given at Delmonico's. In addition to the legislators, about 200 "prominent citizens" were invited, and the main feature of the banquet was an informal contest among the guests to identify unmarked samples of both oleo and butter. From the point of view of the humor magazine *Puck,* however, the most prominent feature of the dinner was the quantity of wine consumed, and it ran a full-page cartoon ridiculing the subsequent decision of the congressmen that oleo was an acceptable article of trade (figure 7).[24]

But by this time even the *Grocer* argued that "there is no doubt that oleomargarine is a legitimate product." After all, oleo had become a significant item of trade for the retail grocers, and one where more profit was possible than with butter. It is also probable that Thurber's old enemy felt free to support oleo because the Commercial Company no longer had a virtual monopoly; in the past year or so half a dozen competitors, each with its own patented variation on the Mège process, threatened Thurber's preeminence in the business. When Congressman John R. Thomas of Illinois introduced a new bill in the House on April

23. *New York Times,* April 10, 1880.
24. *American Grocer,* April 15, 1880, p. 985; *Puck* 7:163 (April 21, 1880), p. 109.

The Great Congressional Oleomargarine Investigation.

Several Members of Congress were much Scandalized at the Audacity of the Oleomargarine Manufacturers.

So They Wrote Speeches Against It—

And Delivered them in Congress, Each in his own Peculiar Style.

Then they were Appointed a Committee to Investigate the Merits of Oleomargarine. They were Receive with Great Politeness by the Manufacturers, and Invited to Partake of a Light Repast.

Result of the Investigation—"Oleo-marsh-rinesh Mush Better'n Butter!"

7. "The Great Congressional Oleomargarine Investigation." From *Puck* 7:16 3 (April 21, 1880), p. 109.

26, to tax oleo at ten cents a pound, the *Grocer* attacked the proposal as merely a selfish maneuver on the part of the dairy interests.[25]

Meanwhile the debate over oleo also proceeded in Albany, where the Assembly had already passed a new oleo bill. At this juncture Francis Thurber decided to support additional legislation. He took the high ground of working against the fraudulent sale of oleo as butter, and he contributed $100 to NAPAB, insisting that his company had never sold the product as anything but oleo and that retailers should be compelled to do the same. This decision put him in seeming disagreement with his comrades in the oleo business, because James Wilson would soon be testifying fervently in Albany, literally waving a copy of his "Oleomargarine" pamphlet in his hand, complaining of the injustice of further restriction upon the manufacture or sale of oleo.[26]

But Wilson's agitation was because of a suggestion *not* incorporated in the state bill Thurber had endorsed: the suggestion that oleo should be distinctively colored by the manufacturer, and thus always be distinguishable from butter. This was a question with which Wilson was not prepared to deal. It had apparently first been publicly suggested by the editor of *Puck*, presumably tongue in cheek, but by May 1880 was being seized upon by the butter men as the answer to their problems. In an editorial jokingly titled "Oilymargarine," *Puck* now ridiculed Thurber's attempt to "cooperate" with the butter interests, unless he was willing to "induce the Oilymargarine manufacturers to color their product pink, red or green, that it may be sold for *what it is.*"[27]

On May 19 the Senate passed the oleo bill. It contained no requirement for distinctive coloration and amended the law of 1877 in only two ways: it corrected the spelling of "oleo-margarin" and specified the characteristics of the label marking the product. Thus the new law must be considered an unqualified victory for Thurber and Wilson. This apparently stimulated a complete reversal of policy on the part of the *Grocer*; the paper now began to

25. *Grocer,* April 16, 1880, p. 546; *New York Times,* April 27, 1880; *Grocer,* April 30, 1880, p. 618.

26. Thurber to Winsor, April 27, 1880, reprinted in *Puck* 7:165 (May 5, 1880), p. 153; Fenner report, p. 261.

27. *Puck* 7:165 (May 5, 1880), p. 153.

condemn *all* oleomargarine, not just the Mège product. It insisted that the federal government had to impose an internal revenue tax on oleo to "protect the legitimate dairy interest."[28]

By the end of the year, however, the *Grocer* was reporting about oleo with ill-concealed glee. The market had suddenly been flooded with cheap western "lard" butter, manufactured from the residue of slaughtered hogs. Since this material, under the new law, had to be labeled "oleomargarine," it was damaging Thurber's sales and driving consumers back to genuine butter. The influx of this inferior competition probably explains a very harsh reprimand addressed to Chandler from Wilson, for now the manufacturers of Mège oleo not only had to fight restrictive legislation but also had to devise some way to dispose of their imitators: "the time has come when there are but two sides to this question, that is those who are for and those who are against us . . . our chemists must stand by us *shoulder* to *shoulder*. . . . The war is upon us."[29]

By 1881 oleomargarine had become the most important food-adulteration issue. In Washington, Congressman Casey Young's report on adulteration, written by George T. Angell, was submitted on February 4. Because Angell perceived Thurber, and Thurber's supporters and hirelings, as his most determined enemies, he retaliated by attacking Thurber's oleo monopoly. Angell portrayed oleo as the most dangerous and insidious adulteration, dismissing the arguments of Thurber's "paid chemists" to the contrary. The irony is that in reality Angell was criticizing the processes employed by Thurber's competitors, those companies using lard and pork offal in their oleo, but it was the Mège monopoly—which specifically avoided these ingredients—that he attacked.[30]

In Albany, fully half a dozen oleo bills were introduced during the 1881 session. The Assembly Committee on Public Health,

28. *New York Times,* May 19, May 20, 1880; Laws of 1880, chap. 439; *Grocer,* July 2, 1880, p. 4; July 16, 1880, p. 70; September 24, 1880, pp. 389–90. See *New York Times,* May 5, May 15, 1880.

29. *Grocer,* December 9, 1880, pp. 741–42; December 16, 1880, pp. 774–75; Wilson to Chandler, November 16, 1880, Chandler Papers.

30. *Adulteration of Food,* 46th Cong., 3d sess., February 4, 1881, H. Rept. 199, p. 15.

chaired by Milton M. Fenner, began an intensive investigation on February 16, indicting oleo as "an injury to the public health, producing an increased mortality." Fenner's determination to condemn oleo shaped the hearings into a forum for the dairymen and the butter dealers. Thus Washington Winsor and T. Mortimer Seaver, of NAPAB, were allowed to select many of the witnesses, and control the direction of the investigation. Winsor, Seaver, and Walter Carr, the Association's vice-president, were the major opposition witnesses, and Thurber's business enemies, such as food wholesaler Frederick W. Leggett, the sponsor of the *Grocer,* were encouraged to testify against oleo.[31]

Wilson responded, in newspaper ads, that the dairy interests were trying to destroy Commercial Manufacturing so as to perpetuate on the market the rancid and inferior butter which oleo threatened to replace. In addition, the company reprinted the scientific testimonials to oleo, claiming they were "not in the least due to any movement on the part of its manufacturers"—a blatant lie. Wilson's hope was that "the American public love fair play, and they will support the manufacturers of oleomargarine in the fight which has been forced upon them."[32]

The Fenner committee now left Albany, accepting Winsor's invitation to continue its sessions in the rooms of the Butter and Cheese Exchange, where numerous New York City witnesses were paraded before it. The committee finally called upon the oleo supporters. But the task of Wilson and Thurber was complicated by the fact that they not only had to defend their own product, but had to draw a distinction between it and "Chicago lard-butter."[33]

When challenged with the possibility of a law prohibiting the coloring of oleo, Wilson argued that "you have no right to impose upon us any color for our product, than we have to impose

31. Fenner report, p. 1; *Minority Report of the Committee on Public Health Investigating Oleomargarine Butter and Lard Cheese,* New York *Assembly Document No. 128* (June 9, 1881), p. 3. It was at this time that the *Grocer,* while still carrying Leggett's price list, dropped it from its "official" status, claiming that this made the paper more "independent" than its competitors.

32. *New York Times,* March 9, 1881. (Although the *Times* would later insist that this three-column letter was placed as an advertisement, at the time it was simply printed as a letter to the editor.) *New York Times,* March 22, 1881.

33. Fenner report, pp. 157, 164.

one upon you for what you call butter." For most of the year, after all, the dairymen themselves added annatto, to imitate the yellow tint of midsummer butter. Wilson's final rejoinder, in response to assorted accusations of unwholesomeness, was to plead the honor and reputability of Thurber and Company: "Who, gentlemen, are our sales' agents? They stand here to-day princes of commerce, the distributors of pure food all over the face of the earth. . . . Is it to be supposed that they can afford to risk their reputation as distributors of pure food to such a vast extent by assuming to distribute oleomargarine if by any known laws of truth, justice or science, a trace of fraud could be found? No, no!" In addition, Wilson named six major stockholders in the company, all of them wealthy, respected New York businessmen and bankers, none of whom would, he claimed, associate themselves with a fraudulent enterprise.[34]

Certainly one remarkable fact about the hearings was the absence of scientific witnesses, although both sides read published "expert" testimony into the record. It is possible that the dairymen could find no reputable professional willing to submit himself to cross-examination. As for Wilson, though he submitted his "Oleomargarine" pamphlet, he brought none of the chemists to testify in person. The *Journal of Commerce* had observed, when the committee moved its investigation from Albany to New York City, "It is believed that a number of leading chemists and sanitarians, employed by the oleomargarine manufacturers, will be produced before the committee." The paper advised the legislators to ask the chemists (1) how they obtained their specimens, (2) if they were paid for their examination, by whom, and how much, and (3) if they, or their relatives, had invested any money in oleomargarine.[35] Perhaps it was for fear that such questions would indeed be asked that Wilson brought no experts with him.

But after the hearings concluded Fenner found himself out-

34. Fenner report, pp. 167, 241–42. Although both Thurber brothers were subpoenaed and testified, the questions asked of them were almost perfunctory. The six stockholders named by Wilson were William Remsen, D. J. Steward, D. S. Appleton, C. M. Field, James D. Smith, and a Mr. Stead.

35. *Weekly Journal of Commerce,* March 25, 1881. For Wilson's and Thurber's legislative "solution," see *Journal of Commerce,* April 5, 1881; *New York Evening Post,* April 15, 1881 (letter to the editor).

voted by his own colleagues; the majority of the committee voted against the oleomargarine bill. Fenner, determined to push the bill through, persuaded the Assembly to discharge the Committee on Public Health from further consideration of the bill and refer it to the committee of the whole.[36] In response, a week later the Board of Aldermen of New York "directed" the city Board of Health to "investigate the subject of oleomargarine." The aldermanic resolution explained that the Assembly committee had been conducting its investigation "by calling as witnesses principally dealers in butter, and have not examined as witnesses medical or chemical experts to determine the value of oleomargarine as food."[37]

It was clearly no coincidence that the aldermen displayed this sudden interest only when the apparently defeated Fenner bill showed new life. Why did the aldermen become involved, when the state Assembly—not the city government—was considering a bill? The "direction" of the aldermen to the Board was clearly a piece of "indirection"—a little sleight-of-hand to give Chandler another opportunity to assert the wholesomeness of oleo. Now Wilson could have his "expert" witnesses, with no embarrassing cross-examination, since the hearings had been terminated. Chandler sent the aldermen a copy of the testimony of the "congregation" of "distinguished chemists," and he declared that the question of the healthfulness of oleo "is one on which there is no difference of opinion among scientific investigators."[38]

Two days later the seven-member majority of the Assembly public health committee issued its own brief report. In describing the manufacture of oleo the majority report specifically referred only to the Mège process, and completely vindicated Commercial Manufacturing and Thurber and Company, even concluding that their oleo was not an "adulteration" or "imitation butter" but a

---

36. *Journal of the Assembly of the State of New York, 104th Session* (Albany, 1881), p. 800 [April 19, 1881]. There does not appear to be a pattern to the committee votes, either geographically or by party. Although Fenner and the other three members supporting the bill were all Republican, the seven-member majority consisted of three Democrats and four Republicans.

37. C. F. Chandler, "Report to the honorable the board of aldermen," letter dated May 3, 1881. The aldermanic resolution "directing the inquiry" is reprinted in Chandler's "Report," and was dated April 28, 1881.

38. Ibid.

safe and healthful product in its own right. They supported the continued use of "butter" coloring for oleo unless the dairymen were also prohibited from using annatto. They opposed instituting any special tax or license fee upon oleo and even went so far as to point out that, since western "lard butter" was an imitation of Mège oleo, the state law should probably be changed to *protect* the Commercial Manufacturing Company.[39]

Undeterred by his own committee's betrayal, Fenner continued to pursue passage of his bill "with a devotion that equals that of the hen with a solitary chicken." Meanwhile, the state Senate concurred in the passage of another oleomargarine bill, which the Assembly had acted upon in March. This bill required all oleo to be distinctly labeled "Imitation Butter," and ordered hotels and boardinghouses serving it to post prominent signs to that effect. Two weeks later the Fenner bill itself, despite its rejection by Fenner's committee, succeeded in passing both houses. Like the earlier bill, Fenner's measure passed with overwhelming majorities. This bill also required the branding of "Imitation Butter" on all oleo packages and tubs, but in addition it prohibited the use of annatto or any other coloring agent.[40]

But on May 30, only three days after the Fenner bill cleared the Senate, Governor Cornell handed down a veto of the first oleo bill on constitutional grounds. Cornell argued that the law of 1880, requiring the labeling of the product as "oleomargarine," was proper, but that the new bill, requiring it to be labeled "Imitation Butter," was a violation of the patent rights of the manufacturers. It was surely this veto, and the anticipation of another for his own measure, that induced Fenner at this time to produce a nineteen-page *Minority Report* on oleo. The report was less an attack on oleo than a diatribe against the "dishonesty, trickery and deception" of Commercial Manufacturing and against Chandler ("the paid chemist of the Oleomargarine Company") and Mott ("the student of Professor Chandler, and brother-in-law to

39. *Majority Report of the Committee on Oleomargarine and Lard Cheese,* New York *Assembly Document No. 105* (May 5, 1881).

40. *New York Times,* May 20, 1881; *Grocer,* May 28, 1881, p. 555. The Fenner bill passed the Assembly 82 to 23 and the Senate by 17 to 3. The *Journal of the Senate of the State of New York, 104th Session* (Albany, 1881), p. 648, shows that Senator Astor, who had sponsored the NBT adulteration bill, which the Senate had just passed on May 10, cast one of the three negative votes.

Mr. Wilson"). The eight visiting scientists were dismissed as "their friends and associates."[41]

The day before the Assembly printed the *Minority Report,* however, Cornell handed down his expected second veto, declaring Fenner's measure "more objectionable than the previous bill." He attacked the bill's willingness to permit coloring for butter, but not oleo, as discriminatory, questioning in what way the bill was for "the better protection of the public health," since if oleo was dangerous, merely prohibiting the use of harmless annatto would not make it less so. He condemned the bill as "an attempt under the guise of protecting the public health to benefit one class of producers at the expense and injury of another."[42]

In the Assembly Fenner tried, unsuccessfully, to override Cornell's veto, claiming that "a rich, cunning, and fraudulent corporation had thus far been triumphant over the hard-working dairyman." Fenner was less harsh on the governor, believing he "had erred, though honestly, in this matter."[43] However, though Cornell's veto messages raised logical objections, he may have been protecting the oleo interests to pay off old political debts.

Cornell was a cold, unlikeable politico who had been vice-president of Western Union, a firm founded by his father. After entering New York politics, he became, by 1870, a "protégé" and "well-entrenched ally" of Senator Roscoe Conkling, the boss of the New York State Republican machine. It was Conkling who, in 1879, had gotten Cornell the governorship, and although relations between the two men began to deteriorate early in 1881, it is possible that Conkling had influenced Cornell's veto.[44] For in the war between Commercial Manufacturing and the dairy interests, and against the "lard-butter" competitors, Conkling used his political influence and his prestige for the Mège monopoly.

Just when Commercial Manufacturing recruited Conkling is un-

41. Assembly *Journal* (1881), p. 1561; *Minority Report,* p. 4.

42. Assembly *Journal* (1881), pp. 1679–80 (June 8, 1881).

43. *New York Times,* June 9, 1881.

44. David M. Jordan, *Roscoe Conkling of New York* (Ithaca, N.Y., 1971), pp. 148, 315–20, 386.

There is no documentation for this speculation. Jordan, p. 365, notes that Cornell "was liberal with the use of his veto power. . . . few were prepared for his square, stubborn resistance to measures he thought wrong." It must also be considered that by the end of July 1881 Conkling and Cornell were enemies.

known. Although he may have been assisting the company through his political influence, it is unlikely that Conkling became intimately involved before the fall of 1881, when he began an intense and lucrative legal practice, specializing in corporate law, after he was prematurely forced to retire from politics. Certainly Wilson was seeking political, as well as legal, assistance, for even while he was fighting the Fenner bill Wilson had declared full-scale war against his imitators, and employed Conkling's "services" in these battles.[45] In addition to trying to persuade the State Board of Health to condemn "sueine, lardine and the other 'ines' of that ilk" as dangers to the public health,[46] Wilson initiated a series of lawsuits against them.

Gustavus Swift first began shipping dressed beef back east from Chicago in the winter of 1875–1876 and soon began using the still-experimental refrigerated railroad cars to create a year-round business. One of the most important consequences of this centralization of cattle and hog slaughtering, of course, was the economic necessity of finding profitable uses for the animal by-products. Swift soon entered the "butterine" business and for a number of years dominated the market; although Armour and Company began manufacturing oleo in 1880—even before it entered the dressed-beef business—until late in the decade its sales of the

45. In 1881 President Garfield, who supported Conkling's enemies within the Republican party, removed Conkling's appointees to the New York Customhouse, the biggest political plum in the nation. Conkling, intending to prove his political strength, resigned from the Senate, assuming that the New York legislature would reappoint him. When his plan fell through, Conkling was left with no alternative and dropped out of politics.

Two of Conkling's efforts on behalf of U.S. Dairy are discussed below, but the full range of his activities remains a mystery. On March 2, 1885, Chandler was served a subpoena to testify on behalf of the company in a suit brought against it by Conkling (Chandler Papers). The *New York Times* (March 2, 1884) reported the initiation of the suit, wherein Conkling was suing Commercial Manufacturing for $10,000 "as the value of legal services rendered by him in 1882 and 1883." The judge in the preliminary hearings ruled that Conkling would have to furnish "a bill of particulars," and describe the "services" he had performed. Conkling's attorney responded, "Mr. Conkling has never kept a detailed and itemized account of services rendered by him to a client."

Neither Jordan nor Donald B. Chidsey, *The Gentleman from New York: A Life of Roscoe Conkling* (New Haven, 1935), discusses Conkling's work for the company.

46. See *Grocer*, April 9, 1881, p. 406; *Sanitary Engineer*, July 1, 1881, p. 355.

product were small compared with Swift's. Thurber could not match the price at which Swift and Armour could market this "lard-butter."[47]

The Chicago "butterine" threatened, not just the supremacy of U.S. Dairy and its subsidiaries, but whatever reputability oleomargarine still retained. These pork products may well have deserved the "trichinosis" and "tapeworm" accusations, and since they were sold as oleo, might drag U.S. Dairy down with them into the abyss of legislative prohibition. Wilson soon sent spies into the "lardine" plants to establish proof of patent infringement; by October the lawyers for Commercial Manufacturing were meeting with Chandler to prepare the case against its competitors.[48]

At the first trial, in November, Chandler was cross-examined regarding his employment by Commercial Manufacturing. His response drew a fine (and possibly perjured) line on the ethics of a public official receiving private compensation:

> I have been employed by the complainants to make investigations in connection with their business . . . and I have received compensation for the time occupied in this work. I have never given them an opinion, however, as far as I can recollect, in regard to the quality of their product; nor have I ever received any compensation for the opinions which I have been called upon to give officially by the legislature, the chairman of a congressional committee, and the board of aldermen of this city. I make it a rule never to give opinions as to the sanitary quality of any article for compensation.

47. Louis Unfer, "Swift and Company: The Development of the Packing Industry, 1875 to 1912" (Ph.D. diss., University of Illinois, 1951), pp. 30–31, 33–36; Mary Yeager Kujovich, "The Dynamics of Oligopoly in the Meat Packing Industry: An Historical Analysis, 1875–1912" (Ph.D. diss., The Johns Hopkins University, 1973), p. 158.

"By 1885 almost as many pounds of dressed beef as livestock were being transported to the East" (Kujovich, p. 178). Two effects of this development, of course, were the displacement of the New York wholesale butchers and the loss of control over meat quality by the health authorities, who could no longer examine the animals on the hoof.

48. Charles D. Deshler to Chandler, April 23, 1881, letters from B. F. Thurston to Chandler, October 1881, Chandler Papers. See New York Tribune, October 6, 1881.

Over the next year or so U.S. Dairy sued a number of other companies and individuals for patent infringement, generally using Chandler as their technical consultant and expert.[49]

Meanwhile, the State Board of Health was in the midst of preparing the twelve food and drug reports for its monumental *Second Annual Report,* as the basis for enforcing the NBT law. Professor G. C. Caldwell's report on butter, cheese, and oils, referring specifically and solely to the Mège product, disparaged criticism that oleo was unwholesome, and it condemned lard-butter as a potentially dangerous adulteration of this "pure" oleo. These judgments are perhaps not terribly surprising, when it is realized that Caldwell was one of the eight expert scientists brought in by Chandler in 1880, and paid to testify as to the wholesomeness and value of Mège oleomargarine.

Thus it should also not be surprising that Chandler never initiated a single prosecution for selling oleo as butter. Still, when the list of exemptions and exceptions was being drawn up by the Board of Health in 1883, Chandler did not wish to risk a discussion of oleo at the meeting between the sanitarians and the wholesalers and manufacturers of food products. When Roscoe Conkling, representing Commercial Manufacturing, approached Chandler in an attempt to get the Board to rule against lard "adulterations" of oleo, Chandler was compelled to refuse. Similarly, Chandler could not use the Board to confiscate competing "oleo" mixtures without imperiling the Mège interests, since the state law did not differentiate between them. He was willing to work for new legislation, but had to refuse Wilson's pleas to circumvent the law.[50]

At this time Chandler was still receiving regular payments from James Wilson. Chandler received a check of $350 to prove—

49. Transcript of trial (*U.S. Dairy vs. Garret Cosine*), Mott to Chandler, June 1, 1882, August 1, 1882, Chandler Papers.

50. Chandler to Conkling, February 23, 1883, Mott to Chandler, August 1, 1882, Chandler Papers. Chandler had apparently met with Conkling only once earlier in regard to oleo. Conkling responded (February 23, 1883, Chandler Papers) that he would not be coming "before the Board" but hoped to see Chandler at another time in regard to restraining the imitators of Mège oleo. After losing their legal battle against Garret Cosine, a manufacturer of a meat/vegetable oil oleo, Wilson and Mott asked Chandler to have the Board of Health inspectors seize and destroy Cosine's product as a deleterious adulteration.

according to his notes of what Wilson required of him—that oleo "is a wholesome product. Is a legitimate industry. Sufferings of the dairymen . . . grossly exaggerated." In December Chandler met with U.S. Dairy officers, Professor Morton, and the company's attorneys once again, to "line out the course of testimony" for additional court cases against imitators.[51]

Meanwhile, however, all was not clear on the legislative front. In February 1882 the House of Representatives Subcommittee on the Internal Revenue Laws, and in April, its parent Committee on Ways and Means, held hearings on oleo. Congressman Thomas of Illinois once again desired to place a ten cent per pound tax on oleo, not for the purpose of raising revenue, but "as the best means . . . of restraining the manufacture of an article which is sold throughout the country under a fraudulent name."[52]

Although federal legislation did not pass in 1882, in the state of New York four separate anti-oleo bills were, this time, signed into law by Governor Cornell.[53] These laws overlapped and conflicted, and they were no more effective than the laws of 1877 or 1880. A total revision of the approach to regulating oleo in New York finally took place in 1884, but only after Francis Thurber voluntarily discontinued his relationship with U.S. Dairy and Commercial Manufacturing. This was sometime in late 1882, or early 1883, after passage of the four new state laws. Thurber no longer acted as the Mège distributor and ceased lobbying against oleo regulation.

Thurber "explained" his action in a July 1885 letter, written *after* his brother Horace had retired from their grocery firm:

51. Chandler's notes, 1883, Deshler to Chandler, December 3, 1883, Chandler Papers.

52. *Oleomargarine. Hearings before the Subcommittee on Changes in the Internal Revenue Laws,* 47th Cong., 1st sess., February 10, 1882 [no doc. no.], p. 2. The committee recommended passage; see *Manufacture and Sale of Oleomargarine,* 47th Cong., 1st sess., June 29, 1882, H. Rept. 1529.

53. Laws of 1882, chaps. 214, 215, 238, 246. Cornell may have simply decided that there was enough support in the legislature to override his veto, though he may have been acting out of anger at Conkling, U.S. Dairy's special attorney, since Conkling had deprived Cornell of the senatorial seat he desired. See Jordan, *Roscoe Conkling,* p. 408; *New York Tribune,* May 29, 1882; *New York Herald,* May 31, August 9, 1882; *Sanitary Engineer,* June 22, 1882, pp. 68–69.

I would say that I have always been opposed to the fraudulent sale of oleomargarine, and have contributed perhaps as much as any one person to compel its honest sale. . . . My brother at one time did have an interest in a small oleomargarine factory, and owing to his influence our firm at one time acted as selling agents for the Commercial Company . . . shortly after my brother's retirement from the head of our firm we stopped selling oleomargarine. . . . I wish to say that my firm will never sell it again. . . . our other business in magnitude is as a thousand to one to any interest we ever had in oleomargarine, and I do not think it is our duty to combat the public prejudice which has been justly evoked by unscrupulous dealers selling it as butter.[54]

This letter, obviously intended for publication, was addressed to James H. Seymour, who, though a leading member of the Butter and Cheese Exchange, had only recently been converted to the anti-oleomargarine campaign. It can best be interpreted as revealing a quid pro quo, for in return for Thurber pleading his previous error (while implying that it was all Horace Thurber's responsibility), Seymour helped him get back into the good graces of the dairy and produce dealers. Seymour testified that he had no doubt that in 1880, when Chandler and the other chemists published their analyses of oleo "as then made by the Commercial Manufacturing Co., when the Thurbers were agents for its sale, the product was a wholesome one, as stated by those chemists; neither have I any doubt that the Thurbers sold the article for what it was, and the position of Mr. F. B. Thurber in connection with oleomargarine has been largely misrepresented."[55]

As of 1884, no leading chemist had declared oleo unwholesome.[56] Nonetheless, in January the New York Senate authorized an investigation of oleo by its Committee on Public Health.

54. *American Grocer,* July 2, 1885, p. 8.
55. Ibid. Seymour was a former president of the N.Y. Mercantile Exchange.
56. See William K. Newton, "The Sanitary Control of the Food Supply," *Public Health Papers and Reports* 9 (1883), p. 160; *Fifth Annual Report of the Board of Health of the State of New Jersey* (Mount Holly, N.J., 1881), pp. 107–9; *Fourth Annual Report of the State Board of Health, Lunacy, and Charity of Massachusetts; Supplement* [July 1882] (Boston, 1883), pp. 27–30. The only exception, among recognized national experts, was Thomas Taylor; see n. 5, above.

The committee clearly intended to rule against oleo: the man appointed as counsel for the hearings was Amasa P. Thornton, counsel for the State Dairymen's Association, which had been lobbying to eliminate oleo from the marketplace. Thornton's argument was that the existing oleo laws were totally ineffective, and that its production and fraudulent sale were growing at a vast pace. Though he at first focused upon Commercial Manufacturing, it was soon learned that the company had just followed F. B. Thurber's lead and had apparently gone out of business.[57]

Thus the hearings concentrated on attacking the Chicago lard-butter manufacturers rather than the Mège companies. In an interesting turnabout, however, T. Mortimer Seaver, who had been the counsel for NAPAB and who had conducted much of Assemblyman Fenner's hearings in 1881, now appeared as "the counsel for the butterine manufacturers." Similarly, Walter Carr, who in 1881 had been vice-president of NAPAB, testified that he now dealt in butterine in his produce business. Carr testified that "when I was opposing oleomargarine I used every argument which I could bring to bear against it; now, I am apathetic; I have been obliged to fall in and sell it."[58]

The "remedy" the committee recommended for this threat to the state's dairymen was "total prohibition." This was legally permissible, they believed, despite earlier arguments that federal patent grants prevented state regulation. They cited a Missouri case of the previous year, in which "Roscoe Conkling was employed as counsel by the [Mège] oleomargarine manufacturers and his great talents were vainly exerted to save them." In that case the federal circuit court ruled that states have the right to prohibit the sale of any product within their borders; patent rights only guarantee "a monopoly to the patentee . . . but [give] no right to manufacture or sell at all, when the same is in conflict with the laws of the State."[59]

The committee's bill—soon signed into law—made it illegal to

---

57. *Report of Committee on Public Health in the Investigation of the Adulteration of Dairy Products,* New York *Senate Document No. 44* (March 21, 1884), pp. 1–4, 23, 68. The committee members were Henry R. Low, Edward G. Thomas, and Henry C. Nelson.

58. Ibid., pp. 211, 234, 249.

59. Ibid., p. 11. The case was *in re* Brosnahon, Jr., Circuit Court of Missouri, June 1883.

sell or manufacture butter substitutes in the state of New York. Most important, the law established a separate enforcement agency, since "the selfish interests of powerful combinations of manufacturers and middlemen" had nullified the six existing anti-oleo laws (which were within the jurisdiction of the Board of Health). To rub salt in the butterine makers' wounds (and perhaps to underscore the ineffectiveness of Chandler's Sanitary Committee, and the entire Board, on this issue), the committee also argued that the new officials "should be chosen from and represent the dairy interests of the State." The men ultimately selected to run the new State Dairy Commission were Josiah K. Brown (as dairy commissioner) and Benjamin F. Van Valkenburgh. Van Valkenburgh, who would in practice be the more active member, was a produce dealer, as well as statistician for the National Butter, Cheese and Egg Association, though he admitted to having sold both oleomargarine and butterine in his business.[60]

The law creating the Dairy Commission gave it jurisdiction over all milk and dairy products, thereby greatly reducing the powers of the State Board of Health. In addition, $30,000 was appropriated for the Commission's use, while Governor Grover Cleveland vetoed the annual appropriation for the Board of Health. On June 23, 1884, the Board "discharged . . . the corps of experts" it had employed to enforce the adulteration laws;[61] in this area the Board was now essentially defunct. By the time the Board's *Fifth Annual Report* was published, the state adulteration law was a dead letter, and the Sanitary Committee extinct.

After half a year in the state courts, the section of the law prohibiting the sale of oleo was declared unconstitutional because it "prevents competition. . . . The sale of a substitute for any article of manufacture is a legitimate business" if conducted without "deception." The constitutionality of the Dairy Commission, however, was not in question, and it remained in existence.[62] More-

60. Laws of 1884, chap. 202; *Senate Document No. 44,* pp. 14, 107; *Journal of the Senate of the State of New York, 107th Session* (Albany, 1884), pp. 559, 583; *Journal of the Assembly of the State of New York, 107th Session* (Albany, 1884), pp. 889–90; *New York Tribune,* March 22, 1884.

61. *Sanitary Engineer,* July 17, 1884, p. 143.

62. *New York Times,* December 25, 1884, March 5, June 17, 1885; Larson, pp. 185–86. The test case was *People v. Morris Marx;* the complete text of the decision appears in *American Grocer,* June 25, 1885, p. 10.

over, even while the case was working its way through the courts a second law was passed, in 1885, making it a misdemeanor to manufacture or sell any non-dairy product "in imitation or semblance of natural butter." As interpreted by Van Valkenburgh, this law prohibited oleo that looked like butter; it would eliminate "deception." Thus the dairymen had resurrected the "coloring" argument of 1880–1881; oleo had to be either white or a distinctive "non-butter" color, in order to be sold legally.[63]

Thurber's associate James Seymour, now an anti-oleo leader, read the Retail Grocers' Union a list, obtained from Van Valkenburgh, of sixty different ingredients named in the various butterine patents, to demonstrate the unwholesomeness of these products (and the superiority of the now-defunct Mège product). Using the new law as leverage, Van Valkenburgh persuaded the members of the Union to sign a pledge not to deal in "oleomargarine" unless it was colored "so that it would not look like butter."[64]

Although the first conviction under the "coloring" law was overturned on appeal, the courts upheld the constitutionality of this regulatory approach, which, apparently, New York was the first state to adopt. By 1887 twenty-nine states and territories had passed some form of anti-oleo legislation, and by the turn of the century twenty-eight had adopted this "coloring" stategy in dealing with oleo, forcing it to be sold either uncolored or dyed pink.[65]

Interestingly, in the test cases for both the 1884 and 1885 New York laws, the chief expert defense witnesses were Professors Chandler and Morton. But it should not really be surprising that these men, who had consistently argued that Mège oleo was the

---

63. Laws of 1885, chap. 183, passed April 30, 1885; *Journal of Commerce,* June 24, 1885; *New York Times,* December 4, 1885; *New York Tribune,* December 17, 1885.

64. *New York Tribune,* December 17, 1885; *New York Times,* December 4, 1885. See *American Grocer,* December 10, 1885, p. 9.

65. *New York Times,* January 27, October 30, 1886; *Produce Exchange Bulletin. Supplement,* July 3, 1886; Jesse P. Battershall, *Food Adulteration and Its Detection* (New York, 1887), pp. 299–307; *Report of the Industrial Commission on Agriculture* (Washington, D.C., 1901), vol. 11, pt. 6, pp. 150–53. The test case was *People* v. *Lipman Arensberg.* New Hampshire was apparently the first state to require that oleo be dyed a specific color—in this case, pink. (See Battershall, p. 304.)

only wholesome butter substitute, and who had been eager witnesses against butterine, should now completely reverse their former stand. Chandler (and presumably Morton as well) had been well paid for earlier testimony on behalf of U.S. Dairy, but as soon as Commercial Manufacturing closed its doors Chandler accepted employment from its lard-butter competitors. He even coaxed an extra $100 from the principal attorney for the butterine manufacturers, who agreed that "the sum named by you as necessary 'to heal your wounds and make you feel that you have not lived in vain,' seems to me very moderate." Over the next few years Chandler received thousands of dollars from an assortment of lard-butter producers, from both New York and Chicago.[66]

In 1886 the dairy interests focused their efforts on prohibiting oleo through confiscatory federal legislation. The times seemed propitious. Reformation of the civil service system, long regarded by most reformers as the key governmental problem of the age, had begun in 1883 with passage of the Pendleton Act. The election of the nominally reformist Democrat Grover Cleveland to the presidency also seemed to bode well for change. Though it would be foolhardy to consider the result of the dairy interests' agitation—the Oleomargarine Tax Law—a triumph for reform, clearly they felt that the time was ripe for legislation similar to Congressman Thomas's failed bill of 1882. But because the opinion had previously been expressed that such legislation was beyond the powers of Congress, the House of Representatives, where such a bill had to originate, referred the question of constitutionality to its Committee on the Judiciary.[67]

The results of that inquiry were not encouraging. The Judiciary Committee ruled that it was unquestionably unconstitutional for the federal government to prevent outright the production of any article of commerce. This left only two alternatives: the regula-

---

66. F. R. Coudert to Chandler, January 20, 1885 (see also Coudert to Chandler, January 31, 1885), Chandler Papers; Chandler Papers, "Butter," box 1. See also Chandler to Cleveland, April 15, 1884, Chandler to Theodore Roosevelt, April 28, 1884, Chandler to state Senator James Otis, April 5, 1884, Chandler Papers; Larson, pp. 182–83.

67. *Adulterated Food Products. Resolution,* 49th Cong., 1st sess., January 11, 1886, H. Misc. Doc. 71. See Ari Hoogenboom, *Outlawing the Spoils* (Urbana, Ill., 1961); John M. Dobson, *Politics in the Gilded Age* (New York, 1972).

tion of the interstate transportation of goods, and the taxing power. But the Committee argued that Congress could not "forbid or restrain the free transportation of any article from one State into another"; *regulation* of commerce did not include the power to interfere with the *right* of commerce. There remained only the fundamental taxing authority of Congress. But even here, the Committee argued that this power should, ethically, only be used to raise a revenue: "merely to strike down a product or an industry, is to abuse a constitutional trust."[68] But the pressure against oleo was now too strong to resist; both houses of Congress ignored the Judiciary Committee's *Report*.

The regulatory bill approved by the House Committee on Agriculture had been presented to Congress by the National Agricultural and Dairy Association, representing twenty-six states, but the bill had been conceived by none other than Francis B. Thurber. At the Association's 1886 convention Thurber outlined the position that the bill's advocates would continue to press throughout the legislative debates. First, Thurber argued that Mège oleo had been a wholesome product, but that more recent "processes and products . . . in which lard and vegetable oils take the place of margarine oil . . . are unwholesome if not dangerous." Second, these products are sold by the retailers as butter: "It was this which made my present firm, some two years ago, decide not to sell any substitute for butter." Third, the states cannot control this "fraud"; federal legislation was necessary. Last, a federal tax of ten cents a pound "would advance the price [of oleo] to a point where the retailer would have no temptation to sell it as butter."[69]

Even before the Association's bill had passed the House, Senator Warner Miller of New York, a farmer and a friend of Thur-

68. *Adulteration of Food. Report,* 49th Cong., 1st sess., April 22, 1886, H. Rept. 1880.

69. Speech of Joseph H. Reall, in *Testimony Taken Before the Committee on Agriculture and Forestry, United States Senate, in Regard to the Manufacture and Sale of Imitation Dairy Products,* 49th Cong., 1st sess., 1886, S. Misc. Doc. 131, p. 1 (this document will hereafter be referred to as Senate *Agriculture* hearings); Hon. Warner Miller, *Butter vs. Oleomargarine,* speech to the U.S. Senate, July 17, 1886, pp. 4–5; *Federal Prohibition of Substitutes For Butter. Proceedings in the House of Representatives,* 49th Cong., 1st sess., May 24, 1886, p. 9; *American Grocer,* March 3, 1886, p. 8.

ber,[70] initiated Senate hearings on behalf of "the representatives of the dairy interests of the country." The tone of the hearings was immediately set by the first speaker, Joseph H. Reall, president of the Association, who attacked the lard-butter makers who had brought the dairy industry "to the verge of destruction" and who could not bring "back to life the innocent people they have killed with the poisonous drugs they have used, nor [restore] to health the thousands who now suffer from the diseases they have entailed." One of the principal anti-oleo speakers was Thurber's defender, James Seymour, who spoke for the "commercial" interests and represented "the Retail Grocers' Association of New York." He refuted the testimony of "expert" defense witnesses Chandler and Morton (who had, once again, been employed by the butterine interests), because their documentation was based on an evaluation of Mège oleo, not the lard-butter counterfeits: "I know of no other test by those parties from that day to the present time."[71]

At the hearings Henry Morton argued that oleo—no matter what its ingredients—"cannot possibly be unwholesome" because rancid ingredients would be "offensive both to the smell and taste." Morton also opposed distinctive coloration for oleo, because "it would affect it greatly as an article of food." (Though coloring was not in the House bill, it was discussed extensively in the hearings as a possible alternative to taxation.) Professor Chandler completely supported Morton. He submitted the documentation prepared for the New York Senate in 1878, his report to the House of Representatives of 1880, the 1880 certificates of the visiting chemists, and his own 1881 report to the New York City aldermen—ignoring the fact that all these reports were based on an examination of Mège oleo, not butterine.[72]

Chandler now thoroughly defended the use of lard in oleo. He claimed that a law merely forbidding oleo's fraudulent sale was

70. This assumption is based on two facts: Miller, throughout the hearings and in all his Senate speeches, always argued that the product of Commercial Manufacturing had been a wholesome article, while vigorously attacking all other oleos; Miller had sponsored, in 1882, a piece of special legislation (S.B. 1727, June 9, 1882) for a substantial postage refund for Thurber's American Grocer Association.

71. Senate *Agriculture* hearings, pp. 1–2, 19–20, 146–47.

72. Ibid., pp. 47, 61; F. R. Coudert to Chandler, May 3, May 6, 1886, oleo manufacturer P. H. van Riper to Chandler, June 18, 1886, Chandler Papers.

sufficient protection, explaining, "There is no one in the United States who has done more to prevent the sale of fraudulent and adulterated food than I have." Chandler also had the effrontery to disparage the attacks on lard-butter by Commissioners Brown and Van Valkenburgh because they were being paid for their efforts. When asked whether he and the other defenders of oleo were testifying merely "as a labor of love," he argued that his "compensation" was different because he had "made investigations in the public interest" and was simply "asked to come before the committee" with expenses paid.[73]

The spokesman for the Chicago lard-butter manufacturers was George H. Webster, a member of the firm of Armour and Company, though at the hearings he also represented Swift and Company, George H. Hammond and Company, N. K. Fairbank and Company, and Samuel W. Allerton, between them the slaughterers of most of the hogs and cattle in the nation and the manufacturers of about two-thirds of the lard-butter. Webster presented virtually identical sworn statements from Philip Armour and Gustavus Swift, describing their methods of manufacture. Both men swore that they did *not* follow the patents granted to them, thus vitiating the effect of Van Valkenburgh's now-infamous "list," which he had presented at the hearings. The patents, Webster explained, had included virtually every conceivable ingredient for the manufacture of oleo, and had been acquired "simply as a matter of protection against the prosecution of the Commercial Manufacturing Company who held the Mége [*sic*] patent in this country. . . . It was a mere *pro-forma* matter, and was never put into practical use."[74]

Webster also presented new "expert" certificates, signed by Cyrus Edson, Dr. Oscar C. De Wolf, New York City health commissioner, and Dr. John H. Rauch, secretary of the Illinois State Board of Health, though he neglected to state how much

73. Senate *Agriculture* hearings, pp. 68, 70–76, 80. A third expert witness was Professor James F. Babcock, the Boston milk inspector, who argued that labeling laws should be the only restriction on oleo. Massachusetts witnesses, and Miller, tore Babcock's testimony apart, pointing to the scarcity of arrests under the Massachusetts labeling law; see Miller, *Butter vs. Oleomargarine,* pp. 29–30.

74. Senate *Agriculture* hearings, pp. 226–27, 107. Frederick Hammond, New England regional manager for the Hammond Company, also testified in person; see pp. 117–23.

these men had been paid for their "visits" to the Armour factory. One piece of testimony Webster later had cause to regret was his admission, upon cross-examination, that at a customer's request Armour branded their tubs "without using the words 'butterine' or 'oleomargarine.' " Thus Armour lard-butter might be shipped to the wholesaler labeled merely "Oakfield Creamery" or "Oakfield Dairy." Senator Miller later quoted this testimony at length to demonstrate the company's participation in widespread fraud, and he also revealed that the Chicago companies were now packaging oleo in one-pound unmarked "rolls" and "prints" to simplify deception on the part of the retailer.[75]

Most of the Senate witnesses were, predictably, anti-oleo men: dairy farmers, produce dealers, representatives of the Grange, and farm association leaders. One point these witnesses tried repeatedly to establish—although it was not germane to the bill—was the unwholesomeness of lard-butter. But even Van Valkenburgh admitted that "by chemistry you cannot prove it to be unhealthful." In 1886 no physiological tests on the effects of oleo had yet been conducted, and there was still no universal agreement as to its healthfulness. At the hearings it was asserted fairly convincingly that various parasites, trichinae, tapeworms, and disease germs may exist in lard-butter when its manufacture is unregulated. Even a supportive study of oleo, published at this time, concluded that consumers had only the word of the manufacturers "that diseased fat is not or can not be used."[76]

By the time the oleo bill came to debate in Congress there seemed little doubt of its passage. In addition to the expected agrarian support—over 100,000 private petitions, and many from Granges and similar organizations, had been received by Congress—many commercial associations, both retail and wholesale, aligned themselves against the "fraud," though other "boards of trade and boards of produce exchange in different large cities"

75. Ibid., pp. 106, 112, Webster responding to questions by Senator Miller; Miller, *Butter vs. Oleomargarine*, p. 7.

76. Senate *Agriculture* hearings, pp. 22, 213–20; H. P. Armsby, "Imitation Butter," *Science* 7:173 (May 28, 1886), p. 472. In contrast to the problems connected with identifying Mège oleo mixed with butter, by 1886 lard-butter could be decisively identified by chemical/microscopical tests.

opposed regulation. On June 3 the House voted, by a healthy majority of 177 to 101, to place a reduced five-cent tax on oleo. But the vote in the Senate to refer the House bill to the Committee on Agriculture succeeded by only a narrow vote of 22 to 21. At this point Thurber persuaded the New York Board of Trade and Transportation to throw its support behind the bill.[77]

On June 9 the House passed an amended version of the oleo bill; the Senate voted for passage on July 28. The bill was signed by President Cleveland on August 2, 1886, and though his message to the House admitted the possibly unjust use of taxation, he insisted that he did "not feel called upon to interpret the motives of Congress." The law called for a "tax" (actually a licensing fee) of $600 on all oleo manufacturers, $480 for wholesalers, and $48 for retailers. The penalities for noncompliance were heavy: a fine of $5,000 for manufacturers and $500 for retailers. Improper labeling was punishable by a fine of $1,000 and two years' imprisonment. But the final tax agreed upon for the sale of oleo had been reduced to only two cents a pound, and no distinctive coloration was required, virtually guaranteeing that the law would not—as the dairymen wished—eliminate the business entirely.[78]

The oleomargarine law of 1886 was the first federal law regulating a domestic food product. It signaled a shift in the fight against adulteration from the state to the federal level. State laws—including the National Board of Trade law in New Jersey, New York, and Massachusetts—had proven ineffective against adulteration. Certainly one of the chief deficiencies of these state laws, as practiced, was their emphasis on prosecuting and harassing the small retailer. Even after Chandler's departure, the New York Board had continued in a similar vein, Thurber's *American Grocer* congratulating it on its efforts and urging the retailers to reform, while *Sanitary Engineer* continued to explain that "as

77. *Federal Prohibition*, pp. 147, 80; *American Grocer*, June 9, 1886, p. 8; June 16, 1886, p. 8. New York state led, with almost 22,000 individual petitions.

78. *Oleomargarine. Message from the President of the United States, Approving House bill 8328*, 49th Cong., 1st sess., August 3, 1886, H. Ex. Doc. 368, pp. 2–3; 24 U.S. Stat. L. 209. The vote was 177 to 99 in the House, and 37 to 24 in the Senate. The law is reprinted in *American Grocer*, August 11, 1886, p. 9; *Journal of Commerce*, August 11, 1886; Battershall, pp. 308–13.

regards adulterations it is generally a necessity to deal with them through the retailers."[79]

The retailers were, of course, cognizant of the one-sidedness of enforcement; this had been the inspiration for the formation of the New York Retail Grocers' Union in 1882. On April 5, 1886, the Union formally incorporated, in the hope of presenting "a solidly aggressive front." In cooperation with the new American Society for the Prevention of Adulteration of Food, Drugs, Medicine, Liquors, &c.—a Philadelphia-based organization—the retailers called for a national food convention. *American Grocer* took this opportunity to urge all retail grocers' unions to appoint delegates, but also congratulated Thurber's New York Board of Trade and Transportation on appointing its own delegates, and it prophetically reendorsed the federal version of the old NBT bill as "the wisest policy" for the convention.[80]

When the call went out for the January 1887 meeting, the convention had been intended to represent retail grocer organizations and health boards. But when the session began, it was dominated by wholesalers and the editors of grocery trade publications, most of which, like *American Grocer,* really represented the interests of wholesalers and manufacturers. Almost immediately Elisha Winter, an associate of Thurber, and Thurber's editor, Frank N. Barrett, succeeded in taking charge of the session, and turned it over to Thurber.

Thurber announced that he had persuaded the National Board of Trade to appoint a special committee to "confer and co-operate" with the convention, to "endeavor to secure well considered legislation" on adulteration. The convention's conference committee consisted of five men: Winter and Barrett, Dr. E. H. Bartley of the Brooklyn Board of Health (a Thurber supporter), H. B. Amerling, a Philadelphian who was one of the founders of the new

79. *Sanitary Engineer,* January 1, 1885, p. 104.

80. "New York Retail Grocers' Union," pamphlet, 1887; *American Grocer,* December 15, 1886, p. 7. The Society was begun in 1885 by H. Wharton Amerling and H. B. Amerling. They published two newspapers, the *Universal Benefactor* and the *Anti-Adulteration Journal.* The Amerlings argued that "everything that we 'taste, touch or handle' is impregnated more or less with poisonous matter, which taken into the body leads gradually, though surely, to disease and death" (*Universal Benefactor* 1:1 [March 1885], p. 1).

Society, and one retail representative, George H. Bond, president of the Boston Retail Grocers' Association. Thus, with Thurber himself chairing the NBT committee, his forces dominated the convention. Virtually the entire session was spent discussing the proposed bill of the "conference committee," a bill that was simply the NBT bill of 1881, modified in recognition that the National Board of Health, which was originally intended to execute the law, was no longer viable. Thurber donated $100 toward the renewed legislative effort. By the time the convention adjourned it had been converted into an organization dedicated to lobbying for Thurber's NBT bill.[81]

When the convention reassembled the following year, representatives of food manufacturers were present, in addition to the retailers and wholesalers. The "great differences of opinion" expressed at this second convention made it the last meeting of the Society. Barrett now argued that "more could be done in the future by quiet, persistent work than by noisy 'brass band' conventions."[82] The last effort of the retailers to draft anti-adulteration legislation in this period had been neutralized.

With the final collapse of the retailers' efforts, leadership of the anti-adulteration movement passed into the hands of Dr. Harvey W. Wiley. Wiley had become chief of the Chemical Division of the Department of Agriculture in 1883, and in 1885 he set his staff to work preparing a massive study of adulteration. In 1887 the first part of *Bulletin 13* of the Division of Chemistry, *Foods and Food Adulterants,* was published, and eventually grew to eight separate parts. *Bulletin 13* was the most complete and responsible of all the treatises on adulteration in the period before 1906.[83]

In the years between 1848, when the federal government had passed the drug import law, and 1886, the legislators in Washington had taken little initiative in the adulteration wars. But the failure of the state efforts, and the growing complexity—the national scope—of the food and drug markets showed that only the

81. *Proceedings of the National Pure Food Convention Held at Washington, Wednesday, January 19th, 1887,* pp. 1, 4–5.

82. Oscar E. Anderson, Jr., *The Health of a Nation* (Chicago, 1958), p. 76.

83. Ibid., pp. 71–75.

federal government could begin to cope with the problem. After 1886 Wiley dedicated his energies, his life, and the resources of the Chemical Division to persuading the government to create effective legislation for this struggle. The eventual result would be the Pure Food and Drug Act of 1906.

12

Conclusion:
The Trout in the Milk

In 1820 Fredrick Accum had identified the threat to justice, order, and morality as being the growing complexity of commerce, which "tended to conceal and facilitate the fraudulent practices" of the unscrupulous. When Professor Lattimore rediscovered Accum's "curious old and somewhat rare book" in 1882, he commented that it "reads as if it had just been written."[1] But if the technological innovations imposed upon the marketplace since Accum's day had intensified the need for regulation, the New York adulteration law was a testing-ground for the limits to which American society was willing to sacrifice its belief in laissez-faire.

By 1883—when the sanitarians of the New York State Board of Health were persuaded by Professor Chandler to yield to the manufacturers and wholesalers by granting exemptions and exceptions to the adulteration law—the brief experiment in regulation was essentially over. Chandler had successfully overcome the reluctance of "unbusiness-like" sanitarians like Elisha Harris, whose objections to Chandler's tactics were seen as efforts "to thwart me at every step."[2] The reformers had surrendered to the

1. Fredrick Accum, *A Treatise on Adulterations of Food, and Culinary Poisons* (Philadelphia, 1820), p. 20; *Second Annual Report of the State Board of Health of New York* (Albany, 1882), p. 594.
2. Chandler to Edward Moore, August 28, 1883, Chandler Papers. When Harris died, a few months later, Chandler did not find it "possible . . . to get away from the city . . . to attend the funeral," though he protested that he had "always been a great admirer of Dr. Harris's indefatigable industry and devotion to the cause of sanitary reform, and I regret extremely that the last years of our inter-

expertise of the chemists, and abdicated their commitment to reforming the marketplace.

In that year William Newton explained that the health boards had been given the task of administering the adulteration laws for two reasons: the simple fact that no other governmental agency existed to which the responsibility could be delegated, and "because a few articles of food are so adulterated as to be injurious to health or life." But, like his colleagues Sharples, Leeds, Johnson, and Chandler, Newton argued that it was time for health boards to turn to other tasks "which properly belong to them," since fraudulent adulterations were not really within the province of the sanitarians and since it had been established that, with rare exceptions, the adulterations in the marketplace touched "only the pocket."[3]

At the 1885 meeting of the American Social Science Association the main speaker on the "The Adulteration of Food" was no longer George T. Angell, but Dr. Charles Harrington of Boston, milk analyst for the Massachusetts State Board of Health, who declared that there "had been an immense improvement in the quality of articles of common consumption." Dr. Newton, speaking next, agreed with Harrington, pointing out that "articles of food are seldom adulterated with poisonous substances. They are adulterated simply to secure large sales, and these would be at once checked by cases of actual poisoning." In other words, the marketplace could safely regulate itself; even truly deleterious practices would be eliminated without the imposition of external regulation. As *American Grocer* argued, "No state law, whether special or general, could accomplish as much" as competition. "Laws will be evaded, but the law of exposure through the rivalry of competing manufacturers and dealers never becomes inoperative."[4]

Francis Thurber, who had shaped and engineered the New

---

course should have been marred by a difference of detail as to the management of certain work in which we were both interested" (Chandler to F. Carmen, February 4, 1884, Chandler Papers).

3. William K. Newton, "The Sanitary Control of the Food Supply," *Public Health Papers and Reports* 9 (1883), p. 169.

4. *Sanitary Engineer*, September 17, 1885, p. 314; *American Grocer*, May 14, 1885, p. 9.

York law, argued in 1883 that "the centralization of power either in the hands of Government or of corporations" was inevitable. Given the choice, Thurber opted for governmental supervision— at least over the reckless power of the monopolies. It was to this end that Thurber had manipulated the state legislature to investigate and control the railroads, and had put himself and his colleagues in the position of conducting the investigation on behalf of the state. In 1885 he argued that "the time for a *laissez faire* policy is past. Our civilization is constantly growing more complex and the forces which now control it must themselves be controlled and directed."[5]

But, like the chemists he employed, Thurber believed that regulation was a temporary expedient, useful for exposing the excesses of the giant corporations and for restraining the behavior of the unscrupulous—those who refused to play by the established rules of the marketplace. Merchants like himself, however, he felt could be trusted to be considerate of the public welfare without the coercion of regulation. After a modicum of supervision, accompanied by publicity to expose the guilty, the nation could safely return to the natural and immutable laws of competition, and be rewarded with fair play in its marketplace.

Thurber was not unique in seeking governmental intervention. Even within the limits of this study, it is clear that many professional (and would-be professional) groups sought two types of external supervision. They sought licensing laws that would grant exclusivity, limit competition, help raise esteem, and enable them to gain greater discretion over fees and pricing. They sought legislative regulation for similar reasons: for example, to attempt to prohibit patent medicines, or to restrain grocers from dealing in them.

More conventional businessmen also sought legislation to help regularize the market, quash negative publicity, improve their public image, eliminate "unfair" competition, and, in general, increase sales. Often these efforts were blatantly self-interested, even if they were couched in terms of the public health: Royal

5. *"Democracy and Anti-Monopoly"—An Address by F. B. Thurber before the Thomas Jefferson Club of Brooklyn* (April 16, 1883), p. 15; *Our Country. A Paper by F. B. Thurber, Read before the XIX Century Club, New York, November 17, 1885*, p. 28.

Baking Powder waged a legislative campaign to outlaw alum in baking powders that lasted for decades. No group wanted to prohibit adulterated sugar more than the large sugar refiners, who supported the NBT bill in 1881 because they could not compete with those who added granulated glucose. The moving forces behind one of the earliest federal laws regulating an imported food—the Tea Adulteration Act of 1883—were the tea importers and wholesalers. The next year they even petitioned Congress to strengthen the law and close loopholes by appointing additional inspectors and by raising their pay. In 1886, while Congress debated the oleo bill, the Millers' National Association drew up a bill for flour labeling, and the National Confectioners' Association sought legislation outlawing deleterious candy adulteration.[6]

Though this study is not broad enough to corroborate more sweeping conclusions about "reform" legislation, in this period it was clearly the packers who beseeched the state, and then the federal, governments for meat inspection legislation. Beginning in 1879, a number of European nations that had provided a substantial market for American meat exports began banning them for health reasons. Though part of the instigation for this prohibition clearly came from the European meat industry, enough cases of trichinosis and hog cholera were proven to validate the claims that American meat lacked proper supervision. When the assurances of the Chicago health authorities proved insufficient to dissuade foreign nations from their ban, the packers turned to the federal government for assistance; the situation was not one of an industry resisting regulation, but of an industry trying to muster enough political support to acquire it.

When Congress failed to legislate such inspection in 1881, the packers turned to the executive branch, which performed a perfunctory "examination" of the industry in that year. When these reassurances also failed to achieve their purpose, the packers persuaded President Chester A. Arthur to appoint a prestigious "impartial and competent commission" to study the question. This five-man commission (which included Professor Chandler as

6. *American Grocer,* January 25, 1883, p. 168; *Adulterated and Spurious Teas,* 48th Cong., 1st sess., March 4, 1884, H. Rept. 665; *American Grocer,* May 19, 1886, p. 7.

the "representative of the New York Chamber of Commerce") conducted a study of slaughtering, packing, and shipping practices, though it relied heavily on the testimony of the packers themselves as to what precautions and policies were followed. When exports failed to respond to this strategy, Congress was forced to act. It established a Bureau of Animal Industry within the Department of Agriculture in 1884, and was finally convinced of the need for broader control, passing inspection acts for meat intended for export in 1890 and 1891. The packers achieved their goal: not only were the European restrictions removed, but the federal government bore the substantial costs of inspection.[7]

Similar problems affected the oleo industry. Commercial Manufacturing's largest business was probably not in the production of oleomargarine itself but in the export of the oil from which the final product was made. For this purpose Commercial maintained foreign factories, especially in Holland. An educated estimate of Commercial's oil exports in 1880 would be approximately 250,000 pounds per week. But England, the largest market for American butter and oleo, was considering import restrictions against both products, because of rumors of large amounts of "counterfeit butter" coming from New York. It was at this time that the "congregation" of scientists gave the Mège product a clean bill of health, and that Thurber gave his support to the New York oleo bill of 1880.

Why didn't the federal oleo law of 1886, which Thurber conceived, and which he initiated through his renewed connections with the dairymen, call for either coloration (following the New York approach of 1885) or complete prohibition? It was estimated that Commercial's production of oleo oil had increased fivefold by 1884. Did Thurber really abandon the oleo business,

7. Gabriel Kolko, *The Triumph of Conservatism* (Chicago, 1967), pp. 98–100; *Swine Products of the United States,* 48th Cong., 1st sess., H. Ex. Doc. 70 (January 31, 1884), H. Ex. Doc. 106 (March 1, 1884), H. Rept. 345 (March 19, 1884); *Inspection of Live Stock,* 49th Cong., 1st sess., April 15, 1886, H. Rept, 1644; *Adulterated Articles of Food, Drink, and Drugs,* 50th Cong., 1st sess., August 25, 1888, H. Rept. 3341; U.S. Statutes 1890, chap. 839; U.S. Statutes 1891, chap. 555. The government appropriated an extra $850,000 for inspection purposes in 1892. The law even provided federal reimbursement for animals confiscated because of exposure to infection.

or did he simply discontinue *domestic* production? Moreover, the new law clearly imposed little restraint upon the Chicago packers. To them, the licensing fee was inconsequential, and the trifling two-cent tax was a virtual guarantee that production would continue unabated. In addition, the law neither regulated the production of oleo oil for export nor taxed exports of the finished product.[8]

Thurber had supported oleo regulation, and the NBT bills, not only to silence reformers like Angell, but also because the activities of the truly unscrupulous threatened the business of the "honest" entrepreneur. But having conceded limitations upon laissez-faire, Thurber immediately sought to place limitations upon regulation. Those who would—as Chandler phrased it—not stop at adulterating sugar with only one part of glucose in five must be supervised. But the legitimate, "acceptable" practices of commerce must be permitted. Thurber sold ten varieties of ground "coffees," only one of which was pure coffee. He defended his mustards as being pure, because he distinguished himself from the scoundrels who colored *their* diluted blends with harmful "arsenical" preparations instead of turmeric. He employed questionable techniques to protect his oleomargarine empire but apparently (and very publicly) withdrew from the business when he felt it had become sullied and disreputable because of the influx of lard-butter from Swift and Armour. Who was to decide which practices were legitimate and which were not?

Chemists such as Chandler had proven their indispensability to the successful operation of the boards of health. When those boards found themselves empowered to enforce the new adulteration laws, it was to these experts that the reformers and sanitarians turned for guidance. All the men appointed by Chandler to conduct the studies of foods and drugs for the monumental 1882 *Annual Report* were fellow chemists, or pharmacists. But if these experts seldom hesitated to render very positive judgments

8. *New York Times,* October 1, 1880, January 15, March 28, 1881; New York State Senate Committee on Public Health, *Investigation of Adulterated Products* (attached to Senate Document No. 44, dated March 21, 1884); *Federal Prohibition of Substitutes For Butter. Proceedings in the House of Representatives,* 49th Cong., 1 sess., May 24, 1886; *American Grocer,* June 16, 1886, p. 8; 24 U.S. Stat. L. 209.

on the healthfulness of the products they studied, they were none-theless groping; their science was primitive and tentative. Ira Remsen publicly denied all of Angell's claims, only to admit privately to Dr. Billings that he really knew very little about adulteration or adulterative practices.

Chandler claimed that alum was dangerous; Dr. Love's report for Chandler's Sanitary Committee denied its danger. By 1884 Love himself condemned it. Yet no chemist had ever conducted an objective, controlled experiment on the use of alum. Chandler claimed that the lactometer was useless; when he realized that his enforcement of the milk laws necessitated its use, he argued that he now trusted the instrument implicitly. Moreover, for every chemist who defended a product or a process, another could be found who condemned it. Yet almost all of these judgments were made on theoretical grounds, rather than being based on scientific experimentation. The chemists could usually *identify* substances; they could not truly *evaluate* them.

Though it would be an error to assume that amateurs like Angell held a monopoly on morality, for the professionals morality also had its practical side. Billings was actively concerned about the dangers of adulteration but also hastened to warn the students graduating from Bellevue that their professional reputations rested on the quality of the medicines they prescribed. Meyer was sincerely concerned about the moral implications of tenement life, but his tenement contest helped perpetuate existing conditions. The resultant law required that all new buildings be equipped with plumbing, while the plumbers' licensing law that Meyer sponsored restricted the competition for installing that equipment in the thousands of dumbbell tenements constructed over the next generation.

The chemists, certainly, were practical men; unlike Angell, Chandler was no Jeremiah of the breakfast table. Ultimately, they saw nothing wrong with mere fraud, and Chandler's difficulties were not with the manufacturers and wholesalers but rather with the sanitarians. As he explained to Board president Edward Moore, Chandler was "almost the only member of the Board who comes in contact with the manufacturers." The sanitarians were less cognizant of the problems and desires of the businessmen. Their reluctance to grant broad exemptions and definitions—a power that Meyer and Chandler had carefully left in the hands of the new enforcers—threatened to alienate "the very persons who secured the passage of the law."[9]

Ultimately, Angell was correct when he argued that the work of eliminating adulteration could not be entrusted to the "boards of health." He had thought that any sincere endeavor would be immediately neutralized by the business interests, "which would either secure their removal or paralyze their efforts."[10] What he did not foresee was that such neutralization would prove unnecessary; not only did the chemists and businessmen agree upon the narrow parameters of the law, but the services of the professionals were readily purchasable. And as Chandler implied in his biting reprimand to Professor Battershall, as long as some professional service was performed for the payment, the businessmen were entitled to exploit the reputation and professional standing of the analyst.

Perhaps the central error made, by both the public and the professionals, was the belief that the experts were capable of self-regulation. Professional pride and codes of ethics were insufficient guarantees of justice and equity. If this early experiment in regulation proved anything, it proved that society needed laws to force the disassociation of the regulator and the regulated, laws that forbade, at a minimum, dual employment. Certainly the boards of health, the first agencies in New York created to regulate the marketplace, served to protect the normative practices of the respectable businessmen by whom the chemists were concurrently employed.

By the end of 1883 the chemists had concluded that the regulation of mere fraud was not the responsibility of the health officials. By 1884 the New York legislature no longer believed that the law was worth its expense; the monies that might have gone to the Sanitary Committee went instead to the politically important Dairy Commission. In that year Governor Grover Cleveland vetoed additional adulteration legislation and asked, "Ought a man be punished who innocently and in good faith has, or even sells, adulterated drugs?"[11]

9. Chandler to Moore, February 5, 1883, Chandler Papers.

10. George T. Angell, "Public Health Associations," *Sanitarian* 7 (1879), p. 131.

11. *Sanitary Engineer,* January 1, 1885, p. 104.

In 1886 Cyrus Edson, appointed to the Board for political reasons despite his lack of qualifications, published an article in which he claimed to have found "toads and small snakes" in watered milk. *American Grocer* took Edson to task for leaving "the reader with the impression that food and drink are 'loaded with poisons.' " The paper argued that only perhaps 1 percent of the foods consumed were "debased," "and of that only a mere fraction can be considered detrimental to health." Thurber's paper reasoned that the consumer was perfectly safe "if he buys of an honest dealer and exercises average common sense and intelligence in the selection of what he eats and drinks."[12]

Edson answered in agreement, and conceded that "adulteration is, no doubt . . . the least dangerous factor to be considered by the sanitarian in his supervision of the food supply." Edson charitably added that "nevertheless it is not to be overlooked or sneered at." Similarly, Albert Leeds had argued that it was time for the courts, not the sanitarians, to enforce the food laws. Yet a contemporary analysis of court activity noted that there was little uniformity in adulteration prosecution; what one court enforced, another ignored.[13]

No one, apparently, would decide which commercial practices were legitimate. But was this first attempt to regulate the marketplace merely a flawed experiment? By 1881 American commerce had achieved modern proportions; New York was dealing with a national problem, but one that came to fruition in that most populous and cosmopolitan state somewhat earlier than in the rest of the nation. Between the time the National Board of Trade law was passed and 1906 nothing really changed, except that the tendencies and technological complexities of modern commerce already present in New York had spread to encompass the rest of the country.

---

12. Cyrus Edson, "Poisons in Food and Drink," *Forum* 1 (August 1886), p. 576; *American Grocer,* August 11, 1886, p. 7; December 15, 1886, p. 9.

13. *American Grocer,* December 29, 1886, p. 9; Albert R. Leeds, "The Adulteration of Foods," *Public Health Papers and Reports* 9 (1883), p. 169; Albert B. Guilbert, "Adulteration of Food," *American Law Review* 22:1 (January–February 1888), pp. 95ff. Guilbert noted, however (p. 104), that "Statutes prohibiting the sale of milk diluted with water have been uniformly sustained."

APPENDIX A

Draft Version of Federal Anti-adulteration Legislation

[Extant portion of what appears to be Dr. J. S. Billings's original draft (located in Wingate Papers).]

The Adulteration of Food

Definition of Food: Any article used for food of man or animals; any article used in the preparation of food, or by admixture with food, before, during or after cooking; any liquid used as a beverage and any article used in the preparation of a beverage.

Definition of the Offense of Adulteration: The manufacture or sale, and the giving or offering for sale, of adulterated articles, and the giving of adulterated articles to persons purchasing of the giver.

Articles are Adulterated as Follows: 1. By addition or substitution of other articles, or of inferior grades or varieties of the same article, so that the name and description assumed do not properly represent the entire material to which such name and description are applied.

2. By dilution, with substances or to an extent concealed from the purchaser or consumer.

3. By removal of the more valuable constituents or portions of articles, such removal not being plainly indicated in the name, label, or description attached or applied to the article.

4. By the application, to any article or grade of article, of a name commonly received or understood as belonging to another article or grade, and tending to deceive the purchaser or consumer.

The Standard of an Article, by which its adulteration shall be judged, shall be a fair and legitimate standard, ensuring such substance and grade and quality as the consumer may properly expect to obtain under the name by which the article is furnished.

The Term Adulteration Does Not Apply to admixtures distinctly and plainly labelled or presented as such, and with a name or description clearly showing the constituents of the mixture, and within reasonable limits the proportions of the constituents.

APPENDIX B

Final Version of National Board of Trade Federal Bill

Board of Trade Bill

To Prevent the Adulteration of Food or Drugs

Be it enacted, etc., That no person or corporation shall knowingly transport, or cause to be transported from the State, district, or territory in which he resides or does business into any other State or territory, or from any foreign country, or other State or territory, into the State or territory in which he resides or does business, for sale or barter, or to be offered for sale or barter, any article of food or drugs adulterated within the meaning of this act, and any person violating the above provision shall be deemed guilty of a misdemeanor, and upon conviction thereof shall be fined not more than fifty dollars for each offence.

SEC. 2. That no person shall, within the District of Columbia, or in any of the territories, or in any fort, arsenal, dock-yard, or reservation, or other place under the jurisdiction of the United States, manufacture, offer for sale, or sell any article of food or drugs which is adulterated within the meaning of this act; and any person violating this provision shall be deemed guilty of a misdemeanor, and upon conviction thereof shall be punished by a fine not exceeding fifty dollars.

SEC. 3. If, on examination of any article of food or drugs imported from any foreign country, it is found to be adulterated within the meaning of this act a return to that effect shall be made upon the invoice, and articles so noted shall not be permitted to pass the custom-house, or be delivered to the consignees unless on re-examination, as provided for in this act, it shall be found that the said articles are not adulterated.

SEC. 4. The owner or consignee shall have the privilege of calling, at his own expense, for a re-examination; and on depositing with the collector of customs such sum as he may deem sufficient to defray such expense, it shall be the duty of the collector of customs to procure a certificate, under oath, from a public analyst, of a careful analysis of the articles in question: and in case the report by certificate of the analyst shall declare the report of the officer who examined the goods to be erroneous, and the said articles to be unadulterated, the said articles shall be returned to the owner or consignee, and passed without reservation on payment of the duties, if any. But in case the officer's return shall be sustained by the analyst, the said articles shall remain in charge of the collector of customs, to be disposed of in accordance with regulations to be prepared by the National Board of Health, and approved by the Secretary of the Treasury: *Provided,* That the owner or consignee, on payment of charges of storage, and other expenses necessarily incurred by the United States, and on giving bond, with sureties satisfactory to the collector, agreeing to remove said articles from the United States, shall have the privilege of re-exporting them at any time within the period of six months after the date of the report of the inspector or public analyst.

SEC. 5. In order to carry into effect the provisions of this act, the Secretary of the Treasury is hereby authorized to appoint from names submitted to him for that purpose by the National Board of Health one or more suitably qualified persons as special inspectors and as public analysts for adulterated food and drugs at such ports of entry as the Secretary of the Treasury may deem expedient, and it shall be the duty of the National Board of Health to prepare instructions governing the work of such inspectors and analysts which, when approved by the Secretary of the Treasury, shall govern their action, and that of collectors of customs, in preventing importation from foreign countries of food or drugs adulterated within the meaning of this act.

SEC. 6. The National Board of Health shall make, or cause to be made, examination of specimens of food and drugs collected under its direction in various parts of the country, and shall publish in its weekly bulletin the results of such analyses. If it shall appear from such examination that any of the provisions of this act have been violated, the Secretary of the Board shall at once report the facts to the proper United States district attorney, with a copy of the results of the analysis duly authenticated by the analyst under oath.

Sec. 7. It shall be the duty of every district attorney to whom the Secretary of the National Board of Health, or any collector of customs shall report any violation of this act, to cause proper proceedings to be commenced and prosecuted without delay for the fines and penalties in such case provided, unless, upon inquiry and examination, he shall decide that such proceedings cannot probably be sustained, in which case he shall report the facts to the National Board of Health; and for the expenses incurred and services rendered in all such cases, the district attorney shall receive and be paid from the Treasury such sum as the Secretary of the Treasury shall deem just and reasonable, upon the certificate of the judge before whom such cases are tried or disposed.

Sec. 8. An article shall be deemed to be adulterated within the meaning of this Act—

a.—In the case of drugs.

1. If, when sold under or by a name recognized in the United States Pharmacopoeia, it differs from the standard of strength, quality, or purity laid down therein.

2. If, when sold under or by a name not recognized in the United States Pharmacopoeia, but which is found in some other pharmacopoeia or other standard work on Materia Medica, it differs materially from the standard of strength, quality, or purity laid down in such work.

3. If its strength or purity fall below the professed standard under which it is sold.

b.—In the case of food or drink.

1. If any substance or substances has or have been mixed with it so as to reduce or lower or injuriously affect its quality or strength.

2. If any inferior or cheaper substance or substances have been substituted wholly or in part for the article.

3. If any valuable constituent of the article has been wholly or in part abstracted.

4. If it be an imitation of or be sold under the name of another article.

5. If it consist wholly or in part of a diseased, or decomposed, or putrid, or rotten animal or vegetable substance, whether manufactured or not, or in the case of milk, if it is the produce of a diseased animal.

6. If it be colored or coated, or polished or powdered, whereby damage is concealed, or it is made to appear better than it really is, or of greater value.

7. If it contain any added poisonous ingredient, or any ingredient which may render such article injurious to the health of a person consuming it: *Provided,* That the National Board of Health may, with the approval of the Secretary of the Treasury, from time to time declare certain articles or preparations to be exempt from the provisions of this act: *And provided further,* That the provisions of this act shall not apply to mixtures or compounds *recognized* as ordinary articles of food, provided that the same are not injurious to health, and that the articles are distinctly labelled as a mixture, stating the components of the mixture.

SEC. 9. It shall be the duty of the National Board of Health to prepare and publish from time to time lists of the articles, mixtures, or compounds declared to be exempt from the provisions of this act, in accordance with the preceding section. The National Board of Health shall also from time to time fix the limits of variability permissible in any article or compound.

SEC. 10. The term "food" as used in this act shall include every article used for food or drink by man.

The term "drug" as used in this act shall include all medicines for internal or external use.

SEC. 11. All the regulations and declarations of the National Board of Health, made under this act from time to time and promulgated, shall be printed in the Statutes-at-Large.

SEC. 12. This act shall take effect ninety days after it shall have become a law.

APPENDIX C

Food and Drug Adulteration Laws of New York and New Jersey

Section 1. No person shall, within this State, manufacture, have, offer for sale, or sell any article of food or drug which is adulterated within the meaning of this act, and any person violating this provision shall be deemed guilty of a misdemeanor, and, upon conviction thereof, shall be punished by a fine not exceeding fifty dollars for the first offence, and not exceeding one hundred dollars for each subsequent offence (for a second and subsequent offences, *N.J.*).

Sec. 2. The term "food," as used in this act, shall include every article used for food or drink by man. The term "drug," as used in this act, shall include all medicines for internal or external use.

Sec. 3. An article shall be deemed to be adulterated within the meaning of this act:

a. In the case of drugs.

1. If, when sold under or by a name recognized in the United States Pharmacopoeia, it differs from the standard of strength, quality, or purity laid down therein.

2. If, when sold under or by a name not recognized in the United States Pharmacopoeia, but which is found in some other pharmacopoeia or other standard work on Materia Medica, it differs materially from the standard of strength, quality, or purity laid down in such work.

3. If its strength or purity fall below the professed standard under which it is sold.

b. In the case of food or drink.

1. If any substance or substances has or have been mixed with

it so as to reduce or lower or injuriously affect its quality or strength.

2. If any inferior or cheaper substance or substances have been substituted wholly or in part for the article.

3. If any valuable constituent of the article has been wholly or in part abstracted.

4. If it be an imitation of, or be sold under the name of another article.

5. If it consists wholly or in part of a deceased or decomposed, or putrid or rotten, animal or vegetable substance, whether manufactured or not, or in the case of milk, if it is the produce of a diseased animal.

6. If it be colored, or coated, or polished, or powdered, whereby damage is concealed, or it is made to appear better than it really is, or of greater value.

7. If it contain any added poisonous ingredient, or any ingredient which may render such article injurious to the health of a person consuming it; *Provided,* That the State board of health may, with the approval of the governor, from time to time declare certain articles or preparations to be exempt from the provisions of this act; *And provided, further,* That the provisions of this act shall not apply to mixtures or compounds recognized as ordinary articles of food, provided that the same are not injurious to health, and that the articles are distinctly labelled as a mixture, stating the components of the mixture.

SEC. 4. It shall be the duty of the State board of health to prepare and publish from time to time, lists of the articles, mixtures, or compounds declared to be exempt from the provisions of this act in accordance with the preceding section. The State board of health shall also from time to time fix the limits of variability permissible in any article of food, or drug, or compound, the standard of which is not established by any national pharmacopoeia.

SEC. 5. The State board of health shall take cognizance of the interests of the public health as it relates to the sale of food and drugs and the adulteration of the same, and make all necessary investigations and inquiries relating thereto. It shall also have the supervision of the appointment of public analyst and chemist, and upon its recommendation, whenever it shall deem any such officers incompetent, the appointment of any and every such officer shall be revoked and be held to be void and of no effect. Within thirty days after the passage of this act, the State board of health shall meet and adopt such measures as may seem necessary to facilitate the enforcement of this act, and prepare rules and regulations with regard to the proper methods of collecting and examining articles of food or drugs, and for the appointment of the necessary inspectors and analysts; and the State board of health shall be authorized to expend, in addition to all sums already appropriated for said board, an amount not exceeding ten thousand dollars (five hundred dollars, N.J.), for the purpose of carrying out the provisions of this act [and the sum of ten thousand dollars is hereby appropriated out of any money in the treasury not otherwise appropriated, for the purposes in this section provided].

SEC. 6. Every person selling or offering or exposing any article of food or drugs for sale, or delivering any article to purchasers, shall be bound to serve or supply any public analyst or other agent of the State or local board of health (any inspector, N.J.) appointed under this act, who shall apply to him for that purpose, and on his tendering the value of the same; with a sample sufficient for the purpose of analysis of any article which is included in this act, and which is in the possession of the person selling, under a penalty not exceeding fifty dollars for a first offence, and one hundred dollars for a second and subsequent offences.

SEC. 7. Any violation of the provisions of this act shall be treated and punished as a misdemeanor; and whoever shall impede, obstruct, hinder, or otherwise prevent any analyst, inspector, or prosecuting officer in the performance of his duty, shall be guilty of a misdemeanor, and shall be liable to indictment and punishment therefor.

SEC. 8. Any act or parts of acts inconsistent with the provisions of this act are hereby repealed.

[SEC. 9. All the regulations and declarations of the State board of health made under this act, from time to time, and promulgated, shall be printed in the statutes at large.]

SEC. 10. This act shall take effect at the expiration of ninety days after it shall become a law. (Section 9. This act shall be deemed a public act, and shall take effect at the expiration of thirty days after it shall become a law, N.J.)

Bibliography

The following bibliography includes only materials actually consulted and employed in the writing of this book; it does not include other materials mentioned in these sources, which are cited in the notes. Additional items, such as miscellaneous periodical advertisements, letters, articles, and clippings and correspondence found in the various manuscript collections are also described only in the notes. The original findings of this study were reached primarily from the examination of the manuscript sources, especially the Chandler and Billings papers.

Manuscript Sources

Atkinson, Edward. Papers. Massachusetts Historical Society. Boston, Massachusetts.

Billings, John Shaw. Papers. Rare Books and Manuscripts Division, The New York Public Library. Astor, Lenox and Tilden Foundations. New York.

Blochman, Lawrence G. Manuscript notes from the Journals of Dr. Edward R. Squibb. Squibb Archives. Princeton, New Jersey.

Chandler, Charles Frederick. Papers. Rare Book and Manuscript Library, Columbia University. New York.

Medical Society of the County of New York. Minutes. 1877–1879. New York.

New York Academy of Medicine. Minutes. 1878–1880. New York.

New York Academy of Medicine. Proceedings of the Council. 1878–1880. New York.

Squibb, Edward Robinson. Papers. Squibb Archives. Princeton, New Jersey.
Wingate, Charles Frederick. Papers. Rare Books and Manuscripts Division, The New York Public Library. Astor, Lenox and Tilden Foundations. New York.

Doctoral Dissertations

Becker, William H. "The Wholesalers of Hardware and Drugs, 1870–1900." The Johns Hopkins University, 1969.
Bruton, Peter W. "The National Board of Health." University of Maryland, 1974.
Cortes, Kathleen F. "Democracy in the American Public Health Association: A Historical Analysis." Columbia University, 1976.
Jamieson, Duncan R. "Towards Cleaner New York. John H. Griscom and New York's Public Health." Michigan State University, 1971.
Kujovich, Mary Y. "The Dynamics of Oligopoly in the Meat Packing Industry: An Historical Analysis, 1875–1912." The Johns Hopkins University, 1973.
Larson, Robert L. "Charles Frederick Chandler, His Life and Work." Columbia University, 1950.
Okun, Mitchell. "Fair Play in the Marketplace: Adulteration and the Origins of Consumerism." City University of New York, 1983.
Unfer, Louis. "Swift and Company: The Development of the Packing Industry, 1875–1912." University of Illinois, 1951.

Published Sources

Accum, Fredrick. *A Treatise on Adulterations of Food, and Culinary Poisons*. Philadelphia, 1820.
Address of the Committee to Promote the Passage of a Metropolitan Health Bill. New York, 1865.
"Adulterations in Food and Drugs." *Hunt's Merchants' Magazine* 41:5 (November 1859), pp. 254–55.
"The Adulterations of Food." *North American Review* 194 (January 1862), pp. 1–40.
"Adulteration of Groceries in England." *Hunt's Merchants' Magazine* 41:5 (November 1859), pp. 252–54.
Alexander, DeAlva S. *A Political History of the State of New York*. Vol. 3. 1909. Rpt. Port Washington, N.Y., 1969.
Alpers, William C. "History of the American Pharmaceutical Associa-

tion, Second Decade 1860–1870." *Journal of the American Pharmaceutical Association* 3 (December 1914), pp. 1625–40; 4 (January 1915), pp. 3–17.

Alsberg, Carl L. "Progress in Federal Food Control." In *A Half Century of Public Health,* ed. Mazyck P. Ravenel. 1921. Rpt. New York, 1970.

American Chemical Society. *Journal of the American Chemical Society,* 1879–1884.

American Chemical Society. *Proceedings of the American Chemical Society,* 1876–1878.

American Grocer, 1869, 1879–1886.

American Pharmaceutical Association. *Proceedings of the American Pharmaceutical Association,* 1871–1886.

American Public Health Association. *Public Health Reports and Papers,* 1879–1886.

Anderson, Oscar E., Jr. *The Health of a Nation.* Chicago, 1958.

Angell, George T. *Protection of Animals.* Boston, 1874.

———. "Public Health Associations." *Sanitarian* 7 (1879), pp. 126–31.

———. *Autobiographical Sketches and Personal Recollections.* Boston, 1892.

Anti-Adulteration Journal, 1886.

Armsby, H. P. "Imitation Butter." *Science* 7:173 (May 28, 1886), pp. 471–75.

Assael, Henry, ed. *The Politics of Distributive Trade Associations: A Study in Conflict Resolution.* Hempstead, N.Y., 1967.

Bailey, M. J. *Report on the Practical Operation of the Law Relating to the Importation of Adulterated and Spurious Drugs.* New York, 1849.

Bailey, Thomas A. "Congressional Opposition to Pure Food Legislation, 1879–1906." *American Journal of Sociology* 36 (July 1930), pp. 52–64.

Battershall, Jesse B. *Food Adulteration and Its Detection.* New York, 1887.

Beck, Lewis C. *Adulterations of Various Substances Used in Medicine and the Arts, with the means of detecting them.* New York, 1846.

Benson, Lee, *Merchants, Farmers, and Railroads.* New York, 1955.

Bernstein, Nancy R. *The First One Hundred Years, Essays on the History of the American Public Health Association.* N.p., 1972.

Billings, John S. "A Century of American Medicine, 1776–1876." In *Selected Papers of John Shaw Billings,* ed. Frank B. Rogers. N.p., 1965.

———. "Address to the Graduating Class of Bellevue Hospital Medical

College." In *Selected Papers of John Shaw Billings,* ed. Frank B. Rogers. 1965.

―――. Introduction. *A Treatise on Hygiene and Pubic Health,* ed. Albert H. Buck. New York, 1879.

Blake, John B., ed. *Safeguarding the Public.* Baltimore, 1970.

Bledstein, Burton J. *The Culture of Professionalism.* New York, 1976.

Blochman, Lawrence G. *Doctor Squibb.* New York, 1958.

Bogart, F. E., et. al. *A History of the National Wholesale Druggists' Association from Its Organization to Nineteen-twenty-four.* New York, 1924.

Boston Herald, 1879.

Boston Medical and Surgical Journal, 1881–1884.

Bowditch, Henry I. "The Future Health Council of the Nation." *Transactions of the American Medical Association* 26 (1875), pp. 301–39.

Brewer, William H. "Glucose in Its Sanitary Aspects." *Public Health Reports and Papers* 10 (1885), pp. 100–5.

Brodman, Estelle. *The Development of Medical Bibliography.* Baltimore, 1954.

Brooklyn Board of Health. *Report of the Board of Health of the City of Brooklyn, 1875–1876.* Brooklyn, 1877.

―――. *Annual Report of the Department of Health of the City of Brooklyn, 1884* [–1885]. Brooklyn, 1885.

―――. *Annual Report of the Department of Health of the City of Brooklyn for the Year 1886.* Brooklyn, 1887.

Browne, Charles A., and Mary E. Weeks. *A History of the American Chemical Society.* Washington, D.C., 1952.

Browne, Junius H. *The Great Metropolis, A Mirror of New-York.* Hartford, 1869.

Buck, Albert H., ed. *A Treatise on Hygiene and Public Health.* 2 vols. New York, 1879.

Buck, Solon J. *The Granger Movement, 1870–1880.* Cambridge, Mass., 1913.

Buel, C. C. "Henry Bergh and His Work." *Scribner's Monthly* 17:6 (April 1879), pp. 872–84.

Burns, Jabez. *The Right and Wrong of Adulteration: The Benefit and Injury of Adulterating: The Use and Abuse of Adulterations.* New York, 1877.

Burrow, James G. *AMA, Voice of American Medicine.* Baltimore, 1963.

Callow, Alexander B., Jr. *The Tweed Ring.* New York, 1965.

Chandler, Charles F. "Report on Dangerous Cosmetics." *Fourth Annual Report of the Metropolitan Board of Health.* New York, 1870.

―――. "Report on Dangerous Kerosene." *Fourth Annual Report of the Metropolitan Board of Health.* New York, 1870.

———. "Report on the Quality of the Milk Supply of the Metropolitan District." *Fourth Annual Report of the Metropolitan Board of Health.* New York, 1870.

———. "Condensed Milk." *American Chemist* 2:1 (July 1871), pp. 25–26.

———. "Report on Petroleum Oil." *First Annual Report of the Board of Health of the Health Department of the City of New York.* New York, 1871.

———. "Report to the honorable the board of aldermen." New York, 1881.

Chidsey, Donald B. *The Gentleman from New York: A Life of Roscoe Conkling.* New Haven, 1935.

Citizens' Association of New York. *Disease and Death in New-York City and its Vicinity.* New York, 1864.

Coleman, Sydney H. *Humane Society Leaders in America.* Albany, 1924.

Collins, James H. *The Story of Canned Foods.* New York, 1924.

Cowen, David L. "America's First Pharmacy Laws." *Journal of the American Pharmaceutical Association* 3:5 (May 1942), pp. 162–69; 3:6 (June 1942), pp. 214–21.

———. "The Role of the Pharmaceutical Industry." In *Safeguarding the Public,* ed. John B. Blake. Baltimore, 1970.

Cummings, Richard O. *The American and His Food.* Chicago, 1940.

Diehl, C. Lewis. "Report on Deleterious Adulterations, and Substitutions of Drugs." In *National Board of Health Bulletin.* Supplement No. 6. Washington, D.C., 1880.

Dobson, John M. *Politics in the Gilded Age.* New York, 1972.

Doremus, Charles A. "Contributions to the Literature of Milk Analysis." *Proceedings of the American Chemical Society* 1:4 (March 1, 1877), pp. 227–52.

Duffy, John. *A History of Public Health in New York City, 1625–1866.* New York, 1968.

———. *A History of Public Health in New York City, 1866–1966.* New York, 1974.

Eaton, Dorman B. *Sanitary Legislation in England and New York.* New York, 1872.

Edson, Cyrus. "Poisons in Food and Drink." *Forum* 1 (August 1886), pp. 572–82.

Edwards, Richard. *New York's Great Industries.* New York, 1884.

Edwards, Richard, and Critten. *New York's Great Industries.* New York, 1885.

Elliott, Arthur H. "Report on the Methods and Apparatus for Testing Inflammable Oils." In *New York State Board of Health Report #45.* Albany, 1882.

Emerson, Haven. "Charles Frederick Chandler, 1836–1925." *Science* 86:2238 (November 19, 1937), pp. 453–61.

Emery, Edwin. *The Press and America*. Englewood Cliffs, N.J., 1972.

An Ephemeris of the Materia Medica, Pharmacy, Therapeutics, and Collateral Information, 1882–1885.

Fairchild, Herman L. *A History of the New York Academy of Sciences*. New York, 1887.

Filby, Frederick A. *A History of Food Adulteration and Analysis*. London, 1934.

Flanders, George L. *Accurate Determination of the Amount of Fat in Milk*. 1909. (Pamphlet)

"Food and Its Adulterations." *Hunt's Merchants' Magazine* 54:5 (May 1866), pp. 340–42.

Forsyth, David P. *The Business Press in America, 1750–1865*. Philadelphia, 1964.

Friedman, Lawrence M. *A History of American Law*. New York, 1973.

Friedman, Lawrence M., and Jack Ladinsky. "Law and Social Change in the Progressive Era." In *New Perspectives on the American Past*, ed. Stanley N. Katz and Stanley I. Kutler. Boston, 1969.

Galishoff, Stuart. *Safeguarding the Public Health*. Westport, Conn., 1975.

Garraty, John. *The New Commonwealth, 1877–1890*. New York, 1968.

Garrison, Fielding H. *John Shaw Billings, A Memoir*. New York, 1915.

German-American Grocer, 1882–1883.

Grant, H. Roger. *Insurance Reform*. Ames, Iowa, 1979.

Griscom, John H. "Anniversary Discourse, Before the New York Academy of Medicine" (New York, 1854). In *Origins of Public Health in America*. New York, 1972.

Grocer, January 1879–December 1886. (Title changed to *Merchants' Review* effective November 12, 1881.)

Guilbert, Albert B. "Adulterations of Food." *American Law Review* 22:1 (January–February 1888), pp. 95–106.

Hart, F. Leslie. "A History of the Adulteration of Food before 1906." *Food-Drug-Cosmetic Law Journal* 7 (January 1952), pp. 5–22.

Hartley, Robert M. *An Historical, Scientific, and Practical Essay on Milk*. 1842. Rpt. [*The Cow and the Dairy*.] New York, 1850.

Haskell, Thomas L. *The Emergence of Professional Social Science*. Urbana, Ill., 1977.

Hassall, Arthur H. *Food and Its Adulterations*. London, 1855.

———. *Adulterations Detected*. 2d ed. London, 1861.

Hedrick, Ulysses P. *A History of Agriculture in the State of New York*. 1933. Rpt. New York, 1966.

Hehner, Otto, and Arthur Angell. *Butter, Its Analysis and Adulterations*. 2d ed. London, 1877.

Historical Statistics of the United States. Washington, D.C., 1975.

A History of the First Half-Century of the National Academy of Sciences. Baltimore, 1913.

Hoogenboom, Ari. *Outlawing the Spoils.* Urbana, Ill., 1961.

Hoskins, Thomas H. *What We Eat: An Account of the Most Common Adulterations of Food and Drink.* Boston, 1861.

House of Commons. *Report from the Select Committee on Adulterations of Food, &c., together with the Proceedings of the Committee, Minutes of Evidence . . .* London, 1856.

Huber, Edward. *Oleomargarine or Bogus Butter.* Richmond, 1880.

Johnson, Samuel W. "Adulterations of Food." *Good Company* 5:12 (August [*sic*] 1880), pp. 546–60; *Journal of Social Science,* 13, pt. 2 (1881), pp. 99–135.

Jordan, David M. *Roscoe Conkling of New York.* Ithaca, N.Y., 1971.

Judge, 1882.

Justice, 1883–1884.

Kebler, L. F. "The Good Work of the Western Wholesale Drug Association (1876–1882) for Honest Drugs." *Journal of the American Pharmaceutical Association* 15:4 (April 1926), pp. 293–97.

Kedzie, Robert C. "The Adulteration and Deterioration of Food." In *National Board of Health Bulletin,* Supplement No. 6. Washington, D.C., 1880.

Kings County Pharmaceutical Society. *Proceedings,* 1877. (Published in *Proceedings of the Medical Society of the County of Kings* 2:10 [December 1877].)

Knickerbocker 53:4 (May 1859), pp. 515–23.

Kolko, Gabriel. *The Triumph of Conservatism.* Chicago, 1963.

Kramer, Howard D. "Early Municipal and State Boards of Health." *Bulletin of the History of Medicine* 24:6 (November–December 1950), pp. 503–29.

Leavitt, Judith W. *The Healthiest City. Milwaukee and the Politics of Health Reform.* Princeton, 1982.

Leeds, Albert R. "The Adulteration of Food." *Third Annual Report of the New Jersey State Board of Health.* Camden, N.J., 1879.

———. "The Adulteration of Foods." *Public Health Reports and Papers* 9 (1883), pp. 166–70.

Leigh, Robert D. *Federal Health Administration in the United States.* New York, 1927.

[Frank] *Leslie's Illustrated Weekly Newspaper,* 1858.

Lydenberg, Harry M. *John Shaw Billings.* Chicago, 1924.

Majority and Minority Reports of the Select Committee of the Board of Health, Appointed to Investigate the Character and Condition of the Sources From Which Cows' Milk is Derived, For Sale in the City of New York. New York, 1858.

Mandelbaum, Seymour J. *Boss Tweed's New York*. New York, 1965.

Martin, Edward W., and Walter Moeller. *Report on Milk and Its Adulterations*. Albany, 1885.

Massachusetts. *Journal of the House of Representatives of the Commonwealth of Massachusetts, Session of 1882*. Boston, 1882.

———. *Journal of the Senate of the Commonwealth of Massachusetts, Session of 1882*. Boston, 1882.

Massachusetts State Board of Health, A Brief History of Its Organization and Its Work, 1869–1912. Boston, 1912.

Massachusetts. *Third Annual Report of the State Board of Health, Lunacy, and Charity of Massachusetts, January, 1882*. Boston, 1882.

———. *Fourth Annual Report of the State Board of Health, Lunacy, and Charity of Massachusetts; Supplement*. Boston, 1883.

———. *Fifth Annual Report of the State Board of Health, Lunacy, and Charity of Massachusetts. Supplement*. Boston, 1884.

———. *Sixth Annual Report of the State Board of Health, Lunacy, and Charity of Massachusetts*. Boston, 1885.

———. *Seventh Annual Report of the State Board of Health, Lunacy, and Charity of Massachusetts. Supplement*. Boston, 1886.

Massachusetts Ploughman and New England Journal of Agriculture, 1879–1881.

Medical News and Library, 1877.

Medical Society of the County of Kings. *Proceedings*, 1877.

Medical Society of the State of New York. *Transactions*, 1878–1881.

Meyer, Henry C. *The Story of the Sanitary Engineer*. New York, 1928.

Minutes of the Proceedings of the Quarantine Convention. Philadelphia, 1857.

Morris, John. *Milk: Its Adulterations, Analysis, Etc.* (Pamphlet, reprinted from *Maryland Medical Journal*, June 15, 1882.)

Mott, Frank L. *A History of American Magazines, 1865–1885*. Cambridge, Mass., 1957.

Mott, Henry A. "Artificial Butter." *Scientific American* 35:22 (November 25, 1876), p. 337.

———. *Complete History and Process of Manufacture of Artificial Butter*. New York, 1876. (Reprint from *Scientific American Supplement* Nos. 48 and 49, 1876.)

———. "Manufacture of Artificial Butter." *Proceedings of the American Chemical Society* 1:3 (November 2, 1876), pp. 154–59.

———. "The Deleterious Use of Alum in Bread and Baking Powders— Alum Being Substituted For Cream of Tartar." *Scientific American* 34:20 (November 16, 1878), p. 308.

———. *The Effect of Alum Upon the Human System, When Used in Baking Powders. Elaborate Experiments Upon Living Dogs. Re-*

searches Made Under the Auspices of the ROYAL BAKING POWDER COMPANY. New York, 1880.

———. "Oleomargarine Butter: The New Article of Commerce." New York, 1880.

———. *The Production of Oleomargarine and Oleomargarine Butter: As Manufactured By the Commercial Manufacturing Co., Consolidated*. New York, 1880.

"Mouthwashes." *Consumer Reports* 49:5 (March 1984), pp. 143–46.

Mullaly, John. *The Milk Trade in New York and Vicinity*. New York, 1853.

Nation, 1878–1881.

National Academy of Sciences. *Report on Glucose*. Washington, D.C., 1884.

National Board of Health. *Annual Reports*, 1879–1882.

National Board of Health Bulletin, June 28, 1879–July 1882.

National Board of Trade. *Proceedings*, 1879–1880.

National Bureau of Economic Research. *Trends in the American Economy in the Nineteenth Century*. Princeton, 1960.

New Jersey. *Third Annual Report of the New Jersey State Board of Health*. Camden, N.J., 1879.

———. *Fourth Annual Report of the Board of Health of the State of New Jersey*. Camden, N.J., 1881.

———. *Fifth Annual Report of the Board of Health of the State of New Jersey*. Mount Holly, N.J., 1881.

———. *Sixth Annual Report of the Board of Health of the State of New Jersey*. Woodbury, N.J., 1882.

———. *Seventh Annual Report of the Board of Health of the State of New Jersey*. Woodbury, N.J., 1883.

———. *Eighth Annual Report of the Board of Health of the State of New Jersey*. Trenton, 1884.

———. *Ninth Annual Report of the Board of Health of the State of New Jersey*. Trenton, 1885.

New Remedies, 1879–1883.

Newton, William K. "The Sanitary Control of the Food Supply." *Public Health Reports and Papers* 9 (1884), pp. 149–65.

New York Board of Trade and Transportation. *Minutes*, 1873–1881.

———. *Proceedings*, 1882–1884.

New York City. *First Annual Report of the Board of Health of the Health Department of the City of New York*. New York, 1871.

———. *Second Annual Report of the Board of Health of the Health Department of the City of New York*. New York, 1872.

———. *Third Annual Report of the Board of Health of the Health Department of the City of New York, 1872–1873*. New York, 1873.

————. *Fourth Annual Report of the Board of Health of the Health Department of the City of New York.* New York, 1874.

————. *Fifth and Sixth Annual Reports of the Board of Health of the City of New York.* New York, 1876.

————. *Seventh Annual Report of the Board of Health of the City of New York.* New York. 1877.

New York Evening Post. April 1881.

New York Herald, selected dates, 1876–1886.

New York Journal of Commerce. Weekly and daily issues, 1874, 1878–1886.

New York Milk Exchange Limited. *By-Laws.*

New York Retail Grocers' Union. New York, 1887. (Pamphlet)

New York State. [First] *Annual Report of the Metropolitan Board of Health. 1866.* New York, 1867.

————. *Second Annual Report of the Metropolitan Board of Health of the State of New York.* New York, 1868.

————. *Third Annual Report of the Metropolitan Board of Health of the State of New York.* New York, 1868.

————. *Fourth Annual Report of the Metropolitan Board of Health of the State of New York.* New York, 1869.

————. *First Annual Report of the State Board of Health of New York.* Albany, 1881.

————. *Second Annual Report of the State Board of Health of New York.* Albany, 1882.

————. *Third Annual Report of the State Board of Health of New York.* Assembly Doc. 110. Albany, 1883.

————. *Fourth Annual Report of the State Board of Health of New York.* Assembly Doc. 89. Albany, 1884.

————. *Fifth Annual Report of the State Board of Health of New York.* Senate Doc. 47. Albany, 1885.

New York State Board of Health. *Manual of the State Board of Health of New York.* Albany, 1880.

————. *Duties and Procedures of Local Boards of Health and Their Officers.* Publication 27. New York, n.d.

————. *Chemistry of Food and Drugs.* Publication 40. Albany, 1881.

New York State Legislature. *Journal of the Assembly of the State of New York,* 1871–1886.

————. *Journal of the Senate of the State of New York,* 1871–1886.

————. *Resolutions Adopted At A Meeting Of The Physicians Of The City Of New York, In Relation To The Sanitary Condition Of Said City.* Senate Doc. 63. Albany, April 18, 1881.

————. *Majority Report of the Committees on Oleomargarine and Lard Cheese.* Assembly Doc. 105. Albany, May 5, 1881.

———. *Minority Report of the Committee on Public Health Investigating Oleomargarine and Lard Cheese*. Assembly Doc. 128. Albany, June 9, 1881.

———. *Testimony Taken Before the Assembly Committee on Public Health in the Matter of the Investigation into the Subject of the Manufacture and Sale of Oleomargarine and Lard-Cheese*. Assembly Doc. 000 [?]. Albany, 1881.

———. *Report of Committee on Public Health in the Investigation of the Adulteration of Dairy Products*. Senate Doc. 44. Albany, March 21, 1884. (Testimony of the *Investigation* appended)

New York State Pharmaceutical Association. *Proceedings*, 1879–1886.

New York Times, 1865–1886.

New York Tribune, selected issues, 1878–1886.

New York World, December 1868–April 1869.

Nitardy, F. W. "Notes on Early Drug Legislation." *Journal of the American Pharmaceutical Association* 23:11 (November 1934), pp. 1122–27.

North, Charles E. "Milk and Its Relation to Public Health." In *A Half Century of Public Health*, ed. Mazyck P. Ravenel. 1921. Rpt. New York, 1970.

"The Oleo-Margarin Industry." *Scientific American* 36:11 (March 17, 1877), p. 168.

Our Dumb Animals, 1879–1880.

Parkes, E. A. *A Manual of Practical Hygiene*. 5th ed. Philadelphia, 1878.

Peabody, Susan W. *Historical Study of Legislation Regarding Public Health in the States of New York and Massachusetts*. Chicago, 1909.

Pearson, Raymond A. *Facts about Milk*. Washington, D.C., 1906.

The People vs Daniel Schrumpf. Misdemeanor, Adulteration of Milk. Record, Testimony and Proceedings. New York, 1881.

The Pharmacopoeia of the United States of America. Boston, 1820.

Plumber and Sanitary Engineer, December 1877–December 1886. (Title changed to *Sanitary Engineer*)

Poole, William F. *Poole's Index to Periodical Literature*. 1882. Rpt. Gloucester, Mass., 1963.

Porter, Glenn. *The Rise of Big Business, 1860–1910*. New York, 1973.

President Chandler and the New York City Health Department, 1866–1883. (Reprinted from *Sanitary Engineer*, May 17, 1883.)

Proceedings and Debates of the Third National Quarantine and Sanitary Convention. New York, 1859.

Proceedings of the National Pure Food Convention Held at Washington, Wednesday, January 19th, 1887.

Produce Exchange Bulletin, selected dates, 1880–1886.

Puck, 1880–1881.

Ravenel, Mazyck P. "The American Public Health Association, Past, Present, Future." In *A Half Century of Public Health,* ed. Mazyck P. Ravenel. 1921. Rpt. New York, 1970.

———, ed. *A Half Century of Public Health.* 1921. Rpt. New York, 1970.

Report of the Council of Hygiene and Public Health of the Citizens' Association. 2d ed. 1866. Rpt. New York, 1970.

Report of the Industrial Commission on Agriculture. Vol. 11. Washington, D.C., 1901.

Report of the Sanitary Committee of the Board of Health on the Concentration and Regulation of the Business of Slaughtering Animals in the City of New York. New York, 1874.

"Repression of Adulteration in America." *Sanitary Record* 3 n.s. (September 15, 1881), pp. 98–99.

Rideing, William H. "How New York is Fed." *Scribner's Monthly* 14:6 (October 1877), pp. 729–43.

Riepina, Sjert F. *The Story of Margarine.* Washington, D.C., 1970.

Riley, Henry A. "Recent Legislation with Regard to Adulteration of Food and Drugs." *Philadelphia Medical Times* 15 (May 2, 1885), pp. 566–70.

Rogers, Everett M. *Social Change in Rural Society.* New York, 1960.

Rogers, Frank B., ed. *Selected Papers of John Shaw Billings.* N.p., 1965.

Rosen, George. *A History of Public Health.* New York, 1958.

———. *From Medical Police to Social Medicine.* New York, 1974.

Rosenkrantz, Barbara G. *Public Health and the State.* Cambridge, Mass., 1972.

Ross, Edward A. *Sin and Society, An Analysis of Latter-Day Iniquity.* Boston, 1907.

Rossiter, Margaret W. "The Charles F. Chandler Collection." *Technology and Culture* 18:2 (April 1977), pp. 222–30.

Rothstein, William G. *American Physicians of the Nineteenth Century.* Baltimore, 1972.

Sanitarian, 1878–1881.

Sanitary Record, 1881–1882.

Schieffelin and Company. *150 Years Service to American Health.* New York, 1944.

Schlesinger, Arthur M. *The Rise of the City, 1878–1898.* 1933. Rpt. Chicago, 1971.

Science: A Weekly Record of Scientific Progress, June 18, 1881.

Scientific American, 1876–1880.

Scribner's Monthly, 1873–1881.

Shaftel, Norman. "A History of the Purification of Milk in New York or

How Now Brown Cow." *New York State Journal of Medicine* 58:6 (March 15, 1958), pp. 911–28.

Sharples, Stephen P. "Specimens of Milk From the Vicinity of Boston." *Proceedings of the American Academy of Arts and Sciences,* n.s. 3, w.s. 11 (May 1875–May 1876), pp. 149–56; n.s. 4, w.s. 12 (May 1876–May 1877), pp. 98–112.

———. "Adulteration of Food." In *A Treatise on Hygiene and Public Health,* ed. Albert H. Buck. Vol. 2. New York, 1879. (Reprinted in *Supplement* to *Fourth Annual Report of the State Board of Health, Lunacy, and Charity of Massachusetts.* Boston, 1883.)

Shaw, R. H., and C. H. Eckles. *The Estimation of Total Solids in Milk by Use of Formulas.* U.S. Department of Agriculture Bulletin 134. Washington, D.C., 1911.

Shryock, Richard H. *The Development of Modern Medicine.* New York, 1947.

———. *Medicine and Society in America, 1660–1860.* New York, 1960.

Smart, Charles. "Report of an Investigation to Determine the Prevalence of Adulteration in Food Supplies." In *National Board of Health Bulletin.* Supplement No. 11. Washington, D.C., 1881.

Smillie, Wilson G. *Public Health.* New York, 1955.

Smith, Stephen. *The City That Was.* 1911. Rpt. Metuchen, N.J., 1973.

Sonnedecker, Glenn. "Controlling Drugs in the Nineteenth Century." In *Safeguarding the Public,* ed. John B. Blake. Baltimore, 1970.

———. *Kremers and Urdang's History of Pharmacy.* Philadelphia, 1976.

Sonnedecker, Glenn, and George Urdang. "Legalization of Drug Standards Under State Laws in the United States of America." *Food-Drug-Cosmetic Law Journal* 8:12 (December 1953), pp. 741–60.

Spalding, James A. *The Life of Dr. Lyman Spalding.* Boston, 1916.

Sproat, John G. *The Best Men.* London, 1968.

Squibb, Edward R. "The Drug Inspectors and the Profession." Editorial. *American Medical Times* 2:28 (1861), pp. 66–68.

———. *List of Preparations of Edward R. Squibb, M.D.* ("Squibb Trade List.") Privately printed, 1861.

———. "Report on the Drug Market." *Proceedings of the American Pharmaceutical Association* 12 (1863), pp. 175–95.

———. "Remarks Upon the Practical Working of the U.S. Drug Law." *Transactions of the American Medical Association* 15 (1865), pp. 142–50.

———. *The American Medical Association and The Pharmacopoeia.* Privately printed, 1877.

———. "Rough Draft of a Proposed Law to Prevent the Adulteration of Food and Medicine and to Create a State Board of Health." *Trans-*

actions of the Medical Society of the State of New York (1879), pp. 209–21.

———. *Proposed Legislation on the Adulteration of Food and Medicines*. New York, 1879.

———. *Semi-Annual Price List of Standard Pharmaceutical Preparations*. Privately printed, 1881.

———. "The Relations of Physicians to their Medical Supplies." *Transactions of the New York State Medical Association* 3 (1887), pp. 84–92.

Starr, Paul. *The Social Transformation of American Medicine*. New York, 1982.

Steele, Zulma. *Angel in Top Hat*. New York, 1942.

Stephen Smith, M.D., LL.D. Addresses In Recognition of His Public Services. 1911. N.p., n.d.

Stieb, Ernst W. *Drug Adulteration: Detection and Control in Nineteenth-Century Britain*. Madison, 1966.

———. "Drug Control in Britain, 1850–1914." In *Safeguarding the Public*, ed. John B. Blake. Baltimore, 1970.

Stone, William L. *History of New York City*. New York, 1872.

Taylor, George R. *The Transportation Revolution, 1815–1860*. 1951. Rpt. New York, 1968.

Taylor, Thomas. "Oleomargarine Under the Microscope." *Scientific American* 38 (June 15, 1878), p. 374.

———. "Oleomargarine and Butter." *American Quarterly Microscopical Journal* 1:4 (July 1879), pp. 294–95.

Thurber, Francis B. *Coffee: from Plantation to Cup*. New York, 1881.

———. *"Democracy and Anti-Monopoly"—An Address by F. B. Thurber before the Thomas Jefferson Club of Brooklyn, April 16, 1883*. N.p., n.d.

———. *Our Country. A Paper by F. B. Thurber, Read before the XIX Century Club, New York, November 17, 1885*. N.p., n.d.

Tobey, James A. *The Legal Aspects of Milk Control*. Chicago, 1936.

Trachtenberg, Alan. *The Incorporation of America*. New York, 1982.

U.S. Congress. House. *Imported Adulterated Drugs, Medicines, &c.* 30th Cong., 1st sess., H. Rept. 664. June 2, 1848.

———. *Operation of the Law to Prevent the Importation of Adulterated Drugs, &c.* 30th Cong., 2d sess., H. Ex. Doc. 43. January 24, 1849.

———. "Representative E. B. Washburne . . ." (Petition of the American Pharmaceutical Association.) 36th Cong., 1st sess., H. Rept. 633. June 15, 1860.

———. *The Adulteration of Articles of Food and Drink*. 45th Cong., 3d sess., H.R. 5916. January 20, 1879.

———. *Adulteration of Articles of Food and Drink*. 46th Cong., 1st sess., H.R. 2014. May 23, 1879.

———. (Substitute for H.R. 2014.) 46th Cong., 2d sess., H.R. 4738. February 25, 1880.

———. *The Manufacture of Articles of Human Food and Drink.* 46th Cong., 2d sess., H. Rept. 346. February 25, 1880.

———. "A Bill Authorizing the President to appoint a commission to examine and report upon the adulteration of food." 46th Cong., 3d sess., H.R. 7005. January 24, 1881.

———. "A Bill to Prevent the Adulteration of Food and Drugs." 46th Cong., 3d sess., H.R. 7040. January 31, 1881. (Hawley bill)

———. *Adulteration of Food.* 46th Cong., 3d sess., H. Rept. 199. February 4, 1881.

———. "A Bill to Prevent the Adulteration of Food and Drugs." 47th Cong., 1st sess., H.R. 1080. December 16, 1881. (Flower bill)

———. "A Bill to Tax and Regulate the Manufacture and Sale of Glucose." 47th Cong., 1st sess., H.R. 3170. January 16, 1882.

———. *Oleomargarine. Hearings before the Subcommittee on Changes in the Internal Revenue Laws.* 47th Cong., 1st sess., no doc. number. February 10, 1882.

———. *Adulterated Food and Drugs.* 47th Cong., 1st sess., H. Rept. 634. March 4, 1882. (Substitutes H.R. 4789 for H.R. 1080)

———. *Manufacture and Sale of Oleomargarine.* 47th Cong., 1st sess., H. Rept. 1529. June 29, 1882.

———. *Swine Products of the United States.* 48th Cong., 1st sess., H. Ex. Doc. 70. January 31, 1884.

———. *Oleomargarine and Imitations of Butter.* 48th Cong., 1st sess., H. Rept. 251. February 7, 1884.

———. *Swine Products of the United States.* 48th Cong., 1st sess., H. Ex. Doc. 106. March 1, 1884.

———. *Adulterated and Spurious Teas.* 48th Cong., 1st sess., H. Rept. 665. March 4, 1884.

———. *Swine Products of the United States.* 48th Cong., 1st sess., H. Rept. 345. March 19, 1884.

———. *Exportation of Imitations of Butter and Cheese.* 48th Cong., 1st sess., H. Rept. 1669. May 29, 1884.

———. *Adulterated Food Products. Resolution.* 49th Cong., 1st sess., H. Misc. Doc. 71. January 11, 1886.

———. *Inspection of Live Stock.* 49th Cong., 1st sess., H. Rept. 1644. April 15, 1886.

———. *Adulteration of Food. Report.* 49th Cong., 1st sess., H. Rept. 1880. April 22, 1886.

———. *Federal Prohibition of Substitutes For Butter. Proceedings in the House of Representatives.* 49th Cong., 1st sess., no doc. number. May 24, 1886. (Debate on H.R. 8328)

———. *Oleomargarine. Message from the President of the United States, Approving House bill 8328.* 49th Cong., 1st sess., H. Ex. Doc. 368. August 3, 1886.

———. *Adulterated Articles of Food, Drink, and Drugs.* 50th Cong., 1st sess., H. Rept. 3341. August 25, 1888.

U.S. Congress. Senate. *Petition of George T. Angell . . . Transportation of Live Stock.* 45th Cong., 1st sess., S. Misc. Doc. 15. December 1, 1877.

———. *Hearings of the Senate Committee on Commerce on Food and Drugs.* 47th Cong., 1st sess., S. Rept. 649. December 20, 1881.

———. "American Grocer Association." 47th Cong., 1st sess., S.B. 1727. June 9, 1882. (Senator Warner Miller, asking for postage refund)

———. *Testimony Taken Before the Committee on Agriculture and Forestry, United States Senate, in Regard to the Manufacture and Sale of Imitation Dairy Products.* 49th Cong., 1st sess., S. Misc. Doc. 131. June 18, 1886. (Hearings on S.B. 1837, identical to H.R. 8328)

———. *Butter vs. Oleomargarine.* Speech of Hon. Warner Miller to the U.S. Senate, July 17, 1886. 49th Cong., 1st sess., No doc. number.

U.S. Department of Agriculture. *Report of the Commissioner of Agriculture,* 1878–1886.

United States Statutes. 9 Stat. L., 237. June 16, 1848. (Imported drugs)

———. 22 Stat. L., 451. March 3, 1883. (Imported tea)

———. 24 Stat. L., 209. August 2, 1886. (Oleomargarine tax)

———. 1890, chap. 839. August 30, 1890. (Livestock inspection)

———. 1891, chap. 555. March 3, 1891. (Livestock inspection)

Universal Benefactor, 1885.

"Upon the Adulteration of Food, Drink and Drugs, From the Chemist's Standpoint." *Journal of the American Chemical Society* 3 (1881), pp. 60–62. (Abstract of discussion by Albert R. Leeds)

Van Ingen, Philip. *The New York Academy of Medicine: Its First 100 Years.* New York, 1949.

Van Stuyvenberg, Johannes H., ed. *Margarine. An Economic, Social and Scientific History, 1869–1969.* Liverpool, 1969.

Waller, Elwyn. "Dangers in Food and Drink." *Century,* 9 n.s. (1886), pp. 303–7.

Wanklyn, J. Alfred. *Milk-Analysis, A Practical Treatise on the Examination of Milk.* New York, 1874.

Warner, Margaret. "Local Control versus National Interest: The Debate over Southern Public Health, 1878–1884." *Journal of Southern History* 50:3 (August 1984), pp. 407–28.

"Water Pipes and Public Health." *Galaxy* 14:5 (May 1872), p. 707.

Weber, Gustavus A. *The Food, Drug, and Insecticide Administration.* Baltimore, 1928.

"What We Eat." *Harper's Weekly* 23:1152 (January 25, 1879), p. 74.

Wiebe, Robert H. *The Search for Order, 1877–1920.* New York, 1967.

Wiley, Harvey W. "The Rotatory Power of Commercial Glucose." *Science: A Weekly Record of Scientific Progress* (February 5, 1881), p. 53.

———. "Glucose and Grape-Sugar." *Popular Science Monthly* 19 (June 1881), pp. 251–57.

———. "Amylose." *Proceedings of the American Association for the Advancement of Science* (August 1881), p. 61.

———. "Mixed Sugars." *Proceedings of the American Association for the Advancement of Science* (August 1881), pp. 61–64.

———. *The History of a Crime against the Food Law.* Washington, D.C., 1929.

———. *An Autobiography.* Indianapolis, 1930.

Wilson, James Q. *Political Organizations.* New York, 1973.

Young, James H. *The Toadstool Millionaires.* Princeton, 1961.

———. "Drugs and the 1906 Law." In *Safeguarding the Public,* ed. John B. Blake. Baltimore, 1970.

Zeigler, Harmon. *Interest Groups in American Society.* Englewood Cliffs, N.J., 1964.

Index